JAPANESE POLITICS

JAPANESE POLITICS
Fixed and Floating Worlds

Timothy Hoye

Texas Woman's University

PRENTICE HALL, UPPER SADDLE RIVER, NEW JERSEY 07458

Library of Congress Cataloging-in-Publication Data

Hoye, Timothy.
    Japanese politics : fixed and floating worlds / Timothy Hoye. —
1st ed.
      p.   cm.
    Includes bibliographical references and index.
    ISBN 0-13-271289-X
    1. Japan—Politics and government—1945- 2. Japan—History—1945-
3. Japan—Civilization—1945- 4. Arts, Japanese—20th century.
I. Title.
DS889.H66   1998
952.04—dc21   98-9690
                                           CIP

Editorial Director: Charlyce Jones Owen
Editor in Chief: Nancy Roberts
Acquisitions Editor: Beth Gillett
Associate Editor: Nicole Conforti
Marketing Manager: Christopher DeJohn
Project Management and Interior Design: Serena Hoffman
Copy Editor: Mary Louise Byrd
Buyer: Bob Anderson
Cover Director: Jayne Conte

This book was set in 10/12 Palatino by Stratford Publishing Services
and was printed and bound by Courier Companies, Inc.
The cover was printed by Phoenix Color Corp.

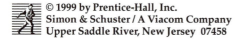 © **1999 by Prentice-Hall, Inc.**
Simon & Schuster / A Viacom Company
Upper Saddle River, New Jersey 07458

Printed in the United States of America

10 9 8 7 6 5 4 3 2 1

ISBN: 0-13-271289-X

Prentice-Hall International (UK) Limited, *London*
Prentice-Hall of Australia Pty. Limited, *Sydney*
Prentice-Hall Canada Inc., *Toronto*
Prentice-Hall Hispanoamericana, S.A., *Mexico*
Prentice-Hall of India Private Limited, *New Delhi*
Prentice-Hall of Japan, Inc., *Tokyo*
Simon & Schuster Asia Pte. Ltd., *Singapore*
Editora Prentice-Hall do Brasil, Ltda., *Rio de Janeiro*

To
Masako Oku Hoye

Contents

3

THE STRUCTURE OF AUTHORITY: JAPANESE GOVERNMENT   62

4

FLOATING STRUCTURES: PARTIES, MASS MEDIA, CITIZEN GROUPS   95

5 THE SCOPE OF AUTHORITY: ISSUES   121

6 SUBJECTS, CITIZENS, OUTSIDERS   153

Preface

Any study of today's Japan might more accurately begin by referring to today's Japans. No other advanced industrialized nation-state in the modern world presents such a complex picture involving both a conscious attempt to preserve tradition and an equally conscious policy of adapting to and leading global changes. This may be nothing more than the continuation of what the modern Japanese state has always managed to accomplish—balancing tradition and modernity. One of the common assumptions among the nation's leadership during the early years of the great Meiji Restoration was that Japan should adopt Western science and technology but maintain its Eastern ethical traditions. Japan is today the oldest monarchy in continuing existence. It is also among the world's leaders in high technology. There are more industrial robots in Japan today, not only than in any other society but in *all* other societies combined. Japan today is saturated with shrines, temples, festivals, rituals, prayers, and other religious practices. It is also saturated with corner video outlets, enormous department stores, countless *pachinko*[1] parlors, karaoke bars, all variety of motorbikes, luxury autos, fast food outlets, convenience stores, and *manga* comics displaying all manner of high- and low-tech violence. Internationally, images of a mystic Japan enveloped in aesthetic traditions created and nurtured by the gentle folk of Lafcadio Hearn's experience compete bewilderingly with images of Japan Incorporated, with postmodern tendencies adapted from the premodern ways of the *samurai* warrior.

Japanese politics today reflects these same tendencies. It, too, bewilders. Japanese politics, since World War II, is multiparty. In recent years, however, it has been tending increasingly toward a two- or perhaps three-party realignment,

---

[1] Japanese terms are italicized throughout the text except where these terms have become familiar, such as karaoke. Also, where Japanese terms have a long "o" sound, they are presented in the text as "ou." Exceptions are place names, such as Tokyo and Osaka, personal names, and terms that have become familiar in English and are customarily written with a short "o," such as *Shinto* and *bushido*. Japanese names are presented in the traditional Japanese style of family name first.

a process expected to accelerate with recently enacted electoral reforms. Japanese politics is traditionally characterized by high voter participation, ranking near the top among democratic nations in voter turnout for national elections. In July 1995, however, turnout reached a postwar low with less than half of eligible voters participating. Japanese politics is traditionally not defined by intense public discussion of controversial issues. This, too, is changing as print and broadcast media editorialize daily on new religions, consumerism, health threats, money politics, continuing corrupt practices, and the foibles of Japanese politics both new and old. Traditionally, dominant individuals do not set the tone and focus of discussion. In the last 20 years, Prime Ministers Tanaka Kakuei, Nakasone Yasuhiro, and to some extent, Hashimoto Ryutaro have been lightning rods for public debate. Ozawa Ichiro, the current leader of the opposition New Frontier Party, has proposed a "blueprint" for a new Japan that has gotten considerable attention both within and outside Japan. Supporters hail his efforts to make Japan a "normal" democracy. Critics have called him the "prince of disorder" (Tamamoto 1995). Traditionally, the center of gravity within Japanese politics is the upper levels of the state bureaucracy; today a shift toward party-centered politics has been observed by numerous scholars, as well as participants. Traditionally, Japanese politics is domestic politics; increasingly it is global politics. Within Japan, centripetal tendencies are traditional—a political dynamic centering in Tokyo—but centrifugal forces more and more pull policy considerations to the prefectural and local levels. There is even much talk of pulling the capital out of Tokyo. Where the traditional Japanese state is "reactive," the emerging Japan is one that can say "no" to outside pressure (*gaiatsu*), especially from the United States. Where some observers see dramatic, unprecedented change, others see politics as usual.

Conceptualization in the social sciences is a complex and controversial affair, not least of all in political science. There is much effort in the direction of structural, phenomenological, and poststructural or deconstructionist theory that challenges basic assumptions about objectivity and science in general. A recent study of basic features of Japanese politics by Kishima Takako, for example, begins from these new perspectives and offers challenging insights. Among innovations in such approaches is the development of new conceptual complexes that distinguish, for example, among *nomos, cosmos,* and *chaos. Nomos* refers to accepted rules and institutions within society; *cosmos* refers to a larger, symbolic order that gives meaning, or originally gave meaning, to *nomos; chaos* refers to the loss of meaning, a disconnection between *nomos* and *cosmos* (Kishima 1991, 3–25). Without accepting all of the nuances of such innovative theories, one can acknowledge the importance of one's worldview in any discussion of power or justice. Theorists such as Michel Foucault, building on the philosophic insights of Edmund Husserl and Alfred Schutz, are often credited with initiating perspectives such as these, perspectives that deemphasize will and rational choice as critical variables—central assumptions in much behaviorist literature—and also the role of structures, economic structures in particular, as is characteristic of Marxist scholars. By this new approach, the overcoming of traditional symbols is not automatically equated with reason and the advance of modernization.

Within the discipline of political science, other scholars have also challenged positivist and Marxist approaches. Also building on the insights of phenomenologists like Husserl and Schutz, but as well on the insights of classical Western political theory with roots in ancient Greek, Hebrew, and Roman cultures, a number of scholars born, raised, and educated in Europe left for the United States in the 1920s and 1930s to escape a decaying European civilization in the wake of fascist political developments. Scholars such as Hannah Arendt, Leo Strauss, Eric Voegelin, Carl Friedrich, Hans Morganthau, Arnold Brecht, and many others have come to be known within the United States as the émigré scholars. Their approach to the study of politics and to modern politics in particular represented a kind of culture shock to the established circles within American political science during the 1940s (Gunnell 1988). But many native American scholars have developed the insights of the émigré scholars into an approach to the study of politics that begins with a philosophical anthropology. Such an approach emphasizes the importance of cultural framework in any study of politics. In other words, the deeper assumptions within cultures, as shaped by religion, language, perspectives on history, the arts, and popular culture, continue to impact political institutions and practices in the modern and postmodern worlds. The focus of analysis is on experience and symbolization.

Among the advantages of such an approach is that it allows a distancing from the perennial scholarly problems of ethnocentrism, social science jargon, and from what some would call positivist assumptions that social and political realities can be studied with the same methods that are appropriate to the physical sciences. All cultures develop symbolic forms that embody, well or poorly, significant human experiences considered lasting and therefore needful of public, or outside, symbolization. Institutions develop to preserve, nurture, and refine these experiences. For example, in ancient Greek and Roman cultures, politics was an experience considered basic. To be human was to be political. Only through experience with others in a common pursuit of a common wealth, a *res publica*, could qualities and characteristics uniquely human be developed. One who did not participate was considered an idiot; one who could not speak well was regarded as a barbarian—like sheep on the hillside, all such a one could say was "bah, bah."

One cannot, however, begin an examination of Japanese experience here. Interestingly, members of the Iwakura mission from Japan to the West in 1871 (discussed in more detail in Chapter 2), glimpsed the importance of the "political" element deriving from the ancient Greek and Roman West. It was considered unique to Western experience and not something characteristic of Japanese experience. Politics points, not always clearly, to some principle of equality, such as in the concept of equal protection of the law found in the Fourteenth Amendment to the U.S. Constitution and much in the center of constitutional debate in the United States today. Such a principle is also clearly evident in the famous inscription chiseled in stone over the front of the entrance to the U.S. Supreme Court building in Washington, D.C. "Equal Justice Under Law" points to a long tradition of equality and rule of law as ideals. Japanese culture, by contrast, has always been characterized by hierarchy and place. One does not leave a private sphere characterized by hierarchy and enter a public sphere aspiring to equality. One leaves a hierarchical interior world (*uchi*) and gently works one's way to an outside world (*soto*). The latter mirrors the former and is similarly hierarchical. At the risk of overstating differences—and the point is more one of focus than essential substance—Western cultures, as part of a larger Western civilization, have at their center an experience of speaking well or poorly in public places on common concerns symbolized as politics and nurtured in institutions that encourage public dialogue by the many (popular assemblies) and the few ("upper" chambers such as the House of Lords in England, the Senate in the ancient Roman Republic, or "higher," even "supreme," courts, such as the U.S. Supreme Court). These institutions are protected by the one (such as a consul in Rome, a president, a prime minister, a dictator, or a generalissimo) who leads auxiliaries whose virtue is courage, not wisdom.

Out of the Western experience develops the mixed constitution of the one, the few, and the many or, in its modern, amended form, the mixed constitution of the executive, judicial, and legislative functions of government. The modern, mixed constitution, as represented by the U.S. Constitution, is a Newtonian refinement of an ancient idea. The mechanical checks and balances are "auxiliary precautions," as James Madison observed in *Federalist No. 51*. The primary check on the power of the state is still the people, that is, the civic virtue of the people. There are variations, sometimes of infinite complexity, between and among presidential and parliamentary forms of modern Western democracy. At the center, however, is the experience of politics as a competitive enterprise channeled, checked, balanced, and otherwise moderated by constitutional, institutional designs. Though parliaments and congresses today are more a setting for the clash of interests than the competition of ideas and principles, faded echoes of the latter ideal are still within the sight and hearing of educators who continue to nurture liberal (or liberating) arts. Virtually every institution of higher education in the world, footnotes to Plato's Academy and Aristotle's Lyceum, continues to challenge entrants to the dual responsibilities of finding careers and finding also their voices as involved citizens.

In traditional Japanese culture, by contrast, aesthetic and family experiences are primary. Traditionally, these primary experiences are symbolized in the institution of the Imperial Court. There, descended from the goddess Amaterasu, the royal family historically symbolizes the larger family of the Japanese people. At court in Kyoto throughout most of Japanese history, a city that symbolizes even today the traditional beauty of Japan, the royal family represented the most fixed of institutions in an otherwise ephemeral world. Reigning, never ruling, the Japanese Emperor represented authority, not power. With the end of the *kokutai* philosophy of the Meiji constitutional era and the implementation of the new 1947 Constitution after the war, institutions reflecting popular sovereignty and the experiences symbolized in the older institutions remain powerful forces in modern, democratic Japan. Even today, in the words of one Japanese scholar: "Anyone intending to enter the political world in Japan, whether male or female, must have a family and children: this is one condition presumed for such activity" (Iwai 1993, 110). Similarly, an unusually high proportion of Diet members are sons, and sometimes daughters, of former Diet and cabinet members. The newest party, as of September 1996, the *Minshuto,* or Democratic Party, is a particularly good example of family politics. It is led by the Hatoyama brothers, whose grandfather was prime minister during the 1950s.

All studies begin with certain assumptions. This introductory study of Japanese politics assumes that politics has both universal and culture-specific dimensions. In its universal, or global, dimensions, politics is about public choices, especially in fundamental areas involving the sources of authority, how basic institutions should be structured, what the scope of state power should be, what citizenship means, and how wider global relations should be developed. How these basic issues are approached, however, is shaped by collective experiences over time, experiences that together form a complex pattern of assumptions about divinity, psychology, ecology, and social propriety—a pattern whose complex particulars are suggested when scholars and participants alike refer to the concept of culture. This study assumes that in its sparest meaning, culture includes experiences as symbolized in language, literature, religion, the arts, and a shared perspective on history, all contributing to the context in which political dynamics take place. Finally, this study of Japanese politics assumes that global political dynamics are moving beyond ideological divisions and in the general direction of what one scholar sees as the potential clash of civilizations, emphasis on "potential" (Huntington 1993).

Like all introductory texts, what follows can only sketch basic dynamics, primary institutions and processes, and the range of political issues confronting the Japanese people today. Errors are errors of fact or judgment on the part of the author. Insights are the reflected and synthesized insights of many scholars, colleagues, friends, and associates, some of whom I would like to mention here.

This study had its beginnings in a National Endowment for the Humanities seminar on "Theory and Practice in Japanese Cultural History" directed by Professors Harold Bolitho and Albert Craig at Harvard University in the summer of 1995. I would first like to thank the Endowment for making outstanding programs such as this possible. I would also like to thank Professors Bolitho and Craig for providing a truly challenging yet warmly collegial setting in which to explore the fascinating world of Japanese cultural history. I would like to thank the other participants as well who helped make the seminar such a memorable one and whose insights and rich experience regarding Japan helped to inspire this effort. Participants were Janice B. Bardsley, Joan E. Fitch, Dorothy H. Guyot, Phyllis Larson, Clayton F. Naff, David Prejsnar, Marjorie Rhine, Michael Seth, Mary Evelyn Tucker, Bernard "Bud" Wellmon, and Benjamin Wren. I want to say a special thanks to Professor Wren of Loyola University, New Orleans, and Professor Seth of Phillips University, who shared the Perkins Hall experience, which meant extended discussions on various aspects of East Asian history and politics outside of Japan, much of it only dimly known to this student.

I would also like to thank the directors of two previous National Endowment for the Humanities seminars. Though the seminars did not bear on Japan, they did focus on developments in early modern political theory and constitutionalism in the West, aspects of which have shaped the basic approach to this study. To Professors Isaac Kramnick of Cornell University and J. G. A. Pocock of Johns Hopkins University, therefore, a sincere thank you. To them I would also like to add a special acknowledgment for their assistance in helping me to secure a Fulbright teaching assignment at Hiroshima University for the 1992–1993 academic year. That experience, perhaps more than anything else, shaped my serious scholarly interest in the world of Japanese politics. Others who helped in my securing that appointment were Professors Ellis Sandoz and Martha Swain. Professor Sandoz, professor of political science and director of the Eric Voegelin Institute for American Renaissance Studies at Louisiana State University, will always be the teacher's teacher to me. It was Professor Sandoz who introduced me to politics as a global activity primarily historical and philosophical in its particulars. Professor Swain, currently professor of history at Mississippi State University, was the colleague at Texas Woman's University who taught all the classes, advised all the students, went to the endless meetings, and still wrote the books. I would like to add here my deep appreciation for the late Professor John H. Hallowell of Duke University, whose mentorship and scholarly example are also especially representative to me of political science, or indeed academics, at its best.

I am grateful for the reviews of the manuscript that were provided by Lawrence Ziring, Western Michigan University; Michael A. Launius, Central Washington University; and Doh C. Shin, University of Illinois at Springfield.

Of the many fine scholars and students I met in Japan, I would like to note here my special thanks to the faculty, staff, and students in the American Studies Program at Hiroshima University. I would like to express the very special debt I feel to Professor Okamoto Masaru for his assistance, and most of all for his friendship. I am sure that it was probably during one of our many conversations on current events in Japan that the idea for this larger study began to take shape. I would also like to thank Professor Yamamoto Masashi of Hiroshima City University for his hospitality, generosity, and conversations about life in Japan and America today.

Thanks also are due to colleagues in the Department of History and Government at Texas Woman's University who were supportive of the project and to students in several courses on Japanese culture and politics. To two colleagues in particular, however, I owe a special thanks. Professor Jim Alexander, department chair, who found ways to release faculty for research and writing projects in what is traditionally a teaching and service intensive environment, and who also supported my trips overseas and to the East Coast to pursue

Japanese studies; and Professor Val Belfiglio, whose constant encouragement, patient listening, and most of all simple friendship helped me to see this project through to completion during busy times. Two other professional colleagues and friends who either encouraged me in this project or helped me to understand through conversations and example the complexities of East Asian political dynamics are Professor Charles Embry of Texas A&M University-Commerce, and Professor Doh C. Shin of the University of Illinois, Springfield. I am also grateful to the staff at Prentice Hall who brought this manuscript through its various stages to completion: Steven Shapiro, Michael Bickerstaff, Nicole Conforti, Serena Hoffman, and Mary Louise Byrd.

Deepest personal thanks go to families on both sides of the Pacific. To my parents, Clement and Mary Hoye, and to my siblings and their families, I express my gratitude for emotional support and appreciation. To my wife's family in Japan, I express a similar gratitude. I especially want to thank my father- and mother-in-law, Oku Shiro and Oku Tsuruko, in Kokura, for their acceptance of and confidence in me, for their personal example, and for their continuing faith in my scholarly efforts. Most of all, I wish to thank my wife, Masako, for her patience, faith, friendship, and contagious interest in Japanese culture and history. This effort is dedicated to her.

Timothy Hoye

Works Cited

Gunnell, John G. 1988. American Political Science, Liberalism, and the Invention of Political Theory. *American Political Science Review* 82 (March): 71–87.

Huntington, Samuel P. 1993. The Clash of Civilizations? *Foreign Affairs* 72 (Summer): 22–49.

Iwai Tomoaki. 1993. The Madonna Boom: Women in the Japanese Diet. *Journal of Japanese Studies* 19 (Winter): 103–120.

Kishima Takako. 1991. *Political Life in Japan: Democracy in a Reversible World.* Princeton, N.J.: Princeton University Press.

Tamamoto Masaru. 1995. Village Politics: Japan's Prince of Disorder. *World Policy Journal* 12 (Spring): 49–60.

JAPANESE POLITICS

1

Japanese Culture/ Japanese Politics

The modern Japanese state may be classified among the liberal democracies of the world. According to Francis Fukuyama's much discussed essay on the "end of history," this is no small matter. For by Fukuyama's reasoning, the twentieth century is ending right where it began—"full of self-confidence in the ultimate triumph of Western liberal democracy" (1989, 3). Japan is, of course, a non-Western liberal democracy. Liberal democracy as a concept may be defined in various ways. Fukuyama presents as a minimal definition a state that "recognizes and protects through a system of law man's universal right to freedom" and one that also "exists only with the consent of the governed" (1989, 4). Michael W. Doyle, sketching what he considers the essential elements of "liberal" states (regimes), draws on the famous German philosopher and political theorist Immanuel Kant. A "liberal" state is one that is "externally sovereign," has a "market" economy based on private property, is populated by citizens "who possess juridical rights," and is "republican." The last term was a globally popular one in the late eighteenth-century world in which Kant lived and today is used interchangeably with the term *democracy*. Whether one refers to "republics" or "democracies," substantive features must include a legislative branch that has "an effective role in public policy," whose members are elected in party competitive elections, and in which voting is based on a reasonably wide suffrage (Doyle 1986, 1164). By any of these standards, Japan is both liberal and democratic. As with the making of public policy, however, the devil—meaning complexity and nuance—is in the details. All modern liberal democracies share essential elements such as those sketched by Fukuyama and Doyle. All are also rooted in larger cultures, however, which give particular character, tone, and texture to what liberal democracy means, both in theory and practice. This is especially true with respect to Japan, whose larger culture is globally famous for its rich, complex, and unique features.

1

The concept of culture, like other concepts covering vast ranges of human experience—concepts like justice, reason, beauty, truth—presents special problems of definition. How does one limit with specific boundaries what by definition is vast and extends beyond traditional boundaries? Once one begins with the observation that politics is an aspect of culture, where does one go from there? There is no widely accepted definition of culture in the social sciences. Etymologically, however, one can point to the general meaning inherent in the concept that it points to those human experiences within a particular people in a particular part of the world that are nurtured or cultivated as especially important. One can also acknowledge, as the noted Japan scholar Merry White has observed, that culture is "more than flavor, and the cultural values that shape lives create patterns that are far from universal" (1987, 152). At a minimum, therefore, and probably with little objection from scholars regardless of field, we can note that language, religion, and a particular, shared history are fundamental elements in culture.

To confine observations here to general contrasts between Western cultures and Japanese culture, one can note the following. With respect to language, and using English as our example of a Western language, there are basic, structural differences. In the English language it is considered natural to distinguish as a matter of course according to number and person. For example, whether one is referring to table or tables (plural) is not implied; rather, it is clearly stated. Introductory lessons in English focus attention on the use of the plural. In Japanese, however, *teburu* (table) could mean one or several tables. Number is implied. With respect to person, English is pronoun rich: I eat, you eat, they eat, we eat, and the rest. In Japanese, "person" is usually implied. Of more importance in Japanese is formality or informality. There are levels of speech according to whether one is addressing a family member, a stranger, a teacher, or the rest. One may speak using honorifics, formal, informal, or casual speech. Written Japanese also clearly distinguishes between concepts indigenous to Japan and concepts, names, and words generally of foreign origin. An entire *syllabary*[1] of characters, called *katakana,* is used to write foreign words. This reflects a cultural tendency to distinguish between inside and outside or insider and outsider, a distinction of considerable importance in politics, especially in matters bearing on citizenship and foreign workers. Such are only examples of numerous distinctions between English and Japanese language as a means of communication within Western English and Japanese cultures. But these examples draw attention to important cultural differences. Hierarchy and formality, for example, are much more important in Japanese culture than in Western English culture.

Without overstating differences or overdramatizing traditional influences, one could digress here at great length on the long shadow of Aristotle's influence in the West and that of **Confucius** in East Asia, including Japan. For

---

[1] Important concepts and historically significant persons, places, and things are highlighted in **bold italics** when first introduced and are defined in more detail in a glossary at the end of the text.

Aristotle, for centuries regarded simply as "the philosopher," human beings are "political" by nature. One must participate in a *res publica* (from the Latin), a commonwealth, to develop human skills and attributes. Today, the liberal arts define required curricula in institutions of higher education where preprofessional ("before professing publicly") programs point beyond undergraduate curricula and core courses encourage the development of good communication skills for effective citizenship, as well as competent jobholders. Law, in the Aristotelian, Western tradition, tends toward statutory and constitutional law in its connotations, types of law where the emphasis is on debate in public assemblies (statutory) and dialogue among jurists using precedents (constitutional).

In the Confucian legacy, family relationships are central. The five basic relationships are to parents, children, spouse, siblings, and emperor, as a symbol of the larger family. The center of duty is not a polis beyond the household; it is the household. The closer something is to the inside (*uchi*), the more hold it has on one's duties. The further outside something or someone is, the less the attachment. *Gaijin,* for example, means "outside" person. Similarly, *gaikoku* is outside, or foreign nation; *gaikokujin* is foreigner; *gaiatsu* is outside pressure; *gaishi* is foreign capital (investment); *gaikou* is diplomacy; and *gaikoukan* is diplomat. Law, in the Confucian tradition, tends toward administrative law. Many general accounts of Japan today characterize the modern nation-state of Japan as an administrative state. Graduates of the law faculties of the top universities in Japan make up the largest proportion of upper-level administrators in Japan. Karel van Wolferen, writing in 1989, observed that over 88 percent of the section chiefs and their superiors in the Finance Ministry were graduates of the **Tokyo University** law faculty. In the Foreign Ministry, the number was 76 percent, with the proportions being equally high in other ministries (van Wolferen 1989, 111).

But politics in Japan is changing. By some accounts it is changing dramatically. Fukushima Kiyohiko, for example, writing in *International Affairs,* sees an emerging era of "big politics" in Japan. He compares Japan today to the United States in the early 1940s, before Pearl Harbor. The United States at that time was being pushed into the international arena after two decades of isolationism beginning with the decision not to join the League of Nations. The postwar fixation of Japanese politics on the small politics of questions regarding the distribution of economic benefits has begun to give way, only since the defeat of the Liberal Democratic Party in 1993, to "broad policy issues" (Fukushima 1996, 54, 55).

With respect to religion, a subject covered more extensively in Chapter 2, traditional Japanese culture represents a unique blend of Shinto, Confucian, and Buddhist influences. Less than 2 percent of Japanese are Christian, though Christianity has had an influence on Japanese culture and society in the modern world, especially in education. Many scholars have pointed to the influence of Christianity in structuring the age of ideologies in Western cultures and the political battles fought among Marxists, liberals, fascists, and others pledged to systematic ideologies, especially in the twentieth century. The absence of a

Christian theological tradition in Japan might explain in part the relative absence of strong ideological battles within Japanese politics. Though the post-war years are certainly famous for the ideological battles between the Liberal Democrats and the socialists, the former have never adhered to a carefully developed ideology, and the socialist agenda was always shaped uniquely by events and circumstances related to Japan's place in twentieth-century global dynamics. The latter point has been dramatically underscored in recent years by high-ranking socialists, such as former Prime Minister *Murayama Tomiichi*, who have all but abandoned previously held ideological positions on issues such as the United States–Japan *Mutual Security Treaty*, the constitutional status of the *Self Defense Forces*, and the status of the Japanese flag. Where a Christian theological tradition is lacking in Japan, indigenous traditions are especially strong. According to Helen Hardacre, Japan is perhaps unique in modern times in its experience with "sponsoring" religion. "Nowhere else in modern history," she writes, "do we find so pronounced an example of state sponsorship of a religion" (1989, 3). As in most cultures, the subject of religious meaning and its relation to politics is vast and complex. The main point here is to underscore the fact that religion in Japan has taken unique paths over the centuries, and whatever the continuing meaning or eroded meanings of these traditions, the results today are also unique.

As with language and religion, the Japanese have a unique sense of history. This is not to suggest that all Japanese share a common understanding of that history. Japan today is a nation of over 125 million people, and despite common introductions to Japan that stress the homogeneity of the people of Japan, there is great diversity as well. Politics, especially democratic politics, is about diversity. Still, there is a strong sense of nation, state, and a common history among the Japanese people that is indeed unique. Among the events that stand out internationally today and that are stressed in virtually all international communications that originate in the Foreign Ministry or other organs of the Japanese state itself, are the atomic bombings, which make Japan unique in world history; the almost complete isolation of the *Edo Period* (1600–1868); the frequency of earthquakes due to Japan's geographic location; the relative absence of natural resources, most notably oil; the continuity of the monarchy, despite its symbolic status under the present constitution; the victories over China and Russia at the turn of the twentieth century; the modernization during the *Meiji* era that caught the world's attention as a rising non-Western power; and the extraordinary economic and technological developments of postwar Japan, developments of such magnitude that references to the Japanese "miracle" are not uncommon. In the 1995/1996 issue of *The Statesman's Yearbook,* Japan follows only Canada and Switzerland in the Human Development Index, an index developed by the United Nations Development Program to track socio-economic measures of national progress. The United States is placed eighth in the same study. Of the ten nation-states ranked highest, of all members of the United Nations, only Japan and the United States have populations over 100 million. Of the nations ranked in the top five, Canada has a population of about 27 million, Switzerland has a population of about 7 million, Sweden, ranked fourth, has a population of about 9 million, and Norway, ranked fifth, has a population of 4.5 million. Also, of the top ten nation-states, Japan is the only non-Western entry (Hunter 1995). The tensions caused by Japanese uniqueness in a shrinking global environment in which many Japanese, and many in the leadership especially, want to play a larger role, a role in guiding global changes into the next century, is a very large element in contemporary Japanese politics. This tension is explored in its various nuances in much of what follows.

To emphasize the uniqueness of Japanese language, religion, and history as aspects of a unique Japanese culture is to caution against too quickly embracing various "convergence" theories regarding East and West and the blending of differences. During the Cold War, it was often argued that the Soviet Union and the United States were slowly moving toward the same goals and that there was a common "modernity" to all advanced systems. Today, the same arguments are often encountered with respect to East Asia, or the Pacific rim, and the West. References to the West usually include the United States, members of the European Union, and Canada, Australia, and New Zealand. Another caution needs noting as well. Stressing the unique features of Japanese culture requires great care in avoiding overstatement and stereotyping. Shinto, for example, is unique to Japan. It does not follow that Shinto is somehow also a definitive key to unlocking the mysteries of the vast tapestry of Japanese culture. Shinto, as a unique element in Japanese experience, is not bizarre, suspect, or pregnant with neo-fascist political messages awaiting rediscovery by right-wing radicals and the like. One must always avoid what Steven Reed calls "mystical cultural explanations" (1993, 4). The modern Japanese state shares many features with other modern democratic states. There are also features not shared, features rooted in a common cultural experience shared, rather, by the Japanese people among themselves over time. Among the most important windows into any culture, where language, religious sensibility, and a particular sense of history combine in a condensed and dramatic form, is literature.

Oe Kenzaburo won the 1994 Nobel Prize for Literature. He was Japan's second recipient of this honor. In 1968, *Kawabata Yasunari* won the prize (see accompanying box). In his acceptance speech in Stockholm, Oe distinguished his work from that of Kawabata in a number of particulars. Most particularly, however, he distinguished his aesthetic sense as deriving more from the Irish poet William Butler Yeats than from any Japanese tradition. Kawabata, on the contrary, drew inspiration more from a medieval *Zen* Buddhist tradition. Oe's comments ranged over a wide cultural terrain. And like his literary works as a whole, his comments in Stockholm could be characterized as suggestive, ambiguous, simple, and fragile. In other words, they were suggestive as opposed to direct or orderly in support of a thesis; what thesis he argued bore on the ambiguity of his feelings and those of the postwar, postmodern Japanese people; illustrative images and stories aimed for simplicity; and the overall impression one receives is of the fragility of all things, not least of the "exquisite"

KAWABATA YASUNARI (1899–1972)

Japan's first Nobel Prize in Literature recipient, Kawabata Yasunari began his public career as a writer with what are called "palm of the hand," or very short stories. He graduated from Tokyo University and remained in Tokyo in the Asakusa district where he wrote many of his earliest, well-known pieces. Kawabata's most famous novel is *Snow Country*, written over a number of years beginning in the mid-1930s. Among his other works are *Thousand Cranes, The Master of Go, The Sound of the Mountain,* and *The Old Capital.* He was also well known outside Japan for a short story originally published in 1927 entitled "The Izu Dancer." He authored about 150 short stories. Kawabata was born in Osaka and died by an apparent suicide. His body was found in a room filled with gas fumes.

---

healing power of art. Among Oe's observations was that in Japan today there is an ambiguous feeling of polarization between past and future that runs like a deep scar that splits "both the state and its people" (1994, 117).

There is much in Oe's speech that suggests it as a good introduction to the vast topic of Japanese culture and Japanese politics in particular. Culture, of course, refers to many things: language, art, religion, philosophy, politics—the complex tapestry that defines human relationships and the connections between and among the human, the divine, and the natural. But all cultures have a center of gravity. One might argue, for example, that Western cultures share a common center in being somewhat ideological. That is, there predominates a seeking after the eternal ideas, for instance, of the good, the true, and the beautiful. This is the context of Alfred North Whitehead's famous insight that all of Western history is as but a footnote to Plato. In the eighteenth and nineteenth centuries, when under the influence of the Enlightenment in Scotland, France, and Germany, Western intellectuals began to look increasingly for developments across time, most famously in the works of Hegel, Darwin, and Marx, the searches often crystallized in various "ideas" of history. Various "logics" of history became the centerpieces of political ideologies such as Marxism and social Darwinism. And much of Asian politics, under Western influences, reflects these influences today. But at the center of Japanese culture one finds more of a sensitivity to aesthetics.

Donald Richie, long-time and distinguished Japan observer particularly acclaimed for his studies of Japanese film, has observed that "aesthetic qualifications become moral qualifications in Japan; beauty becomes honesty" (1987, 79, 80). One has to be careful here to avoid overgeneralization, but even in basic linguistic practices there are good illustrations of these differences between Western and Japanese cultural assumptions. Fumiko Mori Halloran, a Japanese writer, recently observed that the Japanese language is very good for "describing nature and expressing feeling." She observes, for example, that there are several nuanced ways of speaking about rain. *Samidare* means early summer rain; *shigure* is fall rain; *hisame* is a sleet/rain mixture; and *konuka ame* is a foggy, misty rain. American English, by comparison, she observes to be particularly well suited for communicating action. One can run, dash, hasten, rush, speed, gallop, scurry, among other possibilities (Halloran 1995, 23). In the modern West, certainly the American West, all often seems to be "whirl" and sails without anchor.

Modern Japan, however, presents a more complex picture. It was **Donald Keene**, among the most respected of Western observers of Japanese culture, who once observed how difficult it would be "to discuss any aspect of Japanese culture without alluding to the Japanese sense of beauty, perhaps the central element in all of Japanese culture." Based on his study of Japanese aesthetics, Keene cautiously distinguishes four aspects that continue to characterize the Japanese sense of beauty after hundreds of years of development in all of the various forms of Japanese art. Japanese arts tend to be suggestive, avoiding "climactic" moments; irregular, avoiding uniformity; they strive for simplicity, not grandeur; and often focus on "perishability" (Keene 1988). Oe's remarks in Stockholm reflect these tendencies, as do his various, richly textured literary works. One might suggest here that Japanese politics also moves often, certainly not always, along similar lines.

Much can be learned about a particular culture and cultural priorities etched deeply over time by examining children's literature. These stories, told to children generation after generation, can serve as gateways into the various layers of meaning for the people of a particular time and place. Three traditional stories in Japan that reflect some of the above aesthetic elements and that every schoolchild continues to learn are the story of the bamboo cutter and his daughter, Kaguyahime (*Taketori Monogatari*), of the peach boy (*Momotaro*), and of the 47 loyal *ronin*, or masterless **samurai** (*Chushingura*).

These stories represent cornerstones in the Japanese socialization process, a process that traditionally emphasizes "commitment to ethical and aesthetic ideals and service to persons and efforts greater than the particular self." According to Najita Tetsuo, author of *The Intellectual Foundations of Modern Japanese Politics*, these ideals are "central to Japanese culture and shall undoubtedly continue to be so" (1974, 142).

OF SHINING PRINCESSES, PEACH BOYS, AND DEDICATED WARRIORS

The story of the shining princess comes from the late ninth century and is probably "the most famous of the early Japanese tales" (Rimer 1978, 66). An old man, a bamboo cutter, is in the mountains cutting bamboo when he comes upon an open, hollow stalk that has a very bright, shining light emanating from the base. The old man inspects closer and discovers a tiny girl, bathed in light, inside the base of the stalk. He brings the little girl to his wife and they decide to raise her as their own, as they never had children. She grows up very quickly into a most beautiful young woman, a shining princess. Word spreads of her beauty, and young men from all over Japan come to seek her as a wife. Five princes are among the suitors and they each vow to perform virtually impossible tasks to win her hand. Kaguyahime, however, is not of this world. She came from the moon and was banished to the islands of Japan as a punishment for sins committed in a previous life. She tells her five suitors, however, that whoever can please her by performing the deed she instructs will win her hand. One must bring her the begging bowl of the Buddha; one must bring a jeweled branch from Paradise; another must secure a famous robe made of fire-rat fur; another must bring a jewel from the neck of a dragon; and the last must secure the charm of swallows. Each attempts the task, each attempts to deceive Kaguyahime, and each is exposed as a fraud. The emperor himself hears of this shining princess and seeks to meet her. After some difficulty he meets and also falls in love with the princess. But Kaguyahime cannot marry. She must return to the moon, and soon an army will come to retrieve her. Despite the best warriors of the emperor, dispatched to defend her, Kaguyahime returns to her home with the army of the moon. She leaves behind many tears, much sadness, and a letter for the emperor. She also leaves a jar containing a special potion that will give immortality. The emperor, however, in his sadness, writes a poem and gives it, with the potion, to trusted aides whose orders are to take the poem and the potion to the top of the highest mountain in Suruga and burn them. The orders are carried out, and ever since people call that mountain Fuji, meaning "immortal."

Like all works of art, the *Taketori Monogatari*, "Tale of the Bamboo Cutter," is subject to many interpretations. At its core, however, regardless of possible readings, is a theme of beauty and sadness, of a longing to merge with cosmic beauty, frustrated by the limitations of an earthly existence. The tale certainly reflects aspects of the noble truths of Buddhist teaching—that life is suffering, that suffering comes from desire, and that salvation, nirvana, is a painless merger with the cosmos into nothingness. The theme of beauty and sadness is a common one in Japanese literature. *Beauty and Sadness* is the title, for example, of one of Kawabata Yasunari's novels. The cherry blossom, *sakura*, is a cultural symbol cherished by the Japanese as representing both beauty and sadness. Every spring, flower-viewing parties, *hanami*, fill the parks and line the rivers in cities all over Japan in celebration of the flowering blossoms. But the life of the cherry blossom is short and fragile. Sad tales about beautiful young women and tragic circumstances are also common themes in Japanese literature, cinema, and television dramas.

A poignant example is *Ibuse Masuji*'s Black Rain, a novel written in the mid-1960s. The story is of a family, particularly a young woman named Yasuko, struggling to come to terms with the events in their lives and in the life of Japan after the bombing of Hiroshima on August 6, 1945. Yasuko was exposed to the black rain and walked within the city after the explosion to reach her uncle's factory in Ujina. In the years following the war, others with similar experiences become sick and die. Tainted by the bomb, Yasuko cannot marry and has little future. Toward the end of the story she shows signs of the sickness herself and her deterioration accelerates. As she is leaving in an ambulance, her uncle watches in deep sadness the distant sky for a rainbow, for if a rainbow appears, she will recover. Stories, images, sales strategies, television productions, tourism promotionals—virtually every aspect of Japanese culture and society today—mirror well and poorly, in greater and lesser degree, stories of shining princesses and beauty become sadness.

"Peach Boy," **Momotaro**, is probably the most popular of children's stories in Japan today. Like the story of the shining princess, it begins with an elderly couple who have no children. One day the old woman is washing clothes in the river when a giant peach comes floating by. She retrieves it and brings it home to share with her husband for dinner. When he cuts into it, however, they are shocked to find a little boy inside. The boy grows into a strong and courageous young man who vows to go to Ogre Island to defeat the devils there and bring back treasures stolen by them. His mother fixes him some dumplings, and he goes off to fight. On his journey he meets a spotted dog, a monkey, and a pheasant. Each receives some dumplings, and each decides to go along to fight the devils. The pheasant flies over the fort, the monkey sneaks in and opens the gate, and Momotaro and the spotted dog enter the fort, catch the enemy by surprise, and defeat them all. The remaining devils vow never to do wicked things again. Momotaro and his friends take the gold, silver, jewels, and other treasures and return home to live happily.

As with the story of the shining princess, there are many aspects to explore and many possible interpretations. The peach boy, however, is clearly strong, courageous, loyal, generous, and clever. By cooperating with his natural allies, those close to the ground (dogs), those who move in the trees (monkeys), and those who fly above (birds), he can conquer his enemies. He shows both determination and gentleness, characteristics that capture the meanings, respectively, of the verb *ganbaru* (to strive) and the adjective *yasashii* (gentle), Japanese terms daily encountered and that communicate the most essential virtues in Japanese culture today—a commitment to do one's best at all times and to show a gentleness of manner and spirit in encounters with others. There is also in this popular children's story a shared dimension with the story of the shining princess. In both stories, and in many others, a childless elderly couple "adopts" a child of magic possibilities who is divine, meaning from deep within nature.

One of the striking characteristics of Japanese culture and society today is the relationships between young children and those advanced in years, between youth and age. In many respects, both populations are somewhat indulged. Yet the bonds between young children and the elderly, especially grandparents, are among the strongest and most carefully nurtured in Japan. One might observe that the special relationship between the coming and passing generations is a reflection of the deeply entrenched tendency in Japanese culture and society to preserve a careful balance between what is most new—robotics, computer technology, cyberspace communications, changing global markets—and what is most cherished in the traditional culture, the larger Japan.

In the regular session of the Diet in 1996, among the more controversial bills was one involving the civil code that would change basic family law for the first time in half a century. Among its provisions was one providing that married couples could choose to keep their own name or agree on one family name. Traditional law requires that one family name be adopted. The proposed changes are to move Japan in line with changing norms worldwide, especially regarding women in the professions or women who for personal reasons wish to keep their family name after marriage. The bill was not passed in regular session due to controversy. It was to be taken up again in an extraordinary session of the Diet in the fall of 1996. But even as this bill generated opposition, largely due to complications foreseen by some in the Diet regarding children and identity, Prime Minister **Hashimoto Ryutaro** identified as among his biggest priorities his desire to pass legislation to assist the elderly with public insurance for nursing care. He identified it as a top priority in his call for the extraordinary session of the Diet for the fall of 1996.

Any legislation that addresses the very young or the elderly is "extraordinary" by definition. The mature and the middle-aged in Japan, on the other hand, must meet day-to-day challenges with determination and good spirit. They must work hard to secure an environment within which the very young and the very old can develop those deep and precious bonds that reach deep into both nature and history and that are explored in stories like the shining princess and the peach boy.

Youthful renewal and the dignity of age are also powerful themes in Japanese religion. The main building of the Ise Shrine, the most revered of all Shinto shrines, is completely rebuilt every 20 years. The Inner Shrine dates from about the third century, and in traditional belief is said to be home to **Amaterasu Omikami**, from whom the Imperial Family descends. It is founded by the daughter of a legendary emperor named Suinin. The daughter, Yamatohime (Yamato Princess), founded the shrine on orders of the goddess, according to legend. **Yamato** is the traditional name for Japan and refers to the period before **Nara** (710–794). Yamato is a powerful symbol in Japanese thought. During World War II, for example, the Japanese built the largest battleship in the world to that time and named it *Yamato*. In an essay he wrote just one month before he died, Shiba Ryotaro, a popular Japanese novelist, spoke of the Japanese feeling for age and youth. His basic point was that Shinto celebrates youth, and Japanese Buddhism represents age and aging. He pointed out that virtually all of Shinto's rites, myths, and legends are about purification and youth. Buddhist symbols, on the contrary, represent age. He concludes his essay as follows:

> On the one hand, the Japanese celebrate youth. On the other, they revere the mellow austerity of ancient Buddhist statues. These two sensibilities, never integrated into a theoretical framework, reside within everyone. It is the very lack of cohesion, I believe, that is the source of the Japanese people's vitality. (1996, 67)

There is much in Shiba's insight. One might observe the following as well. Children in Japan are regularly brought to Shinto shrines, notably soon after birth and at ages 3, 5, and 7. When one dies in Japan, on the other hand, one is buried according to Buddhist rituals. With respect to politics, one might observe that there is a similar interplay between Japanese party and electoral politics, on the one hand, and Japan's traditional bureaucracy on the other. Dynamics in the one, much like with the rebuilding of the shrine at Ise, center on renewal. A spirit of newness, reform, and starting over prevails. The current proliferation of parties finds its analogue throughout Japanese political development. Dynamics within the bureaucracy, however, are more static. There, a Confucian rule of the sages represents tradition—a theoretical tapestry, like Buddhism, imported from China. Notoriously slow to change and traditionally the object of greater respect than the politicians, Japanese civil servants bear more the burdens of history, tradition, continuity, and the "mellow austerity" of traditional Japanese culture.

Chushingura, the story of the 47 *ronin* (masterless *samurai*), started out as a puppet play (*Bunraku*). It is based, however, on a true story that took place over a 21-month period during 1702 and 1703. Lord Asano Naganori of Ako is in Edo, as the story begins, in order to see to the arrival at the court of the *Shogun* of a special envoy from the Emperor at Kyoto. Inexperienced in such matters, as Ako was a long way from Edo (Tokyo), Asano seeks out the counsel of Lord Kira Yoshinaka, someone well schooled in these affairs. Asano does not deliver an expected bribe, however, and so is taunted and insulted by Kira. Losing his temper, Asano draws his sword and attacks Kira, seriously wounding him. Asano is brought before the Shogun, Tsunayoshi, and is sentenced to die by the traditional *samurai* ritual of *seppuku* for drawing his sword within the castle. Asano's lands are confiscated by the state and his *samurai* become masterless (*ronin*).

The central drama of the play, in all of its forms today, is the revenge plotted by the 47 *ronin* and the masterful way in which through deceit, posturing, determination, and skill they succeed in their plans. On a snowy evening in winter, usually presented as December 14, the *ronin* successfully invade Kira's compound in Edo; they defeat Kira's defenders, kill him, and bring his head to Sengaku Temple where Asano is buried. For their deed, all 47 of Asano's avengers are sentenced to follow their master's fate and commit *seppuku*. They are today buried at Sengaku Temple, with their lord. They are also the focus of many documentaries, movie and television re-creations, and much general discussion.

Part history, part myth, *Chushingura* has become a popular focal point in many discussions, inside and outside of Japan, regarding elements of Japanese culture. Often the discussions center on how the story emphasizes the virtues of loyalty, determination, and dedication to duty. In this respect, *Chushingura* is not unlike the story of *Momotaro*. Others, however, point to the militaristic dimensions of the story and the obsession with exacting revenge. Much has been written on *bushido*, the way of the warrior, as a central element in traditional Japanese culture, and *Chushingura* ultimately represents a celebration of this Japanese warrior ethic. As the code of the *samurai*, the traditional ruling class in Japan, *bushido* taught absolute loyalty, personal honor and duty, courage, skill with weapons, and sacrifice, even of one's life. During the early Edo Period, in the works of Miyamoto Musashi (1584–1645) and Yamago Soko (1622–1685) and in the classic work *Hagakure,* by Yamamoto Tsunetomo, in 1716, the way of the warrior became somewhat codified. During the relatively peaceful Edo Period, the ethic of the *samurai* class developed into a more generalized concept of service to the state. Though the *samurai* class was abolished by the reforms of the Meiji Period, *bushido* survived as a cultural ideal. In 1899, for example, Nitobe Inazo (1862–1933) published *Bushido—The Soul of Japan* and presented his work as an "exposition of Japanese thought." *Bushido,* for Nitobe, was a "code unuttered and unwritten." It developed as an "organic growth" and "fills the same position in the history of ethics that the English constitution does in political history." *Bushido*'s sources may be found in Buddhism's teaching to trust calmly in fate; in Zen Buddhism's additional teaching to seek harmony with the Absolute; in Shintoism's stress on loyalty to the sovereign, reverance for ancestors, and filial piety; in the Confucian doctrine of the five fundamental human relations (see Chapter 2); and, above all, in a concept of "rectitude" or a fundamental sense of justice. *Gishi* means "man of rectitude" and the 47 *ronin,* according to Nitobe, "are known in common parlance as the Forty-seven *Gishi*" (1905, 5–25). Ito Hirobumi, in his "reminiscences" on the drafting of the Meiji Constitution of 1889, expressed the traditional spirit of Japanese culture this way:

> The great ideals offered by philosophy and by historical examples of the golden ages of China and India, Japanicized in the form of a "crust of customs," developed and sanctified by the continual usage of centuries under the comprehensive name of *bushido,* offered us splendid standards of morality, rigorously enforced in the everyday life of the educated classes. The result, as everyone who is acquainted with Old Japan knows, was an education which aspired to the attainment of Stoic heroism, a rustic simplicity and a self sacrificing spirit unsurpassed in Sparta, and the aesthetic culture and intellectual refinement of Athens. (1960, 672)

Ruth Benedict, in her famous study of Japanese culture *The Chrysanthemum and the Sword,* explored what appeared to be contradictions within Japanese culture between aesthetic ideals (the chrysanthemum) and warlike tendencies (the sword). The *Taketori Monogatari* surely expresses the aesthetic dimension and *Chushingura* just as surely expresses the other. But it is also extremely important to note that these stories, and many others with similar themes, are stories from a traditional, preindustrial, predemocratic Japan. Today, as with all modern, industrialized democracies, Japanese culture, society, and politics have been modified by scientific, technological, egalitarian, and historical forces having little to do with shining princesses and dedicated warriors, whether from peaches or *Edo* history. Still, *yasashii* (gentle) voices of Japanese young women fill public buildings, trains, even parks all over Japan, guiding **salarymen**, women, tourists, visiting businessmen and -women, students, and others to their various destinations. Royal weddings, such as that of **Owada Masako** in 1993, evoke images of *kaguyahime.* The virtues portrayed in

Momotaro are daily held up to children as ideals—*ganbatte kudasai* (strive, do your best); *yasashiku shite* (do it gently). Loyalty and dedication to duty are minimal expectations regardless of occupation.

THE "STORY" OF RAMPO EDOGAWA

Japanese films are also important sources for exploring the fundamentals of Japanese culture. Filmmakers such as Kurosawa Akira are well known all over the world (see accompanying box). A recent Japanese film integrates these aspects of Japanese culture and explores the polarization and deep scar to which Oe points in his Nobel speech in Stockholm. The film is entitled *The Mystery of Rampo*. It was directed by Okuyama Kazuyoshi, written by Okuyama and Enoki Yuhei, and stars some of Japan's best known actors and, in the case of the heroine, Japan's best known supermodel, Hada Michiko. Rampo is a reference to one of Japan's most popular mystery writers, Rampo Edogawa, whose real name was Taro Hirai (1894–1965). His first name is taken from one of Taro's favorite writers, the American writer Edgar Allan Poe. In Japanese, Edgar would be pronounced Edoga. The film was one of the biggest hits at the box office in Japan in 1994. On one level, and upon first look, it is the story of a mystery writer exploring the relationship between a story he has written and a real-life event. The story, entitled "The Appearance of Osei," is about a woman named Osei who goes out shopping while her husband, children, and neighboring children play hide and seek. The husband decides to hide in a large chest belonging to Osei, a chest that is called *nagamochi* in Japanese and is like a hope chest where Japanese women traditionally keep memorabilia and precious memories. When the husband closes himself inside the large chest, it latches and he cannot get out. He begins to suffocate. Osei returns and discovers her husband inside the chest, still alive. Spontaneously, Osei decides to slam shut the chest again, thereby suffocating her husband. The police call it an accident. When Rampo submits his story to the government for approval, it is censored. Rampo, in frustration, burns his manuscript. The setting is the first year of *Showa*, 1926.

KUROSAWA AKIRA (b. 1910)

Probably Japan's most famous movie director and screenwriter, certainly outside of Japan, Kurosawa Akira's films are known worldwide for their action, beauty, and originality. Among his best known early works are *Rashomon* (1950), *Ikiru* (1952), and the *Seven Samurai* (1954). More recent works include *Kagemusha* (1980), *Ran* (1985), and *Dreams* (1990). In 1985, Kurosawa was honored with Japan's Order of Culture award, and in 1990, he was presented a special Oscar for his lifetime achievements. Kurosawa was born in Tokyo.

Curiously, it happens that there is a story in the newspaper reporting an event almost identical to the one written by Rampo. A woman has apparently killed her husband by locking him in her *nagamochi*. The newspaper asks whether it was murder or an accident. Rampo, fascinated by this coincidence, locates the woman in the newspaper story and begins to pursue her. He is attracted to her in ways that he does not understand. He is also increasingly ashamed of the work he has done which has the approval of the state. For example, he has written a screenplay about a phantom with 20 faces whose principal character is a detective named Akechi. This detective is Rampo's alter ego and soon Rampo is rewriting his story of the woman who kills her husband, but this time he is basing it on what he learns of the real-life woman whose name is Shizuko and who awakens feelings in him that he has not felt for a long time. The detective, Akechi, becomes a principal character in the new version as there is much to investigate. In the course of writing his new story, Rampo slowly begins to realize that the mystery he is writing about has more to do with himself and much larger events happening around him than anything involving a pulp fiction theme concerning a woman who may or may not have murdered her husband.

Rampo is haunted by images; children and a beautiful woman in mourning dominate. He is plagued by the feeling that he is lost in the woods, in semi-darkness, and cannot find his way out. But he continues to write. A story that resembles his original increasingly becomes something more, something larger. He struggles to give it expression through the investigations of his alter ego, the detective Akechi. On one level, Akechi is investigating the mystery of the woman who may have killed her husband. On another level, however, there seems to be a larger, deeper mystery. Rampo writes of Akechi finding the woman who people say killed her husband newly remarried to a *Marquis*. They live in a huge, Western-style mansion on the coast, high on a cliff overlooking the sea. The Marquis is vulgar, corrupt, poisoned by drugs. He corrupts his wife. Akechi watches. Rampo writes.

In extraordinary sequences where Rampo seems to be getting closer and closer to self-discovery only to lose it, we see detective Akechi getting closer to the truth on Rampo's behalf. Akechi has found a diary in an upstairs bedroom at the mansion of the Marquis. It belongs to the mysterious woman, the Marquis' wife. The heroine, the wife, is ascending the stairs. She is dreaming of being swept far away. She sees Akechi looking through her diary. Akechi turns and says that he was "absorbed" and did not see her. Rampo, too, is absorbed and does not yet see what it is that he is really writing about, what he is really striving to give expression. Events build to a climax with the death of the Marquis. He provides "entertainment" to those who are watching by riding his white steed at full gallop over a cliff and onto the rocks and sea below. The woman at the center of the story asks Akechi to get inside the *nagamochi*. Slowly, then suddenly, Rampo overcomes the polarization between the story he is writing and the story that is happening in the real world of Showa Japan. He races to find Shizuko, only to discover that this real-life woman has become the woman he is now writing about. Art and politics merge and we hurry with Rampo to the Western-style mansion where the mysterious woman is about to commit suicide. Lost at first in the huge house, Rampo finds his way to where Akechi and the woman are located. Is he too late? The woman is lying on the top of the *nagamochi*, having taken a poisonous drink. Akechi is facing Rampo. He says to Rampo, "you finally made it." With a rush of self-realization, Rampo realizes that all of the images that have haunted him, all of the premonitions that he has seen and felt, all of the striving to find his way out of the semidarkness, out of the woods, have led him to this moment and to the imminent threat of death and destruction to everything. He throws himself onto the woman who he now knows is the shining princess that is the spirit of Japan itself, *Yamato*, and tries to protect her from a firestorm, a potential nuclear ending to Japan.

The screen fills with flashbacks and images of potential ruin. Then it is filled with images of fire, wind, and massive destruction. The screen grows dark. But out of the darkness, a small light starts beating, a light that might emanate from the base of a bamboo shoot, as in the classic tale of the bamboo cutter and the shining princess. It grows bright. And within this light, Rampo and the shining princess are one. She says to the literary artist, the guardian of Japanese aesthetics, how happy she is that he finally came. He means "everything" to her. She will lock him inside herself. They embrace. The artist and the shining princess, part history, part myth, all become one harmonious whole beyond time. And in this shining, beautiful moment a bright fire rolls across the screen like a signature—beauty and sadness. One recent study of Japanese culture points to the experience of *aware,* a quietly desperate sorrow, as central to an understanding of Japanese culture and specifically the feeling of *aware* "for the female figure who disappears in silence." According to this study, such an experience is a Japanese "cultural paradigm." By this paradigm, "a woman must disappear in order for sorrow to complete the sense of beauty" (Kawai 1988, 22). The tension created by the potential disappearance of the shining princess in *The Mystery of Rampo* echoes the theme of "The Bamboo Cutter," as well as of modern novels by Ibuse, Kawabata, and **Dazai Osamu**.

The Mystery of Rampo is a many-layered, finely textured work of art not unlike a work by Oe or Kawabata. On one level it is a standard mystery where the detective investigates a crime. On a higher plane, however, it is an extraordinary mystery that investigates the question: Where were the artists, the scholars, the intelligentsia during the early years of Showa? Why were they using their talents to write cheap stories about spouses involved in murder or apparent murders? Why did they not use their artistic talents to save the nation, the culture, the civilization, from fascism? Maruyama Masao, one of Japan's most honored scholars, raised similar questions in the immediate postwar years. The Japanese intelligentsia were, on the whole, "guilty of passivity and impotence" (Barshay 1992, 398). The "mystery" fashioned by the film about Rampo points to that same ambiguity addressed by Oe. The events leading up to and involving the Pacific War (1941–1945) have left a deep scar on the national psyche and continue to split the nation and the people. The Showa period, especially the war years, define for many Japanese a before-and-after sense of history. Stories such as those explored earlier are products of the before; but the story of Rampo, a very recent artistic effort to come to terms with Showa, reaches deep within that old cultural tradition to point the way for Japan's future. The literary artist cannot write without the shining princess; for the latter, the artist means everything. The shining princess is consummate *yasashii* (gentle beauty). The writer Rampo is all determination (*ganbari*).

CULTURE AND POLITICS: MAKING CONNECTIONS

The stories we have been discussing take us inside a culture with deep roots that partially define the context of Japanese politics today. But one must be especially cautious in making connections too neatly. Two cautions are especially important. First, Japanese culture refers to a great deal more, and less, than what is suggested in these narratives. Japanese culture also refers to popular culture and activities as various as karaoke singing bars, new religions, *pachinko*, and the particular nuances of packaged tours. It refers to the use of "night soil" and how it contributed to a clean, urban environment in modern Japan, of waste disposal in general, and of the eclectic designs one sees in prefabricated housing all over Japan. In a recent collection of essays under the title of *The Electric Geisha*, 24 authors contribute their insights on the meaning of the various and complex dimensions of Japanese popular culture today. So many of the stereotypical images of Japanese culture outside of Japan derive from an aristocratic tradition, a court culture, rather than the culture of the larger, urban society of Japanese people (Ueda 1994). Most celebrations of Japanese culture today, such as the Sun and Star Festival in Texas in 1996, incorporate both popular and traditional aspects (see accompanying box).

Second, neat lines directly connecting the aesthetic and warrior ideals of traditional Japan, or of some of the peculiarities in Japanese popular culture, with contemporary politics cannot be drawn. General observations, however, can be made. In July 1996, for example, Prime Minister Hashimoto Ryutaro made a visit to **Yasukuni Shrine**, a famous Shinto shrine dedicated to Japan's war dead. When former Prime Minister Nakasone visited there in the mid-1980s, there were international repercussions, especially in Asian nations. Official visits by the head of the Japanese government to the shrine dedicated to those who served the Japanese war effort were seen as insults to peoples victimized by Japanese aggression during the war. Hashimoto characterized his visit as "private," noting that he had a cousin who died during the war and who was buried at Yasukuni Shrine. But he signed in as the prime minister, an action that raised concerns overseas, as well as at home. The traditional stories, both of the peach boy and the 47 *ronin*, stress the military virtues as do so many traditional stories in Japan.

Regarding a related issue, the Japan Teachers Union, along with most leftist political organizations in Japan, has always opposed the *hinomaru* (rising sun

---

SUN AND STAR 1996

For 100 days, from August through December 1996, Japan and Texas celebrated together the cultural heritage of Japan. Japanese music, arts, theater, sports, and food were all highlighted in numerous exhibits and performances in Dallas, Houston, and Fort Worth. Billed as the largest exhibition of Japanese life and art ever brought to the Americas, the Sun and Star festival featured performances by the Grand Kabuki Theater of Japan, the Tokyo String Quartet, and internationally famous performers such as the violinists Midori and Tamaki Kawakubo, the pianist Minoru Nojima, and the conductor Norio Ohga. The centerpiece of the festival was an exhibit at the Dallas Museum of Art, "Japan's Golden Age: Momoyama." This exhibit included 160 pieces illustrating Japanese painting, ceramics, armor, masks, textiles, and lacquerware. Sixty pieces classified by the Japanese government as National Treasures or Important Cultural Properties were included in the exhibitions. Other exhibits included a large display of *ukiyo e* wood-block prints at the Kimbell Art Museum in Fort Worth and Japanese folk art, clay works, and contemporary arts at other area museums. Sun and Star was four years in the planning and included the cooperation of the Imperial Household Agency and the Agency for Cultural Affairs of the Japanese government. Museums and temples in Japan and scholars and foundations in both countries assisted as well. Corporate sponsors included over 75 companies in Japan and the United States, including major banks, airlines, electronics, and telecommunications corporations.

---

flag) and *kimigayo* (song to the emperor) as symbols of Japan's militarist past. In 1995, however, the Teacher's Union announced its acceptance of both, to the dismay of many and the delight of many others. Another issue where connections can easily be made involves the status and treatment of children in Japan. Among the themes of both the *Taketori Monogatari* and the story of *Momotaro* is that children are divine gifts. Japan today is famous for a cultural propensity to treat "the child as king." These are but a few recent examples of political events, some controversial, which can be related to larger themes in Japanese cultural traditions as reflected in traditional stories.

Other general, but direct connections can also be observed. As there is always hierarchy in Japanese culture, there is always a similar hierarchy in Japanese politics and within the Japanese state. An important distinction in Western politics is that between public and private. The idea of a republic that defines discussions of the principles of good government in the Western tradition until well into the nineteenth century carries this distinction at its core. *Res publica*, "public things," are distinguished from private things. Many stories, Shakespearean ones, for example, explore this distinction. There is a hierarchy where public is higher than private. There is also a fairly hard line distinguishing the two. Though difficult to draw, the line is always present. Brutus, for example, kills Julius Caesar in the play of that name because he was ambitious. As a friend, Brutus loved Caesar. But as Caesar was ambitious, he slew him. Among primary questions in the play is whether in fact Caesar was too ambitious and sought all power as dictator. Brutus says that he was, as do his colleagues in the Roman

Senate. Mark Antony says he was not. A civil war ensues. The tyrant is one who would rule the public realm as a private estate. The psychology of the tyrant is classically portrayed in Book IX of Plato's *Republic*.

In American literature, Herman Melville's novels often explore this fundamental distinction between public and private realms. Ahab, most famously, suffers from a one-eyed reason that runs on iron rails and destroys all that is in its way. In *Moby Dick,* Ahab draws within the vortex of his single-minded navigation all of the delicate balances and checks that secure the *Pequod* against the winds both of sea and fate. In a political sense, ships are often metaphors for the state in Western literature. As the *Pequod* is balanced along the lines of a mixed constitution of fore, aft, and main, so, also, is the American ship of state along legislative, executive, and judicial lines. Distinction without absolute separation of powers is the rule on both ships. Ahab, however, stays below deck, brooding. The action of this and other Melville stories tends to focus on the tension between balancing forces, people, institutions, folkways, rules, and all of the elements that tend toward stabilizing and preserving the *res publica,* the commons, the commonwealth, and the countervailing tendency, often in a central character like Ahab, to draw all of these cultural products into the fire of some private passion or passions. The battle between public and private forces, the difficulty in drawing the line that defines each realm, these are very often the real issues in Western political cultures. In American politics today, for example, questions regarding conflicts of interest by those in power and questions regarding privacy rights are at the very center of public discourse across the ideological spectrum.

In Japanese political culture today, similar battles take place and similar questions are raised. Recent Japanese politics is famous, and infamous, for its scandals. *Lockheed*, Cosmos Recruit, Sagawa Kyubin, the scandals surrounding *Kanemaru Shin*, conflicts of interest involving *Hosokawa Morihiro*, to name but a few, are well known to all Japanese citizens. But there is a sense in which such things are business as usual. Cynics abound in the West as well. But more is expected there of politics, of the *res publica.* In Japan, the distinction between inside (*uchi*) and outside (*soto*) plays a larger role than that between private and public. The latter is present more as a layer imported with Meiji and fragile as such. Political action as a whole partakes more of the outside. Concretely, political institutions such as the Diet and the parties are much less important to the Japanese state than the various organs of the civil service. The former is a product of a constitutional tradition imported from outside a century ago; the latter is a product of a long Japanese tradition with roots extending deeply into Chinese Confucian concepts regarding the rule of the sages and indigenous Japanese ideas regarding the rule of the *samurai* class.

In the early development of the modern Japanese state under the *Meiji Constitution* of 1889, the dynamic of Japanese politics was tension between what were called *transcendental cabinets* and the leaders of the political parties in the Diet. A transcendental cabinet principle conflicted with a party government principle. The former developed from the inside, from the tradition of imperial rule, from the *genro*, mostly from **Satsuma** and **Choshu**, from state organs like the **Privy Council**, and from a long tradition of the rule of the sages. Bureaucrats, prior to World War II, were known as *okami*, or literally those at "the top." The political parties developed mostly from the outside, from constitutional theories brought from the West. During **Taisho** (1912–1926), the latter gained ascendancy. During early Showa, the former gained control, and with the military, complete control. Following the war, and with the writing of the 1947 Constitution, a political culture defined more along Western democratic lines, absent of titles of nobility, has nurtured the party government principle. Yet there is conflict between a professional civil service and party, usually Liberal Democratic Party, governments. As inside is higher than outside, the civil service is higher than the Diet. As inside is higher than outside, personal relationships are of higher importance than political ones. Through a practice known as **amakudari** (descent from heaven), former high-ranking civil servants retire and join large corporations in the private sector—a sort of old-boy network (Schaede 1995). Not wanting to harm future employers, there is generally little friction between national government agencies and large organizations in the private sector. These inside, even cozy, relationships are higher, more important, than any discussions in the Diet, the media, or election campaigns stressing political reform.

Just as traditional Japanese stories emphasize hierarchy, personal relationships, loyalty, hard work, and determination, so also does Japanese politics today reflect these elements. Inside civil servants traditionally shape policy more than publicly elected members of the Diet. Personal connections count for more than ideological agreement. Even within the political arena, personal ties weigh heavily. Politicians in Japan, as in all modern democracies, are expected to bring government spending to their districts. But in Japan, they must also "disperse money at every significant wedding, funeral, and festivity" (Tamamoto 1995b, 56). Practices such as this, nurtured by long cultural traditions that stress the importance of obligations and gift giving, traditions prominently featured in the three traditional stories explored earlier, require great sums of money. This, of course, fuels "money politics." Ideological considerations, on the other hand, do not traditionally count for much. By one recent summation on this point, "Accounts of Japanese politics rarely focus on the conflict of ideas" (Tamamoto 1995b, 51). This has apparently been true since the beginnings of the modern Japanese state. According to George Akita, "There has been in Japan since about the 1890s a deeper gulf between intellectuals and politics than in most Western countries" (1967, 2). Loyalty and personal connections are especially important within the parties where *habatsu* (cliques) further divide party members. Hard work and determination are expected of all, but are more truly expected (*honne*) of the civil service than the Diet. And as the writers, the scholars, the intellectuals, in the manner of Rampo, explore the polarizations and the deep scar left by mid-twentieth-century politics, the politicians debate political reform. Some leaders, such as **Ozawa Ichiro**, see a Japan modeled more after the West. In his *Blueprint for a New Japan*, Ozawa sees a Japanese political culture with less corruption, less money politics, fewer factions, more economic competition, and more competition especially between and among ideas. Others see naïveté in such visions. One scholar, Tamamoto Masaru, sees in Japan today a kind of stateless people whose only conception of the state is that it is something associated with bureaucrats (1995a, 16).

FIXED AND FLOATING WORLDS

One way of conceptualizing Japanese politics that is taken from Japanese culture itself is to see it defined by an often subtle distinction between a more "fixed" institutional world and a more "floating" one. The latter is often somewhat illusory, though not lacking in substance. This distinction between fixed and floating worlds is reflected in everyday language in the much observed Japanese conceptual distinction between *honne* (true feelings) and *tatemae* (apparent feelings). The former is reserved, mostly, for discussions with intimates and friends and other relationships based over time and held together by mutual trust. The latter is more difficult to define with precision but it points to "principles" or outward displays of agreement or conformity designed to promote harmony above all else. It is sometimes presented as "false front," though this denies the legitimacy of its claims in a "floating" world of appearances.

The concept of a floating world originates with Buddhism, though the connotations of the concept have evolved somewhat over time. It is generally related to the Buddhist emphasis on life as ephemeral, a major theme in the famous *Tale of Genji*. One might compare here the lotus, or water lily, in Buddhist imagery to the cross in Christian symbolism. As the latter is a powerful symbol for death and resurrection, so also is the lotus a symbol for the concerns of human life, mostly illusory concerns, floating on vast expanses of water, or, symbolically, nothingness. The lotus is a water plant found in marshes, ponds, and paddies all across Japan. Because the lotus flower floats on the water but has deep, unseen roots beneath the water and within the mud below, it is traditionally seen as a powerful symbol for the capacity of the human spirit to rise above the dark, the formless, the routine. It can rise in forms both sublime, as in the traditional Buddhist quest for nirvana, and somewhat foolish, as in the modern quest for escape in entertainment. In either case, the lotus suggests a world of illusion, a floating world of impermanence and unreality.

Water is also a particularly powerful symbol in Japanese life, from the daily bathing ritual to weekend trips to *onsen* (hot springs) in the mountains. Water symbolizes a more lasting environment. William LaFleur (1992), in a recent and provocative study of the abortion issue in Japan, and in his examination of the extraordinary practice in Japan of increasing reliance on *mizuko jizo* as protectors of aborted fetuses, stresses the continuing force of a Buddhist concept of "liquid life" and the "world of water and words" in Japanese culture. The continuing force of Buddhism in the lives of many Japanese is illustrated by pilgrimages which continue from the eighth century (see accompanying box).

SHIKOKU'S 88 BUDDHIST TEMPLES

There is a 750-mile course around the island of Shikoku, the smallest of Japan's four main islands, which marks the trail for pilgrims desiring to visit 88 Buddhist temples in the same manner as others have done for centuries. About 100,000 people make the pilgrimage each year, some—though few—by foot. Kukai, from Shikoku and the founder of Shingon Buddhism, is said to have begun the practice of visiting all the temples back in the late eighth century. The temples are located both along the coast and up in the mountains, making for an arduous journey. People make the journey today for a variety of reasons. Some pray for deceased family members, some pray for personal health or job promotions, and some take the journey for the same reason they might climb Mt. Fuji—for the adventure. Japanese have made pilgrimages like this one for centuries, the most famous being ones to the Ise Shrine.

In the traditional Buddhist world, the mundane concerns and anxieties of human life are more illusory than real, more "floating" than "fixed." The more substantive aspects of life are beneath the surface, within the heart, and largely unknowable. They are protected through elaborate patterns of accepted rites and rituals. There is a proper way of everything in traditional Japanese culture. There is the way of the warrior, *bushido;* there is the way of tea, *sadou.* In traditional Buddhist teaching, *ukiyo* (floating world) refers to a world of sorrows, a view that reflects the primary teaching that life is suffering. In the early urban culture of cities like Osaka, Kyoto, and Edo, however, *ukiyo* came to mean the floating world of pleasures, activities through which one escapes sorrows. The concept of a floating world increasingly came to refer to the pleasures associated with the entertainment districts in the large cities (see accompanying box).

During the middle years of the Edo Period (1600–1868), with the full emergence of an urban class and an urban culture, the concept of a floating world

HOKUSAI KATSUSHIHA (1760–1849) AND *UKIYO E*

Hokusai Katsushiha is widely regarded as among the greatest of the "floating world" wood-block artists of the Edo Period. His most famous prints are landscapes, such as his *Thirty-six Views of Mt. Fuji* and other outdoor scenes of waterfalls, birds, ocean waves, and bridges. Much commercial art in Japan today features Hokusai images. He worked under other names at different times in his career. He also did book illustrations, among them the *One Hundred Views of Mt. Fuji. Ukiyo e* prints, especially those depicting life in the entertainment districts of large cities, were extremely popular within the merchant class of Edo in the late eighteenth and early nineteenth centuries. These prints later became popular in the West and influenced a number of European artists, especially among the French Impressionists.

came to be associated exclusively with pleasure and with the pleasure quarters of the cities. When a particular art form was developed, using woodblocks to make prints, many of the themes of the prints were taken from the pleasure quarters. These prints representing *ukiyo e* (floating world pictures), as they came to be called, developed into a distinctive element in the emerging popular culture of Edo Japan. They became popular in the West in the late nineteenth century and helped shape the Impressionist school of French painting. Claude Monet was especially taken by these prints, and his water lily paintings are among his most famous. Over the years, the concept of a floating world, therefore, came to be associated with a particular aesthetic tradition of wood-block prints and of artists such as **Hokusai** and **Utamaro**. It also came to suggest chic or avant-garde. A rising, bourgeois merchant class increasingly embraced the symbolism of life in the floating world of pleasure and illusion as life itself. Yet, within the new symbolic connotations there remained the distant Buddhist association with illusion, pale reality, and brevity. The opening line in the medieval *Tale of the Heike* points to the traditional meaning: "The bell of the Jetavana Temple tolls in every man's heart to warn him that all is vanity and evanescence" (Rimer 1991, 59).

The political dynamic in most modern democracies is defined by a competition between and among political parties, which compete for votes and seek to control national or regional governments in the service of ideology. The system may be a two-party one, as in the United States, or a multiparty one, as in France, Italy, or Germany. In Japan, however, the political dynamic might be better conceptualized as competition between fixed and floating structures, such as the various ministries, on the one hand, and the various parties, on the other. The emphasis within fixed structures is on stability, continuity, and long-range planning. These are structures that are rooted deep within East Asian cultural traditions. The emphasis within the floating party structures is on tracking change, responding to shifting voter alliances, and short-term accommodations. Emphasis in party politics is on the new. In times of great social change, new parties form and re-form. The electoral system itself becomes re-formed. In the dynamic at present, the floating party structures are assuming a larger role in the Japanese state. Power and authority are shifting away from the bureaucracy and toward the parties. But the shift is slow and subtle and will probably remain incomplete. One recent study notes that the power of the national bureaucracy, "from a local voter's or local politician's perspective, . . . is still quite formidable" (Fukui and Fukai 1996, 276). In traditional Japanese culture, lines are drawn less sharply and the emphasis is placed on seeking harmony rather than encouraging competition. And as the dynamic between fixed and floating structures defines the internal world of Japanese politics, so also is there a dynamic between a vast Japanese culture defined by a common language, history, and religious traditions and the world of Japanese politics. In this sense, all of Japanese politics is like a world afloat upon the sea of Japanese culture.

A recent event that illustrates the traditional and changing relationships between the administrative and legislative organs of the modern Japanese state involves the Ministry of Finance and reform members of the Diet. Traditionally, the Ministry of Finance is among the most important and influential of government agencies. As a reporter for the *Wall Street Journal* recently observed, the Japanese Ministry of Finance combines in one agency the activities performed in the United States by the Federal Reserve, Congress, the Internal Revenue Service, the Treasury Department, the Securities and Exchange Commission, the Federal Deposit Insurance Corporation, the U.S. Trade Representative, and state regulators, among other agencies. Recently, the Ministry of Finance has come under severe criticism for its handling of a number of fiscally related issues, most notably the banking crises over bad loans, especially those involving the *jusen* (mortgage lending companies), and restrictions to foreign companies seeking access to the huge financial services markets in Japan. Led by the *Sakigake* (New Party Harbinger), a small but influential new party that is part of the governing coalition with the Liberal Democratic Party and the Social Democrats in 1996, reform members of the Diet began urging the breakup of the Ministry of Finance. Early in 1996, the breakup seemed imminent. But due to careful, often behind-the-scenes maneuvering, ministry officials managed to blunt the reform efforts by diverting public attention to the Bank of Japan. The result was a decision in the Diet to grant more autonomy to the Bank of Japan and to dilute calls for the breakup of the Finance Ministry (Sapsford 1996, A1, A4).

This is one example of reform politics—rooted in the authoritative concerns of citizens, encouraged in the press and within new parties, championed by representatives of the reform agenda in the Diet—running into the established traditions of an administrative state sustained by well-trained, well-connected bureaucrats representative of a much older legacy vaguely reminiscent of the Confucian rule of the sages. Events such as these fuel both Western and Japanese critics who say that modern Japan, no less than traditional Japan, is run by an inner elite with little or no meaningful connection to voters, citizens, and the electoral process. This perspective suggests that though the 1947 Constitution states clearly that the people are the sovereign power, the real power in the modern Japanese state is in an elitist bureaucracy with little accountability to anything but itself. Other recent events in Japan, beyond the *jusen* crisis and the credibility of the Ministry of Finance, have eroded public trust in the bureaucracy and encouraged more reform dialogue in the press and within the parties. Health and Welfare Ministry officials are under fire for denying the existence of files warning them as early as 1983 on the dangers of imported, unheated blood products. Within the last few years, close to 2,000 of about 5,000 hemophiliacs in Japan have tested positive for HIV, and about 400 have died of AIDS. Under pressure from Diet members, most associated with the *Sakigake* Party, a number of files have recently been "discovered" that point to negligence within the ministry. Defense Agency officials similarly denied for years that the Imperial Japanese Army forced women into prostitution as "comfort women" during the war. A college professor in Tokyo, however, in 1992, discovered records in the National Institute for Defense Studies proving the contrary. In recent years, the comfort women issue has been among the most publicized in Japan and remains steeped in controversy. Related concerns over bureaucratic responses, or lack of responses, to nuclear power issues, emergency preparedness, the rise of dangerous new religions, food poisoning, and defense policy have contributed to a climate of reform that increasingly means administrative as well as electoral reform.

One could, however, juxtapose here a recent event in American politics. In June 1996, the U.S. Supreme Court ruled that three U.S. House of Representatives districts within the state of Texas were unconstitutionally drawn. The Court ruled that the Texas legislature, in overly stressing race as a factor in drawing district boundaries, violated the equal protection clause of the Fourteenth Amendment. It was not originally clear what exactly the practical impact of this decision would be in Texas. Should scheduled elections for November 1996 proceed in the three districts, or should special elections be called based on redrawn districts? Should the Texas legislature be called into special session to redraw the districts? In August, a federal district court in Austin ruled that 13, not 3, of the 30 U.S. House districts in Texas would have to be redrawn before the November elections. The Austin court redrew the lines temporarily and directed the state legislature to draw permanent districts by June 1997. Based on the original decision of 9 justices on the U.S. Supreme Court and by 3 federal district court judges in Austin, 13 of 30 U.S. House districts in Texas were completely changed, affecting over 40 percent of Texas voters, 13 incumbent members of the U.S. House, including Majority Leader Dick Armey, and 13 challengers nominated by their party's voters in spring primaries.

One could present this as but one more example in the long-established traditions of judicial review and judicial activism in American political history. The balance wheel in modern American democracy is the judiciary, the bench, and the bar. Just as scholars can point to bureaucrats, including especially those in the Ministry of Finance, as the real midwives of the industrial revolution and, later, the postwar, economic miracle in Japan, so also can scholars point to jurists, especially on the U.S. Supreme Court, as the true architects of industrialization in late nineteenth- and early twentieth-century America. The Lochner era is a well-established term for referring to American constitutional development during the period of rapid industrialization. The reference is to the case of *Lochner* v. *New York* (1905) where the U.S. Supreme Court rejected a law in New York state that regulated the hours that bakers could work as an excessive interference with the right of contract protected by the Fourteenth Amendment's due process clause. Liberty meant liberty of contract during the Lochner era. The interpretation by the Court was nurtured less by the Fourteenth Amendment, however, than by a social Darwinist jurisprudence widely shared by the Court and pointed out by Justice Oliver Wendell Holmes in his famous dissenting opinion. Competition was considered the law of nature and, also, of the

American state. Cooperation and harmony are the law of nature in traditional Japanese thought, a view that permeates virtually every aspect of Japanese culture today. Activist judges nurtured by schools of jurisprudence balance electoral political dynamics in America today; reserved, entrenched, traditional bureaucrats, ministry officials nurtured by long-established administrative traditions, balance electoral political dynamics in Japan.

The United States–Japan Treaty of Mutual Cooperation and Security, as written in 1960, pledges both governments to uphold "the principles of democracy, individual liberty, and the rule of law." Focusing only on the last of these three principles, it is clear that *rule of law* as a fundamental concept carries very different meanings and shades of meanings within the two national heritages. Balancing the electoral and participatory dynamics in modern Japan is the Japanese bureaucracy; in modern America, it is the federal judiciary. Decision-making processes in the respective cultural traditions are the products of developments over centuries, developments originating in ancient China and ancient Greece, respectively. The "sources of authority" in traditional Japanese culture are the subject of Chapter 2.

THE FOCUS OF JAPANESE POLITICS

Defining politics is a tricky business. Like all fundamental concepts it is not susceptible to easy characterizations. Problems of definition are compounded by the need to consider politics in a non-Western setting such as Japan. Politics is, after all, a concept Western in origin. It derives from the Greek term *polis,* meaning "city." In its classical Greek origins it suggested action, rather than inaction, and public as opposed to private action. Without overstating differences, it might be noted that cultures deriving from Western origins tend to emphasize action and public discussion even today. There is little striving after still points; in large measure, all is whirl. This is certainly not a place where such large issues can be explored in any detail. But as *Edwin Reischauer* has noted, Japan is indeed modernized but not "Westernized." There are substantial Western aspects, and many of the tendencies in Japan today are clearly Western tendencies, especially among younger Japanese. Yet, for the larger part of its history, Japan developed in almost complete isolation from Western influences. Though there is certainly action in traditional stories such as the *Taketori Monogatari, Momotaro,* and *Chushingura,* there is more emphasis on beauty and sadness, hierarchy, gentleness of character (*yasashii*), determination, and personal loyalty. This combination of Eastern and Western influences is part of that complex ambiguity to which Oe refers in his Stockholm speech. And from those Eastern influences, from Confucian and Buddhist traditions, from Shinto, from its experience as an East Asian people unified by a common geography, history, and language, much of what is traditionally Japanese does not stress action and public discussion. In a recent poll, Japanese citizens were asked if "civic responsibility" and "public morals" were being observed in Japan today. Fully 61 percent responded "no." When asked to identify a specific example to illustrate the decline in civic responsibility, the largest response, 56 percent, pointed to "roads and rivers . . . littered with trash" (Ladd 1995, 27). A similar poll in the United States or in Western Europe might be expected to illicit some concern with voter turnout or apathy toward important political issues. The Japanese response is more of an aesthetic one.

It has already been noted that the bureaucratic organs of the modern Japanese state share more the tone and tendency of principles and practices Confucian in origin. But even the "floating" structures in modern Japanese politics—the parties, the media institutions, the interest groups—tend to organize less around debate and discussion than around personal loyalties and what could be called private rather than public connections. This is perhaps the context of Ozawa's stress on more issue politics, on Japan becoming a "normal" democracy—meaning Western democracy—and Hashimoto's more cautious approach. Often in articles discussing Hashimoto, the emphasis is as much on his previous connections—personal loyalties—than on his views regarding specific issues. For example, Hashimoto served as president of the Japan War Bereaved Families Association, a veterans' organization designed to give support to survivors of World War II veterans. So politics in Japan includes a wider range of activities than suggested by some famous definitions popular in the political science literature. Japanese politics is more than who gets what, when, how (Harold Lasswell). It also includes both more and less than the authoritative allocation of scarce resources (David Easton). Gary Allinson presents politics in Japan as encompassing a wide "field of action" where numerous interests, some well organized, some poorly organized, pursue their interests. The emphasis in his approach is more on how power is exercised than on who or what has power. This approach reflects the changing nature of Japanese society and politics and the increasing role of "quasi-formal" organizations such as the *shingikai* (Allinson 1993b, 1–14).

As noted in the Preface, all studies must begin with certain assumptions. This one accepts the definition of politics offered by Leslie Lipson (1993) that politics, regardless of nuances according to time, place, and cultural context, always involves active attempts to resolve problems associated with five "great issues." These issues have to do with the sources of authority, the structures of authority, the proper scope of government, the meaning of citizenship, and the role of the state in international relations. It is intriguing that, as the Japanese state today moves toward internal reform and more external involvement, as it seeks to find a balance between Asian and Western aspects of its identity on the global stage, it also wrestles with each of these great issues. The assumption here is that the context within which each of these issues is examined, debated, and ideally resolved is shaped by a culture that is unique to Japan. Chapter 2, for example, examines the sources of authority in today's Japan. Any consideration of sources of authority in the West would have to examine the legacy of antiquity in Greece and Rome, notably Greek philosophy and Roman law. The practice of judicial review in the United States, for example, shows the faded traces of rule by philosopher rulers in Plato and the tendency to tie things back to the founding of Rome. In Japan today, the constitution grants the power of judicial review to judges, but it is a power rarely used. Instead, high-ranking civil servants craft most bills that become law in the Diet, laws that are almost never challenged on constitutional grounds in the courts. The rule of the sages in ancient China is an important basis of the modern administrative state in all East Asian nation-states, including Japan. But Japan is also influenced by Western concepts. Chapter 2, therefore, explores the influence of both sages and citizens as sources of authority in today's Japan. The world of the sages is more "fixed"; the world of citizens more "floating."

Chapter 3 analyzes the structure of Japanese government under the 1947 constitution. Unlike many Western democracies, such as the United States, Canada, Australia, and Germany, Japan is not a federal union of semi-independent states. Prefectures have no reserved powers, such as states within the American union. Japanese government today is overwhelmingly national government, though the precise nature regarding where power is or how it operates is not always clear. Still, directives from Tokyo are the daily routine. Among the reform proposals advanced by Hosokawa and the founders of the Japan New Party is more independence for prefectural and local governments, proposals now embraced by many. But traditionally, at least since the Meiji reforms that began in 1868, Japanese government is highly centralized, and remains so today. Precedents both for centralized structures and more autonomy in the regions can be found in Japanese history. Also, Japan's parliamentary design conforms more with Japanese cultural tendencies to stress harmony rather than competition. In other words, there is no separation of powers and competition between and among branches such as one finds in the United States or in France. There is also no tradition of strong, individual rule, such as one might associate with presidents in France or the United States. Chapter 4 examines floating structures—parties, interest groups, media, *koenkai*. Marxist parties, inspired largely by developments in Western philosophy and political theory, are the exception to the larger rule of nonideological parties in Japan. Even among Marxists, ideology tends to be more flexible as exemplified in the recent "conversion" of Prime Minister Murayama and other party members on previously essential socialist principles.

Nowhere, perhaps, is the influence of non-Western cultural traditions more pronounced in Japanese politics than in questions regarding the scope of government authority. For example, competition, even hostility, between government and business is the norm in the West. In Japan, as with other East Asian nations, government and business work together. Some refer to the Japanese approach as state capitalism. Others express frustration in finding any suitable categories within which to place the Japanese approach to government and business relationships. On a broad range of issues, one sees Japanese cultural traditions shaping assumptions that guide discussion in the Diet, the public realm, and within the bureaucracy. Social and family issues, personal issues, often outweigh economic ones to the great frustration of outside negotiators desirous of opening notoriously closed Japanese markets. Many businesses in Japan are small businesses, mom and pop operations, not the famous giants such as Mitsubishi, Toyota, Sony, Nissan, and the like. Much state regulation is designed, traditionally, to protect these family-owned businesses from competition from large retailers. The latter can charge lower prices based on volume sales. But mom-and-pop businesses preserve families and neighborhoods. On other issues such as education, crime and punishment, public safety, transportation, health, and taxes, to name some, traditions deeply rooted in Japanese history and reinforced by language, religion, and aesthetics continue to shape policy decisions.

Generally, the scope of authority granted to the government, or assumed by the government, is much wider in Japan than in Western democracies. A good illustration is Japan's national health care system. In the United States, when President Bill Clinton attempted a dramatic overhaul of the role of the national government in health care, there was a fierce battle in the Congress and ultimately no major legislation changing the status quo. In Japan, the state assumes responsibility for a minimum health care safety net but at great cost. In 1984, 9.9 percent of the population of Japan was aged 65 or over. In 1994, the proportion had risen to 14.1 percent. Projections show Japan in 2025 with 25.8 percent of its population at age 65 or over, a projection that many have referred to as a looming catastrophe and that is behind several controversial measures passed in the Diet, such as the *consumption*, or sales, *tax* back in 1989.

All states have to define citizenship. What factors distinguish insiders from outsiders? What are the rights and duties of citizenship? Chapter 6 addresses these issues in the modern Japanese state. Japan today is, of course, one of the world's leaders in defining, promoting, and developing human rights. But as with other Asian nations, Japan sometimes approaches these issues differently from Western nations. Questions regarding gender, nationality, and age, among other factors, are weighed based on cultural traditions sometimes unique to Japan. Women today in Japan are among the most vocal in working for change, and more and more women are finding their way into positions previously held by men. Korean and *burakumin* minorities continue to fight for recognition in a society that for reasons not found in other modern nation-states have traditionally been discriminated against. Foreign workers in Japan often complain about difficulties based on traditional prejudices found only in Japan. Unspoken but widely recognized hierarchies based on age and family connection also play continuing and large roles in Japanese society and politics. These and other issues are studied in Chapter 6.

Among the biggest issues in Japan today are those related to Japan's role in international relations. The Japanese government, with support from the United States and other Western democracies, seeks a permanent seat on the United Nations Security Council. Japan is currently second only to the United States in monetary contributions to the United Nations. But due to interpretations given to *Article 9* of Japan's constitution, a comparable measure of support to peace-keeping missions where troops are required has not been forthcoming. This is among the most divisive issues in Japan today. Should Japan spend more on defense, recruit more of its young people for military service, and commit more troops to UN peacekeeping missions overseas? Limited missions in recent years to Cambodia, Mozambique, El Salvador, the Golan Heights, and Somalia drew strong negative responses from Japanese mindful of the war years. Asian neighbors are not eager to see Japan again commit troops to overseas missions. Yet, given the increasing role of the United Nations in places like the Middle East, Africa, Southeast Asia, and Bosnia-Herzegovina, what should Japan's responsibility be as a potential member of the permanent Security Council?

On a related matter, questions regarding the Japan–U.S. security alliance are back in the center of bilateral discussions between Tokyo and Washington. The Cold War is over, by most accounts, and the utility of the Japan–U.S. alliance is under review in the wake of changing global alignments. How important is a strong Pacific presence by the United States to Japan, and should Japan get out from under the American umbrella in the new global order? Relations with the United States have become especially strained as well due to growing concerns regarding the behavior of American military personnel in Japan, especially on Okinawa. In September 1995, three U.S. servicemen were arrested, indicted for, tried, and convicted for the rape of a 12-year-old Okinawan girl. This incident, and others in recent years involving criminal activity, have heightened demands for renegotiating the terms of the defense alliance. In April 1996, President Clinton traveled to Japan to sign a new agreement that reasserts basic principles which have governed the relationship since 1960 but which also agree to reductions in Okinawa. Some in Japan, however, argue that the new agreement alters the fundamental nature of the role of Japanese defense commitments, a subject explored in Chapter 7. These and other considerations involving trade balances and imbalances, cultural exchanges, and political and commercial treaties are also addressed in Chapter 7.

All of these "great issues" of politics are debated or not debated within the institutional settings and basic, underlying assumptions of Japanese culture. The cultural forces involving language, religion, a sense of history, aesthetics, and social dynamics—forces that shape basic perspectives on human relationships in all of their nuances—do not determine politics. They do, however, determine politics to a considerable extent and in powerful ways. One must always avoid overstating cultural values and differences between and among cultures, while at the same time noting important dimensions of particular cultures. With respect to Japan, non-Western sources of authority blend with Western ones in unique and complex ways.

JAPANESE POLITICS TODAY: AN OVERVIEW

The decade of the 1990s has been marked by a proliferation of new parties and shifting alliances in Japan. Most scholars refer to the period from 1955 to 1993 as the *55 system*. During this period, Japanese politics was virtually the one-party rule of the Liberal Democratic Party (LDP). The leading opposition party was the Japan Socialist Party (JSP). Other parties competed for votes and gained representation in the Diet, but the LDP and the JSP represented the "in" and "out" parties and set the agenda for national political debate. The *Komei* party, founded in 1964, made significant inroads during the 1960s and 1970s with its emphasis on "clean government" and its constituency base in the large Buddhist sect called *Soka Gakkai*. The LDP in the Diet organized around different factions, each headed by a strong leader. The faction headed by Tanaka Kakuei, prime minister during the mid-1970s, played the leading role right through the breakup of the system in 1993. Kanemaru Shin, *Takeshita Noboru*, Ozawa Ichiro, and Hashimoto Ryutaro all trace their origins to the Tanaka faction. Japanese politics today, in fact, could be characterized as a competitive struggle between those associated with Ozawa and his New Frontier Party (NFP) and those aligned with the traditional LDP under Hashimoto's leadership.

The 55 system began to break up for a variety of reasons. Pressures to raise taxes led to an unpopular consumption (sales) tax in 1989; pressures from outside Japan to open markets, especially in agriculture, threatened the LDP's traditional strength among rural voters, especially rice farmers; continued reports of corruption which often included questions of possible linkages between LDP officials and *yakuza*, eroded public confidence; the end of the Cold War also meant an end to the traditional competition between the LDP and the Socialists within the Diet; and, most of all, the Kanemaru scandal. In the early 1990s, rumors began to circulate that the LDP might split into two or more parties. Such became the case when Ozawa and *Hata Tsutomu* led 44 LDP Diet members out of the party in 1992 and formed the Japan Renewal Party (*Shinseito*). At about the same time, Hosokawa was organizing the Japan New Party (*Nihon Shinto*). Soon after, another, smaller group of LDP broke away and formed the Japan New Party Harbinger (*Sakigake*). The LDP lost a confidence vote in the summer of 1993 under Prime Minister *Miyazawa Kiichi*, and elections were held in July. In that election, for the first time in 38 years, the LDP lost its majority in the House of Representatives. All three of the new parties elected members to the Diet and a coalition government with Hosokawa as prime minister was formed.

The new coalition government proved to be very popular at first. Polls showed wide support for Hosokawa and his reform agenda. To the shock and dismay of almost everyone, however, Hosokawa admitted wrongdoing in the spring of 1994 involving a personal loan, and resigned. Unprecedented realignments began to take place over the next few months. For a very brief period, Hata became prime minister, but a fragile coalition soon broke apart. A most unlikely coalition involving the LDP, the Social Democratic Party (the JSP changed its English name to SDPJ), and the New Party Harbinger named Murayama Tomiichi, a Socialist, prime minister. Throughout the period of the 55 system, the LDP and the Socialists were often bitter adversaries. Their positions on numerous issues were at polar opposites. The LDP never fully supported the 1947 Constitution, the Socialists did; the LDP supported a strong

Japan–U.S. security alliance, the Socialists stressed their pacifist roots and consistently criticized the alliance; the LDP supported the traditional symbols of the Japanese state such as the flag (*hinomaru*) and the unofficial national anthem, the *kimigayo,* while the Socialists never recognized these. Differences on domestic issues covered the entire spectrum. Yet, from the summer of 1994 through the end of 1995, this unlikely coalition governed Japan. Prime Minister Murayama announced his change of opinion on a wide range of issues, as did many other Socialists, a shift in policy which Masumi Fukatsu, writing for the *Japan Quarterly,* called "astronomical" (Masumi 1995), and many critics began writing off the Social Democrats as finished.

Increasingly, parties began to realign yet again. Most notably, in December 1994, nine different groups within the Diet joined to form the New Frontier Party (*Shinshinto*) under the leadership of Ozawa and **Kaifu Toshiki**. Their intention was to offer a conservative alternative to the LDP and to usher Japan into a new age of two-party politics. The New Frontier Party dramatizes its mission in terms of leading a third "new opening" of Japan in the modern era. According to Ozawa, the coming of Commodore Perry in 1853 marked the first opening; the American occupation and the writing of the new constitution marked the second; and the formation of the NFP marks the third. Only the last is indigenous with the Japanese themselves. In terms of policy focus, the vision painted is one of continuing the development of *civilization and enlightenment* begun during the Meiji era with particular designs on developing Japan as a "normal" democracy and a global leader. The LDP, under Hashimoto's leadership, also seeks reform, but at a slower pace. Many of the differences separating the two parties have more to do with scope and timing than substance.

As the twenty-first century approaches, Japanese-style democracy appears to be characterized by three dominant features: first, a recentering from the bureaucracy and toward party government and other less formalized, or less "fixed," structures such as *shingikai* (advisory commissions)—toward what Gary Allinson calls the "negotiated polity" (1993a, 17–49); second, party politics dominated by two conservative parties and a possible third party on the left made up of remnants of the socialist, communist, and harbinger (*Sakigake*) parties; and third, a continuing national dialogue on Japan's place in global affairs in the wake of the end of the Cold War. Recent electoral reforms that dramatically reshape lower house districts will affect Japanese politics in ways yet to be seen (Christenson 1994). First elections under the new scheme were held in October 1996. A complex scheme of electing Diet members from multimember districts has been replaced by 300 single-member districts and 11 regions from which an additional 200 members are chosen based on party votes. (Old and new systems are examined in Chapters 3 and 6.) Supporters believe that the new system will bring a new politics based less on money and personalities and more on public dialogue on issues. Critics believe that it is more show than substance and that real reform will come only when stricter campaign finance laws aimed directly at traditional money politics (*kinken seiji*) are enacted. Other critics look deeper. A recent study of grassroots political dynamics in Okayama and Toyama Prefectures concludes that "Japanese voters are mobilized at election time mainly by the lure of pork barrel, only marginally by policy issues, and even less by ideals and visions" (Fukui and Fukai 1996, 268, 269). Another study emphasizes the role of "young Turks" within the parties, not disillusioned voters, as the source of recent reform efforts, a sort of revolution from within (Wolfe 1995).

Summary

The modern Japanese state may best be classified as a liberal democracy. At a minimum, this means a widespread acceptance of the rule of law, an ideal of human freedom, and consent of the governed. Whereas Japan shares these and other basic features with other modern liberal democratic states, it is also defined by a larger culture somewhat unique in many of its features. Japanese language, religious traditions, historical experiences, and traditional arts, especially literary arts, are among representative elements within this larger culture. These elements represent forces that have shaped the development of liberal democracy as it is practiced in Japan today. Aspects of the Japanese language include tendencies toward formality, the expression of feeling, and the recognition of hierarchy. Japanese religious traditions include Shinto, Buddhist, and Confucian influences, with little exposure to Christian, Islamic, Jewish, or other more Western religions. Japanese history, as with any nation-state, also has particularly unique features. Especially noteworthy are experiences with a long period of isolation during the Edo Period, frequent earthquakes, a scarcity of natural resources, the atomic bombings, the long reign of an Imperial House, and rapid postwar economic development. Among literary arts, traditional children's stories in Japan stress virtues still important in the socialization process. Prominent among these virtues are the importance of effort, gentleness, loyalty, and a sensitivity both to beauty and sadness. Popular contemporary films, such as *The Mystery of Rampo,* also dramatize the importance of these traditional virtues. The Nobel writer Oe Kenzaburo is a modern literary artist whose work reflects many aspects of Japanese culture but also points beyond them to the challenges brought by Western influences. Among other results, Western influences have caused something of an ambiguous feeling regarding past and future that splits the thoughts and feelings of many Japanese people today.

Many of these aspects of Japanese culture are reflected in Japanese politics. One way of conceptualizing the complex world of Japanese politics today is to see it as shaped somewhat by the dynamic interplay between fixed and floating worlds, an image taken from Japanese Buddhism, history, and the arts. A fixed world characterized by administrative traditions with roots in ancient Chinese civilization balances a more floating world dominated by institutions more Western in origin, such as the political parties and organs of mass media.

This is somewhat different from Western models of liberal democracy where competition between and among parties representing different ideological traditions and visions of the good society is more the center of the political drama. Despite cultural differences, however, the focus of Japanese politics today tends to be centered on universal political issues regarding sources of authority, the structure of governing institutions, the legitimate scope of state authority, the meaning of citizenship, and the role of the state among the nations of the world. More specifically, a brief overview of Japanese politics today would highlight the proliferation of new parties, shifting alliances within old parties, the breakup of the 55 system, a shift of power from administrative to party institutions (a shift probably temporary), and recent electoral and administrative reform efforts.

Suggested Readings

Benedict, Ruth. 1946. *The Chrysanthemum and the Sword: Patterns of Japanese Culture.* New York: World.

Booth, Alan. 1995. *Looking for the Lost: Journeys Through a Vanishing Japan.* New York: Kodansha International.

Doi Takeo. 1973. *The Anatomy of Dependence.* Trans. John Bester. Tokyo: Kodansha International.

Dore, Ronald Philip. 1978. *Shinohata: A Portrait of a Japanese Village.* London: Allen Lane.

Ikegami Eiko. 1995. *The Taming of the Samurai: Honorific Individualism and the Making of Modern Japan.* Cambridge, MA: Harvard University Press.

Keene, Donald. 1984. *Dawn to the West: Japanese Literature of the Modern Era.* New York: Holt, Rinehart, & Winston.

LaFleur, William R. 1992. *Liquid Life: Abortion and Buddhism in Japan.* Princeton, NJ: Princeton University Press.

Najita Tetsuo. 1974. *The Intellectual Foundations of Modern Japanese Politics.* Chicago: University of Chicago Press.

Nakane Chie. 1970. *Japanese Society.* Berkeley: University of California Press.

Nitobe Inazo. 1905. *Bushido—The Soul of Japan: An Exposition of Japanese Thought.* New York: Putnam's.

Oe Kenzaburo. 1995. *Japan, The Ambiguous and Myself: The Nobel Speech and Other Lectures.* Tokyo: Kodansha International.

Ohnuki-Tierney Emiko. 1993. *Rice as Self: Japanese Identities Through Time.* Princeton, NJ: Princeton University Press.

Reed, Steven R. 1993. *Making Common Sense of Japan.* Pittsburgh: University of Pittsburgh Press.

Reischauer, Edwin O., and Marius B. Jansen. 1995. *The Japanese Today: Change and Continuity.* Cambridge, MA: Belknap Press of Harvard University Press.

Richie, Donald. 1987. *A Lateral View: Essays on Contemporary Japan.* Tokyo: The Japan Times.

Rimer, J. Thomas. 1978. *Modern Japanese Fiction and Its Traditions.* Princeton, NJ: Princeton University Press.

Works Cited

Akita, George. 1967. *Foundations of Constitutional Government in Modern Japan, 1868–1900.* Cambridge, MA: Harvard University Press.

Allinson, Gary D. 1993a. Citizenship, Fragmentation, and the Negotiated Polity. In *Political Dynamics in Contemporary Japan,* ed. Gary D. Allinson and Yasunori Sone, 17–49. Ithaca, NY: Cornell University Press.

———. 1993b. Introduction: Analyzing Political Change: Topics, Findings, and Implications. In *Political Dynamics in Contemporary Japan,* ed. Gary D. Allinson and Yasunori Sone, 1–14. Ithaca, NY: Cornell University Press.

Barshay, Andrew E. 1992. Imagining Democracy in Postwar Japan: Reflections on Maruyama Masao and Modernism. *Journal of Japanese Studies* 18 (Summer): 365–406.

Christenson, Raymond V. 1994. Electoral Reform in Japan: How It Was Enacted and Changes It May Bring. *Asian Survey* 34 (July): 589–605.

Doyle, Michael W. 1986. Liberalism and World Politics. *American Political Science Review* 80 (December): 1151–1169.

Fukui, Haruhiro, and Shigeko N. Fukai. 1996. Pork Barrel Politics, Networks, and Local Economic Development in Contemporary Japan. *Asian Survey* 36 (March): 268–286.

Fukushima Kiyohiko. 1996. The Revival of "Big Politics" in Japan. *International Affairs* 72 (January): 53–72.

Fukuyama, Francis. 1989. The End of History? *The National Interest* (Summer): 3–18.

Halloran, Fumiko Mori. 1995. Escape to Another World: Glimpsing Truth Through Writing. *Japan Update,* June, 22–23.

Hardacre, Helen. 1989. *Shinto and the State, 1868–1988.* Princeton, NJ: Princeton University Press.

Hunter, Brian, ed. 1995. Japan. In *The Statesman's Yearbook, 1995–1996,* 818–826. New York: St. Martin's Press.

Ito Hirobumi. 1960. Reminiscences on the Drafting of the New Constitution. In *Sources of Japanese Tradition,* compiled by Ryusaku Tsunoda, Wm. Theodore de Bary, and Donald Keane, 671–676. New York: Columbia University Press.

Kawai Hayao. 1988. *The Japanese Psyche: Major Motifs in the Fairy Tales of Japan.* Dallas: Spring Publications.

Keene, Donald. 1988. *The Pleasures of Japanese Literature.* New York: Columbia University Press.

Ladd, Everett C. 1995. Japan and America: Two Different Nations Draw Closer. *The Public Perspective: A Roper Center Review of Public Opinion and Polling* 6 (no. 5): 18–36.

LaFleur, William R. 1992. *Liquid Life: Abortion and Buddhism in Japan.* Princeton, NJ: Princeton University Press.

Lipson, Leslie. 1993. *The Great Issues of Politics: An Introduction to Political Science.* Englewood Cliffs, NJ: Prentice Hall.

Masumi Fukatsu. 1995. The SDPJ's Astronomical Shift in Policy. *Japan Quarterly* 42 (January): 70–82.

Najita Tetsuo. 1974. *The Intellectual Foundations of Modern Japanese Politics.* Chicago: University of Chicago Press.

Nitobe Inazo. 1905. *Bushido—The Soul of Japan: An Exposition of Japanese Thought.* New York: Putnam's.

Oe Kenzaburo. 1994. Japan, the Ambiguous, and Myself. Trans. Hisaaki Yamanouchi. In *Japan, the Ambiguous, and Myself: The Nobel Speech and Other Lectures*, 105–128. Tokyo: Kodansha International.

Reed, Steven R. 1993. *Making Common Sense of Japan*. Pittsburgh: University of Pittsburgh Press.

Richie, Donald. 1987. *A Lateral View: Essays on Contemporary Japan*. Tokyo: The Japan Times.

Rimer, J. Thomas. 1978. *Modern Japanese Fiction and Its Traditions*. Princeton, NJ: Princeton University Press.

———. 1991. *A Reader's Guide to Japanese Literature*. Tokyo: Kodansha International.

Sapsford, Jathon. 1996. The Way a Bureaucracy Beat Back Reform Says Volumes About Japan. *Wall Street Journal*, 2 August, 1 (A), 4 (A).

Schaede, Ulrike. 1995. The "Old Boy" Network and Government-Business Relations in Japan. *Journal of Japanese Studies* 21 (Summer): 293–317.

Shiba Ryotaro. 1996. Age, Youth, and Japanese Sensibilities. *Japan Echo* 23 (Summer): 67.

Tamamoto Masaru. 1995a. Reflections on Japan's Postwar State. *Daedalus* 124 (Spring): 1–22.

———. 1995b. Village Politics: Japan's Prince of Disorder. *World Policy Journal* 12 (Spring): 49–60.

Ueda, Atsushi, ed. 1994. *The Electric Geisha: Explaining Japan's Popular Culture*. Trans. Miriam Eguchi. Tokyo: Kodansha International.

van Wolferen, Karel. 1989. *The Enigma of Japanese Power: People and Politics in a Stateless Nation*. New York: Knopf.

White, Merry. 1987. The Virtue of Japanese Mothers: Cultural Definitions of Women's Lives. *Daedalus* 116 (Summer): 149–163.

Wolfe, Eugene L. 1995. Japanese Electoral and Political Reform: Role of the Young Turks. *Asian Survey* 35 (December): 1059–1074.

2

Sages and Citizens: Sources of Authority

All modern states derive their authority from sources unique to each state or from sources shared with a larger civilization. For example, a primary source of authority in the United States is the widespread acceptance of a concept of the *rule of law*. This concept is most dramatically embodied in the U.S. Constitution, which defines the bedrock of authority in the modern American state. When the president of the United States takes the oath of office he pledges to preserve, protect, and defend the principles written into this document. For a true understanding of the concept of the rule of law, however, and how it works through institutionalized practices such as judicial review, one would have to study the classical political and legal theories of Greece and Rome. In other words, one would have to study the origin and development of the concept of the rule of law in a larger Western civilization of which the modern American state is a part. Samuel Huntington argues that there are eight world civilizations that increasingly define the dynamics of global politics in the late twentieth century. Interestingly, only one of these civilizations is contained within the boundaries of a single nation-state—Japan. So, if Huntington is correct, Japan is uniquely situated among the nations of the world in its self-identity as both a civilization and a nation-state (Huntington 1993).

The authoritative base of the modern Japanese state is to be found in four traditions, one unique to Japan and three derived from outside. Unique to Japan is Shinto or the way of the gods. Shintoism is a pantheistic religion with roots deep within Japanese tradition. Shintoist belief does not draw clear distinctions between human and nonhuman things in nature. *Kami*, or gods, are everywhere according to traditional Shintoism. But there is hierarchy among the gods, and chief among them is the sun goddess, Amaterasu, from whom the Japanese nation descends, as recorded in the *Kojiki*, an early history of Japan written in A.D. 712 (see accompanying box). According to the *Meiji Constitution* of 1889, the Japanese Emperor represents "a lineal succession unbroken for ages eternal." Writing at the time of the maturity of state Shinto, Japanese Professor

ISE SHRINE

In a heavily wooded area in the city of Ise in Mie Prefecture is the Ise Shrine, which dates from the third century. Home in Shinto belief to Amaterasu Omikami, the sun goddess from whom the Imperial Family descends, the inner shrine (*Naiku*) is rebuilt every 20 years in a ritual called *shikinen sengu*. Every year, in October, special rites to mark the coming in of the year's rice crop are performed. Traditionally, new emperors take part in special ceremonies at the Ise Shrine as well. With the constitutional separation of church and state under the present constitution, however, this ritual is no longer sanctioned by the Japanese government. In a private ceremony in November 1990, however, after his official inauguration as Japan's 125th Emperor, Akihito took part in a traditional ceremony at Ise. Similarly, in his first trip following his wedding to Owada Masako, in June 1993, Crown Prince Naruhito visited Ise.

Matsunami Niichiro observed for foreign readers that the reason for promulgating the Meiji Constitution on February 11, 1889, was because that day marked the 2,549th anniversary of the accession of *Jimmu Tenno*, the first Emperor of Japan (1940, 9). Shintoism played an enormously important role in the founding of the modern Japanese state during the Meiji transformation. By justifying the tremendous changes needed to bring Japan into the modern era by rooting those changes in the restoration of the Emperor as the locus of state sovereignty, the leaders of early *Meiji* moved Japan both forward and backward at the same time, thus effecting a kind of temporal and psychological stability. In addition to Shintoism, three other authoritative traditions have shaped the modern Japanese state: Buddhism, Confucianism (both from China or largely from China in the case of Buddhism), and constitutional and political theories from the West. Of these three traditions, Buddhist influence has probably been the least authoritative, and Confucianist thought the most in defining the foundations of the modern Japanese state.

NARA AND THE ASCENT OF MT. HIEI:
THE BUDDHIST TRADITION

The relationship between religion and the state is always problematic. The first real capital of Japan was at *Nara* in the *kansai* region of the main island of Honshu, not far from Kyoto. In the sixth century, Buddhism arrived in Japan at Nara and soon made its political presence felt. Though today Buddhism is the least vital of the sources of political authority, such has not always been the case. In fact, during the Nara Period (A.D. 710–794) Buddhism came close to becoming an official state religion under an early Empress, an event that precipitated the move of the capital to Heian (today Kyoto) in 794. (See Table 2–1 for a periodization of Japanese political history.) At Nara, a large complex of Buddhist temples

TABLE 2–1
Political Chronology of Japan

Period	Years
Nara	710–794
Heian	794–1185
Kamakura	1185–1333
Muromachi	1333–1568
Momoyama	1568–1600
Edo (also called Tokugawa)	1600–1868
Meiji	1868–1912
Taisho	1912–1926
Showa	1926–1989
Heisei	1989–

was constructed prior to the move of the capital, a complex that includes the five-story *Horyuji Temple* and other buildings recognized as the oldest wooden buildings in the world (Reischauer and Jansen 1995, 43).

At the new capital, Kyoto, a monk by the name of *Saicho* was given permission by the court to establish a temple and schools on Mt. Hiei, just outside of Kyoto to the northeast. At his mountain schools, Saicho developed a curriculum for his young students that came to distinguish them into three classes. At the top were what were called the national "treasures." These were students who had developed skill in both speech and action. They were to remain on Mt. Hiei. Those students skillful in speech but not action became teachers in the communities surrounding the temple. Students with skills more suited to action contributed to the building of roads, irrigation projects, and other such projects useful to the surrounding communities. This ascent to Mt. Hiei by Saicho and the tradition maintained by his followers symbolized the "otherworldly" focus of Buddhism and its distancing from the world of politics. Soon, however, other sects engaged in activities closer to the court life in Kyoto. The Buddhist priest *Kukai*, for example, developed what came to be known as the *Shingon* sect of Buddhism. The Shingon sect developed more along aesthetic lines, whereas the sect associated with Saicho, which came to be called *Tendai* Buddhism, emphasized morality. The Shingon sect was more popular at the court.

Without overstating differences between Tendai and Shingon Buddhism, one might examine a fifteenth-century play by the *Noh* master *Seami* to illustrate the potential within the Shingon sect of becoming too involved with politics and the state. The play, *Sotoba Komachi,* explores the character of a woman of legend named Komachi. According to the legend she had many lovers to whom she was not especially kind. One of them, Shosho, was told that she would take him seriously only if he came to her house on 100 different nights. And so Shosho came, through hail and snow and all the other challenges of a hostile nature for 99 nights. But on the one-hundredth night he died. In old age, Komachi wanders somewhat in madness and on one occasion is approached and questioned by priests of the Shingon sect. The play opens with a priest saying: "We who on shallow hills have built our home in the heart's deep recess seek solitude." Then, turning to the audience, he continues: "I am a priest of the Koyasan. I am minded to go up to the Capital to visit the shrines and sanctuaries there. The Buddha of the past is gone, and he that shall be Buddha has not yet come into the world." Arthur Waley, in a footnote, explains that the Koyasan, Kukai's original temple, is "not so remote as most mountain temples" (1921, 150). As the play unfolds, we witness a spirited dialogue between the old woman Komachi and the Shingon priests. One dimension of this complex interaction is the dramatization of Komachi's superior insight that compassion is the true heart of Buddhist teaching. By comparison, all things of this world, external manifestations, are virtually meaningless.

One must be careful not to read too much into one possible interpretation of one Noh play. Still, the various temples of virtually all the Buddhist sects were by the fifteenth-century deeply involved in the things of this world and, more specifically, the things usually reserved to the state, or carefully licensed by the state, such as raising taxes, collecting tolls, creating schools, lending money, and amassing huge areas of land. By the late sixteenth-century, the power of the Buddhist temples had become so great that *Oda Nobunaga*, one of the three great unifiers of early modern Japan, virtually made war on the temples. In that campaign, in 1571, he completely razed the complex on Mt. Hiei, which had grown to over 3,000 structures, and massacred hundreds, including women and children (McMullin 1984). With the coming of the Meiji era (1868–1912), Buddhism was considered by the political leadership to be a religion in opposition to needed changes and even "decadent" (Ketelaar 1990).

The Buddhist tradition in Japan is long, complex, and rich in both the sophistication of its teachings and in its impact on the development of Japanese culture. Buddhism is, for example, an important element in Lady Murasaki's famous *Tale of Genji* (see accompanying box). And, like Christianity in the West, it developed many different schools or sects over the centuries with some gaining more adherents than others. But central to all of Buddhism are common teachings regarding the four noble truths, the three treasures, and the eightfold path. That life is painful, that pain derives from desires, that desires can only be overcome by the Buddha's teachings, and that nirvana (nothingness) or the transcending of pain is nothing less than the merging of oneself with the larger cosmos represent the truths of traditional Buddhist teaching. The treasures are the person of the historical Buddha (which means enlightened or awakened one), *Gautama Siddhartha* (c. 560–480 B.C.), the teachings of Buddhist literature (the "law"), and the monastic orders or priesthood. As origin, doctrine, and example, these treasures define the pillars of Buddhism in traditional Japanese culture. The eightfold path consists of right understanding, right thought, right speech, right conduct, right livelihood, right application, right consciousness, and right concentration.

LADY MURASAKI AND THE *TALE OF GENJI*

Very little is known of the details of Murasaki Shikibu's life, but her *Genji Monogatari* is known the world over as the ultimate expression of medieval Japanese court life and ideals. Lady Murasaki is known to have been a member of the Fujiwara family and to have lived within court circles in Kyoto in the late tenth century. She wrote poetry as well as the tale for which she is famous. The tale is over 1,000 pages of detail regarding the life of Prince Genji and of a young man named Kaoru who becomes the primary character after the prince's death. Genji is the son of the Emperor but is not allowed royal status. Readers follow the life, romances, and marriage of the Prince against a social and political background shaped by basic elements in Japanese culture such as the Imperial House and Shinto and Buddhist religious beliefs. The tale inspired many Noh dramas and is still drawn on by contemporary artists. It is widely regarded as one of the best introductions to a study of traditional Japanese culture.

Among the most popular and influential sects in traditional Japan are those founded by the great reformers of the **Heian** (A.D. 794–1185) and **Kamakura** (A.D. 1185–1333) periods. Among the former are **Kuya, Ryonin**, and **Genshin**; among the latter are **Honen** and **Ippen**. The Heian reformers, and Ippen during Kamakura, developed what is called Pure Land Buddhism, an interpretation that stresses equality, simplicity, the arts, and salvation in the hereafter. Honen and his disciple Shinran developed True Pure Land Buddhism, a sect that was banished from Kyoto because of unprecedented doctrinal changes, such as the marrying of priests. Both of these traditions, Pure Land and True Pure Land, stress the otherworldly duties of the faithful. Another sect that developed during the Kamakura Period, and which took this transcendental focus to its highest logic, was **Zen**. Both of the great Zen pioneers, **Eisai** and **Dogen**, emphasized meditation and the importance of studying the way of the Buddha by studying one's own self. Zen Buddhism became the preferred approach of the *bushi* or *samurai* class and contributed much to the development of *bushido*, the way of the *samurai*. *Nichiren* Buddhism, finally, also dates from the late Kamakura Period. The contemporary *Soka Gakkai* trace their origins to this sect. As the formative influence in the creation of the Komei political party, the *Soka Gakkai* represent the most direct influence of Buddhist authority in contemporary Japanese politics.

Perhaps because of the large landholdings, former political involvements, and earlier formations of large armies of defenders called *sohei*, the leaders of the Meiji reforms passed a number of laws to diminish the size and influence of the Buddhist temples and priests. From 1871 to 1876 the number of temples fell from 465,000 to about 72,000, and the number of Buddhist priests fell from about 76,000 to about 19,500. Both of these reductions were brought about by direct state intervention (Davis 1992). Yet these changes were almost certainly also due to the old-fashioned and otherworldly characteristics of a traditional source of authority that seemed to the Meiji leaders to have no place in the development of a modern Japanese state that could compete with the West. Politics, despite the political involvements of various temples throughout the centuries, was for traditional Buddhism part of the *ukiyo* or "floating world" of illusion and impermanence. It was the name given to what is undoubtedly the most popular and best-known Japanese art form. The *ukiyo e* or floating world pictures of the early modern *Edo Period* (1600–1868), though originally inspired by the transient texture of the rising commercial class's lifestyle, came to mean chic, stylish, even modern. One might wonder today if, similarly, the illusive style of Japanese politics from the dawn of the Meiji era to the present might be in the early stages of evolving from a floating world of illusions into something more meaningful, modern, even postmodern.

THE RULE OF THE SAGES: CONFUCIANISM IN JAPAN

Of all of the sources of authority in modern Japan, Confucianism may well be the most authoritative. Such a statement is not without controversy. Many would argue that Japan today as a modern, progressive state, is more the product of Western theories than anything in its Confucian past. Yet few can deny that Japan is among the most determined among modern states to encourage the importance of education, competitive exams, group harmony, loyalty to one's group, and family values as the bedrock values of modern society. All of these are characteristic of traditional Confucianist thought. Some even argue that Confucianism continues to play a role in the religious consciousness of Japanese people, that Confucianism is a "forgotten religion" (Kaji 1991).

Confucius (551–479 B.C.) taught that good government required a ruling class of wise administrators devoted to duty. He also stressed the importance of loyalty in one's personal relationships, especially those involving sovereign and subject, father and son, husband and wife, older brother and younger brother, and friend and friend. Later Confucianists taught the importance of the classic texts by Confucius, the *Analects*, for example, and by the famous early commentator *Mencius* (371–289 B.C.). Confucianism also teaches hierarchy, stability over change, and the fundamental importance of education, especially education in classic texts. Confucianism first came to Japan from Korea in the fifth century A.D. Its early influence at the court can be seen in the constitution promulgated by *Shotoku Taishi* in the early seventh century and in the Taika reforms of 645. But Confucian thought played a secondary role to Buddhism until the beginnings of the Edo Period.

Among the many changes brought by the *Tokugawa* Shogunate (1600–1868) was the official recognition of Confucianism as a guiding ideology. *Hayashi Razan* built a school and a shrine to Confucius in Edo and began to teach a particular approach to Confucianism associated with the teachings of the thirteenth-century scholar *Chu Hsi*. This neo-Confucianism, or *shushigaku*, as it came to be called, provided the conceptual framework for the Tokugawa state.

One was born into a particular place in society and had to accept the duties appropriate to that place. All was strict hierarchy. At the top was the Shogun in Edo, and in the domains the local *daimyo* ruled. Successive Tokugawa Shoguns developed and refined a political system called *Bakuhan* in which 260 *daimyo* shared power and authority with the shogunal government. The central government was able to secure control of the outer domains through various practices, such as the *sankin kotai* (alternating attendance) and the permanent residence of *daimyo* wives and children at Edo. The great expense of maintaining these dual residencies and the virtual hostage status of *daimyo* families kept distant plottings to a minimum. Through various seclusion acts, Tokugawa Shoguns also forbade travel abroad, forbade the return of Japanese already abroad, and banned Christian teaching. Underlying and justifying the ordered and hierarchical world of the *Bakuhan* system was the neo-Confucianist orthodoxy (Tucker 1989, 14–16).

A recent study of one of the new religions in Japan, the *Gedatsu-kai*, shows the fundamental debt of even the newest religions in Japan today to the basic teachings of neo-Confucianism. A belief in "three fundamental bonds and five cardinal virtues" lies at the center of these teachings. The "fundamental bonds" are the first three in traditional Confucian teaching: the bonds of ruler and subject, father and son, and husband and wife. The five cardinal virtues are loyalty, filial piety, benevolence, righteousness, and propriety. The neo-Confucian ideal was, therefore, "for all people to be mindful of these three ethical bonds and develop personally the five cardinal principles (or virtues), for the purpose of promoting a harmonious society" (Earhart 1989, 29). There is no upward mobility according to neo-Confucianist teachings. In the late seventeenth century, however, new interpretations began to challenge established views. The most dramatic challenges came from *Ogyu Sorai* (1666–1728).

According to Sorai, the principal focus of Confucianism as a way of governance had been lost sight of under neo-Confucianist teachings. Sorai wanted to return to the classics and read them in their purity, without the overlay of centuries of interpretation. This Ancient Learning School found in the classics of Chinese philosophy a way of the sages wherein the state was conceived as artificial and subject to reform. In other words, under Sorai's influence, Confucianism increasingly became a philosophy of experimentation and change, particularly with respect to reforming state institutions. Among Sorai's proposed changes were to abolish the *sankin kotai*, the alternating attendance of *Daimyo* in Edo which the *bakufu* required as a way of keeping a close eye on *daimyo* activities, to return *samurai* to rural areas, and to remove the hereditary succession to office. These proposals were not heeded by the *bakufu*. But they showed Sorai's concern with dramatic changes in Japanese society that were not being addressed. Principal among the changes was the growing power and influence of a rising merchant class and the concurrent demise of the *samurai*. A new concern with social forces as a proper subject for the historian created a climate within which less orthodox versions of Japanese history could be written and taken seriously by educated classes. One such history was written by *Rai Sanyo*

(1781–1832). Called *Nihon Gaishi, an Unofficial History of Japan,* Sanyo's work argued that "each house flourished to the extent that it was loyal to the emperor and then fell when it became disloyal" (Embree 1988, 319). This was among the primary works that circulated among the young *samurai* in places like **Choshu** and **Satsuma** during the period immediately preceding the monumental events of the Meiji transformation, which ushered Japan into the modern era and a much larger world.

The primary concern of the Meiji leadership was to bring Japan into a larger world defined by Western ideas and values. But a reluctance to accept all things Western led to a serious reconsideration of traditional values such as were especially embodied in Shinto and Confucianism and the teachings of Yoshida Shoin (see accompanying box). Even where Western ideas were adopted, they were often interpreted "in ways that were meaningful within the Confucian intellectual heritage, with its ideas of social hierarchy and the responsibility of leaders to rule the nation in the interests of the nation as a whole" (Inoue 1991, 67). The Confucianist influence was particularly evident in the *Imperial Rescript on Education* announced in 1890. It reads like a summary of the main tenets of Confucianism, as the following excerpt shows:

> Ye, our subjects, be filial to your parents, affectionate to your brothers and sisters; as husbands and wives be harmonious, as friends true; bear yourselves in modesty and moderation; extend your benevolence to all; pursue learning and cultivate arts, and thereby develop your intellectual faculties and perfect your moral powers; furthermore, advance the public good and promote common interests; always respect the constitution and observe the laws; should any emergency arise, offer

---

YOSHIDA SHOIN (1830–1859)

Behind many of the actions taken by young *samurai* in the tumultuous years leading up to the Meiji Restoration was the young teacher Yoshida Shoin and the small, private school he founded in Hagi called *Shoka Sonjuku.* Born near Hagi, a small castle town in Choshu, in what is today Yamaguchi Prefecture, Yoshida developed as a tireless scholar, writer, and teacher whose influence became a driving force in the critical years of the Restoration. Influenced by the Mito School of Shinto and Confucianist philosophies, Yoshida developed a national vision of Japan with the Emperor restored to the center of the national government and of a *kokutai* philosophy captured in the phrase *sonno joi* (honor the Emperor; expel the barbarian). Because of various political activities, numerous writings, unapproved travels, and acts in defiance of law—such as attempting to stow away on Commodore Matthew Perry's flagship in 1854—Yoshida was placed under house arrest in his home at Hagi. Due to alleged involvement in a plot to assassinate a high government official, he was later ordered to Edo (Tokyo), where he was tried, convicted, and executed. He is honored today at shrines in Hagi and in Tokyo. Among his students at the humble school in Hagi were Ito Hirobumi, Japan's first prime minister, and Yamagata Aritomo, a leading *genro* of the Meiji Period. A museum in Hagi chronicles his life, his influence, and his times.

yourselves courageously to the state; and thus guard and maintain the prosperity of our Imperial throne, coeval with heaven and earth. ("Imperial Rescript on Education" 1973)

The last admonition refers to the divine origins and office of the Japanese Emperor. In preparing the Meiji Constitution of 1889, the leaders of the government decided to anchor what was to be a modern Japanese state in a very ancient concept of the Imperial House as presented in the *Kojiki*, or Record of Ancient Matters, completed in A.D. 712.

STATE SHINTO AND *KOKUTAI*

When *Ito Hirobumi*, Japan's first prime minister (see accompanying box), wrote his *Commentaries* on the Meiji Constitution, he expressed clearly and concisely that the words "reigned over" and "governed" in Chapter 1 of the constitution, on the Emperor, meant "that the Emperor on His Throne combines in Himself the sovereignty of the State and the government of the country and of His subjects" (Ito 1906, 3). Though the new constitution was written in accordance with all kinds of advice from Western sources, largely German, and sought to embody some aspects at least of modern democratic theory, it was in its fundamental character neither very democratic nor very Western.

In the development of the constitution, a concept of *kokutai*, or national essence, came into increasing use and prominence. A concept saturated with mythical suggestions emphasizing the harmony and uniqueness of the Japanese state, *kokutai* came to embody everything non-Western. Some Japanese

---

ITO HIROBUMI (1841–1909)

Japan's first prime minister and architect, by most accounts, of the modern Japanese state, Ito was among the young men of Choshu who studied at the *Shoka Sonjuku* with Yoshida Shoin in Hagi. He became active in the *sonno joi* movement to topple the Tokugawa government. He stowed away on a voyage to England as a young man and learned of Western technological strength firsthand. He served in a number of official posts during the early years of Meiji, including governor of Hyogo Prefecture. He was a member of the Iwakura mission in the early 1870s. With the death of Saigo Takamori in the Satsuma rebellion in 1877, and the deaths of Kido Takayoshi and Okubo Toshimichi shortly after, Ito became increasingly influential at Tokyo. In 1882, with others, Ito went to Europe to study Western constitutionalism, especially in lectures by and discussions with Rudolf von Gneist and Lorenz von Stein. On returning, he was a leading figure in bringing to completion the Meiji Constitution of 1889. He served as prime minister on four different occasions and ended his career in government as Japanese resident general in Korea. In Manchuria, in 1909, he was assassinated by a Korean nationalist.

---

intellectuals in the early twentieth century sought to give a more precise meaning to Japanese uniqueness—for example, the writer *Tanizaki Junichiro* (1886–1965) and the philosopher *Watsuji Tetsuro* (1889–1960). For Tanizaki, best known for his novels *Some Prefer Nettles* and *The Makioka Sisters,* Japan was unique in its aesthetic sense. In a famous essay written in 1934, "In Praise of Shadows," Tanizaki explored the meaning of shadow and half light in the Japanese sensibility. According to Tanizaki, and unlike the Western quest for light and precision, the Japanese quest was for "beauty not in the thing itself but in the patterns of shadows, the light and the darkness, that one thing against another creates" (Harootunian and Najita 1988, 754). The philosopher Watsuji, who taught at Kyoto and Tokyo universities for many years, developed a kind of Japanese version of a Nietzschean critique of the West. As Nietzsche looked back to the ancient Greece of Western civilization for inspiration, so also did Watsuji look to ancient Japan. Drawing on differences in climate, geography, and concepts of space, Watsuji developed a theory of Japanese uniqueness with respect to the particular "space" of the Japanese house and household. In an elaborate exposition of the deeper meaning of this sense of space in Japanese thinking, he pointed out, among other things, that the Japanese had not and probably would not develop a sense of the "public" in the sense that it existed in the West. Watsuji rejected both liberalism and Marxism as inappropriate Western ideologies for Japan (Harootunian and Najita 1988, 743–749).

Another writer, *Dazai Osamu* (1909–1948), echoed these themes in his work. Usually identified with the Japanese "romantic school," Dazai is most famous for the novels *Setting Sun* and *No Longer Human.* In the *Setting Sun,* in particular, Dazai examines and critiques Japan's tragic relationship with the West. The main characters in the novel, which Donald Keene, the translator, says is among the best for seeing how Japan is today, are Kazuko, her brother Naoji, and their mother. The story is set in immediate postwar Japan and is filled with flashbacks to the war years and before. Naoji is a drug addict who has returned from the Pacific War, Kazuko is a single woman, divorced, in her late twenties, who seeks a child from a once famous artist associate of her brother, and the mother is the last "aristocrat" in Japan. Through complex character studies, flashbacks, rich symbolism, dream narrations, diaries, and a compact style of writing in the tradition of *haiku* and *tanka* poetry, Dazai takes the reader into the psychological despair and drama of postwar Japan.

In his "Moonflower Journal," Naoji tells the reader of his despair over being a phony "aristocrat," a reference to the nobility of his family under the Meiji Constitution, a nobility artificially created after a Western model. In the manner of Tanizaki on shadows, we have the life of thoughts that grow in the half light of the moon, like moonflowers. And among the thoughts that grow are those that see hypocrisy, conceit, duplicity, and vanity everywhere. "All men are the same." This thought in particular tears at Naoji and forms a center around which all other thoughts coalesce. He is a phony aristocrat, but in Japan there is the sensibility that could form the basis of a true life of excellence. "They say the wisteria of Ushijima are a thousand years old, and the wisteria of

Kumano date from centuries ago." "My heart dances only in those clusters of wisteria blossom" (Dazai 1984, 62). Dazai here points to that long tradition of Japanese aesthetics that is central to Shinto, central to the thought of the eighteenth-century philosopher **Motoori Norinaga** (1730–1801), central to the *kokugaku* (national studies) movement of the same period, and central to the *kokutai* concept.

And at the heart of this aesthetic tradition is the concept of **mono no aware**, a concept difficult to translate, but which means something like a "thing's sadness or pity" (Matsumoto 1970). In Dazai's *Setting Sun,* to continue with that example, we see much that is sad and pitiful. Yet there is also strength. Kazuko, Naoji's sister, is in many ways sad, pitiful, and strong. Like her mother, she is the center around which the *uchi* world will grow well or poorly, and, writ large, the greater *uchi* of Japan. The name Kazuko has in its principal Chinese character, or *kanji,* the meaning of great harmony. It is the same character as the principal character in **Yamato**, the original name for Japan. She courts a corrupted artist named Uehara in numerous and clever letters to the effect that she wants a child. In the end a child is expected, though what hope this child symbolizes is surrounded densely by complex images suggesting caution.

Dazai's work is about many aspects of Japanese psychology and culture, but at its heart is the theme of Japan in transition and the major characters are, in Kazuko's words, victims of a transition in morality. The political overtones are striking. In the recent, often dramatic exchanges regarding observances of the fiftieth anniversary of the end of World War II, it was noted that events related to Europe often had a sense of closure and resolution about them but events related to Japan were conspicuous by an opposite tone. Many Japanese continue to see themselves more as victims than victimizers, referring not only to their unique status as the only victims of atomic bombing but also as victims—along with other East Asian nations—of Western colonialism and imperialism. Dazai is among those literary artists who skillfully take their readers inside this political psychology, thereby placing contemporary Japanese political culture in a larger historical framework.

Tanizaki, Watsuji, and Dazai are but three examples among many to illustrate the cultural self-study that characterizes so much of the literature and scholarship of the first half of the twentieth century in Japan. Even as Japan was demonstrating to the world that it could catch up and modernize in step with the Western powers, even that it could defeat them on the battlefield as evidenced by the victory over Russia in the war of 1904–1905, many Japanese scholars and writers yearned for a clearer expression of Japanese uniqueness, or non-Western characteristics. Framed by the larger *kokutai* philosophy of a unique Japanese state, much of this literary effort found inspiration in the Shinto past of a traditional Japan looked after by many gods and a truly benevolent Emperor. Early Meiji political leaders saw in traditional Shinto "a tool useful in the legitimization of the political regime" (Hardacre 1989, 59). According to Joseph Pittau, the *kokutai* philosophy stressed "the absolute homogeneity of Japanese culture, characterized by the link of loyalty and love between the people and the emperor" (1967, 2). In the beginning of the Meiji era (1868–1912), however, it was a hunger for knowledge of the West that motivated Japan's leaders.

THE IWAKURA MISSION TO THE WEST

In November 1871, a group of about 50 Japanese left on a tour of Europe and the United States. Among the group were Ito Hirobumi, *Kido Takayoshi*, and *Okubo Toshimichi*, each of whom would play a leading role in the design of the new Japanese state. The mission was named after *Iwakura Tomami*, who organized it and was among its leaders. They were gone for nearly two years, and in that time they learned a great deal about the West and about Japan in comparative perspective. The mission visited 11 countries and over 100 cities and towns in the United States and Western Europe. Among the representatives who went on the mission were five young girls. Countries visited were the United States, France, the Netherlands, Sweden, Belgium, Russia, Germany, Denmark, Austria-Hungary, Italy, and Switzerland. The mission visited museums, schools, libraries, factories, government offices, courts, banks, military establishments, even zoos, and shipyards. Mission representatives attended circus performances, ballets, banquets, and speeches. Among many lessons learned was that the government itself should be active in pursuing industrial enterprises. In 1878, a five-volume account was published called *A True Account of the Tour in America and Europe of the Special Ambassador.*

The *Iwakura Mission* was one of the most dramatic diplomatic missions ever attempted and dramatically illustrates the zeal with which the Meiji leadership undertook *"civilization and enlightenment"* (Japan Information and Culture Center 1996, 8). While they were away, more conservative forces had been working on plans for the invasion of Korea. So a two-edged crisis developed in Japan during the mid-1870s. On the one hand, the power and cultural differences of the West were better understood, provoking a critical sense of potential threats from the West; on the other hand, internal dissent regarding the nature and pace of change was threatening to undermine the entire Restoration. *Saigo Takamori*, the Satsuma leader, and *Itagaki Taisuke* of Tosa both resigned from the government. Saigo returned to Satsuma to organize disgruntled *samurai*, and Itagaki returned home to organize the *Minkento*, or People's Rights Party, Japan's first political party. Whereas Saigo was inspired by nostalgia for a traditional Japan, Itagaki and his followers were inspired by Western democratic and progressive theories of politics. Saigo led an open rebellion in 1877, was defeated, and died with the assistance of an aide in traditional *samurai* fashion. Itagaki led the fight for the creation of a legislative assembly elected by the people.

Much of the reform agenda of the period was set by the official report of the Iwakura mission, the five-volume study published in 1878 and called *Jikki*, for short (Soviak 1971, 8, 9). Divided into specialty groups, the mission visited the various countries mentioned earlier. Some members went to special exhibitions, such as the International Exhibition in Vienna. Perhaps most importantly, members for the first time made contact with the German *Rudolph von Gneist* and the Austrian *Lorenz von Stein*, scholars who would later play an important role in shaping the Meiji Constitution. Among the deeper impressions in the Iwakura reports is the observation that Western progress is cumulative and that the deeper source of Western success is to be found in ancient Rome. "Even though England, France, and Germany are flourishing now, the basic factors responsible for their enlightenment are naturally traceable to ancient Rome" (Soviak 1971, 25). The reports note that a distinctive worldview derives from the long history that separates the modern West from its ancient roots and that such a view is greatly at odds with the worldview of Eastern peoples. Forms of government evolve over time according to these respective worldviews and rapid changes in technology and industry must not also bring a too-rapid transformation of social and political institutions. Among the greatest challenges to the leaders of the new Meiji state would be the balancing of rapid modernization in some areas with great caution in others. This combined attitude of modernization and caution especially characterized the deliberations of the decade of the 1880s over the philosophical and institutional design of Japan's first modern constitution.

Western constitutionalism, though it embodies many modern improvements over the ancients, has its origins in the Western classical tradition which originates in Greece and Rome. Prior to the European Enlightenment of the seventeenth and eighteenth centuries and the great democratic revolutions of the late eighteenth and early nineteenth centuries was the Renaissance. In the rebirth of ancient learning characteristic of the Renaissance certain basic insights of the ancients regarding good government came to be widely accepted as wise. Among these insights were that first importance in any state should attach to the rule of law, not men. Also, that a good constitution of government would be a mixture of the one, the few, and the many, as in the ancient Roman Republic of the consul(s), senate, and assembly; that standing armies should be discouraged as a threat to republican institutions; that a periodic return to first principles would stabilize a republic over time; and that a spirit of civic virtue, widely distributed among the larger population, should inform the whole (Pocock 1972). This civic humanist paradigm was a large part of the Western worldview with its roots in Rome glimpsed by representatives of the Iwakura mission.

But the worldview that cautioned those representatives was shaped by sources of authority very different from those in the ancient West. Rule of the sages as taught in the Chinese Confucian tradition was as deeply rooted in Eastern assumptions about good government as rule of law was in the West. John Haley, in his study of the Japanese concept of law, begins by observing that it would be difficult to overstate Japan's "institutional debt to imperial China." A large part of that debt was a concept of law "as an instrument of government control quite separate from any moral or religious order serving the interests of those who exercised paramount political authority." The Japanese "paradigm" was that of an "administrative state" (Haley 1991, 19). The Western idea of balancing the one, the few, and the many, an idea easily seen in both the "high culture" of Shakespearean tragedy, as in *Julius Caesar*, or the middle-class culture of the *Wizard of Oz*, is somewhat foreign to a worldview that stresses the authority of the few wise over all the rest.

Cautions in the West over standing armies easily translated into strict civilian rule of the military as one aspect of legislative over executive authority. Where executive authority predominates, as in the Confucian worldview of the rule of the sages, such cautions are less a part of tradition. The idea of a periodic return to first principles focuses attention on the clear delineation of principles at a founding and the measuring of legislative and executive acts against those principles as in, for example, judicial review in the U.S. constitutional tradition. There is little of such reasoning in traditional Shinto, Buddhist, or Confucian thought as it bears on politics and law. Modernization, and the tendency within it to think of reason as technological and progressive, discourage such thinking by definition. As for civic virtue, it is the very center of Western constitutional thought. This is perhaps best expressed by James Madison in *Federalist No. 51*: "The virtue of the people is the primary control on the government, but experience has taught mankind the importance of auxiliary precautions." The auxiliary precautions are the mechanical checks and balances derived from modern science, the Newtonian balancing of centripetal and centrifugal forces in a mechanical universe defined by forces to which man must also conform. Yet these are but constitutional safety mechanisms. The primary check on the government is the virtue of the citizenry in their participation in the life of the state as citizens. In the Meiji Constitution, a constitution given by the Emperor and not drafted by representatives of the larger society in conventions, the first chapter defines the Emperor as sovereign and the second chapter defines the "rights and duties" of "subjects," not "citizens."

Japan's first, or Meiji, constitution embodied a constitutional design that failed to reflect the premodern dimensions of Western constitutionalism, dimensions difficult to perceive from within a worldview nurtured by Shinto, Buddhist, and Confucian sources of authority—dimensions, also, losing their meaning within the West itself. For it might be argued that one of the more tragic aspects of Japan's encounter with the West in the late nineteenth century is that forces of industrialization and modernization, accompanied by the widespread acceptance of a new philosophy of social Darwinism, were eroding the very foundations that had contributed so much to Western success. The late nineteenth century in the West was defined more by expansionism and imperialism than by rule of law. As Hannah Arendt has observed, imperialism was not so much the last stage of capitalism, as Lenin observed; rather it was the "first stage in political rule of the bourgeoisie" (1951, 138). It was this type of rule, rather than the rule of law characteristic of a long evolution of Western constitutional doctrine, from which the Japanese of the early Meiji era learned their political theory. The idea of a merchant, or bourgeois, class ruling the land of the *samurai* was especially disturbing to the traditional thought of the outer *daimyo* who led the Meiji Restoration in the first place. This became the context within which Saigo led his ***Satsuma rebellion***.

WESTERN SOURCES OF AUTHORITY

When Commodore ***Matthew C. Perry*** arrived in Japan in July 1853, Japanese exposure to Western influence was minimal. There had been some contact with ***Dutch Learning*** by way of Nagasaki during the Edo Period. The Dutch were allowed to settle on and conduct trade from the island of Dejima in Nagasaki harbor. This was the only opening to the West during the long period of isolation that characterized the Edo Period. Western medicine was introduced to Japan by the Dutch, and the Dutch language was the only foreign language available for study during this period. ***Fukuzawa Yukichi, Saionji Kimmochi,*** and ***Okuma Shigenobu*** were among those heavily influenced by Dutch Learning (see accompanying box). For the most part, however, there was little interest in or exposure to Western ideas until after Perry's arrival. But in the next 40 years, a new generation of political leaders would midwife tremendous changes in Japanese culture, society, and politics in the name of "civilization and enlightenment." Largely, this meant Western civilization and Western enlightenment. Fashions, architecture, manners, technology, and, perhaps most importantly, political institutions were all reexamined in the light of Western concepts.

At the center of political reform was the call for a constitution of government for Japan, such as those found in the West. As early as 1868 the new Meiji Emperor called for a constitution in his ***Charter Oath***. In 1881, an Imperial

---

FUKUZAWA YUKICHI (1835–1901)

Founder of what is today's Keio University, Fukuzawa was among the most important of the leaders of the civilization and enlightenment movement during the Meiji Period. From the study of Western weaponry in his youth in the 1850s to the study of Western classics and Western science later in his life, Fukuzawa always championed Western learning. He benefited from the Dutch Learning of his youth and went on to study chemistry, anatomy, physics, and English. He sailed to America in 1860 with the first Japanese mission to the West and later to France, England, Holland, Portugal, and Russia, absorbing as much Western culture as he could. His most famous work is the ten-volume study of *Conditions in the West,* published in the late 1860s. He also published a newspaper and championed the rights of women. Though he never served in a government position, his influence ranks among the highest in shaping the modern Japanese state. Other important works include an *Outline of a Theory of Civilization* and *The Autobiography of Yukichi Fukuzawa,* both only recently translated into English.

---

proclamation promised a written constitution and a representative assembly by the year 1890. Questions regarding the nature and timing of such a constitution divided the early Meiji political leadership. Okuma, for example, wanted to move quickly for a constitution and a national assembly along the lines of the English Parliament. Ito Hirobumi favored more caution and leaned toward a Prussian model. Okuma's influence in the inner circle declined rapidly and Ito's surged. In 1882, Ito and nine others left on another mission to the West, this time to study Western constitutions.

Among the others was *Saionji Kimmochi* (1849–1940), who would later be called the "last *genro.*" Saionji was born in Kyoto of a *seiga* family, a family related to the Emperor. In his youth, Saionji read Rai Sanyo's *Nihon Gaishi* and, like many of his contemporaries, was captivated by it. He was similarly captivated by the works of Fukuzawa Yukichi. Fukuzawa, probably more than anyone else of the entire Meiji era, popularized, interpreted, and generally nurtured Western learning in Japan (Craig 1968). Saionji, like many of his generation, developed a hunger for more and more Western learning. In 1870, therefore, he went to Paris—just in time to witness the *Paris Commune*. He stayed in Paris for ten years, studying with the liberal lawyer Emile Accollas. Among his youthful friends in Paris was Georges Clemenceau, the future president of France. Upon returning to Japan, Saionji joined the *Freedom and People's Rights Movement* where he nurtured his interest in Western political and constitutional theory. In his life and public career, Saionji represented all of the complexities of a traditional Japan making the transition to a modern, urban, industrialized, and democratic nation-state. The transition to democracy would prove to be especially difficult. In 1882, Saionji joined Ito and the others on the trip to Europe in search of a deeper understanding of Western constitutional theory and to gather basic information on Western constitutions.

In Europe, the Ito entourage split into groups and called on scholars in France, Germany, Austria, and, briefly, England. They spent a year and a half on their journey. Most of the serious attention was focused on lectures by two scholars in particular: Rudolf von Gneist in Germany and Lorenz von Stein in Austria. The general effect of these lectures was to reinforce Ito's belief that Japan should follow a Prussian model rather than a British, French, or American one. Primarily this meant a strengthening of Imperial authority and a careful design of more democratic institutions so as to prevent too quick a democratization of the Japanese state. The actual drafting of the Meiji Constitution took place between 1886 and 1888 and was the work of a small number of men that included a Prussian adviser, *Carl Friedrich Hermann Roessler*. It was submitted to a newly created *Privy Council* headed by Ito where it was debated between May and December of 1888 with the Emperor present.

Some of the more specific features of this first constitution of Japan will be examined in later chapters. It is especially important to note here that the Meiji Constitution was not submitted to constitutional conventions for debate, nor was it at any time submitted to voters for ratification. It was presented as a gift from the Emperor. In his *Commentaries* on the Meiji Constitution, Ito presents the following summation of his thoughts on the role of the Emperor in the Japanese state, a summation that also reflects his view that the deeper sources of authority lie in Japan's particular history wherein ministers of state "assist" the sovereign (Emperor). Anything so new as a representative assembly (Diet) may merely give "advice":

> In our country, the relations between Sovereign and subject were established at the time that the state was founded. The unity of political powers was weakened, during the middle ages, by a succession of civil commotions. Since the Restoration (A.D. 1868), however, the Imperial power has grown strong and vigorous; and the Emperor has been pleased to issue decrees proclaiming the grand policy of instituting a constitutional form of government, which it is hoped will give precision to the rights and duties of subjects and gradually promote their well-being, by securing unity to the sovereign powers of the Head of the State, by opening a wider field of activity for serving (the Emperor), and by prescribing, with the assistance of the Ministers of State and the advice of the Diet, the whole mode of the working of the machinery of State in a due and proper manner. (1906, 1)

But this view of the Imperial Throne as the supreme source of authority, a view that included a residual concept of the rule of the sages in the form of *genro* who were firmly established as the leadership in the administrative organs of the state, did not go unchallenged.

Led in the beginning by **Itagaki Taisuke** of **Tosa**, in **Shikoku**, and **Okuma Shigenobu** of **Hizen**, in **Kyushu**, the various popular rights movements eventually crystallized into the first political parties in Japan. The first truly national party was led by Itagaki and was called the *Jiyuto*, or Liberal, Party. Okuma, after falling out with Ito in the early 1880s, organized the *Kaishinto*, or Progressive, Party. Okuma also established a school that developed into **Waseda University** in Tokyo, today one of the most prestigious private universities in Japan and still noted for its development of political leaders. Okuma would go on to serve as prime minister on two occasions. The first time, in 1898, he formed Japan's first political party cabinet. Though the two original parties underwent many changes, and name changes, one can still recognize them as the originals, respectively, of the post–World War II Liberal and Democratic parties. In 1955, these two parties merged to form the Liberal Democratic Party (LDP). From 1955 to 1993, the LDP was the governing party in the Japanese Diet. It remains the largest party represented in the Diet.

The early parties led by Itagaki and Okuma were inspired by Western models of popular sovereignty and people's rights. From the first Diet election, held on November 29, 1890, the early years under the Meiji Constitution saw continuous struggle between the lower house in the Diet and what were called *transcendental cabinets*. The latter were made up mostly of the *genro* and mostly those from Satsuma and Choshu. They were called the *Satcho* clique for short. It would be an oversimplification to say that the sources of authority in the new Japanese government under the Meiji Constitution derived from an administrative tradition rooted in Confucian teachings, on the one hand, and an emerging democratic tradition rooted in Western theory and practice, on the other. It would take many years, for example, for the Diet to establish itself as a legitimate contender for power. Still, the Confucian and Western traditions defined the main currents of Meiji political theory and practice. There were other currents. And among them was the current that carried the strong voices of authoritative women.

WOMEN OF AUTHORITY

According to Chinese sources, women in positions of leadership was common in third-century Japan. Ruling empresses can be found into the eighth century. In literature, **Lady Murasaki Shikibu** is world renowned for the *Tale of Genji*, often called the world's first novel and cited as a basic source for understanding Japanese aesthetic and psychological tendencies. Lady Sarashina's "diary," which dates from the eleventh century, is another literary source famous for its insights into *Heian* court life and also for its literary style of mixing poetry and prose. Sei Shonagon's *Pillow Book* is contemporaneous with *Tales of Genji* and is renowned for its wit and psychological insights. The shining princess, Kaguyahime, is known to all Japanese children from the "Tale of the Bamboo Cutter" (see Chapter 1). In all corners of Japan today, from anchor desks on evening news programs to loud speakers hung in trees in otherwise remote mountain settings, the voice of authority is very often a woman's voice. This is not to diminish the truth that women in Japanese society have had more often than not to play a secondary role and, under Confucian influence, a deeply subordinate one; rather, it is to note that Japanese women have always played authoritative roles and, increasingly, in the world of public and political events. With respect to the latter point, Merry White has observed that women are today "the most visible, and audible, agents of change" in Japanese society (1992, 62).

But women have often been in the forefront of change in Japanese society. *Tsuda Umeko*, for example, was among five young women to go abroad on the Iwakura mission in 1871. She returned to America later and graduated from Bryn Mawr. Back in Japan she tutored in the household of Ito Hirobumi and also in one of the top Imperial schools for 15 years before resigning to open her own school for girls, the forerunner of Tsuda College. *Yoshioka Yayoi* founded the Tokyo Women's Medical College in 1900 to help women who sought medical training and careers as physicians. These efforts in establishing opportunities for women in higher education represented dramatic departures from the Confucian-inspired *onna daigaku*—women's higher learning—of the Edo Period. According to *onna daigaku*, women should be obedient to parents, then husband, then sons.

In politics, **Kishida Toshiko** was among the leaders in the Freedom and People's Rights Movement, *Fukuda Hideko* was among the leaders of early socialist activity in Japan, and **Hiratsuka Raicho** founded the **Bluestocking Society**, the first feminist organization in Japan. There was also a Women's Suffrage League, founded in the 1920s, that fought for wide-ranging reforms in Japanese law as it affected women. Generally, however, from 1890 to 1945, women faced a severely uphill battle to gain the right to participate in Japanese public life. During the Popular Rights Movement of the 1880s, women could take part through voting and the holding of office in "a few towns and villages" (Garon 1993, 10). But toward the end of the decade, limits began to be imposed. In 1888, the Law on the City System and the Law on the Town and Village System limited the franchise and the holding of office to males. In 1890, prior to the meeting of the first Diet, the Law on Assembly and Political Association prohibited women from active participation in political associations. They could not attend meetings where any political discussion took place. The Police Law of 1900 strengthened these restrictions.

The place of women in Japanese society was to be that of the "good wife and wise mother." This had been the overwhelming assumption within Japanese culture since the middle of the Tokugawa Period and the acceptance of the *onna daigaku* (higher education of women) concept that taught the subservience of women to fathers, husbands, and sons. Although reformers such as Fukuzawa Yukichi challenged this ideal, it was very difficult to displace. On three different occasions, the lower house of the Japanese Diet under the Meiji Constitution passed amendments to the fundamental law that would eliminate restrictions on women attending political meetings, sponsoring such meetings, and joining political groups. Each time, however, the amendments were vetoed by the upper House of Peers made up largely of *genro* and former *daimyo*. Despite the fact that between 1895 and 1920 the number of girls of elementary school age who were in school doubled from 43.9 to 98.8 percent, and the number of young women enrolled in institutions of higher education showed comparable gains, it was not until 1922 that the basic law was amended to allow women to attend and sponsor political meetings. By and large, despite grassroots tendencies to the contrary, the Japanese government "used its extensive powers to shape the contours and strategies of the women's movement from the 1880s through World War II" (Garon 1993, 5–41).

Under the 1947 Constitution, women are not only guaranteed the right to vote but also "the essential equality of the sexes." Among the principal architects of provisions in the 1947 Constitution that extended women's rights was Beate Sirota, an Austrian woman who spent most of her childhood in Japan, was fluent in Japanese, and worked tirelessly to convince the appropriate sections of U.S. General Douglas MacArthur's staff of the justice of such changes in Japanese fundamental law (Pharr 1987). Still, today, women in Japan are less represented in public institutions than women in other advanced, democratic nations. Worldwide, according to a recent study, women average 14.6 percent of parliamentary seats. In Japan, the average is 3.9 percent. Occasionally, however, there are surprises. In 1989, in upper house elections, women candidates represented 21.79 percent of all candidates running. Twenty-two women were elected to the House of Councillors (upper house) in that election, 17.46 percent of the total. This phenomenon has been referred to by one scholar as the "Madonna boom" (Iwai 1993).

Among the biggest issues in recent years in Japan is that of the "comfort women." An estimated 200,000 women from East Asian nations occupied by the Japanese Imperial Army during the war years were forced into prostitution by the Japanese army. In August 1996, payments were begun to victims by a private foundation, the Asian Women's Fund, payments accompanied by a letter from Prime Minister Hashimoto expressing sincere apologies for the actions. Many victims, however, in South Korea, Taiwan, and the Philippines refused to accept the payments. Many want the Japanese government to accept the recommendation of the United Nations Commission on Human Rights in April 1996, to conduct a complete investigation as a first step in redressing the grievances of victims. The official position of the government has been that previous war compensation packages have settled all claims from the war years. Surviving comfort women have become strong voices of authority not only in Japan but worldwide.

CONSTITUTIONALISM AND DEMOCRACY IN JAPAN TODAY

There are lively debates among scholars today on the extent of Japan's commitment to constitutionalism and democracy. Both concepts are still relatively new to Japan, being products of the Meiji era. Joseph Pittau sees in the foundations of the modern Japanese state a "new theory of the state." For him, the Meiji Constitution represented fundamentally "an uneasy marriage of absolute ideas with modern constitutional principles bound together by mythical traditions" (1967, 198). With respect to constitutionalism, and as noted earlier, Japan's early efforts resulted in a constitution with but the most rudimentary elements of modern democratic practice. And though these elements were given depth and character with the coming of party cabinets, with the reforms associated with *Hara Takashi*, the "commoner" prime minister, and with the widespread democratic reforms of the *Taisho* Period (1912–1926), those same elements were all but crushed by events like the enactment of the Peace Preservation Law in 1925, the occupation of Manchuria, the assassination of Prime Minister *Inukai Tsuyoshi* in the May 15 "incident" of 1932, and the rise of the military to power during the 1930s.

The concept of a rule of law transcending immediate political dynamics and capable of offering a deep, cultural resistance to groups determined to assume power was not part of Showa political culture. The Japanese legal tradition as a whole, from its earliest development, was largely a product of Chinese sources, sources that did not include a higher or natural law tradition, appeals to which could check the power of state authorities. A tradition of constitutionalism in the Western sense of legal limits on the power of the state was simply not an aspect of Meiji constitutional theory or practice. When Japanese scholars first encountered French and German civil and commercial codes during early Meiji, they generally failed to understand the concept of private rights independent of state authority. Similarly, in the first several sessions of the new Japanese Diet in the 1890s, impassioned debates over the various codes, especially the civil code, delayed implementation. Primary concerns of critics focused on the radical individualism assumed in many of the provisions that originated in Western jurisprudence (Haley 1991, 72–77). Even in 1996, debates over changes in the civil code bearing on family matters were postponed due to controversy within the ruling coalition parties.

With the 1947 Constitution, however, a constitution largely drafted by Americans under General MacArthur's command during the occupation (1945–1952), Japan has what many believe is among the most progressive constitutions in the world. The famous *Article 9*, for example, renounces war; its provisions guaranteeing equality for women have already been noted. It is also true, however, that the 1947 Constitution is the product of occupation and outside authorship. According to one participant, the "entire job was finished in two weeks." Echoing the sentiments of others, Mark Gayn proceeded to observe the following in his *Japan Diary:* "What is wrong—disastrously wrong—is that this constitution does not come from the Japanese grass roots. It is an alien constitution foisted on the Japanese government, and then represented as a native product, when any Japanese high-school student simply by reading it can perceive its foreign origin" (1973, 19–24). As Oe Kenzaburo noted in his Nobel speech at Stockholm, even though "we now have the half-century-old new Constitution, some popular sentiment for the old one lives on in some quarters" (1995, 7).

These are aspects of Japanese constitutionalism that occasionally flare into political issues, as will be discussed in a later chapter. From its beginning, the Liberal Democratic Party has called for the rewriting of the constitution, and the Japan Socialist Party—now called the Social Democratic Party of Japan—has defended the constitution. Only in January 1995, as part of its coalition with the SDPJ, did the LDP renounce its call for a new constitution (Tamamoto 1995b, 60). There is even disagreement as to what sections of the constitution were intended to mean. According to one recent study, the current Japanese constitution reads very differently in Japanese than in English and is the product of considerable misunderstanding between MacArthur's staff and the Japanese leadership of the time. Kyoko Inoue argues that the "Japanese version" of the "new" constitution is "more compatible with Japanese social and political values than the English version" (1991, 2).

In 1994, a number of calls for revision of the Japanese constitution were published. In the spring, the Kansai Association of Corporate Executives called for "rethinking" the constitution. In the summer, an institute headed by former Prime Minister Nakasone included constitutional reform in its considerations of Japan's future. Most notably, however, the *Yomiuri Shimbun*, Japan's most widely circulating newspaper, published a completely new constitution for consideration in its November 3 issue. The newspaper had been studying constitutional revision since 1992. Much of the impetus for the initiative was provided by Japan's response, and lack of response, to the war in the Persian Gulf. Though most revisionists since the inception of the constitution in 1947 have focused on Article 9, the *Yomiuri Shimbun* offered also a more concise preamble, a provision on privacy, another on environmental issues, and structural changes in the Diet and courts that would give the upper House of Councillors more responsibilities and create a "constitutional court" with the power to rule on the constitutionality of legislation passed by the Diet. These recommendations, among others, generated considerable debate, especially among competing newspapers. While the *Asahi Shimbun* and *Mainichi Shimbun,* Japan's second and third largest newspapers, were somewhat critical of hasty revisions, the *Sankei Shimbun,* Japan's sixth largest paper, urged reforms that would reflect "Japan's culture and traditions more faithfully" ("Editorials" 1995).

With respect to democracy, the picture is even less clearly defined. But this is a problem that is global in character. The concept of democracy itself is subject to extensive debate, especially in this era of postindustrial, postmodern, post–Cold War global politics. According to Edwin Reischauer, Japan's political heritage "includes no experience with the concepts and practices of democracy" (Reischauer and Jansen 1995, 231). A more recent study claims that there are, indeed, "no citizens in Japan because they never concerned themselves with political associations in the first instance" (Tamamoto 1995a, 16). Though the Diet has now functioned for over 100 years as a representative assembly for the people of Japan, there are those who argue that it is in practice more the representative assembly for the particular interests of select groups. For Karel van Wolferen, for example, whose *Enigma of Japanese Power* is among the most often cited *revisionist studies* of Japan, the "elusive" Japanese state is a "rigged one-party system" (1989, 25–30). The reference is to the Liberal Democratic Party and its near 40-year control of the lower house of the Diet. Though Japan is clearly recognized as a modern democracy with all of the implications regarding such things as regular elections, rule of law, human rights, and party competition, still, the Japanese experience with "the concepts and practices of democracy" is relatively new when compared with that of other modern, democratic nations. In addition, certain features of traditional Japanese culture (much of it explored earlier) remain as either counterweights or modifying influences on the development of democratic political culture in Japan. For example, in the Japanese version of the 1947 Constitution, according to the Inoue study, "the people do not command the government not to infringe their rights and liberties." Rather, the Japanese version "affirms the responsibility of the Japanese government to establish a democratic government, and the people and the government together affirm the necessity of protecting individual rights and liberties" (1991, 103). The difficulty here, and in analyzing East/West relations generally, is to avoid either overstating or understating the importance of cultural differences. As Robert J. Smith put it in a recent article on "Culture as Explanation," culture is neither "all nor nothing" (Smith 1989).

With respect to the concept of equality, for example, Japan presents something of an enigma. Economically, Japan has been ranked with Sweden and

Australia as having the smallest income gap between richest and poorest. Also, class consciousness is weak. On the other hand, there is much greater stress on hierarchy in Japanese society than in almost any other modern democracy. Nakane Chie, in her often quoted study of *Japanese Society,* distinguishes two basic types of human relations: horizontal and vertical. As examples, she offers the following: "the parent-child relation is vertical, the sibling relation is horizontal; the superior-inferior relation is vertical, as opposed to the horizontal colleague relation" (1970, 23). From this conceptual base she analyzes the internal structure of the group in Japanese society and illustrates the complex and often subtle process through which ranking and hierarchy take place. "Without consciousness of ranking," she writes, "life could not be carried on smoothly in Japan, for rank is the social norm on which Japanese life is based" (31). Much of this emphasis on ranking derives from the Confucian tradition. Even mass protests, such as the rice riots of 1918, are often motivated less by a consciousness of "rights" being denied than by a perception of superiors failing in their duties regarding benevolence. Michael Lewis, examining mass protest in Imperial Japan, observes that the rice riots "can be better understood by referring to Confucian benevolence and the responsibilities of social 'superiors' rather than to Lockean notions of inalienable rights to life, liberty, and property" (1990, xix). Although the roles of *amae, on,* and *iegara*—complex terms referring to personal relationships and their larger effects—certainly play continuing parts in structuring Japanese society and its hierarchical aspects, the larger force of historical change is in the direction of egalitarian, or horizontal, relations.

Japan today represents a particularly complex example of modern democratic governance, a phenomenon largely the result of the traditional sources of authority either unique to Japan (Shintoism) or uniquely transformed by Japanese experience (Buddhism, Confucianism, Western constitutional and democratic theories). As subsequent chapters will explore in more detail, virtually all of the various agencies, institutions, practices, and polemics that characterize democracy in Japan today reflect in some measure the continuing influences of the sources of authority here sketched.

Summary

All modern states have institutions and practices considered authoritative. These derive from sources often ancient. In the United States, for example, a concept of the rule of law derives from ancient Greek and Roman civilizations. Sources of authority in modern Japan derive primarily from Buddhist, Confucian, and Shinto religious traditions and from Western influences. Buddhism in Japan dates from the sixth century and was heavily influential during the Nara, Heian, Kamakura, and Muromachi periods. Though complex in its development, Japanese Buddhism teaches common principles regarding certain noble truths, three treasures, and an eightfold path. Sects such as Pure Land, True

Pure Land, and Zen Buddhism share other common features, such as a belief in equality, simplicity, artistic sensibility, and salvation in the hereafter. The meditation, self-reflection, and aesthetic cultivation characteristic of Zen Buddhism was especially popular among the *samurai* and became an important influence in defining *bushido*, or the way of the *samurai*. During the Momoyama Period, and again at the beginning of the Meiji Period, Buddhist influence declined due to state actions directed against it. Today it is probably the least authoritative of the traditional sources of authority in Japan. Confucianism, however, is perhaps the most influential of traditional sources. Teachings such as the desired rule of the sages, the importance of education, the priority of personal relationships, especially to parents, spouse, children, siblings, and sovereign, the first importance of harmony, and personal loyalty—all continue, in greater or lesser degree, in modern Japan. Shinto, during the Meiji, Taisho, and early Showa periods developed into State Shinto with a mystic *kokutai* philosophy as its defining feature. By this philosophy of the state, "loyalty and love between the people and the emperor" was the cardinal principle of politics. During the same period, Western influences, largely through the efforts of leaders like Fukuzawa Yukichi, produced a movement toward civilization and enlightenment. The Meiji Constitution of 1889 reflects all of these traditions, notably the Confucian, Shinto, and Western, largely German, influences.

The role of authoritative women in the development of the modern Japanese state should not be overlooked. From ruling empresses in early Japan, through the world-renowned literary works of Lady Murasaki and Sei Shonagon, to the contemporary role of women as agents of change, especially in perceptions of the war years and the injustices suffered by "comfort women," Japanese women have often been among the most authoritative of voices.

Suggested Readings

Akita, George. 1967. *Foundations of Constitutional Government in Modern Japan, 1868–1900.* Cambridge, MA: Harvard University Press.

Bellah, Robert N. 1957. *Tokugawa Religion: The Values of Pre-industrial Japan.* Glencoe, IL: Free Press.

Blacker, Carmen. 1975. *The Catalpa Bow: A Study of Shamanistic Practices in Japan.* London: Allen and Unwin.

Bolitho, Harold. 1974. *Treasures Among Men: The Fudai Daimyo in Tokugawa Japan.* New Haven, CT: Yale University Press.

Craig, Albert M. 1961. *Choshu in the Meiji Restoration.* Cambridge, MA: Harvard University Press.

Earhart, H. Byron. 1989. *Gedatsu-kai and Religion in Contemporary Japan: Returning to the Center.* Bloomington: Indiana University Press.

Fairbank, John K., Edwin O. Reischauer, and Albert M. Craig. 1989. *East Asia: Tradition and Transformation.* Boston: Houghton Mifflin.

Gluck, Carol. 1985. *Japan's Modern Myths: Ideology in the Late Meiji Period.* Princeton, NJ: Princeton University Press.

Haley, John Owen. 1991. *Authority Without Power: Law and the Japanese Paradox.* New York: Oxford University Press.

Hardacre, Helen. 1989. *Shinto and the State, 1868–1988.* Princeton, NJ: Princeton University Press.

Inoue, Kyoko. 1991. *MacArthur's Japanese Constitution: A Linguistic and Cultural Study of Its Making.* Chicago: University of Chicago Press.

Ramseyer, J. Mark, and Frances M. Rosenbluth. 1995. *The Politics of Oligarchy: Institutional Choice in Imperial Japan.* Cambridge: Cambridge University Press.

Sansom, George B. 1936. *Japan: A Short Cultural History.* New York: Appleton Century.

Tucker, Mary Evelyn. 1989. *Moral and Spiritual Cultivation in Japanese Neo-Confucianism: The Life and Thought of Kaibara Ekken, 1630–1740.* Albany: State University of New York Press.

Works Cited

Arendt, Hannah. 1951. *The Origins of Totalitarianism.* New York: Harcourt, Brace and World.

Craig, Albert. 1968. Fukuzawa Yukichi: The Philosophical Foundations of Meiji Nationalism. In *Political Development in Modern Japan,* ed. Robert E. Ward, 99–148. Princeton, NJ: Princeton University Press.

Davis, Winston. 1992. *Japanese Religion and Society: Paradigms of Structure and Change.* Albany: State University of New York Press.

Dazai Osamu. 1984. *Setting Sun,* trans. Donald Keene. Tokyo: Charles Tuttle.

Earhart, H. Byron. 1989. *Gedatsu-kai and Religion in Contemporary Japan: Returning to the Center.* Bloomington: Indiana University Press.

"Editorials." 1995. The Constitution: Four Newspapers Speak Out. *Japan Echo* 22 (Spring): 35–39.

Embree, Ainslee T., ed. 1988. *Encyclopedia of Asian History.* New York: Charles Scribner's Sons. S.v. "Rai Sanyo," by Bob Tadashi Wakabayashi.

Garon, Sheldon. 1993. Women's Groups and the Japanese State: Contending Approaches to Political Integration, 1890–1945. *Journal of Japanese Studies* 19 (Winter): 5–41.

Gayn, Mark. 1973. Drafting the Japanese Constitution. In *Postwar Japan: 1945 to the Present,* ed. Jon Livingston, Joe Moore, and Felicia Oldfather, 19–24. New York: Pantheon.

Haley, John Owen. 1991. *Authority Without Power: Law and the Japanese Paradox.* New York: Oxford University Press.

Hardacre, Helen. 1989. *Shinto and the State, 1868–1988.* Princeton, NJ: Princeton University Press.

Harootunian, Harry D., and Tetsuo Najita. 1988. Japanese Revolt Against the West: Political and Cultural Criticism in the Twentieth Century. In *The Cambridge History of Japan.* Vol. 6, *The Twentieth Century,* ed. Peter Duus, 711–774. Cambridge: Cambridge University Press.

Huntington, Samuel P. 1993. The Clash of Civilizations? *Foreign Affairs* 72 (Summer): 22–49.

Imperial Rescript on Education. 1973. In *Imperial Japan: 1800–1945,* ed. Jon Livingston, Joe Moore, and Felicia Oldfather, 153, 154. New York: Pantheon.

Inoue, Kyoko. 1991. *MacArthur's Japanese Constitution: A Linguistic and Cultural Study of Its Making.* Chicago: University of Chicago Press.

Ito Hirobumi. 1906. *Commentaries on the Constitution of the Empire of Japan,* trans. Baron Miyoji Ito. Tokyo.

Iwai Tomoaki. 1993. The Madonna Boom: Women in the Japanese Diet. *Journal of Japanese Studies* 19 (Winter): 103–120.

Japan Information and Culture Center. 1996. Venturing into a New World. *Japan Now* 6 (June): 8.

Kaji Nobuyuki. 1991. Confucianism, the Forgotten Religion. *Japan Quarterly* 38 (January): 57–62.

Ketelaar, James E. 1990. *Of Heretics and Martyrs in Meiji Japan: Buddhism and Its Persecution.* Princeton, NJ: Princeton University Press.

Lewis, Michael. 1990. *Rioters and Citizens: Mass Protest in Imperial Japan.* Berkeley: University of California Press.

Matsumoto Shigeru. 1970. *Motoori Norinaga (1730–1801).* Cambridge, MA: Harvard University Press.

Matsunami Niichiro. 1940. *The Japanese Constitution and Politics.* Tokyo: Maruzen.

McMullin, Neil. 1984. *Buddhism and the State in 16th-Century Japan.* Princeton, NJ: Princeton University Press.

Nakane, Chie. 1970. *Japanese Society.* Berkeley: University of California Press.

Oe Kenzaburo. 1995. Japan, the Ambiguous, and Myself: Nobel Lecture 1994. *World Literature Today* 69 (Winter): 5–9.

Pharr, Susan. 1987. The Politics of Women's Rights. In *Democratizing Japan: The Allied Occupation,* ed. Robert E. Ward and Sakamoto Yoshikazu, 221–252. Honolulu: University of Hawaii Press.

Pittau, Joseph, S.J. 1967. *Political Thought in Early Meiji Japan, 1868–1889.* Cambridge, MA: Harvard University Press.

Pocock, J. G. A. 1972. Virtue and Commerce in the Eighteenth Century. *Journal of Interdisciplinary History* 3 (Winter): 119–134.

Reischauer, Edwin O., and Marius B. Jansen. 1995. *The Japanese Today: Change and Continuity.* Cambridge, MA: Belknap Press of Harvard University Press.

Smith, Robert J. 1989. Culture as Explanation: Neither All nor Nothing. *Cornell International Law Journal.* 22 (3): 425–434.

Soviak, Eugene. 1971. On the Nature of Western Progress: The Journal of the Iwakura Embassy. In *Tradition and Modernization in Japanese Culture,* ed. Donald H. Shively, 7–34. Princeton, NJ: Princeton University Press.

Tamamoto Masaru. 1995a. Reflections on Japan's Postwar State. *Daedalus* 124 (Spring): 1–22.

———. 1995b. Village Politics: Japan's Prince of Disorder. *World Policy Journal* 12 (Spring): 49–60.

Tucker, Mary Evelyn. 1989. *Moral and Spiritual Cultivation in Japanese Neo-Confucianism: The Life and Thought of Kaibara Ekken, 1630–1740.* Albany: State University of New York Press.

van Wolferen, Karel. 1989. *The Enigma of Japanese Power.* New York: Knopf.

Waley, Arthur. 1921. *The No Plays of Japan.* London: Allen and Unwin.

White, Merry. 1992. Home Truths: Women and Social Change in Japan. *Daedalus* 121 (Fall): 61–82.

3

The Structure of Authority: Japanese Government

Among the most basic of political issues are those relating to the structure of government. The structure of Japanese government today is unitary, with the central government located in Tokyo (see accompanying box). This has almost always been the case. First **Nara**, then **Heian** (Kyoto), then **Kamakura**, and finally **Edo**, renamed Tokyo with the **Meiji Restoration**, have served as central governments for Japan. Under the Shogunate, Japanese Emperors in Kyoto reigned but did not rule. Power was centralized in the hands of the *shogun* until the end of the *Tokugawa* reign in 1868. Even with the coming of the *genro* during *Meiji* and the *Satcho* clique, laws were promulgated in the name of the Emperor but the Meiji Emperor had no real power. Under the 1947 Constitution, all sovereignty lies with the Japanese people as represented in the Diet. Still, in Japan today, one can see the faded traces of Shinto and Confucian sources of authority in the continuing structures of the Imperial House and the state bureaucracy.

The 1947 Constitution provides for a parliamentary form of government. Unlike the separation of powers idea central to American political theory and practice, parliamentary forms stress more cohesion between the executive and legislative functions, a style of governance more in keeping with Japanese experience under the *Meiji Constitution*, despite the breakdown in practice. Parliamentary systems require majority parties, or coalitions in the absence of a one-party majority, to form a government. The leader of a majority party or coalition then names a cabinet that runs the various state ministries. Elections for the House of Representatives are scheduled every four years but only if the government does not lose a confidence vote. Under the Japanese constitution today, if a majority in the House votes no confidence in the government, fails to sustain a confidence motion, or if the prime minister chooses to dissolve the House, then an election for the House must be held within 40 days from the date of the dissolution. It is customary for the prime minister to give a policy speech prior to dissolving the House. In September 1996, however, Prime

CHIYODA WARD
(NAGATACHO)

Tokyo is a city of wards, districts, and sections each specializing in some particular function or activity. Asakusa, for example, dates from the Edo Period and is centered around the Sensoji Temple. The famous pleasure quarter, Yoshiwara, was nearby. It is home to the Sanja festival every May in which 100 portable shrines are paraded through the streets. Minato Ward is where the Roppongi district is located, home today of some of the liveliest and most popular nightspots in Tokyo. Chiyoda Ward is where one finds the Imperial Palace, Tokyo Station, and the Nagatacho district where most of the important national government buildings are located. The Diet building, completed in 1936, is there along with the Supreme Court and various ministry headquarters. Nagatacho is the central axis point of Japanese politics today.

Minister *Hashimoto Ryutaro* broke with precedent and dissolved the House for an October election without the speech. Leaders of his coalition partners, the Social Democrats and the *Sakigake* (New Party Harbinger), reluctantly agreed to the action. Following the election, the Diet must meet within 30 days. These are all general features of parliamentary forms of government similar to those found in all parliamentary systems. The emphasis is on popular sovereignty as expressed through the election of representatives both from single-member and multimember districts.

POPULAR SOVEREIGNTY: THE JAPANESE DIET

The Japanese Diet was created by the Meiji Constitution of 1889. The first Diet met in 1890 following the first election. It is the oldest national assembly in Asia. Like other organs of state government of that time, the Diet was modeled after Western precedents and based on observations that various Japanese leaders made on several trips to Europe beginning with the *Iwakura* mission. German constitutional precedents were favored by *Ito Hirobumi* as reflected in the choice for the name of the representative assembly. The first Diet consisted of an upper and a lower house, as does the present Diet. All titles of nobility, however, were abolished at the end of World War II. Early Diet sessions were not especially representative. Only about 1.5 percent of the population was eligible to vote for members of the lower house. Early sessions only lasted about three months. Today's Diet consists of a House of Representatives, which consists of 500 members—beginning with the election under the new election law in 1996—and a House of Councillors consisting of 252 members. House members sit for four-year terms or until elections resulting from no-confidence votes are called. Upper house members sit for six-year terms with half of the total elected every three years. The last upper house election was held in the summer of 1995. Today, the Diet, the legislative branch of the national government, is the "highest organ of state power" and is the "sole law-making organ of the state."

The history of the House of Representatives is a microcosm of the history of the democratization of Japanese politics. In the first election for the House on July 1, 1890, only 450,852 Japanese citizens were eligible to cast votes. Eligibility meant males with one-year residency in their district and who had paid a qualifying tax of 15 yen. The districting system was a dual one where 214 seats were from single-member districts and the remaining 86 seats were from 43 two-seat districts. By 1902, the number of eligible voters had risen to 982,868. In addition, the number of representatives was increased to 376 and enlarged so that the total number of constituencies was reduced from 257 (214 plus 43) to 105 (a complex combination of single-member and multimember districts). The residency requirement was dropped to six months and the tax was reduced to 10 yen. By the February election in 1928, after the reforms and tendencies of the period often referred to as *Taisho* democracy (1912–1926), the proportion of voters and number of seats had risen dramatically to over 12 million voters electing 466 members. Eligible voters by 1928 represented 20 percent of the population. These democratic tendencies were interrupted, of course, by the events of the 1930s and 1940s and the war years. For the April 1946 election, the first postwar election, eligible voters reached almost 37 million. This was due to the reforms brought by the American occupation which included the enfranchisement of women. But the prewar figures show that the Japanese Diet, and the principle of popular sovereignty, were developing in Japan independent of direct outside pressure. Native democratic tendencies had developed such that postwar reforms were building on precedent as well as promoting revolutionary change. On balance, however, the changes brought by the 1947 Constitution were indeed revolutionary (Ramsdell 1992, 7, 8).

The 1947 Constitution put the principle of popular sovereignty squarely at the center of the postwar Japanese state. This also placed the Diet at the center of the decision-making process, at least in theory. The introductory section of the new constitution reflects the terms of the *Potsdam Declaration* of July 26, 1945, which Japan accepted officially on August 14, bringing the war to an end. The section states clearly that the "Japanese people, acting through our duly elected representatives in the National Diet . . . do proclaim that sovereign power resides with the people and do firmly establish this Constitution." Chapter 4 of the constitution, Articles 41 through 64, describes the structure, powers, and general operations of the Diet. The Diet shall be the "highest organ of state power, and shall be the sole law-making organ of the state" (Article 41). Electoral districts shall be "fixed by law" (Article 47). Bills become laws "on passage by both Houses, except as otherwise provided by the Constitution" (Article 59). A bill passed by the House of Representatives but not agreed to by the House of Councillors becomes law if passed again by a two-thirds majority of members present in the House (Article 59). Budgets must "first be submitted to the House of Representatives" (Article 60). These provisions all indicate clearly the intent of the constitution to place primary responsibility for state decision making in the House of Representatives of the Diet.

Among controversial aspects of the Diet's structure is the ratio of citizens per representative in both the lower and upper houses. As in the United States, the Japanese courts for many years ruled that the apportionment of districts for the Diet was a political question and not subject to review by the judicial branch of government. In the United States, with *Baker* v. *Carr* (1962), this situation changed with the establishment of the famous "one man, one vote" precedent. A reapportionment "revolution" ensued in the United States. In Japan, well into the 1980s, disparities between over- and underrepresented districts continued, with rural voters continuing to have a disproportionate voice in the Diet. In 1985, however, the Japanese Supreme Court ruled that the disparity in the House of Representatives between rural and urban districts, a disparity that had reached a level of 4.4 voters to one, was unconstitutional. The Diet responded to the decision by passing legislation to give urban voters eight new seats in the House and to deny rural voters seven previously held seats. This action also increased the total number of seats in the House by one, bringing the total House seats to 512 (Curtis 1988, 50). In 1996, the Supreme Court ruled that the ratio of 6.59 to 1 in the House of Councillors was also unconstitutional. Neither of these decisions, however, voided elections.

The organization of the Diet is bicameral and has been since its creation. The first Diet, however, had an "upper" House—called the House of Peers (*Kizokuin*)—based on a peerage system created in 1884. By this action, five ranks within a new aristocracy were created: prince, marquis, count, viscount, and baron. These new titled nobles were added to an earlier nobility created in 1869 following the Meiji Restoration. These earlier nobles included members of the royal family, court nobles, and former *daimyo*. The newer nobility were often given such status based on distinguished service to Japan. The House of Peers also originally included members appointed by the Emperor—or, more often, in the Emperor's name—for their contributions to Japan as especially large taxpayers. The House of Peers and the peerage system were abolished after the war and replaced with a House of Councillors. It is important to note the prior existence of a House of Peers, however, as an example of the institutionalization of hierarchy characteristic of traditional Japanese culture and history.

The House of Councillors today shares power with the House of Representatives, but the latter chooses the prime minister and has virtual control of the budgeting process. When a budget package passes the lower house, for example, it automatically becomes law within 30 days even if the upper house fails to act or votes against it. In addition, the lower house has the power to override, by a two-thirds vote, any attempt by the House of Councillors to negate actions of the lower house. The House of Councillors consists of 252 members who serve six-year terms. Half of the total number are elected in national elections every three years. As under the new system for the House of

Representatives, voters in upper house elections have two votes, one for an individual and one for a party. In a national election, of the 126 seats up for election, 50 are filled nationally based on the proportion of votes cast for parties. On July 23, 1995, the coalition government's parties—the LDP, the Social Democrats, and the *Sakigake*—managed to win 68 of the 126 contested seats, 4 more than the number needed for a majority. Among the noteworthy results of the election was the showing of the Social Democratic Party of Japan, which only won 16 seats in the election, a result that foreshadowed its dismal showing in October 1996 in the House election. Another noteworthy result was the relatively strong showing of the New Frontier Party in its first big test. In head-to-head competition with the LDP in the party vote for the national seats, *Ozawa*'s party won 18 seats to the LDP's 15. As the results in the House election in October of the following year showed, however, the New Frontier Party could not sustain its early successes. In all contests in the July 1995 race, the LDP won 46 of the 126 seats and the New Frontier Party won 40. Table 3–1 shows the balance of power in the House of Councillors as of January 1997.

In the actual policymaking process, the Diet more often than not takes up legislation originally drafted in one of the various ministries. At the beginning of the Diet sessions, custom dictates that the prime minister and members of the cabinet present policy statements to members of both houses. These statements identify priority concerns in both domestic and foreign policy areas and reflect the views of the majority party's leadership—traditionally the Liberal Democratic Party's leadership—or the coalition government's leadership. These views

TABLE 3–1
House of Councillors, Party Balance
(as of January 20, 1997)

Party	Number of Seats
Liberal Democratic Party	112
Heiseikai*	61
Social Democratic Party	22
Democratic Party and Shin-Ryokufukai*	22
Japanese Communist Party	14
Niin Club*	4
Jiyunokai*	4
New Party Sakigake	3
New Social Party–Alliance for Peace	3
Taiyo Party	3
Independents	4
Total	252

*The Heiseikai is a loose association of New Frontier Party, Komei members who stayed with that party, and others. The Shin-Ryokufukai, Niin Club, and Jiyunokai are similar associations within the chamber.

SOURCE: Secretariat, House of Councillors (Web page).

also reflect the positions of senior ministry officials who work closely with cabinet ministers and the leadership of the ruling party or parties. Other parties also present their agendas and critiques. As much of the specific content of these presentations deals with budget matters, controversial differences on key issues often erupt in Budget Committee meetings. A good example is the recent confrontation between Ozawa's New Frontier Party and the Hashimoto-led coalition over the *jusen* bailout proposal. Differences reached the point where Ozawa's supporters physically blocked access to the assembly room where meetings were being held. This action had the effect of seriously damaging the New Frontier Party's standing in public opinion and hastened Prime Minister Hashimoto's decision to dissolve the extraordinary session of the Diet in late September 1996 and call a national election for October 20.

An important consideration with respect to the Diet as an institution representative of popular sovereignty is whether and to what extent members of the Diet increasingly see their membership as a kind of professional membership. This is a growing concern in all modern democratic states and is mirrored in the United States in recent efforts to impose term limits for members of representative institutions. Some argue that professionalism is a positive development in an increasingly complex world of public policy making. Experience is needed to learn the ways of internal, institutional negotiation as well as the complex nuances of issues, especially issues like nuclear power generation, public health financing, and monetary policy. Critics contend that what supporters call professionalism is in fact the entrenchment of well-organized, well-financed interests often with little connection with or regard for the larger public good. In Japan, the occupation government prohibited numerous former members from standing for a Diet election. As a consequence, 82 percent of those elected to the Diet in the April 1946 election were first-timers. With the restoration of Japanese sovereignty in 1952, many prewar members returned to the Diet, bringing their experience and adding a certain professionalism to the Diet through the 1950s and 1960s. According to Daniel Ramsdell's detailed study of the first 100 years of the Japanese Diet, 1890 to 1990, the prewar Diet "was mostly made up of amateurs with little experience." Since the end of the postwar occupation, however, the Diet has "steadily become more and more professional" (Ramsdell 1992, 85–103).

Party balances within the House of Representatives have shifted dramatically in recent years due to global changes in the post–Cold War environment and domestic crises involving corruption, economic stagnation, an aging society, administrative failings, and voter disillusionment. On the eve of the 1996 national election for the House of Representatives on October 20, the largest bloc of seats belonged to the Liberal Democratic Party with 211. Next was the New Frontier Party with 160. These two blocs were led by Hashimoto Ryutaro, the prime minister, and Ozawa Ichiro. Each party made its appeal in the national election of that year to the conservative voters, but with some significant differences. The LDP continued its support of the scheduled rise in the consumption tax from 3 percent to 5 percent in April 1997. The New Frontier Party promised to delay implementation of the tax increase and, in fact, offered a tax cut given control of the House. The third largest force in the House going into the election was the newly formed *Minshuto,* or Democratic Party of Japan, with 52 seats. These members were all previously affiliated with other parties, most with the Social Democrats or the *Sakigake* (New Party Harbinger). The Social Democratic Party of Japan was reduced to 30 seats by defections. Doi Takako was back at the head of the party and leading the campaign in the national election. But the long fall of the party was dramatically illustrated by the fact that it was only running 48 candidates (8 women) for the House election. The Japan Communist Party held 15 seats but was showing new vitality by running over 300 in the October election, including 66 women candidates. The *Sakigake* was down to 9 seats, after defections to the *Minshuto,* and a scattering of minor party and independent representatives rounded out the total. From this balance a coalition government was formed in which the LDP, the Social Democrats, and the *Sakigake* were members. With the complete transformation of the latter two parties in the coalition, the postelection government promised to be substantially changed.

On October 20, the LDP increased its number of seats to 239, just 12 short of an absolute majority. This all but assured that Hashimoto would continue as prime minister. Prospects for continuing the coalition with the Social Democrats and *Sakigake* were diminished, however, by the poor showing of both parties and the views expressed by SDPJ leader Doi that she would not immediately agree to continuing the coalition. The SDPJ won only 15 seats in the election, only 4 of which were won in the new single-member districts. The *Sakigake,* already reduced to 9 members in the House from defections going into the election, managed to hold only 2 seats, both single-member seats. The New Frontier Party saw its numbers decrease to 156, raising questions about Ozawa's continued leadership of the party. Among the bigger surprises was the election of 26 Japan Communist Party candidates, 24 of them from proportional lists. Most analysts predicted that the single-member districts would work to the advantage of large parties, a prediction that generally held true. Of the 300 seats contested, the LDP and New Frontier parties won a combined total of 265, or 88 percent of the seats. The 200 proportional seats were expected to work to the advantage of smaller and newer parties. In addition to the JCP benefiting, so also did the *Minshuto.* The latter kept its 52 seats in the election, securing 35 of them in the proportional voting.

The election signaled the almost certain dissolution of both the Social Democratic and *Sakigake* parties. The demise of the former was particularly noteworthy, as it was the Social Democrats, previously under its English name of the Japan Socialist Party, which defined the opposition to the LDP throughout the days of the **55 *system***. It was also largely the Socialist Party that upheld the peace constitution and kept the pressure on the government to renegotiate the **Mutual Security Treaty**. Many agree that the demise of the party was brought on by the changes of position announced under the **Murayama** administration on all of the key issues where the Socialist Party had always differed with the LDP. Others point to the shrewd machinations of the LDP in approving the Murayama government as a sort of transition government through which the Socialist Party would lose credibility even as the LDP would gain strength through its willingness to work with former opponents.

As for Ozawa and the New Frontier Party, speculation in the days after the election centered on whether Ozawa would remain as the party's head, or even if the party would continue to exist. Many analysts projected numerous, or at least significant, defections from the party, many returning to the LDP from whence they came. Such an event would create the prospect of the LDP gaining its majority after all. It is highly likely that the New Frontier Party's relatively poor showing was a direct result of its actions in the House chambers and in the budget hearings earlier where members, under Ozawa's leadership, physically blocked access to places where debate and voting could take place. As the symbol of popular sovereignty, the Diet represents the forum and focus of democracy in modern Japan. In a time of increasing criticism of the bureaucracy, and increasing sensitivity to the need for elected representatives to assume a greater role in policy formation, a time in which, as *Minshuto* election ads framed it "the citizen is protagonist," many saw in the New Frontier Party's tactics the tactics of prewar Japanese politics. In late December, owing to these and other frustrations, Hata Tsutomu and 12 other members of the New Frontier Party (a total of 10 from the lower house and 3 in the upper house) broke away and formed yet another new party, which they called the *Taiyoto*, or "sun," Party.

The continuing proliferation of new parties also reflects the deep frustrations among many former LDP Diet members under the 55 system. Ten of the new *Taiyoto* members were formerly LDP representatives. Voters are also showing increased frustration with the Japanese political system. Many did not participate at all in the October 20 election. The turnout of just over 59 percent marked a postwar low for turnout in a national House election. This continued a slide begun in 1993 and that continued in the upper house election of July 1995. For many, the poor showing of women candidates was also a disappointment. With the proportion of women members in the Diet already among the smallest for an advanced nation, the October national election represented nothing less than an embarrassment. Of the 153 women candidates, only 23 were elected, the largest number (8) running as New Frontier Party candidates. Only 7 of the women winning seats won them in single-member districts. Still, the 1996 election was an improvement over July 1993, when only 14 women won seats in the House. Table 3–2 shows the party balance of power in the House of Representatives as of January 1997.

As the representative institution most expressive of the principle of popular sovereignty, the House of Representatives reflects the tone and texture of the larger society at any given time. That a more "fixed" party, the LDP, is increasingly in the role of negotiating coalitions with the "floating" representatives of Japan's ever changing party landscape is but a current miniature within the Diet of the larger dynamic involving the fixed and floating worlds of traditional Japanese politics.

TABLE 3–2
House of Representatives, Party Balance

Political Party	Representation in the House of Representatives before October 20, 1996	Representation in the House after October 20, 1996	Representation in the House as of January 16, 1997
Liberal Democratic Party (LDP)	211	239	240
New Frontier Party (*Shinshinto*)	160	156	142
Democratic Party of Japan (*Minshuto*)	52	52	52
Japan Communist Party (JCP)	15	26	26
Social Democratic Party	30	15	15
Taiyo Party	0	0	10
21 Seiki	0	0	4
New Party Harbinger (*Sakigake*)	9	2	2
Others	16	10	9
Totals	**493***	**500**	**500**

*There were 18 vacancies in the House at the time of the election. The previous House membership, prior to implementation of election reforms, was 511.

SOURCE: Secretariat, House of Representatives (Web page).

THE PRIME MINISTER AND HIS CIRCLE: THE CABINET

The cabinet is recruited from the Diet and is largely made up of senior members of the ruling, majority party, or members of coalition parties as under Prime Minister Hashimoto. The first Hashimoto cabinet, established in January 1996, consisted of 11 Liberal Democratic Party ministers, 6 Social Democratic Party of Japan members, 2 New Party Harbinger members, and 1 non-Diet minister. There are presently 20 cabinet positions. Leading the government in 1996 was Hashimoto Ryutaro, whose previous experience included serving as minister of health and welfare, transportation, finance, and, most recently, minister of international trade and industry. Other high-profile cabinet ministers were Ikeda Yukihiko, the foreign minister, whose previous experience included head of the Defense Agency; Kan Naoto, health and welfare minister, who made headlines for his investigation of the HIV tainted blood supply issue and, later, for his defection from *Sakigake* to the new *Minshuto;* and Kubo Wataru, deputy prime minister and finance minister, Japan's first Socialist minister of finance. A June 1996 poll showed that although LDP popularity was only at 35 percent and New Frontier Party popularity, the leading opposition party under Ozawa

Ichiro, was at only 9 percent, the cabinet enjoyed a 50 percent approval rating ("Japan's Opposition Blunders" 1996). There may be echoes here of Japanese history and a tradition that puts more confidence in institutions tied to the bureaucratic, administrative structures—firm, rather than floating, structures. The second Hashimoto cabinet, named in early November following the October 20 election, consisted of all LDP appointments, the first such LDP cabinet in three years. Ikeda continued as foreign minister.

The cabinet (*Naikaku*) originated with changes to the original system of government set up at the beginning of the Meiji Restoration to implement the dramatic changes brought by restoring the Emperor, at least nominally, to power. The primary institution created for that purpose was called the *Dajo-kwan* and governed until 1885. In that year, a cabinet was created to take its place. It was in the newly created cabinet, with Ito Hirobumi as minister president, that the *genro* from Satsuma and Choshu established their authority. Of the original ten members, four were from Satsuma and four were from Choshu. The change to the new cabinet was justified as a "return to the ancient Japanese polity." Shortly after, in 1888, a **Privy Council** was created with the primary purpose of approving the final draft of a constitution for Japan and of advising the Emperor on matters of state (McLaren 1965, 112–132).

The Meiji Constitution, of course, does not reflect the real power and authority of what actually constituted Japanese national government at the turn of the twentieth century. Few dispute this. Yet, some scholars today, notably Chalmers Johnson, argue that the 1947 Constitution is similarly misleading. According to Johnson, Article 41 of the current constitution on the powers of the Diet is "not only untrue, it also conflicts with the Japanese political culture inherited from Japan's century of defensive modernization." A more accurate answer to the question of who governs Japan is for Johnson "Japan's elite state bureaucracy" (Johnson 1995, 13). A recent study of industrial finance in Japan by Kent Calder challenges this view, however. Calder sees the Japanese state as more "reactive" than proactive. Private institutions compete among each other and so do state bureaucracies. For example, generally speaking, the Ministry of International Trade and Industry tends to favor intervention in the economy, while the Finance Ministry tends to favor regulation (Calder 1993). Hayao Kenji, in a recent study of the prime minister's office in Japan, similarly stresses the "reactive leadership" in Japan (Hayao 1993, 3–27). Another scholar who challenges Johnson's view is Margaret McKean. Her recent study of "State Strength and the Public Interest" leads to the conclusion that a "pluralization of participation" in Japanese policymaking is evident in recent years and that this development is "enhancing Japanese democracy" (McKean 1993, 103). Traditionally, public servants in all of the agencies of national government are recruited from the top law departments of the best universities in Japan and compete through rigorous examinations. Through the drafting of most legislation, these bureaucratic agencies more accurately define the axis of public policy decision making in the modern Japanese state. Many commentators observe that reform politics in Japan today, such as exemplified in the new electoral reform legislation, is designed to change the balance of power from the bureaucracy to the Diet. Skeptics see little prospect of such a dramatic change.

The prime minister under the 1947 Constitution is defined as the head of the cabinet. He or she must be a civilian and must be chosen by the Diet from among its membership. The prime minister appoints ministers of state, with a majority coming from the Diet membership, and removes them. He or she submits bills on behalf of the cabinet, reports on affairs of state, controls administrative business, and countersigns all laws and cabinet orders. The prime minister does not have the veto power. The Office of Prime Minister under the Japanese constitution is usually regarded as somewhat typical among parliamentary systems, though the holder of the position in Japan is often, as one recent study puts it, "a remarkably weak and passive figure" (Hayao 1993, 26). Cabinets, on the other hand, have substantial power, including the power under Article 7 of the constitution to dissolve the House of Representatives and call a general election. This was done in late September 1996. The relationship between the prime minister and cabinet members is complex, one that reflects the party balances within the House. During the 55 system, the relationship between prime minister and cabinet ministers was more often smooth than not. Recent governments, on the other hand, have been the unstable mirror reflection of a changing Japanese society and political scene. Table 3–3 shows Japanese prime ministers since 1982.

Both the prime minister and the cabinet are responsible to the Diet, and all ministers must resign en masse if the House passes a no-confidence resolution or rejects a confidence motion. This happened only twice during the 55 system. The most dramatic instance was in 1993, when the subsequent national election denied the Liberal Democratic Party a majority in the House and effectively ended the 55 system. The no-confidence vote in June 1993 was followed by

TABLE 3–3
Japanese Prime Ministers, 1982–1997

Name	Party	Tenure
Hashimoto Ryutaro	Liberal Democratic Party (LDP)	1996 (January)–
Murayama Tomiichi	Social Democratic Party of Japan (SDPJ)	1994 (June)–1996 (January)
Hata Tsutomu	Japan Renewal Party (JRP)	1994 (April)–1994 (June)
Hosokawa Morihiro	Japan New Party (JNP)	1993 (August)–1994 (April)
Miyazawa Kiichi	Liberal Democratic Party	1991 (November)–1993 (August)
Kaifu Toshiki	Liberal Democratic Party	1989 (August)–1991 (November)
Uno Sosuke	Liberal Democratic Party	1989 (June)–1989 (August)
Takeshita Noboru	Liberal Democratic Party	1987 (November)–1989 (June)
Nakasone Yasuhiro	Liberal Democratic Party	1982 (November)– 1987 (November)

a walkout of 44 LDP members led by Hata Tsutomu. This group became the nucleus of the Japan Renewal Party (*Shinseito*) and, later, was a major force in the formation of the New Frontier Party (*Shinshinto*), founded in December 1994.

From the breakup of the LDP majority and the subsequent realignments among traditional parties and the creation of new parties, there was little stability in the Prime Minister's Office or in the cabinet through the mid-1990s. From Miyazawa Kiichi's resignation following the no-confidence vote and the election of July 18, 1993, to January 1996, Japan had four prime ministers and four cabinets. *Hosokawa Morihiro*'s cabinet represented a coalition of seven parties and only lasted eight months. During the Hosokawa government, the emphasis was on reforming both the electoral system and the bureaucracy. With respect to the first, a comprehensive election reform bill was eventually passed in 1994. With respect to the second, little changed. There was, however, a high-profile confrontation between the minister of MITI (Ministry of International Trade and Industry), Kumagai Hiroshi, and a high-ranking career civil servant, Naito Masahisa, who directed the Industrial Policy Bureau within MITI. Kumagai forced Naito to resign over allegations of improper promotions within the bureau. The actions of the minister were hailed by reform advocates as a victory for the reform agenda and for the prospect of elected officials actually taking control of the policy process from entrenched bureaucrats (Sterngold 1993, A, 3). But the celebratory mood was brief. In April 1994, Hosokawa resigned as prime minister over questions regarding financial matters from years before. Ensuing months brought Prime Ministers *Hata Tsutomu* and *Murayama Tomiichi* and their cabinets. The Murayama cabinet represented one of the strangest coalitions of unlike-minded ministers in the history of Japanese politics and foreshadowed the demise of the Social Democratic Party of Japan and the rise of the *Minshuto*.

All of these events illustrate the especially "floating" or ephemeral nature of recent cabinets and the great difficulty in achieving stable governments in the Japan of the mid-1990s. In any case, prime ministers and their cabinets have not, as a rule, lasted that long in postwar Japan. From the end of World War II until Miyazawa resigned in 1993, Japan had 21 prime ministers in 48 years. Longest terms were served by Yoshida Shigeru (7 years), Sato Eisaku (almost 8 years), and Nakasone Yasuhiro (5 years). Yoshida served on two different occasions. With these exceptions, however, cabinets are short-lived as a rule.

A recent study by Hayao Kenji of the Prime Minister's Office in Japan and its role in making public policy distinguishes three types of leadership: technocratic, political, and reactive. The first is the approach of the problem solver. This approach takes policy challenges seriously. The leader as technocrat encourages cost/benefit analyses and aspires to rational choice. This approach does not so much set the agenda as find solutions for an assumed agenda. This approach is characteristic more of bureaucratic than political behavior. The political leader, on the other hand, emphasizes policy changes and agenda setting. There are attempts here to express in policy the aspirations of large segments of society. Reactive leadership, finally, is neither setting agendas nor actively seeking solutions to presumed problems. The reactive leader brings to bear what support and expertise he or she can to a given problem, but it is done only in reaction to agendas set by others and involves a kind of brokering with respect to details. It is this third, or reactive, style of leadership that one typically finds in the office of the Japanese prime minister. There are exceptions, such as Ikeda Hayato's famous income doubling plan of the 1960s. More often, however, outside pressure (*gaiatsu*) or domestic circumstances prompt ministerial reaction (Hayao 1993, 3–27).

There is evidence that more "political" prime ministers will emerge in the postreform world of Japanese politics. Many observers note that the times require it. Entrenched bureaucracies hold courses and deal with adjusting to minor changes. Whether or not one accepts Ozawa's dramatic characterization of Japanese politics today as entering a third great phase in which Japanese leaders must take the initiative rather than respond to outside, Western pressures, it is clear that major changes are taking place. Regional and national security issues in the emerging post–Cold War global environment beg careful consideration of defense and foreign policy positions; the rising tide of nationalist and specifically Okinawan resentment over the continued presence of American bases requires leadership in the bilateral relationship with the United States; recent bank failures and public bailout proposals present unprecedented challenges in the areas of monetary and fiscal policy; a rapidly aging population continues to call forth creative approaches to stave off emergency shortfalls in care for the elderly in the not-too-distant future; and crises of confidence among citizens both in political and administrative organs of the Japanese state beg for more vision and more leadership from the prime minister and his cabinet. The single-member districts under the 1994 reforms are designed to encourage more issue politics from the campaigns through Diet deliberations. Specific reform proposals were promoted by candidates for the LDP, the New Frontier Party, and the new *Minshuto* in their October 1996 campaigns. These proposals often focused on reorganizing and generally shrinking the administrative organs of the state. Critics, however, noted often and loudly that the specifics were hard to find. As for the other critical areas of concern, they got little attention in "politics as usual" campaigns in which promises of new roads and other public works for particular constituencies squeezed out broader, national, and long-term issues. The Japanese public appears to be responsive to bold leadership proposals, as polls by the *Yomiuri Shimbun* suggest. When Prime Minister Hosokawa Morihiro took office on reform pledges to redesign electoral politics, pledges that translated in 1994 to the passage of the election reforms under which the national House election of October 1996 took place, public support for his new administration—the first non LDP administration in 38 years—was at 71.9 percent. This was the highest show of support since the newspaper started taking the poll in the early 1970s. By contrast, the highly unusual and somewhat controversial coalition administration of Murayama Tomiichi, beginning in June 1994, received only 37.1 percent public support (Masamura 1996, 61).

Late in 1996, there was strong evidence that more political prime ministers and party leaders who aspire to the post will attempt to energize the creative potential of party followers in the Diet. In his policy speech to the Diet upon becoming prime minister, for example, Hashimoto Ryutaro began by telling his audience that reform is "Japan's most pressing need today." He proceeded to stress Japan's aging population, the "collapse" of Cold War structures, the challenge of rebuilding Japan's gloomy economic situation, the prospects represented by rising Asian economies, the need for "thoroughgoing deregulation," the need for a "proactive" foreign policy, and the desirability of reforming government administration. With respect to the last item, Hashimoto urged that "the government administration itself first achieve a major transformation of its values in line with the changing times." He also proposed amendments to the Cabinet Law to "strengthen the Cabinet system." In his concluding remarks he presented a vision of Japan in the next century as a place where "the ideals of freedom and responsibility take precedence over those of regulation and protection, when qualitative enhancement is seen as more important than quantitative expansion, and when the community and home take precedence over the company or other economic organization" (Hashimoto 1996, 62–65).

Ozawa Ichiro, leader of the New Frontier Party, also offered a somewhat detailed plan, highlights of which are included in his "policy manifesto" of December 1995, when Ozawa was chosen president of his party. Also emphasizing reform, Ozawa pledged himself to a ten-year plan that included income tax cuts, land tax cuts, more research and development funding, more public works projects, and a delay in implementation of the rise in the consumption tax from 3 percent to 5 percent. On security matters, the emphasis was on strong ties with the United States, development of a United Nations police force for UN peacekeeping activities, reorganization of the *Self Defense Forces*, and development of a crisis management system to deal more effectively with earthquakes and other civil emergencies. Social pledges included more people with their own homes, shorter working hours, reemployment opportunities for women, care for the elderly, and school reform, including reform of the "examination hell" process, among other pledges. On administrative reform, Ozawa envisioned stronger local governments and a leaner central administration of 15 ministries and agencies. He also supported the relocation of the capital outside of Tokyo. On the subject of "responsible politics," Ozawa wants politicians and parties to be "the prime actors in making policy decisions, and they will bear final responsibility for these decisions" (1996, 66, 67).

There are many more details in both policy statements, but these representative illustrations point to a common concern among major players in Japanese politics to energize the parties and the Diet, reform administrative structures, and address the major, broad issues facing Japan at the beginning of the twenty-first century.

Under the 55 system, selecting the prime minister was virtually the same as picking the head of the Liberal Democratic Party. Traditionally, this meant that one of the heads of various factions would be chosen to head the whole party. Toward the end of the system in the early 1990s, however, two relative unknowns emerged as party head and prime minister, Uno Sosuke and *Kaifu Toshiki*. All of the major faction leaders had been implicated directly or indirectly in the Recruit Cosmos scandal. Party members who become president of the LDP have always been members of the House of Representatives, though there is no formal provision prohibiting House of Councillors members from serving either as party president or prime minister. Also, they typically have more than 20 years' service in the House. Because the safest seats have tended to be rural ones, few postwar prime ministers are from heavily urban areas. Hashimoto Ryutaro, for example, is from Okayama Prefecture. Technically, the party president is chosen at a convention that is held every two years. Hashimoto was chosen party president of the LDP in September 1995, in a contest with Kono Yohei, who was party president at the time and also foreign minister and deputy prime minister. In balloting for prime minister in the House in January, Hashimoto defeated his closest rival, Ozawa Ichiro of the New Frontier Party, by over 100 votes. The outcome was never in question. The previous prime minister, Murayama Tomiichi, in a very different kind of contest, was chosen in a highly competitive and emotionally charged environment that shocked many veteran analysts of Japanese politics. Murayama, head of the Social Democratic Party of Japan, was chosen on the second ballot, defeating former LDP Prime Minister Kaifu Toshiki by a vote of 261 to 214. A dramatic element in the vote was Kaifu's departure from the LDP just hours before the vote. He could not support the Socialist Murayama for prime minister. Some LDP party members, including former Prime Minister Nakasone, also could not endorse Murayama and voted for Kaifu. These events foreshadowed the formation later, in December 1994, of the New Frontier Party (*Shinshinto*), which seeks to challenge the LDP for the conservative middle of the Japanese political scene.

THE EMPEROR AND HIS FAMILY AS SYMBOLS OF STATE

Chapter 1 of the 1947 Constitution, like that of the Meiji Constitution of 1889, is on the Emperor. The present constitution, however, which went into effect on May 3, 1947, states clearly that the Emperor "shall be the symbol of the State and of the unity of the people." Under the Meiji Constitution, the Emperor was afforded a different status by law. He was alternatively "sacred and inviolable"; "head of the Empire"; he exercised "legislative power with the consent of the Imperial Diet"; he gave "sanction to laws"; he opened, closed, and dissolved the House of Representatives; and had the power to issue, on all manner of occasions, Imperial ordinances. He determined the organization of the administration, appointments to national service, and salaries of government officials, had "supreme" command of the army and navy, declared war and peace, and concluded treaties, among other powers. The first 17 articles of the Meiji Constitution, of a total of 76, deal with the powers and status of the Emperor. Under the Meiji Constitution, the Emperor was truly *tenno*, the heavenly sovereign. In practice, however, the *genro,* mostly from Satsuma and Choshu, ruled Japan through *transcendental cabinets.* No other feature of the present Japanese constitution dramatizes the different structure created by the two constitutions than the respective sections on the Emperor.

There was much controversy following World War II on whether the Showa Emperor, *Hirohito,* should continue in any public capacity. Some urged his trial on war crimes. Ascending the Imperial Throne upon the death of his father, the *Taisho* Emperor, in December 1925, Hirohito served as Emperor of Japan for 62 years, the longest reign in Japanese history. Perspectives differ on his role and responsibility during the military governance of Japan during the 1930s and 1940s. Most accounts present Emperor Hirohito as moderate to liberal in his political views but kept isolated from and uninvolved in affairs of state during his early reign. Three exceptions to this pattern have been noted. The first involved the resignation of Prime Minister Tanaka Giichi in 1929 over actions taken and not taken to punish Japanese army officers in Manchuria for the assassination of a warlord. Emperor Hirohito was publicly critical of the prime minister, which led to the latter's resignation. The second exception, often noted, was the suppression of a coup attempt by young army officers in the famous 2-26 incident. On February 26, 1936, a group of junior officers had attempted an overthrow of the national government. Expected support from senior officers was not forthcoming, however, and the coup attempt failed. The Emperor called for swift action to suppress the rebellion. During the three-day incident in Tokyo, which involved about 1,400 troops, the finance minister and several other high government officials were assassinated. The prime minister barely escaped only because of mistaken identity. The final example is the famous vote by the Emperor to accept the Potsdam Declaration in August 1945, ending the war. At war's end, after much debate, the Imperial institution was continued but only as a symbol. The Imperial Household Ministry, once at the center of power and prestige in the Japanese state, has been replaced by the Imperial Household Agency under the Prime Minister's Office.

The present *Heisei* Emperor, *Akihito,* is the 125th Emperor and is, by all accounts, a popular symbol of the Japanese state. With the Empress *Michiko,* their three children, and two daughters-in-law, the royal family today spends much time performing ceremonial and diplomatic duties. The widely publicized and celebrated weddings of *Prince Akishino* to *Kawashima Kiko* in 1990 and of *Crown Prince Naruhito* to *Owada Masako* in 1993 have reinforced the popularity of the royal family in Japan almost inversely proportional to the declining popularity of the royal family in England (see accompanying box). Empress Michiko, who married then Crown Prince Akihito in 1959, is the first commoner to become Empress and symbolizes for many Japanese the democratization of modern Japan. Emperor Akihito was enthroned to the Chrysanthemum Throne on November 12, 1990. On November 22 and 23, he also participated in the *daijosai,* a traditional Shinto rite performed upon the ascension of a new Emperor. Unlike in the past, however, this was a private ceremony, not a state ceremony.

A ROYAL WEDDING

The Crown Prince Naruhito, at age 33, married Owada Masako in a Shinto ceremony on the grounds of the Imperial Palace on June 9, 1993. For the first time, it was much noted, the Empress-to-be was a woman with a career. A Harvard University graduate who also studied at Oxford, the new Crown Princess represented the new Japanese woman deeply involved in economic as well as political affairs. She had most recently worked in the Foreign Ministry and often worked at the highest levels of diplomacy as a negotiator and as a translator. On her wedding day she was a symbol also of traditional Japan, however, as she wore the customary 12-layered silk kimono of Heian fashion while millions watched on television. The day was declared a national holiday. Much debate in the media questioned how the new Crown Princess would adjust from the cosmopolitan worlds of Harvard, Oxford, and the Foreign Ministry to the highly sheltered and ritualized world of the Imperial Palace.

Emperor Akihito traveled to the People's Republic of China in the fall of 1992, the first Japanese Emperor to visit China. That visit has come to symbolize in many ways the increasingly Asian focus of much Japanese diplomacy and trade. In April 1993, the Emperor went to Okinawa where as many as 200,000 Japanese died during the final weeks of World War II. His reception there was polite, though far from enthusiastic. Many Okinawans continue to feel bitterness toward Tokyo over war memories and, today, over defense issues involving American bases there. In the summer of 1994, the Emperor and Empress visited the United States on a two-week tour the highlight of which was a state dinner in the White House Rose Garden on June 13. It was the first state dinner for the Clinton White House. Among scheduled stops in the early planning for the trip was one at Pearl Harbor, Hawaii. This was canceled by the Japanese government, however, to avoid political controversy. Both the China trip and the one to the United States sparked protests from those who continue to point to events in World War II. Much was written of the "apology that wasn't" on the China trip, and protestors in the United States held signs and expressed displeasure in other ways at several points on the American tour. These and other trips abroad highlight the increasing importance of the Japanese Emperor today in high-level diplomacy.

No institution of state is more "fixed" than the Imperial House. Though the Emperor today is but a symbolic figure who reigns but does not rule, this is not unusual in the larger history of the Japanese state. According to legend, the first Japanese emperor was *Jimmu*. Along with the next 13 emperors, Jimmu is not considered an actual, historical figure. Historically verifiable Emperors of Japan date from the early sixth century with Kimmei. During most of the Heian Period (794–1185), a regency developed around the Imperial Throne such that a single family, the *Fujiwara*, virtually controlled the Imperial office and sustained themselves through intermarriage with the royal family. Toward the end of the Heian Period, the Taira (or Heike) family, followed by the Minamoto (or

Genji) family, assumed similar roles. The great conflict between the latter two families is the subject of the famous *Tale of the Heike*. The victory of the Minamoto family brought the **Kamakura** Shogunate to power and reduced the role of the Imperial institution in the actual governing of Japan until the Meiji Restoration. The only real Imperial challenge to the Shogunate in the interim was the attempt by the Emperor Go-Daigo in the fourteenth century that restored the Emperor to power for a very brief period. With the reunification of Japan in the late sixteenth century through the efforts of **Oda Nobunaga**, **Toyotomi Hideyoshi**, and **Tokugawa Ieyasu**, the long equilibrium between a reigning Emperor at Kyoto and a ruling Shogun at Edo was established. The Tokugawa Shogunate remained in power until the great events of the Meiji Restoration brought the return of the Emperor, in a manner of speaking. Though the Meiji Constitution of 1889 gave virtually all power to the Emperor, the real power was with the *genro,* who governed through transcendental cabinets. All of this changed with the 1947 Constitution.

ADMINISTRATIVE AGENCIES/ADMINISTRATIVE STATE?

In positioning themselves for election or reelection to the House of Representatives in the days leading up to the national election in October 1996, candidates for all three major parties—the LDP, the New Frontier, and the newly formed *Minshuto*—competed with each other on plans to trim, subdue, reshape, modify, abolish, or otherwise reconstruct the Japanese bureaucracy. This national bureaucracy has been the focus of increased controversy in recent years due to high-profile crises, cases of mismanagement, and resistance to investigation. Questions regarding the Health and Welfare Ministry's handling of the unheated blood scandal in which hundreds died from the AIDS virus; questions regarding the Finance Ministry's role in the many bank failures and in the *jusen* bailout; questions regarding various agency coverups, denials, and incompetencies related to the "comfort women" issue, the nuclear power issue, the Kobe earthquake and its aftermath, the Tokyo subway and Matsumoto poison gas attacks, among other issues—all point to the need for administrative reform in some measure. These questions and calls for reform aim at the core of the traditional, fixed world of Japanese government. Administrative rule, or at least guidance, has been the norm throughout the better part of Japanese history. Most legislation that passes the Diet originates in the bureaucracy. For example, as reported in the *Japan Times Online* (19 June, 1996), the Diet session that ended on June 19, 1996, passed 99 bills and 8 treaties sponsored by bureaucratic agencies of the national government and only 11 bills sponsored by members of the Diet. According to John Haley, this is really not dramatically different, however, than parliamentary systems in the United Kingdom, Germany, or France, where similarly high proportions of legislation originate in the executive branch (1991, 140).

Under the Meiji Constitution, the national bureaucracy was modeled after that of Prussia. Civil service examinations were given to prospective government employees and preparation for careers in the civil service was provided by national universities, such as Tokyo and Kyoto universities. Todai, or *Tokyo University*, was founded in 1877 as Tokyo Imperial University and was established primarily to educate national civil servants. Most senior level administrators were graduates of these two universities. Most laws were drafted within the various agencies and then submitted to the Diet as required by the Meiji Constitution. Imperial ordinances, however, were also issued. Though the latter were subordinate to Diet statutes under the constitution, emergency Imperial ordinances carried equal authority with statutes. All ministers under Japan's first modern constitution were appointed by the Emperor as well. In practice this meant that the *genro* controlled ordinances and appointments. This system was not especially unique to the early modern Japanese state under the Meiji Constitution. From the seventh to tenth centuries, Japan was governed by what is called the *ritsuryo* system borrowed from China. This system featured administrative hierarchy and strict governance from the top. At the top was the *Dajokan*, the Grand Council of State. With the Meiji Restoration, and prior to the implementation of the Meiji Constitution in 1889, the *genro* referred to their collective governance as *Dajokan* as well. In 1885, the *Dajokan* was replaced by the cabinet.

Today, the Japanese bureaucracy is organized according to the National Government Organization Law of 1948. This law provides for the creation of four types of administrative agency: ministries, the Office of Prime Minister, agencies, and commissions. Twelve ministries define the center of the national bureaucracy each headed by a cabinet minister appointed by the prime minister. Each ministry represents a particularly important aspect of the modern Japanese state or economy. Some, such as the Ministry of Finance and the Ministry of International Trade and Industry, have historically played greater roles in Japanese government. The Ministry of Finance is responsible, for example, for budgeting, taxes, customs and tariffs, insurance, banking, securities, and monetary policies. Founded in 1869 and alternatively headed by some of the leading Restoration statesmen such as Ito Hirobumi and Okubo Toshimichi, it remains among the most important of government organs. Because of its traditional status and power, however, and because of its recent failures regarding banking and investments (*jusen* crisis), the Ministry of Finance is at the top of the administrative reform agenda among virtually all party politicians.

The Ministry of International Trade and Industry (MITI) is also among the traditionally most important organs of the Japanese state. This ministry develops and implements industrial and trade policies, among the most contested issue areas in Japanese politics and diplomacy. Critics have argued that MITI is the central coordinating organ of Japan, Incorporated, and the real engine of Japan's postwar economic development. Environmentalists also regularly target MITI for not being sensitive to the ecological costs of many of its policies. MITI was created only in 1949, though prewar agencies, such as the Ministry of Commerce and Industry and the earlier Ministry of Agriculture and Commerce, had similar, if broader functions. Since 1964, MITI has worked closely with the

Industrial Structure Council, an advisory body made up of members from both the public and private sectors of the economy, to plan long-term policy objectives and means for implementing them. This is an example of the role of *shingikai,* or deliberative councils, which are playing an increasing role in administrative planning today. Much of MITI's power derives from its use of administrative guidance, a legally nonbinding device whereby administrative agencies give directions, make warnings, make requests, ask for cooperation, give suggestions, and issue opinions—all of which are traditionally accepted as authoritative and compelling by affected groups in the private sector. This power has been diminishing in recent years due to the enormous success of private enterprises in a more global economy.

MITI also keeps numerous statistics on the Japanese economy invaluable for examining strengths, weaknesses, balances, and trends. This reflects the large planning role that MITI plays, a role substantially more activist than most Western nation-states where government and industry more often collide or compete. For example, regarding balances, MITI statistics reveal, as of 1991, that in the manufacturing sector of the Japanese economy, production by small and medium-sized establishments, those employing less than 300 persons, represented a higher percentage of total production than large firms employing over 300 persons. The smaller companies produced 51.8 percent of the total and the larger companies 48.2 percent. The smaller firms produced in especially large proportions in such areas as publishing and printing, pulp and paper manufacturing, metal products, foodstuffs, textiles and apparel, and leather products. Large manufacturers accounted for larger percentages of production in chemicals, precision machinery, rubber products, steel, electrical machinery, energy products, and, of course, transportation. These figures are noteworthy as a balance to the often stereotypical view of the Japanese economy as dominated by the giants in partnership with the national government (JISEA 1995, 21).

Other particularly important ministerial organs of the national bureaucracy are the Ministry of Agriculture, Forestry, and Fisheries, the Ministry of Foreign Affairs, and the Ministry of Health and Welfare. The first, MAFF, is responsible for assuring Japan's food supply and for both promoting and protecting Japanese agricultural, lumber, and seafood products and markets. It is famous and notorious as the ministry responsible for price supports and subsidies, especially for domestic rice. The subject of rice in Japan traditionally evokes somewhat mystical and religious images. A rice culture in early Japan virtually dictated social and political arrangements still evident in Japanese culture, society, and politics today. Prices on rice are largely controlled by the national government. Rice farmers sell most of their crops to the national government, which then sets the price for retail sales. Imports are largely prohibited, barring emergency shortages, such that rice has become a symbol for Japan's trade partners of Japan's closed markets. The Ministry of Foreign Affairs is also often in the center of controversy. Founded in 1869, the Foreign Ministry was early among the most important in the national government due to the outside pressures on Japan notoriously symbolized by the *unequal treaties*. Today, economic issues often define concerns in the Foreign Ministry. Ten bureaus within the ministry deal with such areas as cultural affairs, Asian affairs, North American affairs, other regional affairs, economic affairs, treaties, and the United Nations. The ministry operates 165 embassies in other countries, 65 consulates-general, 2 consulates, and 6 missions. The Ministry of Health and Welfare, as noted earlier, is at the center of the reform movement for two high-profile cases from 1995–1996: the unheated blood and tainted food crises. This agency is routinely responsible for the implementation of social welfare programs and the maintenance of public health. It oversees the welfare and medical systems, licenses physicians, nurses, and other health care professionals, approves and regulates drugs, and has the largest single budget of all the ministries.

The other ministries are Construction, Home Affairs, Transportation, Education, Posts and Telecommunications, Justice, and Labor. The Ministry of Education, or **Mombusho**, is today the Ministry of Education, Science, Culture and Sports. It is still referred to most often, however, as simply the Ministry of Education. With responsibilities over Japan's schools, it is often in the center of national attention, especially with reports of deaths due to *ijime* (bullying) which periodically appear in national headlines. Continuing and growing concerns over textbooks, curricula, and scheduling also keep Mombusho in the public eye and in political discussion. Attached to the ministry is the Agency for Cultural Affairs, which promotes cultural activities. The Ministry of Home Affairs coordinates the relationship between the national government in Tokyo and the various prefectures. It also administers election laws. These are two areas often targeted for reform. Decentralization is a popular theme given higher status recently by actions and inactions in Okinawa Prefecture relating to U.S. bases there. The electoral reforms of 1994 have created an entirely new election system for the House of Representatives the implications of which are still not clearly known. The Ministry of Transportation has an ever growing responsibility to administer all laws bearing on harbors, bridges, tunnels, airports, airlines, inspection of ships, automobiles, trucks, and all international transportation. The Ministry of Justice administers the prison system, the registration of families, and the registration of aliens and represents Japan in all litigation involving the national government. The Public Prosecutor's Office is located within the Justice Ministry and was much in the news in the mid-1990s with its prosecution of the leader of the *Aum Shinrikyo* cult, **Asahara Shoko**.

The largest ministry, in terms of personnel, is the Ministry of Posts and Telecommunications with over 300,000 officials. The smallest is the Ministry of Home Affairs with less than 600 (JISEA 1995, 99). The Construction Ministry may well be the most controversial among the ministries in the last 20 years. Huge public works projects have been used periodically to stimulate a sagging economy, and bidding for these projects is less than open. In 1995, in what the *Economist* called a "costly battle against recession," the Japanese government spent $88 billion on public works, the largest amount on record ("A Costly Battle" 1996). Through a system called *dango*, carefully developed relationships among contractors, Diet members, and bureaucrats all but close public works contracts to foreign companies. This is the subject of Brian Woodall's recent study of *Japan Under Construction*. According to Woodall (1996), internal, unwritten bidding arrangements involving dozens of Japanese contractors stack the deck against public works projects going to anyone else.

Ministries often have overlapping jurisdictions, and crisis situations can require coordinated efforts to find a resolution. One example is the spread of the O-157 *E. coli* bacillus in the summer and early fall of 1996. Schools in Osaka and Iwate prefectures experienced large numbers of food poisoning cases ultimately linked to salads served in school lunches. The Ministry of Health and Welfare, which oversees all health-related issues, took primary responsibility for tracing the source of the poisonings. The Ministry of Education, concerned that methods of delivery and preparation were related to the poisonings, began a review of the school lunch system and mass production methods in particular.

Among agencies in the Japanese government today are the Imperial Household Agency, with about 1,100 officials; the Defense Agency, with approximately 300,000 personnel; the Economic Planning Agency, about 500; the Science and Technology Agency, 2,100 personnel; and the Environmental Agency, with just under 1,000 officials. All of these agencies are under the Prime Minister's Office. The Imperial Household Agency is responsible for the affairs of the Emperor and his family. The Defense Agency dates from 1954 and is today responsible for Japan's Self Defense Forces. The director-general of the agency must be a civilian and is under the command of the prime minister. Both the Defense and Economic Planning agencies are cabinet-level agencies. The latter is responsible for developing economic strategies and keeping statistics tracking economic activities. Every year it prepares and publishes a *White Paper on the National Life.* The income doubling plan of the 1960s originated in this agency and was then approved by the cabinet. Working closely with this agency is a *shingikai* named the Economic Council. The Science and Technology Agency dates from 1956 and has cabinet-level status also. Among responsibilities are to implement and enforce laws regulating nuclear energy policy and to oversee the National Space Development Agency. Finally, the Environment Agency, a cabinet-level agency, enforces antipollution laws, establishes quality standards regarding the environment, and keeps statistics. Regarding the latter, for example, agency statistics show that in 1991 Japan accounted for 5 percent of carbon dioxide emissions globally, compared with 23.3 percent by the United States and 11.2 percent by the People's Republic of China (JISEA 1995, 96).

Often, agencies and ministries work together to resolve problems. For example, in the summer of 1996, the Japan Youth Federation, a right wing affiliate among those who sponsor the sound trucks in Tokyo that broadcast all manner of propaganda loudly, built a small, makeshift lighthouse on one of the **Senkaku Islands**, which lie about 400 kilometers southwest of Okinawa. These eight small islands are uninhabited but controversial due to their being contested by Japan and China. After a Chinese activist died (drowned) near the disputed lighthouse while protesting its construction, anti-Japanese protests began in Beijing and Hong Kong. Officials in the Foreign Ministry and in the Defense

Agency and Maritime Safety Agency met and decided not to recognize the lighthouse.

Commissions are also part of the executive branch of Japanese government. One commission of note, attached to the Prime Minister's Office, is the Fair Trade Commission (FTC), staffed by just under 500 officials. The primary responsibility of the commission is to enforce the antimonopoly law, or the Law Concerning the Prohibition of Private Monopoly and Preservation of Fair Trade. Enacted in 1947, this law is periodically in the news, as its interpretation and enforcement, or laxity of enforcement, are related to the whole area of Japanese domestic markets and fair trade practices, a subject covered in Chapter 7. Often, the Fair Trade Commission's interpretation of a particular business practice runs counter to interpretations in the Ministry of International Trade and Industry. Under the antimonopoly law, for example, entrepreneurs cannot engage in practices "contrary to the public interest." The FTC view is that the public interest is harmed "whenever free competition is substantially restrained in any market for any reason." MITI's view, however, is that the public interest must be determined "by a balancing of various interests within the economy" (Itasaka 1983, 66).

Administrative reform, in late 1996, was more than a political campaign issue in the House of Representatives election of October 20. A government advisory panel, considering proposals to amend Japan's public disclosure law, recommended that the names of senior administrators receiving public funds for entertainment expenses be disclosed. This recommendation came in response to numerous reports of high-ranking civil servants spending large sums or seeking reimbursement for nonexistent expenses. The recommendation called for officials above the rank of director to have their names disclosed when they claimed travel and entertainment expenses. Interestingly, the recommendations of the panel did not include any statement regarding its approval of a public's "right to know." Several civic groups were pushing for recognition of the right in the panel's report ("Senior Bureaucrats" 1996, 16–19).

Criticisms of bureaucratic behavior also go beyond reform proposals, such as amending disclosure requirements. The chief of the Biologics and Antibiotics Division of the Health and Welfare Ministry faced a criminal investigation in October 1996 by the Tokyo District Public Prosecutor's Office for his failure to warn medical institutions of the risks associated with using unheated blood products in the mid-1980s. The investigation focused on the official's responsibility in the deaths of two patients from AIDS, one in 1991 and one in 1995 ("Ex-Official Faces" 1996, 2–5). Earlier, in July, the director-general of the Banking Bureau, Nishimura Yoshimasu, retired after only two years in that position within the Finance Ministry. As reported in the *New York Times* (4 July, 1996, sec. D, p. 15), it was Nishimura who acknowledged that the Finance Ministry waited six weeks before telling American regulators about Daiwa Bank losing over $1 billion in unauthorized bond trading. Earlier in the year, Prime Minister Hashimoto was reported to be having difficulty finding someone to accept the post of finance minister. Outgoing minister, Takemura Masayoshi, refused reappointment amidst the scandal-shrouded atmosphere surrounding the ministry (WuDunn 1996, 2). In addition to the *jusen* bailout, the Ministry of Finance is blamed for massive mismanagement and failure to prevent the extraordinary recent rise in bad debts. The entrance gates to the ministry were bolted shut early in 1996, and from mid-January to mid-March there were often protestors outside the building. According to one account, a Japanese motorist deliberately crashed his car into a public building in January and upon getting out, looking confused, said to police: "I thought this was the Ministry of Finance" (Rafferty 1996, 31). Between February and June 1996, as reported in the *New York Times* (14 June, 1996, sec. D, p. 3), the three coalition parties debated the issue of removing bank regulation and inspection from Finance Ministry jurisdiction and announced in June that it planned to submit a reform bill to the Diet in the summer of 1997.

Calls for reform are also being heard at the grass roots level. On August 4, 1996, voters in the small city of Maki on the Sea of Japan voted in Japan's first local referendum. On the ballot was the question of whether or not residents would support construction of a nuclear power plant. The vote was not legally binding, but the vote against construction sent a powerful signal to Tokyo that its plans for the continued development of nuclear power generation are in trouble. It also drew attention to the gap between a traditionally administrative state and a rising political consciousness seeking to thwart the plans of state administrators. A month later, on Okinawa, a similar referendum vote not to accept Tokyo's acceptance of the new Japan–U.S. security treaty sent an even louder message from the grassroots that the traditional pattern of bureaucrats shaping policies that are never seriously modified in political debate, either in campaigns for the Diet or deliberations in the Diet, was headed for change.

The approximately 1.2 million officials who work in the national bureaucracy are placed according to the provisions of the 1947 National Civil Service Law and as administered by the National Personnel Authority. Three commissioners appointed by the cabinet and confirmed by both chambers of the Diet run the authority. The civil service is divided into different grades and services. Recruitment is by competitive examinations followed by oral interviews.

JAPANESE COURTS

The judicial branch of Japanese government consists of a Supreme Court, 8 high courts, and 50 district courts. In addition, there are 50 family courts and 452 summary courts. The Supreme Court was established by the 1947 Constitution. Other courts are established by statute. The high courts have 6 branches, and the district and family courts have 201 branches. The structure of the Supreme Court consists of a chief justice and 14 associates. They are appointed by the cabinet, although the chief justice is technically appointed by the Emperor after being designated by the cabinet. The Supreme Court, under Article 77 of the constitution, determines rules of procedure and administers all judicial affairs.

All Supreme Court judges are subject to confirming elections at the first national election for the House of Representatives following their initial appointment. After such an election, they stand again for confirmation by the voters in the first national House election after ten years' service on the bench. If a majority of voters vote against a judge continuing in service, the judge is dismissed. Lower court judges are also appointed by the cabinet but from a list prepared by the Supreme Court. Lower court judges hold ten-year terms and may be reappointed. The Japanese judicial system does not use juries. All cases that come before the Supreme Court are appeals.

Article 81 of the constitution specifically grants to the Supreme Court the power "to determine the constitutionality of any law, order, regulation or official act." That is, the Supreme Court has the power of judicial review. This was first exercised in the national police reserve case of 1952. The reserve was established in response to the beginning of the Korean War by command of Douglas MacArthur acting as Supreme Commander of the Allied Powers. This action was challenged by one of the leaders of the Japan Socialist Party who claimed that such a command was in violation of Article 9 of the constitution, which prohibits "land, sea, and air forces." The Supreme Court, however, upheld the creation of the reserve and the legal status of the 75,000 men recruited for it. The court avoided the direct question regarding the reserve as a "land force" by categorizing the new organization as an ally of domestic police in maintaining internal order. In the same year as the court decision, the reserve changed its name to National Safety Forces and, two years later, to the present Self Defense Forces under the Defense Agency. Opposition to the constitutionality of the Self Defense Forces by the Japan Socialist Party, later the Social Democratic Party of Japan, continued until 1994 when Prime Minister Murayama reversed the party's position to accord with the LDP's position and to help solidify the coalition government. Despite the Supreme Court having the power of judicial review, it has only invalidated Diet actions on a handful of occasions.

Two more recent high-profile cases, one in the Supreme Court and one in a Tokyo District Court, gained international attention. The Supreme Court decision involved the land dispute over base leases on Okinawa. Thirty-five landowners on Okinawa controlling over 35,000 square meters of land within the perimeters of 13 U.S. military facilities on Okinawa refused to sign leases. In addition, Governor Ota Masahide, siding with the protestors, refused to order their signatures. A high court in Fukuoka, Kyushu, earlier ordered Ota to sign but the decision was appealed. In August 1996, the Supreme Court, noting the exclusive jurisdiction of the national government in such matters, ruled that there were no violations of the constitution in the leases issue and ordered Ota and the landowners to sign. In the Tokyo District Court, in April 1996, Japan's "trial of the century" got underway. Asahara Shoko, leader of the cult *Aum Shinrikyo,* went on trial facing 17 felony charges related to the Tokyo subway sarin gas attack and an earlier incident in Matsumoto. On the day the trial began, according to the *New York Times* (24 April, 1996), 2,000 police were gathered in Hibiya Park in central Tokyo to control a crowd of spectators estimated at near 12,000. The courtroom held only 48 seats and they were assigned by lottery.

In early April 1997, the Supreme Court made a ruling regarding the relationship between religion and the Japanese state. For years, the prefectural government of Ehime, on Shikoku, made public offerings to Shinto shrines within the prefecture. This practice was not unlike the practice in Tokyo of giving similar public offerings, meaning taxpayer funds, to support the Yasukuni Shrine dedicated to the 2.6 million war dead in Japan. In 1982, a case was brought against this practice as a violation of Article 20 of the 1947 constitution which prohibits religious education or other religious activities on the part of the state. In the courts for many years, the Supreme Court finally ruled that such a practice does indeed violate the constitution and must not continue. Supporters of the decision hailed it as a decisive vote for the Peace Constitution in the fiftieth year of its existence. Critics noted that offerings had always been small and that they had always been accepted as within "cultural" exceptions to the separation of religion and the state in previous precedents ("Supreme Court Rules" 1997).

JAPANESE LOCAL GOVERNMENT: PREFECTURES, MUNICIPALITIES

In 1871, the national government of the early Meiji Period abolished the feudal domain system of the *daimyo* and established in its place a system of prefectural governments. The intent of the action was to centralize power in the new capital and to end the regional powers of the *daimyo*. Among other actions of the period was the abolition of domain armies and the end of hereditary claims by *daimyo* families. From the new law, prefectural governors would be appointed by the national government. This was all achieved in steps and culminated in the creation of the prefectures. By these actions, the 261 feudal domains of the Tokugawa era were transformed into over 300 prefectures. This number was reduced shortly after to 72 prefectures and eventually to the current 47. Okinawa became the forty-seventh prefecture when it was returned to Japanese sovereignty from United States occupation in 1972. The Taisho Period, famous for democratizing tendencies in general, was also a period during which stronger, more autonomous local governments were developed. In 1926, for example, building on momentum from the Taisho years, two major changes took effect. The provisions of the universal male suffrage legislation of 1925 were extended to include local elections as well; also, a number of restrictions on local prerogatives were lifted, allowing more flexibility to local officials. For example, the home minister was no longer in charge of appointing mayors; rather, mayors began to be selected by local assemblies. Three years later, in 1929, home ministers were no longer able to "item veto" prefectural budgets. Most of these gains were eroded during the war years with the increased power of the *Imperial Rule Assistance Association*. But the seeds of local autonomy had been planted, and when the occupation began its work of democratization after the war, its focus on developing strong grass-roots organizations and local governments had much already in place to work with.

Among the early actions of the occupation government was the abolition of the Home Ministry in December 1947. Early reorganization efforts targeted the police and education functions of local government for reform. The Police Law of 1947 established rural and municipal police forces under a National Public Safety Commission appointed by the prime minister with Diet consent. Commissions were also established at the prefectural and municipal levels. Schools were reorganized under elected boards in 1948. From 1947 through 1952, the period of the occupation, laws were passed on local autonomy, local finance, local elections, local public services, and local public enterprises. The intention of all of these laws was to give citizens more control of and access to government at the prefectural and municipal levels. Prefectural assemblies were given the veto override power and the power to approve more gubernatorial appointments.

The high point of the occupation efforts to give life to the constitutional requirement to strengthen the autonomy of local governments was the work of the Local Administration Investigation Committee established in late 1949. Under the leadership of Kambe Masao, a professor at Kyoto University and a former mayor of Kyoto, this committee continued the work of earlier studies, visited the United States to observe local governance there (three of the five commissioners going), and submitted a comprehensive report to the Diet and the cabinet in December 1950. This was an important document in that it painstakingly outlined the necessary steps to make autonomous local government in Japan, at both the prefectural and municipal levels, a reality. The commission called for the clear definition of the functions of each of the three levels of government, the municipal, the prefectural, and the national. It also emphasized the importance of municipal governments and stressed that any functions of government that could efficiently be handled at the municipal level should be carried out there. It also called for appropriate financing of each level independent of the other two. According to one study, the Kambe report represented "the flowering of the last rose in the Indian summer of local autonomy reform" (Steiner 1973, 56).

Due to resistance within the traditional, national bureaucracy, many of the reforms were not fully implemented or failed to work as intended. Soon after the occupation, the traditionalists moved to recentralize as much administration as they could. Despite opposition from the Socialists, labor unions, scholars, and media critics, the Police Law in 1954 and Board of Education Law of 1956 replaced occupation programs with centralized administrative boards to oversee police and school issues. Most controversial in these changes was the return of curriculum and textbook decisions to the Ministry of Education, a controversy that in many respects continues to the present. The new education law had the effect of diluting the influence of the leftist Japan Teachers Union. Other legislation of the 1950s facilitated the amalgamation of cities, towns, and villages in the name of administrative efficiency. In 1953, there were 9,582 towns and villages. By 1956, there were 3,975. In 1989, the number was down to 2,590.

The desire of some in the national ministries, agencies, and bureaus to divide Japan into broad administrative regions to replace the prefectures has been successfully resisted over the years by strong prefectural interests. During the 1960s and 1970s, the centralizing tendency continued, however. A major element in this tendency was the expansion of public corporations controlled by the national government. Examples of these corporations are the Japan Highway Public Corporation and the Housing and Urban Development Corporation, both of which come under the jurisdiction of the Ministry of Construction. The Construction Ministry has five bureaus all of which actively develop land use and building plans, especially in urban and coastal areas. The activities of the ministry and the public corporations leave little for local governments to plan in areas such as housing, transportation, and general land use. Much of local government work in these areas has become work directed from Tokyo. The Japan Highway Public Corporation, for example, plans, builds, maintains, and supervises the major toll roads in Japan. Today this means over 3,000 miles of expressways and hundreds of miles more of general roads. The Metropolitan Expressway Public Corporation serves the same function in the Tokyo Metropolitan area.

The Housing and Urban Development Corporation dates from 1981 but absorbed two earlier corporations dating from 1955 and 1973. This corporation was among five targeted for abolition in the year 1999 by a special LDP task force on administrative reform in its report of March 27, 1997. Submitted directly to Prime Minister Hashimoto, the report represents a concrete proposal for trimming the national bureaucracy in the interest of administrative reform. Two items reported in the *Japan Times Online* (27 March, 1997), however, point to "floating" aspects in the report. First, the announcement was made just five days prior to the scheduled rise in the consumption tax from 3 to 5 percent, a circumstance suggesting an attempt by the LDP leadership to "deflect public criticism that the government is trying to tax its way out of national deficit"; and second, the possibility was strong that a new government corporation would be established as well—one to manage the reforms ("Bold Streamlining Plan Penned" 1997). The Housing and Urban Development Corporation builds housing complexes and develops surrounding areas. Public works projects, in fiscal year 1994, represented 15.3 percent of total general account outlays of the national government. Only social welfare, interest on the debt, and total grants to local governments represented larger national expenditures. The public works figure for 1994 was up 29.6 percent from the previous year, reflecting the largest percentage increase in any area in the national government's outlays. This increase illustrates the tendency in recent years for the government to increase public works spending during times of economic slowdown. Such spending also heightens concerns, especially among foreign contractors, over the *dango* system of bidding on such projects.

Today, prefectural government structures and operations are the subject of the broad provisions of Chapter 8 in the constitution on local self-government. Today, also, many are calling for the strengthening of local governments, especially given the problems both in *Nagatacho* and in *Kasumigaseki*. Decentralization is the spirit of the times in all advanced democratic states. For the Japanese, according to Margaret McKean, local politics is traditionally "of greater concern than national politics" (1981, 11). Each of the 47 prefectures is classified by legislation as one of four types. *To* refers only to Tokyo; *do* refers only to Hokkaido; *fu* refers to Osaka and Kyoto prefectures; and *ken* refers to the remaining 43. In addition to the prefectures, there are also over 3,000 cities, towns, and villages, all classified as municipalities. There are no unincorporated areas in Japan. Table 3–4 lists the largest cities in Japan today. Whereas approximately 1.2 million officials work in the national government, over 3.2 million local government officials staff prefectural and municipal offices (JISEA 1995, 94). Unlike the parliamentary system in the national government, prefectural governments are "presidential." That is, chief executives, governors, are elected independently of the prefectural assemblies. The same is true of municipal governments, where mayors serve as chief executives. On the municipal level, there are variations on a national norm. Tokyo combines the prefectural and municipal governments. Also, within large cities such as Tokyo there are wards designated as "cities" given substantial powers. In terms of size, prefectures tend on average to be smaller than the American states and do not, of course, have "reserved powers" in a federal union. Japanese government is unitary. The largest prefecture is Hokkaido and the smallest is Tottori, in western Honshu. Local revenues come mostly from the national government with only about one-third or less coming from local taxes. The Ministry of Home Affairs must approve any borrowing by local governments. National legislation that affects local government

TABLE 3–4
Japanese Cities with 1 Million or More Population

City	Population
Tokyo	7.87 million
Yokohama	3.27 million
Osaka	2.5 million
Nagoya	2.1 million
Sapporo	1.7 million
Kobe	1.5 million
Kyoto	1.4 million
Fukuoka	1.2 million
Kawasaki	1.2 million
Hiroshima	1.1 million
Kitakyushu	1.0 million

SOURCE: Brian Hunter, ed., "Japan," in *The Statesman's Yearbook, 1996–1997* (New York: St. Martin's Press, 1996), pp. 759–760.

generates organized interest, for or against, by local governments, but in acting as interest groups they are "not particularly influential." There are six organized bodies of local officials who lobby the national government. The National Governors' Conference and the National Conference of City Mayors are more effective, generally, than similar organizations for prefectural assembly chairs, city assembly chairs, town and village mayors, and town and village assembly chairs. If compared to other unitary states, according to Steven Reed, "Japanese local governments have a somewhat larger grant of authority than is the norm." They also tend to have a "stronger financial base" (1986, 22–43).

Sometimes local governments use their grants of authority to do creative things at the grass roots that send a signal to higher levels. Among the larger issues in Japan in recent years is the place of foreign workers and students in Japanese society. They must carry registration cards and be fingerprinted, and they have very little voice in shaping policies either in private or public forums. In Kawasaki, in the spring of 1996, the Personnel Commission for the city, which administers civil service examinations for municipal job applicants, scrapped the requirement that only Japanese nationals may sit for the exams. The new rule covers applicants beginning with jobs for fiscal year 1997 and is

TABLE 3–5
Regions and Prefectures in Japan

Region	Prefecture	Region	Prefecture
Hokkaido	Hokkaido		Yamanashi
	Aomori	Chubu	Gifu
	Akita		Aichi
Tohoku	Iwate		Shizuoka
	Yamagata		Tochigi
	Miyagi		Ibaraki
	Fukushima		Gunma
	Niigata	Kanto	Saitama
	Toyama		Tokyo
Chubu	Ishikawa		Chiba
	Nagano		Kanagawa
	Fukui		
	Kyoto		Fukuoka
	Shiga		Oita
	Hyogo		Kumamoto
Kinki	Osaka	Kyushu	Saga
	Mie		Nagasaki
	Nara		Miyazaki
	Wakayama		Kagoshima
	Tottori		Ehime
	Shimane	Shikoku	Kagawa
Chugoku	Okayama		Tokushima
	Hiroshima		Kochi
	Yamaguchi	Okinawa	Okinawa

limited to applicants for positions below the level of department chief. Still, it represents a breakthrough at the municipal level that could have implications at the national level in time. The Ministry of Home Affairs, the national agency that oversees local governments, opposed the change in Kawasaki. Twelve other cities were planning similarly to open civil service exams to non-Japanese in 1996. Kawasaki's actions remain in dispute, however, as in May 1996, a Tokyo District Court ruled that non-Japanese citizens have no constitutional right to hold jobs in the public sector (Ebitsubo and Nakamura 1996, 114).

Summary

Japanese government is unitary with the central government in Tokyo. It is also parliamentary. The representative assembly, or Diet, consists of a House of Representatives, with 500 members, and a House of Councillors, with 252 members. Elections for the House are normally held every four years. A no-confidence vote or dissolution of the House by the prime minister results in an earlier election. The last election of the House of Representatives was held in October 1996, the first under a new election system. Members are elected from single-member districts (300) and multimember, regional districts (200 representatives from 11 regions). Elections for the House of Councillors are held every three years, with half the membership standing for election. Primary power in the Diet rests with the House of Representatives. Most legislation, however, is initially prepared within the various administrative agencies. In 1997, the LDP held the most seats in both chambers, but short of a majority. The prime minister is the head of the cabinet and chooses cabinet ministers. Prime Minister Hashimoto's second cabinet, in 1997, consisted of all LDP members. Japan has had five prime ministers between 1993 and 1997.

Under the 1947 Constitution, the Emperor is a symbol of the Japanese state and holds no real power. The present Emperor, Akihito, is the 125th Emperor and the first to visit China. The present era is called Heisei and dates from 1989. Crown Prince Naruhito married Owada Masako in June 1993. Administrative agencies in Japanese government today are classified as ministries, agencies, and commissions. There is also the Office of the Prime Minister. Ministries include Finance; MITI; Agriculture, Forestry, and Fisheries; Foreign Affairs; Health and Welfare; Construction; Home Affairs; Transportation; Education; Ports and Telecommunications; Justice; and Labor. Among agencies are the Imperial Household Agency, the Defense Agency, and the Economic Planning Agency. A key commission is the Fair Trade Commission, which enforces Japan's antimonopoly law. Administrative reform refers to efforts to reconsider and revise the entire administrative structure of the Japanese state. Principal courts in Japan are the Supreme Court, 8 high courts, and 50 district courts. Judges are appointed by the cabinet with Supreme Court judges standing for periodic confirming elections. The judicial system in Japan does not use the jury system. The Supreme Court has the power of judicial review, though it is rarely exercised. Japan is divided into 47 prefectures each classified as either *to, do, fu,* or *ken*. Prefectural governors are elected independent of prefectural assemblies. There are over 3,000 municipalities in Japan, with 11 having populations over 1 million. There are no unincorporated areas in Japan. Public corporations, such as the Housing and Urban Development Corporation, are controlled by the national government and are among the major targets today of reform advocates.

Suggested Readings

Calder, Kent E. 1993. *Strategic Capitalism: Private Business and Public Purpose in Japanese Industrial Finance.* Princeton, NJ: Princeton University Press.

Fraser, Andrew, R. H. P. Mason, and Philip Mitchell. 1995. *Japan's Early Parliaments, 1890–1905: Structure, Issues and Trends.* London: Routledge/Nissan Institute.

Hayao Kenji. 1993. *The Japanese Prime Minister and Public Policy.* Pittsburgh: University of Pittsburgh Press.

Johnson, Chalmers. 1995. *Japan: Who Governs?* New York: Norton.

———. 1982. *MITI and the Japanese Miracle.* Stanford, CA: Stanford University Press.

Kato Junko. 1994. *The Problem of Bureaucratic Rationality: Tax Politics in Japan.* Princeton, NJ: Princeton University Press.

Kim, Hyung-ki, Michio Muramatsu, T. J. Pempel, and Kozo Yamamura, eds. 1995. *The Japanese Civil Service and Economic Development—Catalysts of Change.* Oxford: Clarendon Press.

Large, Stephen S. 1992. *Emperor Hirohito and Showa Japan: A Political Biography.* London: Routledge.

Okimoto, Daniel I. 1989. *Between MITI and the Market: Japanese Industrial Policy for High Technology.* Stanford, CA: Stanford University Press.

Ramsdell, Daniel B. 1992. *The Japanese Diet: Stability and Change in the Japanese House of Representatives, 1890–1990.* Lanham, MD: University Press of America.

Reed, Steven R. 1986. *Japanese Prefectures and Policymaking.* Pittsburgh: University of Pittsburgh Press.

van Wolferen, Karel. 1989. *The Enigma of Japanese Power.* New York: Knopf.

Webb, Herschel. 1968. *The Japanese Imperial Institution in the Tokugawa Period.* New York: Columbia University Press.

Woodall, Brian. 1996. *Japan Under Construction: Corruption, Politics, and Public Works.* Berkeley: University of California Press.

Works Cited

Bold Streamlining Plan Penned for Public Entities. 1997. *Japan Times Online,* 27 March.

Calder, Kent. 1993. *Strategic Capitalism: Private Business and Public Purpose in Japanese Industrial Finance.* Princeton, NJ: Princeton University Press.

A Costly Battle Against Recession. 1996. *Economist,* 8 June, 40, 41.

Curtis, Gerald L. 1988. *The Japanese Way of Politics.* New York: Columbia University Press.

Ebitsubo Isamu, and Nakamura Tokuji. 1996. Chronology. *Japan Quarterly* 43 (July): 106–117.

Ex-Official Faces HIV Investigation. 1996. *Asahi e News,* 4 October, 2–5.

Haley, John O. 1991. *Authority Without Power: Law and the Japanese Paradox.* Oxford: Oxford University Press.

Hashimoto Ryutaro. 1996. Prime Minister's Policy Speech. *Japan Echo,* 23 (Spring): 62–65.

Hayao Kenji. 1993. *The Japanese Prime Minister and Public Policy.* Pittsburgh: University of Pittsburgh Press.

Itasaka Gen, ed. in chief. 1983. *Kodansha Encyclopedia.* Tokyo: Kodansha. S. v. Antimonopoly Law, by Matsushita Mitsuo.

Japan Institute for Social and Economic Affairs (JISEA). 1995. *Japan, 1995: An International Comparison.* Tokyo.

Japan's Opposition Blunders. 1996. *Economist.* 15 June, 35, 36.

Johnson, Chalmers. 1995. *Japan: Who Governs?* New York: Norton.

Masamura Kimihiro. 1996. A Caretaker Administration. *Japan Echo,* 23 (Spring): 61.

McKean, Margaret A. 1981. *Environmental Protest and Citizen Politics in Japan.* Berkeley: University of California Press.

———. 1993. State Strength and the Public Interest. In *Political Dynamics in Contemporary Japan,* ed. Gary D. Allinson and Yasunori Sone, 72–104. Ithaca, NY: Cornell University Press.

McLaren, Walter Wallace. 1965. *A Political History of Japan During the Meiji Era, 1867–1912.* New York: Russell and Russell.

Ozawa Ichiro. 1996. A Policy Manifesto. *Japan Echo,* 23 (Spring): 66, 67.

Rafferty, Kevin. 1996. Laughing a Siege to Scorn. *Look Japan,* 42 (September): 31.

Ramsdell, Daniel B. 1992. *The Japanese Diet: Stability and Change in the Japanese House of Representatives, 1890–1990.* Lanham, MD: University Press of America.

Reed, Steven R. 1986. *Japanese Prefectures and Policymaking.* Pittsburgh: University of Pittsburgh Press.

Senior Bureaucrats to Face the Wrath of Disclosure Law. 1996. *Asahi e News,* 4 October, 16–19.

Steiner, Kurt. 1973. Occupation Reforms in Local Government. In *Postwar Japan: 1945 to the Present,* ed. Jon Livingston, Joe Moore, and Felicia Oldfather, 42–56. New York: Pantheon.

Sterngold, James. 1993. Who Really Runs Japan? Stay Tuned. *New York Times,* 24 December, 3 (A).

Supreme Court Rules Ehime's Shrine Offerings Unconstitutional. 1997. *Japan Times Online,* 2 April.

Woodall, Brian. 1996. *Japan Under Construction: Corruption, Politics, and Public Works.* Berkeley: University of California Press.

WuDunn, Sheryl. 1996. Few Takers for Japanese Finance Post. *New York Times,* 10 January, 2 (D).

4

Floating Structures: Parties, Mass Media, Citizen Groups

Structures of authority in Japanese politics are both fixed and floating. Among the latter are the political parties, the myriad interest groups and *koenkai,* citizen groups, and the various mass media. These institutions are more floating in that they respond more quickly to surface changes in Japanese society. Political parties in Japan have their origin in the early days of the **Meiji Restoration** and, specifically, in debates over the nature and timing of a constitution for the new Japanese state. The *Jiyuto,* or Liberal Party, is considered the first political party in Japan. It was formed out of a coalition of ex-*samurai,* small landowners, peasants, and some large merchants in 1881. From the short-lived Liberal Party evolved the *Seiyukai* in 1900 to which the Liberal Democratic Party traces its origins. Today, Japanese political parties are at the center of dramatic changes in Japanese society and culture, both as products and producers of those changes.

PARTY POLITICS IN JAPAN: OLD AND NEW FRONTIERS

Early in December 1994, in Yokohama, one of Japan's largest "new parties" announced its entry onto the stage of Japanese politics. Presenting itself as the leader of modern Japan's third great opening to the world, the New Frontier Party identified itself with the grandest possible historical significance. The first opening was that brought by Commodore **Matthew C. Perry** in 1853, an event that signaled an end to Japan's isolation under the **Tokugawa** Shogunate and the beginning of Japan's participation in global, balance of power politics. The second opening was that imposed by the U.S. occupation following World War II. Both of these events were led by Western outsiders. The third great opening, the New Frontier Party, represents the first led by the Japanese themselves. An examination of the party's Japanese name, however, suggests a less grand challenge to the existing Japanese political status quo. A literal translation of *Shinshinto* is "new, new party," a circumstance that has led the English journal

THE "VERY NEW" PARTY

On December 10, 1994, the New Frontier Party of Ozawa Ichiro was launched as the newest of Japan's recent wave of new parties. Within a very brief period in the early 1990s, Japan became home to the creation of the Japan Renewal Party (*Shinseito*), the Japan New Party (*Nihon Shinto*), and the New Party Harbinger (*Sakigake*), all claiming the reform label and calling for a new, more open, more democratic Japan. Intended as a conservative alternative to the Liberal Democratic Party, the New Frontier Party has gotten off to a slow start in election results. The Japanese name for the party is *Shinshinto*, which literally means "new, new party." There was some debate on what the English designation of the party should be before New Frontier Party was chosen. This prompted the *Economist*, in its December 17, 1994 issue, to call the party the "very new party" (38).

Economist to call the new party the "very new party" ("The Very New Party" 1994). The satirical reference is to the fact that the New Frontier Party was the fourth major new party in Japan since **Hosokawa Morihiro** formed the Japan New Party (*Nihon Shinto*) in 1992 (see accompanying box).

In addition to Hosokawa's party and the New Frontier Party, the Japan Renewal Party (*Shinseito*) and the New Party Harbinger (*Sakigake*) were breakaway parties from the once dominant Liberal Democratic Party (*Jiminto*). The latter, after a series of scandals, lost its control of the Diet after 38 years in the national election of July 1993. Following the October 1996 House election, however, the Liberal Democratic Party appeared to be reestablishing itself. After working in a coalition government with the Social Democratic Party of Japan and the New Party Harbinger (*Sakigake*) for two years, the LDP presented itself in the 1996 election as the "new" LDP under **Hashimoto Ryutaro**'s leadership. And even though it would need to continue to work within a coalition, the LDP had regained its role as the leading party in the Diet with 239 seats. Following the same election, on the other hand, the New Frontier Party, led by *Ozawa Ichiro*, found itself on the verge of early extinction. Even though it managed to win 156 seats in the 1996 election, the total represented an overall loss of 4 seats. In the aftermath of the election, other leaders in the New Frontier Party, such as former Prime Ministers Hosokawa Morihiro and Hata Tsutomu, were threatening to bolt the party unless Ozawa resigned as president. In late December, Hata did leave, bringing 12 colleagues with him to form the *Taiyo* Party. A major element in the composition of the New Frontier Party's support is the 12 million strong membership of the Buddhist organization **Soka Gakkai**. Among the New Frontier candidates running in the proportional balloting in the July 1995 election, 7 of the top 15 listed candidates had connections with the *Soka Gakkai* (Blaker 1996).

As discussed in Chapter 2, the Liberal Democratic Party represents a fusion of the old Liberal and Democratic parties in 1955. The predominance of the resulting LDP has been such that most studies of postwar Japanese politics refer to the *55 system*. In a 1989 study comparing 25 "liberal democracies," Japan is not included. Instead, Japan is grouped among six "nominal" liberal democracies. According to Alan Ware, referring to Japan: "The dominance of one party in the system is so institutionalized that it is arguable that voters there are unable to exercise an effective choice" (1989, 14, 15). Other scholars are less critical. Writing at the same time, Gerald Curtis described a "transformation" of the party system in Japan from 1955 through the late 1980s. Curtis describes a system of "striking contrasts," one of which is that between "one-party dominance and intense interparty competition" (1988, 4). Curtis identifies "three phases" of LDP rule: one from 1955 to the mid-1960s, which was characterized by ideological battles; a second phase to the mid 1970s marked by a decline in polarized politics between parties and the rise of the *Komeito* as an entirely new and different party; and, finally, the period from the mid-1970s to the late 1980s where old levels of support return but in an environment free of ideological extremes. Among reasons for LDP success, Curtis cites the inflexibility of the opposition, continuing support from rural voters, and the party's ability to track change and respond.

Another reason for LDP success is what Kent Calder calls "compensation." This is, perhaps, a new conceptualization of an old practice, one that Muramatsu Michio calls the "politics of reciprocity" and others call "patron-client" relations. Calder defines compensation as "material benefits, usually distributive in character, extended to support groups exerting strategic political effects on behalf of the grantor" (Calder 1988, 159, n. 4, 5). Examples are public works projects, small business loans, and agricultural price supports. This politics of compensation reinforces the "personalistic dimensions" of Japanese politics as well. The ability to translate political support from support groups (*koenkai*) into government services in the district is essential to any Diet candidate. Failure to deliver through the "pipe" can end a Diet career quickly. Curtis downplays this process as an explanation for LDP success, suggesting that the LDP's popularity "has risen along with heightened public interest in issues that transcend parochial constituency concerns" (Curtis 1988, 223). A study by Bradley Richardson on "Constituency versus Parties In Japanese Voting Behavior" reinforces this view (1988).

From the late 1980s, however, LDP popularity began to decline rapidly in the wake of public criticism over LDP issue positions and, more seriously, from scandals. Among the issues were agricultural policies that put foreign demands over domestic farmers and a 3 percent *consumption tax*. With respect to the first, the Japanese government was under increasing pressure to open its markets to selected products, such as beef, oranges, and rice. With respect to the consumption, or sales, tax, the LDP was seeking additional sources of revenue for services such as health care for a rapidly aging population. During the 1986 national elections, the LDP had promised not to support such a tax. Most serious among the scandals were the Recruit Cosmos scandal, which brought down Prime Minister *Takeshita Noboru* in 1989, and bribery charges against former LDP "kingmaker" *Kanemaru Shin*.

KANEMARU SHIN (1914–1996)

Perhaps no public figure in Japan better symbolizes what is wrong with Japanese politics today than Kanemaru Shin. His highest political positions were as vice president of the Liberal Democratic Party and as deputy prime minister. But he epitomized for many the back room kingmaker and wheeler dealer who made and unmade prime ministers and other government leaders. Following his resignation from the Diet as an LDP member of the House and during investigations into his possibly illegal activities, investigators found hundreds of pounds of gold, cash, and securities valued in the tens of millions of dollars in his home and office. In his resignation from the Diet, he admitted taking bribes from a trucking company, actions for which he was indicted in 1993. His trial was still in progress when he died in March 1996, at 81. Kanemaru was born in a village northwest of Tokyo, and his father was a *sake* brewer. He served in Manchuria during World War II and entered the Diet in 1958. He rose quickly as a close associate of Tanaka Kakuei.

Following a series of very high profile investigations and court cases, voices of reform from both within and outside the LDP began to challenge politics as usual in Japan. With the creation of Hosokawa's party and the splitting off from the LDP of Ozawa's group (the Japan Renewal Party, *Shinseito*) and the New Party Harbinger (*Sakigake*), the LDP faced its biggest test since 1955 in the national election of July 1993. For the first time, the LDP lost its majority in the lower house of the Diet. Following two very fragile coalition governments under Hosokawa and **Hata Tsutomu**, the LDP reemerged in the summer of 1994 as the largest partner in a coalition that included the Social Democratic Party of Japan and the New Party Harbinger. This extraordinary grouping led one commentator to wonder "whether any political bed in any country has ever accommodated stranger bedfellows" (Blaker 1995, 2). **Murayama Tomiichi**, chair of the SDPJ, became prime minister. It was only the second time in postwar Japan's history that a Socialist assumed the office of prime minister. The first time was immediately after the war. Early in 1996, Hashimoto Ryutaro became prime minister, thus returning the LDP to its traditional postwar role of shaping the government.

The Social Democratic Party of Japan was formerly called the Japan Socialist Party (JSP). In 1991, responding to the worldwide decline of Marxist parties, the JSP changed its English name to Social Democratic Party of Japan, though it retained its Japanese name of *Nippon Shakaito*. In the beginning, this did not affect the party's positions on issues. Traditionally, for example, the JSP defined its positions on crucial issues according to a strict application of Marxist-Leninist ideology. Among important issues, the JSP called for an "unarmed neutrality" in foreign policy, opposition to the **Mutual Security Treaty** with the United States, and opposition to the official recognition of South Korea. The party also refused to acknowledge the legitimacy of the **Self Defense Forces** under **Article 9** of the constitution. Largely because of these positions, regarded by many as rigid and unrealistic, the JSP played the role in postwar

Japanese politics of what Gerald Curtis calls "perpetual opposition." Following the 1993 election and the subsequent formation of a coalition with the LDP, the newly named SDPJ began also to revise its position on numerous issues. For example, Prime Minister Murayama, shortly after the election, announced that he now supported the SDF, the national flag, the national anthem, and the security treaty with the United States. This turnabout caused a split within the SDPJ and helped set the stage for the formation of the New Frontier Party in December 1994. It also contributed to the growing cynicism of Japanese voters whose turnout in the House of Councillors election of July 1995 was a postwar low.

The alliance of the LDP and SDPJ, however fragile, is a dramatic illustration of the changing dynamics in current Japanese politics. Throughout the early years of the 55 system, the center of gravity in Japanese politics was the ideological division between a largely conservative LDP, with roots in prewar Japanese politics, and a largely radical JSP, with roots in the Marxist tradition. Today, the socialist tradition seems to have little future in Japan, and the LDP competes with the New Frontier Party for the attention of the more conservative Japanese voter. Attempting to define alternatives on the left are the remnants of the old JSP and the New Party Harbinger (*Sakigake*). In September 1996, after much discussion and planning, various members of the ruling coalition's Social Democratic Party and New Party Harbinger, along with others from various affiliations, announced the formation of yet another "new" party. Led by Hatoyama Yukio, formerly secretary-general of the New Party Harbinger, Kan Naoto, Health and Welfare Minister in the Hashimoto cabinet and a leader in the New Party Harbinger Party, and Hatoyama Kunio, brother of Yukio and a former member of the New Frontier Party, the new party adopted the name of *Minshuto*, or Democratic Party.

The name is reminiscent of a pre–55 system party founded in 1954 in which the Hatoyama brothers' grandfather, Ichiro, was a member and leader. Hatoyama Ichiro, in fact, was prime minister from December 1954 to December 1956. His party, the *Nihon Minshuto*, merged in 1955 with the *Jiyuto* to form the LDP and launch the 55 system. Just as the earlier *Minshuto* was formed in opposition to Prime Minister Yoshida Shigeru (see accompanying box) and all that Yoshida represented, so also the new *Minshuto* aims at basic reforms, especially of the Japanese bureaucracy. Among platform pledges of the new party were to build greater trust between Japan and neighboring Asian countries, especially with respect to war issues such as the "comfort women" issue, and to reform the administrative structures of Japanese government. Campaign ads for the October 1996 national election dramatized the theme that "citizens" are the protagonists in Japan today. Another theme of particular interest is that of a *Heisei* "Restoration." Playing on the powerful symbolism of the Meiji Restoration, this theme of *Minshuto* suggests a moving forward toward more "democratization" as a concurrent restoration of unfulfilled aspirations.

On the eve of the October election in 1996, the *Minshuto* was already showing strong support in public opinion polls. In an *Asahi Shimbun* poll taken in late September, less than a month prior to the election and within a week of

YOSHIDA SHIGERU (1878–1967)

"One Man" Yoshida was prime minister from May 1946 to May 1947 and again from October 1948 to December 1954. As the best known postwar public figure in Japan, Yoshida had a long career in the Japanese bureaucracy before his emergence as a party politician and party leader after the war. Married to Okubo Toshimichi's granddaughter in 1909, and a graduate of Tokyo University's Law Faculty, Yoshida embarked on a career in government service and served in overseas assignments in Mukden, London, and Rome, among other places. He became the ambassador to Italy in 1931, serving less than two years, and later ambassador to Great Britain. An opponent of the Tojo government and a critic of the war, Yoshida was placed under arrest and held by military police for two months toward the end of the war. He served as foreign minister after the war and then prime minister. He published a four-volume set of his memoirs in the late 1950s. Due to his strong presence, and numerous contributions in the difficult years of postwar occupation and the return of sovereignty in 1952, the postwar years in Japanese politics are often referred to as the Yoshida Era.

the official formation of the party, the *Minshuto* was the second choice of those polled. As reported by the *Asahi e News* (1 October 1996), of the people who were asked which party was their "favorite," 9 percent chose the new *Minshuto*. The LDP was the preferred party of 28 percent. The New Frontier Party showed only a 7 percent support. Of the remaining parties, 5 percent named the Social Democrats, 3 percent the Japan Communist Party, and 1 percent the fading coalition partner New Party Harbinger. In the same poll, 40 percent of respondents said they were "undecided" as to which party they would support in the upcoming election, though fully 64 percent said they would "definitely vote." Surprisingly, the *Minshuto* showed 18 percent of those responding within Tokyo. This compared to only 8 percent for the New Frontier Party, which came in second. The new party, as other new parties, is making its appeal mostly to urban voters who continue to be interested in political reform, especially and increasingly administrative reform.

In the October campaign, the LDP ran ads showing *kendo* scenes, the traditional martial art in which Hashimoto Ryutaro is expert. The thrust of the ads is to focus on idealism, "Japan Dream," and the importance of effort. The finale of the *kendo* scenes shows Hashimoto removing his "mask" so that all can see that he is the featured performer in the scenes. Ozawa's New Frontier Party ads in the October election focused on two issues: the scheduled increase in the consumption tax in April 1997 to 5 percent, and the bailout of the *jusen* mortgage lending companies. Regarding the first, ads showing a women's volleyball team defending against a ball marked 5 percent were run with the defending woman's team wearing red and white uniforms, the colors in the Japanese flag. In other words, to defend against the increases is to defend Japan. On the failed *jusens*, the ads show orange juice being squeezed from oranges by machine, suggesting a bureaucratic machine squeezing Japanese citizens through the public funding of the *jusen* rescue.

It was Ozawa's New Frontier Party that blockaded sessions on the issue in the spring to draw attention to the matter. Going into the election, the Social Democratic Party was on the verge of extinction. In an attempt to solidify what base it still held, the party named Doi Takako its head again shortly before the election. As speaker of the House of Representatives, she was nonaligned according to party. But with the dissolution of the House in late September and the announcement of the election for October, she was persuaded to take again the top position in the Social Democratic Party of Japan. She spearheaded the national campaign of the party in the October election. Results of that election, however, proved disappointing for the Social Democrats and also for Ozawa and the New Frontier Party. For the *Sakigake* Party, they were catastrophic. The LDP, on the other hand, was a big winner, increasing its position in the House from 211 to 239 seats. The Japan Communist Party also showed surprising gains, almost doubling its representation in the House from 15 to 26 seats. The Social Democrats dropped to a meager 15 seats in the House, and the *Sakigake* held onto only to 2 seats. Among the bigger stories coming out of the election was the relatively disappointing showing of the New Frontier Party. Not only did they lose four seats in the election, but there was already serious talk of the party dissolving over internal disputes.

THE MARXIST TRADITION AND PARTY STRUCTURES

In September 1996, just a month before the national election, Doi's Social Democratic Party of Japan issued its first official history. The volume is over 1,200 pages and begins coverage from 1945. There is some irony in the timing of the book in that although the Social Democrats represented the second largest party within the governing coalition at the time of publication, most scholarly and media accounts were writing the obituary of the party. Heavy losses in 1993 in lower house elections and again in the upper house elections of 1995; ideological switches on basic issues like the legal status of the Self Defense Forces and the United States–Japan Security Treaty, changes brought on by the end of the Cold War and shifting global dynamics; and the expected realignments caused by electoral reform legislation all signaled the doom of the Social Democrats, even as they chronicled their achievements.

The Social Democratic Party of Japan is the successor to the Japan Socialist Party (JSP), founded in 1906, though the early party was forced to break up by government order within a year of its formation. Over the next several years, various factions organized and dissolved under various names sharing, however, something of a common Marxist vision. The modern, postwar party was founded in November 1945, and, after winning over 30 percent of lower house seats in the 1947 election, shared the power of a coalition government for

15 months during 1947–1948. **Katayama Tetsu** (1887–1978) served as prime minister for eight months during that period, one of only two Socialist prime ministers in Japanese political history. Like many of the earlier Socialists, Katayama was a Christian. He was active in Socialist causes prior to World War II and was among the founders of the postwar party. He was instrumental in the revision of the criminal code after the war, in creating the Ministry of Labor, in the passage of the Labor Standards and Antimonopoly laws, and in ensuring the breakup of the *Zaibatsu*. Later he helped create the **Democratic Socialist Party** in 1960.

In the 1949 election to the lower house, largely due to internal disputes that divided the party along more conservative and more radical lines, the Japan Socialist Party lost almost 100 seats. The divisions within the party became ever more acute in subsequent years, leading eventually to two contending groups each claiming the name of Japan Socialist Party. The biggest element in the dispute was disagreement over two sensitive policy issues: the peace treaty and the security treaty with the United States. More radical Socialists opposed both treaties and supported a strict interpretation of Article 9 of the 1947 Constitution which "renounces" war and prohibits "land, sea, and air forces" and other "war potential." The more conservative group supported the peace treaty and remained flexible on other issues. It was not until 1955 that the two groups reunited, an event with three particularly important consequences: First, the party was able to gain a third of the seats in the House of Representatives in the 1955 election, thus establishing itself as a legitimate contender for control of the postoccupation government; second, electoral success allowed the party to frustrate widespread desires among other Diet members to revise the constitution; and third, the reunited party forced non-Marxist parties to work toward their own unification. This second influence led to the merger of the Liberal and Democratic parties and the creation of the Liberal Democratic Party (LDP) and the 55 system that governed Japan from 1955 to 1993. The role of the Japan Socialist Party during this period became that of "perpetual opposition" (Curtis 1988, 117–156). Reacting to what they believed were increasingly radical tendencies within the party, a group within the JSP broke away in 1960 to form the Democratic Socialist Party.

With other Marxist groups, the Japan Socialist Party was very active in the battle over renewal of the United States–Japan Security Treaty in 1960. The confrontation over that renewal is often referred to as the biggest political issue, sometimes "crisis," in postwar Japanese political development. There were many dimensions to the crisis, but at the center of concern by opponents was fear that Japan would become a large Pacific military base for the United States and that a large U.S. military presence in Japan would provoke communist regimes in the region and involve Japan in a third world war and nuclear devastation. Japan, in 1960, was once again an independent nation-state with sovereignty and was responsible for its own decisions. Japan would be held responsible for the nature of the alliances that it chose to create. Related concerns focused on problems arising from the concentration of foreign troops on

Japanese territory and criminal activities involving those troops, concerns that have resurfaced recently, as discussed in Chapter 7. The Japan Socialist Party, along with dozens of other groups, staged demonstrations opposing the treaty revision. In May 1960, the JSP boycotted the Diet session at which the LDP majority voted to approve the treaty extension. Demonstrations opposed to the action of the Diet continued outside the Diet building and reached crowd levels estimated at a quarter of a million and more. On June 15, students forced themselves into the House of Representatives chamber and were met by police. In the confrontation, a woman student was killed, trampled to death. The events surrounding the renewal of the treaty marked a turning point in postwar Japanese politics at which ideological divisions between an entrenched Liberal Democratic Party and an opposition Japan Socialist Party became accentuated, divisions that mirrored the larger, global reality of the Cold War.

LDP POLITICS: THE 55 SYSTEM

Japan's Liberal Democratic Party (*Jiminto*) was founded in November 1955, when the Liberal Party (*Jiyuto*) and the Japan Democratic Party (*Nihon Min-shuto*) merged. From 1955 to the summer of 1993, this party governed through holding a majority of seats in the House of Representatives. Founders of the two postwar parties that joined to form the LDP were mostly affiliated with the *Seiyukai* and *Minseito* parties of prewar Japanese political developments. The *Seiyukai* dates from 1900 and the **Minseito** from 1927. Together these two parties alternated in forming governments during the early *Showa* period. Historically, the *Seiyukai* is especially symbolic of Japan's political development toward a modern democratic state. Founded by **Ito Hirobumi**, it brought together party politicians and members of the national bureaucracy in an alliance between the competing institutions of the bureaucracy and the new Diet; it was the party of **Saionji Kimmochi**, one of the most experienced and distinguished of the founding *genro*; and it was the party of **Hara Takashi**, the "commoner" prime minister, assassinated at Tokyo Station in 1921. It is also historically associated, on the other hand, with opening the door to a larger military presence in the government by its virulent attack on the opposition *Minseito* government's endorsement of the London Naval Treaty of 1930. The 1930 treaty limited Japan's prerogative to build more battleships to give it parity with the Western powers. The *Minseito* is historically identified also with the assassination of Prime Minister Hamaguchi Osachi in 1930 and its attempts to resist the growing demands of the military in the early 1930s. Though the modern LDP was founded in 1955 and established what is universally referred to as the 55 system, its origins predate the war and its history contains major events in the larger development of the modern Japanese state.

The 1955 merger was largely a response to the reunification of the Socialists earlier in the year. Among the early platform positions of the LDP was one calling for the revision of the 1947 Constitution. In 1956, a special commission was formed to study the need for possible revisions in the constitution. The commission was made up of members of the Diet, as well as legal scholars. The opposition Socialists boycotted the commission's work as biased in favor of change. It was not until 1965 that the commission reported its findings, largely inconclusive, to the Diet. A rival group of more liberal scholars, the Constitutional Problems Study Group, operated concurrently with the official government commission. Though no revisions were forthcoming from these different study groups, various aspects of the 1947 Constitution continue to divide public opinion today. As reform agendas proliferate in the post–Cold War climate of current debate, especially as calls for reform turn more toward structural, administrative reform, the issue of constitutional revision will likely gather momentum. The new *Minshuto* has placed such administrative reforms at the top of its agenda.

During the 1960s, the LDP enjoyed considerable support among voters, largely due to its economic policies. It also drew considerable strength from its alliance with large businesses, rice farmers, and small shopkeepers. The LDP benefited, perhaps most of all, from the anachronistic and overly ideological appeals of its primary opposition. The Japan Socialist Party (JSP), as already noted, traditionally drew its inspiration from a Marxist tradition that emphasizes world historic class dynamics. Such an orientation can easily lose an audience in times of economic prosperity and "income doubling" plans. During the Cold War, the LDP was the party of capitalism, economic development, and a free press. The Socialists were the party of confrontation, planned economies, and internal turmoil characteristic of the Soviet Union and the People's Republic of China. This "first phase" of the *55 system* was noted for its ideological politics.

It was also known for cozy relationships between and among the LDP, bureaucratic agencies, and large corporations in the business world. A network of what are often called "iron triangles" was established wherein "tribes" (*zoku*) of LDP policy specialists, support groups in particular industries/companies related to the policy area, and civil servants in the appropriate administrative agency would work out policy details to the mutual advantage of each other. LDP Diet members benefit from large campaign contributions, companies benefit from policies that restrict market access, either domestic or foreign, and bureaucrats make connections in the private sector, thus paving the way for their later "descent from heaven" (*amakudari*). Recent crises involving tainted blood products, bank failings, and overly restrictive regulations preventing foreign competitors from entering Japanese markets have directed increased attention to the development of these cozy relationships. One Japanese scholar, Shimada Haruo, refers to the setup as "sham democracy." He argues that the 55 system hurt the Japanese people in three major ways: First, the "backroom deals" squeezed the majority out of the decision-making process; second, citizens lost basic trust in the political system; and third, people became generally demoralized knowing that what passed as popular sovereignty and representative government was basically "just a show" (Shimada 1994, 5–10). This is the context, perhaps, of the "Japan Dream" advertisement run by the LDP in the October 1996 campaign for the House of Representatives. Among the punch lines of the *kendo* action–dominated piece with Hashimoto in the lead is that this is the "new LDP."

LDP FACTIONS

Writing on *The Voice of Japanese Democracy*, in 1918, Ozaki Yukio observed that when political parties are established in the East, "they at once partake of the nature of faction, pursuing private and personal interests instead of the interests of the state" (1960, 690). Factions, or *batsu* in Japanese, are "in-groups" and are common in all aspects of Japanese society, not just politics. They are always hierarchical and tightly bound by traditional obligations of *kobun* (child) and *oyabun* (parents) or *kouhai* (junior) and *sempai* (senior). The former owe respect and loyalty to the latter, who reciprocate with various kinds of help. In traditional Japan, these tightly bound and hierarchical relationships were the building blocks of virtually all organizations, including political ones. Famous *batsu* in the development of the modern Japanese state during early Meiji were the *hambatsu,* or domain factions—meaning mostly the domains of Choshu and Satsuma—and the *zaibatsu,* or financial cliques. To a large extent the organization of various institutions into factions continues in modern Japan. *Habatsu,* more specifically, refers to the factions within political parties such as noted by Ozaki. During the 55 system, the various factions within the ruling Liberal Democratic Party were the true center of political dynamics in the Diet. Usually numbering about half a dozen, these factions competed for power within the party and, ultimately, for the Office of Prime Minister. The president of the LDP was almost always chosen by the House as prime minister. Competition among factions was also a large factor in driving money politics. LDP factions, according to Gerald Curtis, have, throughout the party's history, "provided the primary political community for Japan's political elite, providing a setting of intimacy and common purpose" (1988, 80, 81).

Famous factions were headed by Tanaka Kakuei in the 1970s and Takeshita Noboru in the 1980s. Both Hashimoto Ryutaro and Ozawa Ichiro were formerly associated with the Takeshita faction of the LDP. Many of the recent new parties, such as Ozawa's and Hata's Japan Renewal Party, have their origins in factional disputes. The Takeshita faction during the late 1980s and early 1990s was hit especially hard by charges of corruption, since Kanemaru Shin was also a Takeshita faction insider. But factionalism is not confined to the LDP or the 55 system. One recent analysis of Ozawa's New Frontier Party characterizes the internal disputes following the 1996 House elections as a "series of factional activities organized by Hosokawa, Hata and others who have had their fill of Ozawa's high handed leadership" (Wakamiya 1997, 7). In James Madison's famous *Federalist No. 10,* he observed that among the most important tests of any plan of government was whether and to what extent sufficient remedies for controlling the power of factions was provided. This remains a challenge for reformers in Japan today.

OTHER POSTWAR PARTIES

From the first postwar election on April 10, 1946, until the last election prior to the creation of the 55 system on February 2, 1955, and limiting the number to parties holding at least five seats in the House of Representatives following an election, there were at least ten parties fielding candidates for the House with some success. "At least" refers to problems of classification. Some parties would split and re-form later, or temporarily take on an adjective. Major parties included the Progressive, Liberal, Cooperative, Socialist, Communist, Democratic, National Cooperative, Democratic Liberal, Labor Farmer, and Reform. The most successful among these in the ten-year period between the end of the war and the formation of the Liberal Democratic Party were the Liberal and Japan Democratic parties and the Socialist Party, though it split in the early 1950s. As for the others, they represented what Curtis has called "a bewildering series of party splits and mergers among conservative politicians." Much of the confusion was brought on by the occupation and actions of *SCAP*, such as the purge in January 1946 of some 35,000 former officials in the prewar Diet and local governments (Curtis 1988, 6).

The first really significant new parties were formed after the 55 system was in place. Following the May 1958 election to the lower house, the LDP controlled 287 seats and the Japan Socialist Party 166 seats. The Japan Communist Party held one seat and the rest went to mostly independents. Three parties formed to challenge the two dominant parties in the period 1960–1976. In 1960, the Democratic Socialist Party broke away from the Japan Socialist Party, largely over the events surrounding the 1960 renewal of the Mutual Security Treaty. In 1964, the *Komei* Party was formed as a political organ of the large and growing Buddhist sect called *Soka Gakkai*. In 1976, the New Liberal Club broke away from the LDP. The Democratic Socialist Party and the *Komei* were among the parties that joined the New Frontier Party in 1994. The New Liberal Club, in the beginning led by Kono Yohei, started out with only six members of the Diet. After some early success in recruiting supporters from the "post-ideology" generation of educated, younger, urban voters, it soon folded itself back into the LDP and ceased to exist after 1986 (Curtis 1988, 30–35).

A groundswell of calls for reform of money politics, conflicts of interest, centralized government, entrenched bureaucracy, and a host of other problems led to unprecedented realignments in the Japanese political party landscape in the early 1990s. Hosokawa Morihiro, former governor of Kumamoto Prefecture on Kyushu, formed his Japan New Party first and managed to collect about 8 percent of the votes in the July 1993 House of Representatives election, enough to translate into 35 seats (JISEA 1995, 98). It was also enough to put him in a position to negotiate with several other parties in the formation of a coalition government, Japan's first since the long reign of the LDP. These negotiations ended with Hosokawa being selected prime minister. It was during Hosokawa's short reign that the electoral reforms driving the 1996 House election were implemented. Shortly after the formation of the Japan New Party, two groups split from the LDP, one under the leadership of Ozawa Ichiro and Hata Tsutomu and the other, smaller group, under Takemura Masayoshi called the *Sakigake* (New Party Harbinger). Ozawa and Hata formed the Japan Renewal Party (*Shinseito*) and succeeded in capturing 55 seats in the 1993 election for the House based on about 10 percent of the votes cast (JISEA 1995, 98). The *Sakigake* won only 13 seats and about 2½ percent of the vote in the subsequent House election, but managed a place in the coalition that continued through the Hashimoto government (JISEA 1995, 98). The Japan Renewal and Japan New parties formed the core of the New Frontier Party launched in December 1994. The *Sakigake*, vastly depleted by defections to the *Minshuto*, managed only two seats in the 1996 House election and was facing a very uncertain future in the aftermath of that election. In the aftermath also, the New Frontier Party was showing serious signs of internal dissent and conflict between Ozawa, on one side, and Hosokawa/Hata, on the other.

MASS CULTURE/MASS MEDIA

Though references to Japanese culture usually evoke images from a traditional culture such as women in kimonos, traditional arts such as *ikebana* (flower arranging), and the tea ceremony, traditional religions such as are reflected in the countless shrines and temples that cover the Japanese landscape, and the various other elements explored in Chapter 1, Japanese culture today also encompasses all of the characteristics of mass culture that one encounters in all modern industrial societies. Surfaces in Japan today, in fact, are somewhat noisy, smoky, and littered, especially by neon signs in urban landscapes. Also, everything is mediated by electronic images. Particularly noticeable aspects of mass culture are fast-food operations, video rental outlets, urban shopping arcades, video game and pachinko parlors, coffeehouses, noodle shops, *danchi* (apartment complexes) as far as one can see in some quarters, and, of course, *manga* comics. In mass culture, whether the activity is entertainment, business, travel, or politics, the emphasis is on speed, consumption, and large numbers of people. Mass communications, for example, is defined in *The International Encyclopedia of Higher Education* as "the effective transmission of ideas, information, and experience to large groups of people" (Knowles 1977, 2750). This is all made possible, of course, by a changing technology. Traditional concepts like journalism and broadcasting have largely given way to the concept of mass communications in virtually all discussions of contemporary communications. The biggest single element in these changes is the development of television as a mass medium. As prices continue to fall, and the number of Web sites contin-ues to grow, however, on-line time by home computers may soon rival televi-sion time in the average home.

Television in Japan is both public and private. Television broadcasting in Japan began in 1953. Since then, public and private stations have engaged in healthy competition. NHK, the Japan Broadcasting Corporation, receives almost all of its revenues from fees paid for television reception. NHK is orga-nized under the 1950 broadcasting law, which was designed by occupation authorities to break the government's monopoly of communications in the pre-war Japanese state. NHK, prior to the war, was Japan's only broadcast outlet and it was controlled by the state. The 1950 law encourages private, commercial development, competition, and political neutrality. NHK today is the "second largest broadcast agency in the world," after the British Broadcasting Corpora-tion (BBC). It is governed by a board of governors appointed by the prime minister yet "autonomous from, but somewhat accountable to, government" (Krauss 1996, 90). Today, according to *Forbes* magazine, Japan is the "world's greatest growth market for cable television." In 1995, 63 percent of homes in the United States were wired for cable. By comparison, in the same year, only about 6 percent of Japanese homes had cable. In the years to come, the percentage of wired homes in Japan will rise dramatically, however. The reason is that Japa-nese bureaucrats have decided to deregulate telecommunications in fundamen-tal ways. In 1993, the Ministry of Posts and Telecommunications deregulated the cable television industry in Japan, making it possible for the industry to get a foothold. Among changes allowed were to allow single companies to own more than one cable system; to allow cable systems to offer telephone service; and to raise the allowable percentage of foreign-owned cable systems to 33 per-cent, up from only 20 percent. These deregulatory actions are expected to result in Japan reaching comparable levels of cable-wired homes as in the United States within a decade. Several U.S. companies are expected to benefit from this decision, most in joint ventures with Japanese companies. For example, Jupiter Telecommunications Company is a joint venture within which Sumitomo owns a 60 percent share and U.S.–based Telecommunications International owns 40 percent. Other American companies involved in joint ventures include Time Warner, U.S. West, and, in satellite broadcasting, Hughes Communications (Weinberg 1995, 44, 45). The stakes for these companies are high. In 1995, 99 per-cent of Japanese households had color television sets and 75 percent had VCRs (JISEA 1995, 83).

As in other industrialized nations, one effect of television in Japan has been to enhance the social status of widely recognizable television "personali-ties." In the spring of 1995, the highlight of local elections across Japan was the election of the "no party"—or independent—candidates for governor in Japan's two most populous prefectures. Aoshima Yukio was elected governor of Tokyo Prefecture and Yokoyama "Knock" was chosen governor of Osaka Prefecture. Though many political analysts emphasized the snub that these elections repre-sented for the major parties, particularly the LDP and the New Frontier, each competing for the conservative middle in the post–55 system world of Japanese politics, some pointed to another aspect of the elections. Both Yokoyama and Aoshima are well-known television personalities. According to Fujitake Akira, a professor of sociology at Tokyo's Gakushuin University, Aoshima's fame largely rested on "his skill as a script writer for TV variety shows, on his lyrics for hit songs, and on his role as an old woman who was the heroine of the TV version of the popular comic strip 'Mean Old Woman.'" Similarly, Yokoyama was best known for his work as a "member of a cross-talk comedy trio." Fujitake contends that the use of TV in Japanese politics, traditionally, is different from that in the United States in that the prime minister, cabinet officials, and Diet members rarely appear on TV. Also, as officials, and younger politicians, tend to appear more in recent years, they do so more often as guests on entertainment programs rather than to present, promote, or discuss issues (Fujitake 1995, 14, 15). Donald Richie has written of Japanese television that it tends to be, like much else in Japan, "relentlessly conciliatory" (1987, 184). In a time of voter distrust and heightened cynicism, it is little wonder that younger politicians would seek exposure in entertainment formats on television. A more positive perspective on the role of television in Japan is offered by ***Edwin Reischauer***. He argues that it is television, more than anything else, that has "smoothed out the contrasts in values and attitudes between rural and urban dwellers, which were so divisive in prewar Japan" (Reischauer and Jansen 1995, 218).

According to Susan Pharr, a recent study of various politically active groups in Japan, groups that included government bureaucrats, business leaders, political party leaders, union officials, and leaders in various social movements, revealed that each one, with the exception of leaders in the media itself, ranked the Japanese media first in "power and influence" (Pharr 1996b, 19). But how much of this power is directed at shaping policy or in presenting a particular view of the Japanese state? Ellis Krauss has done a study of NHK performance in this area. Between 1983 and 1985, he examined the television news coverage that NHK devoted to Japanese politics and the Japanese state in general. As in the United States, television news is the primary news source for most Japanese citizens. Among his findings were that over half of news items and three-fifths of air time were devoted to politically related events; over a third of stories pertained in some way to the state bureaucracy or its various advisory councils; the Japanese state, generally speaking, is presented as "impersonal," "paternal," and somewhat a "conflict manager." This portrayal of the state compares, according to Krauss, with a more "executive"-centered view in American news (1996, 89–129). Another recent study of editorial cartoons in Japanese newspapers tends to confirm a similar portrayal of the Japanese state. An examination of cartoons of prime ministers appearing in the *Yomiuri* and *Asahi* newspapers, papers with a combined circulation of over 25 million readers, suggests that from Suzuki Zenko (1980–1982) through Hosokawa Morihiro (1993–1994) these papers gave increasingly more attention to the prime minister as an object of newsworthiness, but that the resultant images of these men collectively were more often than not images of "weak" and "confused" leaders, generally "lacking in confidence." The prime minister is more a "manager" than a "charismatic leader." Prime ministers, according to this study, tend to avoid conflict more than anything else (Feldman 1995, 571–580).

With a national literacy rate at 97 to 99 percent, Japanese newspapers enjoy a wide readership. Japan, in fact, has "the highest total newspaper circulation in the world and twice the daily circulation per capita in the U.S." (Budner and Krauss 1995, 348). The Japanese newspaper business began essentially with modern Japan and the Meiji Restoration. Prior to 1868, only papers published by foreigners and containing mostly foreign news were published. Domestic papers carrying news about Japan began in 1868 with publications in major cities such as Tokyo, Osaka, and Kyoto. The first daily newspaper was published in Yokohama in 1871. These early papers tended to focus on politics and calls for a Japanese national assembly. The *Yomiuri Shimbun* was launched in 1874 and the *Asahi Shimbun* in 1879. Today, these are Japan's leading newspapers in terms of circulation. As of 1993, the *Yomiuri* newspaper had a circulation of 9,874,000 for the morning edition and 4,513,000 for an evening publication. The *Asahi* paper also publishes morning and evening editions with circulation figures at 8,229,000 and 4,532,000, respectively. Other large newspapers are the *Mainichi, Chunichi, Nihon Keizai,* and *Sankei* publications. All of these papers publish morning and evening editions. English-language publications include the *Japan Times,* about 68,000 circulation for a morning edition; the *Daily Yomiuri,* 52,000 in the morning; the *Mainichi Daily News,* 47,000 morning subscribers; and the *Nikkei Weekly,* about 36,000 subscribers. The *Asahi Shimbun* publishes the only evening edition in English, with a circulation of about 39,000 (JISEA 1995, 94).

As with most businesses and professions in Japan, journalists are initially hired through competitive examinations among applicants with university degrees. The competition is fierce, with hundreds of applicants for a relative handful of openings at any given time. Once hired, reporters are assigned to very specialized assignments and become members of press clubs. There are over a thousand of such clubs in Japan today and they serve as both places for business, as in conducting interviews or making announcements, and also as social meeting places. Critics maintain that the "cooperative" atmosphere in such clubs contributes to a homogenous style in Japanese journalism with little distinctiveness among newspapers.

It is difficult to say just how much power Japanese newspapers have. As noted in Chapter 2, the *Yomiuri Shimbun,* the largest circulating, published in the November 3, 1994, issue the complete text of a proposed new constitution for Japan. Though other newspapers and many scholars took note and offered editorial endorsements or criticisms, virtually nothing has been proposed within government administrative agencies, within the Diet, or in campaigns for the House in October 1996. In late July 1995, following the national House of Councillors election, all five large national dailies called for an immediate election for the lower house to give stability to Japanese politics ("Awaiting the New Order" 1995). Yet, it was not until October 1996 that such an election was actually held.

TABLE 4–1
Japanese Newspaper Circulation, 1993

	Circulation (morning and evening editions combined)
In Japanese	
Yomiuri	14.3 million
Asahi	12.5 million
Mainichi	6.0 million
Nihon Keizai	4.6 million
Chunichi	4.4 million
Sankei	2.9 million
In English	
The Japan Times	68,000
The Daily Yomiuri	52,000
Mainichi Daily News	47,000
Nikkei Weekly	36,000
Asahi Evening News	39,000 (evening only)

SOURCE: JISEA 1995, 94.

Togo Shigehiko, a Tokyo correspondent for the *Washington Post* since the mid-1970s, offers some interesting comparisons between Japanese and American journalistic practices. In a talk in 1994 at the Japan Information and Culture Center in Washington, D.C., he made the following observations. In America, there are about 370 institutions of higher education offering courses in journalism, whereas in Japan there are "very few such schools." Also, American journalists write as a career and remain as writers. Japanese journalists are usually "promoted" to executive positions with seniority. He also noted that, generally speaking, Japanese television is "far less critical than the print press in Japan." As for those who criticize the Japanese press for being too "chummy" with their press clubs and social activities, Togo reminded his audience that the media in Japan were principally responsible for bringing down three prime ministers, Tanaka, Takeshita, and Uno; that they were relentless in their investigations of the Lockheed, Recruit, and other scandals; and that the media played a "major role" in ending the LDP dominance of party politics in Japan.

During the period leading up to the July 1993 election, which brought the Hosokawa coalition to power, the "morning TV talk shows broadcast hours of discussion on the political situation, featuring politicians, economists, entertainment personalities and other well-known figures." Those broadcasts, according to Togo, had "a major impact on public opinion" (Japan Information and Culture Center 1994, 4). This view is reinforced by Kristin Kyoko Altman in her study of "Television and Political Turmoil: Japan's Summer of 1993." She begins her study by noting that in October 1993 millions of viewers all over Japan watched as Tsubaki Sadayoshi, an executive at TV Asahi, began testimony before the Diet concerning whether his network had slanted its coverage of the election in July (Altman 1996, 165–186).

Some studies find remarkable balance in Japanese newspaper reporting. One study, for example, of Japanese newspaper coverage of Japan–U.S. trade friction found that one-sided reporting is relatively rare both in the Japanese and American presses. In a comparative study of articles in the *Asahi, Yomiuri,* and *Nihon Keizai* papers in Japan and in the *New York Times, Washington Post, Wall Street Journal, Los Angeles Times,* and *USA Today* in the United States, the authors examined reports on the FSX fighter plane controversy in 1988–1989, the purchase of Columbia Pictures and Rockefeller Center in New York City by Japanese investors in 1989, and the **Structural Impediments Initiative** talks of 1989–1990. Other findings in the study included the observation that Japanese reports tend to be shorter and cite fewer sources than American reports. They also note that coverage often depends as much on the nature of the issue as on any journalistic standards. Most notably, but cautiously, the authors note that "Japanese news reports were more likely to be one-sided than American ones" (Budner and Krauss 1995, 342).

English-language newspapers also have a long history in Japan beginning with the port cities of Nagasaki, Yokohama, and Hyogo (Kobe), which were opened to foreign trade under the commercial treaties of 1858. The English-language papers were first published in these ports to inform and entertain foreign visitors. The first such paper was the *Nagasaki Shipping List and Advertiser* begun in June 1861. The *Japan Herald* followed, in Yokohama, followed by the *Daily Japan Herald.* These early papers were largely to publicize shipping schedules and advertisements. Over time, they and others publicized overseas events. Early Japanese newspapers often drew much of their overseas information from these English-language newspapers. When Japanese papers became heavily censored by the Meiji government, beginning in 1875, the English-language newspapers were overlooked. An example of their "independence" was the support of the *Japan Overland Mail* for the *samurai* in Kagoshima during the **Satsuma Rebellion** of 1877 (Haruhara 1994, 474–484).

As noted in Chapter 2, the *Yomiuri* newspaper, Japan's most widely circulated, presented in its November 3, 1994, edition the complete draft of a new constitution for Japan. This was in part related to the approaching fiftieth anniversary of the 1947 Constitution, which went into effect on May 3, 1947. May 3 is Constitution Day in Japan. But bigger reasons for the publication of a new draft were the reform climate of Japanese politics, relative silence on the subject among politicians and bureaucrats, the major changes facing Japan brought on by changing global conditions and Japan's need to participate more in the international arena, and the need to loosen up entrenched bureaucrats at home. In 1992, the *Yomiuri* newspaper established a Constitution Study Council for the purpose of looking into the whole subject of constitutional revision. Its recommendations, however, were to proceed cautiously and to focus only on provisions showing clear need of change. The paper, however, decided to reexamine on its own the entire constitution and to publish its recommendations for an entirely new document. The group offering the draft was headed by Take-moto Iinuma, director of the Yomiuri Research Institute. As one scholar in Japan has noted, "sooner or later the Japanese will have to decide what to do about their supreme law" (Matsuzaki 1995, 22–25). When that time comes, the *Yomiuri* draft will undoubtedly be a major item in the debates over specifics. If Japanese television tends to avoid issues and controversy, to be "conciliatory" in Donald Richie's view, then Japanese newspapers are tending increasingly to be more provocative. In *About Face,* the American journalist Clayton Naff describes his experience working for the *Japan Times* in often humorous terms to challenge the perception that Japanese newspapers—especially ones with large numbers of foreign correspondents—are "stooges" for the establishment. His experience was that the *Japan Times* "was as independent as any other Japanese newspa-per—which is to say that it was not adversarial toward the Establishment, but neither was it a stooge" (Naff 1996, 119, 120).

Major recommendations in the *Yomiuri*'s draft for a new constitution include clearer statements on Japan's role in international peace keeping, secu-rity, and humanitarian projects and, specifically, the role and limits of the Self Defense Forces. Also, changing conceptions regarding human rights, espe-cially with regard to privacy and the environment, ought to be incorporated. Diet reforms, including a strengthening of the cabinet, are recommended. And, finally, judicial reforms, complete with specifics, are encouraged. An interesting general suggestion is that constitutional provisions related to the Emperor as a symbol of the Japanese state follow, rather than precede, provisions on popular sovereignty. This proposed clarification of the fundamental law's opening chap-ter "to clarify that sovereignty rests with the people" is the draft plan's "first point" (Constitutional Studies Group 1995, 26–28).

Other mass media institutions in Japan today include publishers of jour-nals, magazines, books, videos, motion pictures, and *manga.* Among magazines, one might distinguish between "high-brow" monthly magazines, such as *Sekai* and *Bungei Shunju,* which include news, social and political commentary and analysis, and various reviews, and "popular" magazines, such as *Shukan Asahi* and *Focus.* These latter include the *manga* magazines (Pharr 1996a, 6). *Manga* popularity dates from what one source calls the "revolution of the late 1960s" (Natsume 1996, 20). *Manga,* or cartoons, were originally created for children. Today they are aimed at everyone, everywhere. As for content, they run from silly to perverse, from apolitical to politically violent. They have been assaulted as pornographic and defended as artistically avante-garde.

Manga as media may well dramatize as well as any type of mass medium in today's world can the complex and problematic nature of mass communica-tions in modern democracies. For those who hail the technological transforma-tions within the communications industry that have brought television, radio, motion pictures, and now cyberspace as mediating forces that will midwife more democratic political processes due to their power to reach large masses of people with even larger masses of information, one might ask why, then, the proportionate rise in what seem somewhat mindless comics among the world's most literate people. One thinks here of Erich Kahler's analysis of the "overpopulation of the surfaces" as among the greater problems in modern, mass society" (1989, 93–97). Are *manga* in Japan but an escape for the bewildered on crowded buses, trolleys, and trains, themselves but metaphors for crowded worlds in which people increasingly live? If this is so, then there might be some inverse logic with respect to the future of democracy in Japan, and perhaps elsewhere, that the bigger, the faster, the more sophisticated, the more overwhelming mass media communications become, the smaller, the slower, the more simplistic will be the response of citizens over time. For the less cynical, however, *manga* might be examined more closely for its political and wider, cultural content. One recent, if brief, analysis of the work of Tsuge Yoshiharu by Natsume Fusanosuke, for example, finds in Tsuge's drawings and stories "a representation in manga form of the murky psychological landscape of the Japanese as they go through the violent social upheavals of modernization." He further sees Tsuge's influence in the "more refined form" of the "entertainment manga of later years" (Natsume 1996, 20, 21).

CITIZEN ACTION GROUPS

Among the more interesting developments in Japanese politics under the postwar constitution is the increased activity of citizen action groups, or citizens' movements. Mobilized in the beginning on behalf of environmental causes, these groups, of both urban and rural Japanese citizens, cut across all traditional organizational lines in Japanese politics and illustrate the wider democratization of Japanese society. Margaret McKean, in her classic study of these "citizens' movements," identifies five important characteristics of Japanese political culture out of which the citizens' movements emerged. Drawing on the work of other scholars, such as Bradley Richardson, Scott Flanagan, Sidney Verba, Norman H. Nie, and Jae-on Kim, she observes in Japan a tradition of community-based participation, meaning citizens who are neither typically urban or rural but more typically bound together in "closely knit" communities; also, "apolitical groupism," a tendency to put group affiliations ahead of resource considerations; a high degree of cohesion, rather than conflict, within segments; and "passive formalism." With respect to the last element she observes that "most Japanese had learned democratic norms as ideals but had not yet internalized these norms through personal experience" (McKean 1981, 10–17). Yet the environmental anxieties brought on by rapid modernization, industrialization, and rebuilding after the war mobilized citizens into action groups like the Citizens' Conference of Usuki, which battled against construction of a cement factory in Oita Prefecture, the Liaison Movement to Prevent Petroleum Development in the Osumi Peninsula (Kagoshima Prefecture), the Society to Protect Nature and Culture in Oiso (Kanagawa Prefecture), and the Movement to Decrease Garbage in Chuo Ward (Tokyo). These are but a few of the movements that organized and acted in defense of their communities and the environment in McKean's study. They point to the democratization at the grass roots in Japan brought on by community responses to perceived crises.

Other, more recent protests by citizen action groups were against the development of the *shinkansen* (bullet train). Concerned both with the expansion of the bullet train's routes and the consequent environmental impact, and with noise and vibration caused by existing routes, these groups organized protests in Nagoya, Tokyo, Toda, Urawa, and Yono. Working with local governments, neighborhood associations, political parties, representatives of the Japan National Railway, and Ministry of Transportation officials, attempting to increase media coverage, and developing their own "mini-media" were all strategies employed by these citizen action groups. According to David Groth, about 130,000 households have suffered some form of pollution-related problem along the *shinkansen* corridor from Tokyo to Kyushu. This, and similar statistics, illustrate why between the late 1960s and the early 1980s, the period of the greatest development of the *shinkansen* lines, about 100 different citizen action groups were organized in protest (Groth 1996). Many of these activists are women and housewives in particular. In her study of "The Rise of the Housewife Activist" (1992), Mary Noguchi profiles six such women who personify the volunteer at the grass roots whose "apolitical groupism" can become carefully focused political action when issues threatening to her community and home enter her vision.

INTEREST GROUPS AND *KOENKAI*

Interest groups in Japan, as in all modern liberal democracies, attempt to influence public policy formulation in their own interest. Traditionally, interest groups in Japan concentrate their energies on the various organs of the national bureaucracy and on the Liberal Democratic Party. Perhaps the most powerful interest group in Japan today is *Keidanren*, or Federation of Economic Organizations. This group represents the largest corporate interests in Japan. Created in 1946, *Keidanren*'s primary objective is to make proposals to the national government that are in the best interests of the national economy as a whole. Another large business group is *Nikkeiren*, or Federation of Employers Association. Since 1948, *Nikkeiren* has represented management concerns in negotiations with labor unions. It recommends labor policy to the Diet and various administrative agencies. Every spring, labor unions all over Japan submit wage proposals to various employers. *Nikkeiren* coordinates corporate responses and issues guidelines for management. Other large business groups are the *Keizai Douyukai*, which represents corporate executives, and the Japan Chamber of Commerce and Industry. The last is the oldest business group in Japan, dating from 1922. Individual chambers of commerce for cities like Osaka, Tokyo, and Kobe, however, date from early Meiji. All of these associations would be classified in the United States as economic interest groups particularly interested in management and market concerns.

Concerns of workers are represented by the various labor unions. There is much diversity, more complexity, and less influence, generally, when it comes to organized labor in Japan. Though labor unions in Japan date from the 1890s, it was not until the Allied occupation after World War II that labor unions were actually encouraged. Unions in Japan, like so much else, are organized somewhat according to a family model. Unions are mostly enterprise or company unions today. That is, each company or enterprise has unions whose membership is restricted to company workers. If someone loses a job, he or she also loses membership in the union. There are also federations, however. Following major realignments during the 1980s, the Japanese Trade Union Confederation (*Rengou*) was formed and is today the largest federation of unions. Among member unions is the powerful Japan Teachers' Union, which joined in 1989. Another federation, the National Confederation of Trade Unions (*Zenrouren*), is closely affiliated with the Japan Communist Party. A third, *Zenroukyou*, National Trade Union Council, was also organized in the late 1980s and includes most railway workers. About one-fourth of Japanese workers belong to unions. This compares with about 16 percent in the United States (1992), 43 percent in the United Kingdom (1991), and 42 percent in Germany (1991) (JISEA 1994, 70). Agricultural interests are promoted through *noukyou,* agricultural cooperative associations. These associations represent among the strongest supporters of the Liberal Democratic Party and have recently been at the center of national attention due to involvement in the *jusen* crisis (discussed in Chapter 5). They have also been a powerful source of opposition to the liberalizing of rice importation laws and those governing other aspects of the agricultural sector of the economy.

In the early 1990s, amid the many calls for reforming Japanese politics, *Keidanren* and *Rengou* were particularly active and supportive of reform efforts. *Keidanren,* following the 1990 House election, refused to contribute any more funds to the Liberal Democratic Party factions. *Rengou,* in the 1993 House election, implemented a policy of "selective endorsement" of candidates and withdrew all support to left wing Social Democratic Party candidates. On the other hand, candidates supported by Ozawa Ichiro, mostly in the Japan Renewal Party, benefited much from *Rengou* support (Otake 1996, 271, 272).

If large, traditional interest groups like *Keidanren* and *Rengou* were among the champions of electoral reform, the many LDP–related *Koenkai* groups were consistently opposed to it. *Koenkai* are the political support organizations for Diet members. They emerged during the occupation period with all of the dramatic changes which that period brought to the Japanese political landscape. Former local leaders in the communities were often purged from holding any office, more offices were created by the democratic reforms, land reforms led to the demise of once powerful landlords who could formerly deliver votes, and the electorate was greatly expanded with the extension of suffrage to women. All of these changes led to the emergence of *koenkai,* or political support groups. Some have called these groups a modern substitute for the old landlords and a support system for the "new ruling class." LDP *koenkai* will often include local political leaders and elected officials. *Koenkai* can be quite large and have several divisions. They are created and financed by politicians who like to preserve the "fiction" that they are in fact grass-roots organizations mobilized for his or her support (Curtis 1971, 126–131). One scholar calls *koenkai* "associations of vote-gatherers." But they also perform other tasks. Drawing on the example of Tanaka Kakuei's group, called *Etsuzankai*, Karel van Wolferen portrays *koenkai* activities as including such things as tracking funerals, weddings, and birthdays in the district and assisting the unemployed and underemployed to find jobs (1989, 131). But there are also strong feelings among *koenkai* members. They "are not only the core of spoils distribution; they are also characterized by strong bonds among their members, nurtured through sharing and surviving the passionate experience of elections" (Otake 1996, 279). Because of a deep, vested interest in maintaining the system as it was, *koenkai* resisted election reform in the early 1990s.

Summary

Among "floating" structures in Japan are political parties, mass media institutions, citizen action groups, interest groups, and *koenkai*. From the *Jiyuto* of early Meiji to the *Taiyoto* of late 1996, the history of Japanese political parties is one especially marked by the formation of new parties. The party system today remains multiparty, though reform advocates are urging changes in the direction of a two- or three-party system with more attention to issues and less attention to factions and money politics. The Liberal Democratic Party controlled the Diet from 1955 to 1993 and governed Japan in what is called the 55 system. During the 55 system, the Japan Socialist Party was the dominant opposition party. Today the JSP is called the Social Democratic Party of Japan (SDPJ) in English and has been greatly reduced in influence in recent years. Because of LDP dominance during this period, factions (*habatsu*) within the party became the center of Japanese politics. In-fighting between and among these factions heightened pressures for raising larger and larger sums of money, a circumstance that drove money politics and eventually led to the end of the 55 system in 1993 over repeated charges of corruption. Other significant parties in the postwar state were the Democratic Socialist and *Komei* parties. Both of these parties folded within the New Frontier Party in 1994. The New Frontier Party, headed by Ozawa Ichiro, is today the second largest party and offers itself as a conservative alternative to the LDP. The *Sakigake*, Japan Communist Party, and the new *Taiyo* Party are significant minor parties that occasionally have substantial impact on particular issues. The *Minshuto*, or Democratic Party, was founded on the eve of the 1996 national House election and is the largest of the new parties.

Mediating the political messages, though more often the commercial and "pop" messages of mass culture, are a wide assortment of mass media institutions. Television in Japan is both public and private. The NHK, the public broadcasting company, is the second largest broadcasting company in the world. Among trends in television broadcasting is the rapid increase in the growth of cable television, an area where Japan has been slow to develop. Television in Japan, as in other industrial nations, has accelerated the trend toward more and more widely recognizable television "personalities" running for political office. Recently, this has contributed to the "no party" movement in Japan whereby many turn away from the traditional parties and turn toward well-known personalities who run as independents. Governors of Tokyo and Osaka prefectures elected in 1995 were former television personalities without party backing. Newspaper circulation in Japan is the highest in the world, and Japan's literacy rate is between 97 and 98 percent. The *Yomiuri, Asahi, Mainichi,* and *Chunichi* papers are the largest circulating. The *Yomiuri* has led efforts in recent years to propose a new constitution for Japan. Journalists in Japan are praised for their professionalism and criticized for their "chumminess." Among other especially noteworthy mass media organs in Japan today are the *manga* comics. These widely circulating and slickly produced publications are the subject of much discussion inside and outside of Japan. The often violent and earthy themes raise questions regarding the political depth of an otherwise highly literate citizenry.

Citizen action groups, interest groups, and *koenkai* also impact public policy in Japan in various ways. Citizen action groups began with deep concerns regarding environmental pollution and today are among the more dramatic of Japan's political institutions. Interest groups are many and well organized as in any modern liberal state. Efforts traditionally focus more on administrative agencies than Diet committees and members, with the exception of LDP members. *Keidanren* (business), *Rengou* (labor), and *Noukyou* (farmers) are among the most important of these groups. *Koenkai,* or citizen supporting groups, date from the occupation period and democratization. They get out the vote for their Diet representatives, but they also track personal achievements and noteworthy events in the lives of constituents on behalf of the Diet member. They generally opposed recent electoral reform efforts.

Suggested Readings

Curtis, Gerald L. 1971. *Election Campaigning Japanese Style.* New York: Columbia University Press.

————. 1988. *The Japanese Way of Politics.* New York: Columbia University Press.

Feldman, Ofer. 1993. *Politics and the News Media in Japan.* Ann Arbor: University of Michigan Press.

Flanagan, Scott C. 1991. *The Japanese Voter.* New Haven, CT: Yale University Press.

Hrebenar, Ronald J. 1986. *The Japanese Party System: From One Party Rule to Coalition Government.* Boulder, CO: Westview.

Kishima Takako. 1991. *Political Life in Japan: Democracy in a Reversible World.* Princeton, NJ: Princeton University Press.

Krauss, Ellis S., and Takeshi Ishida. 1989. *Democracy in Japan.* Pittsburgh: University of Pittsburgh Press.

McKean, Margaret A. 1981. *Environmental Protest and Citizen Politics in Japan*. Berkeley: University of California Press.

Pharr, Susan J., and Ellis S. Krauss, eds. 1996. *Media and Politics in Japan*. Honolulu: University of Hawaii Press.

Richardson, Bradley M., and Scott C. Flanagan. 1984. *Politics in Japan*. Boston: Little, Brown.

van Wolferen, Karel. 1989. *The Enigma of Japanese Power: People and Politics in a Stateless Nation*. New York: Knopf.

Works Cited

Altman, Kristin Kyoko. 1996. Television and Political Turmoil: Japan's Summer of 1993. In *Media and Politics in Japan*, ed. Susan J. Pharr and Ellis S. Krauss, 165–186. Honolulu: University of Hawaii Press.

Awaiting the New Order. 1995. *Economist*, 29 July, 25.

Blaker, Michael. 1995. Japan in 1994: Out with Old, In with the New? *Asian Survey* 35 (January): 1–12.

———. 1996. Japan in 1995: A Year of Natural and Other Disasters. *Asian Survey* 36 (January): 41–52.

Budner, Stanley, and Ellis S. Krauss. 1995. Newspaper Coverage of U.S.–Japan Frictions: Balance and Objectivity. *Asian Survey* 35 (April): 336–356.

Calder, Kent. 1988. *Crisis and Compensation: Public Policy and Political Stability in Japan, 1949–1986*. Princeton, NJ: Princeton University Press.

Constitutional Studies Group. 1995. A Proposal for a Sweeping Revision of the Constitution. *Japan Echo* 22 (Spring): 26–28.

Curtis, Gerald L. 1971. *Election Campaigning Japanese Style*. New York: Columbia University Press.

———. 1988. *The Japanese Way of Politics*. New York: Columbia University Press.

Feldman, Ofer. 1995. Political Reality and Editorial Cartoons in Japan: How the National Dailies Illustrate the Japanese Prime Minister. *Journalism and Mass Communication Quarterly* 72 (Autumn): 571–580.

Fujitake Akira. 1995. TV Democracy: Media Skip Policy and Make Politics a Spectacle. *Japan Update*, June, 14, 15.

Groth, David Earl. 1996. Media and Political Protest: The Bullet Train Movements. In *Media and Politics in Japan*, ed. Susan J. Pharr and Ellis S. Krauss, 213–241. Honolulu: University of Hawaii Press.

Haruhara Akihiko. 1994. English-Language Newspapers in Japan. *Japan Quarterly* 41 (October): 474–484.

Japan Information and Culture Center. 1994. Japan's Media: A Unique Brand of Journalism. *Japan Now* 4 (April): 4.

Japan Institute for Social and Economic Affairs (JISEA). 1994. *Japan, 1994: An International Comparison*. Tokyo.

———. 1995. *Japan, 1995: An International Comparison*. Tokyo.

Kahler, Erich. 1989. *The Tower and the Abyss: An Inquiry into the Transformation of the Individual*. New Brunswick, NJ: Transaction Books.

Knowles, Asa S., ed. 1977. *International Encyclopedia of Higher Education*. San Francisco: Jossey-Bass. S.v. Mass Communication (Field of Study), by John Wicklein.

Krauss, Ellis S. 1996. Portraying the State: NHK Television News and Politics. In *Media and Politics in Japan*, ed. Susan J. Pharr and Ellis S. Krauss, 89–129. Honolulu: University of Hawaii Press.

Matsuzaki Tetsuhisa. 1995. A Newspaper Rewrites the Constitution. *Japan Echo* 22 (Spring): 22–25.

McKean, Margaret A. 1981. *Environmental Protest and Citizen Politics in Japan*. Berkeley: University of California Press.

Naff, Clayton. 1996. *About Face: How I Stumbled onto Japan's Social Revolution*. Tokyo: Kodansha International.

Natsume Fusanosuke. 1996. The Night Grabs. *Look Japan* 41 (February): 20, 21.

Noguchi, Mary Goebel. 1992. The Rise of the Housewife Activist. *Japan Quarterly*, 39 (July): 339–352.

Otake Hideo. 1996. Forces for Political Reform: The Liberal Democratic Party's Young Reformers and Ozawa Ichiro. *Journal of Japanese Studies* 22 (Summer): 269–294.

Ozaki Yukio. 1960. Factions and Parties. In *Sources of Japanese Tradition*, comp. Tsunoda Ryusaku, Wm. Theodore de Bary, and Donald Keene, 689–690. New York: Columbia University Press.

Pharr, Susan J. 1996a. Media and Politics in Japan: Historical and Contemporary Perspectives. In *Media and Politics in Japan*, ed. Susan J. Pharr and Ellis S. Krauss, 3–17. Honolulu: University of Hawaii Press.

———. 1996b. "Media as Trickster in Japan: A Comparative Perspective." In *Media and Politics in Japan*, ed. Susan J. Pharr and Ellis S. Krauss, 19–43. Honolulu: University of Hawaii Press.

Reischauer, Edwin O., and Marius B. Jansen. 1995. *The Japanese Today: Change and Continuity*. Cambridge, MA: Belknap Press of Harvard University Press.

Richardson, Bradley M. 1988. Constituency versus Parties in Japanese Voting Behavior. *American Political Science Review* 82 (September): 695–718.

Richie, Donald. 1987. *A Lateral View: Essays on Contemporary Japan*. Tokyo: Japan Times, Ltd.

Shimada Haruo. 1994. The Flaws of the 1955 Setup. *Economic Eye: A Quarterly Digest of Views from Japan* 15 (Spring): 5–10.

Van Wolferen, Karel. 1989. *The Enigma of Japanese Power: People and Politics in a Stateless Nation*. New York: Knopf.

The Very New Party. 1994. *Economist*, 17 December, 38–40.

Wakamiya Yoshibumi. 1997. Hashimoto Administration's Clouded Future. *Japan Quarterly* 44 (January): 4–10.

Ware, Alan. 1989. Parties, Electoral Competition and Democracy. *Parliamentary Affairs: A Journal of Comparative Politics* 42 (January): 14, 15.

Weinberg, Neil. 1995. Cable Comes to Fuchu. *Forbes*, 6 November, 44, 45.

5

The Scope
of Authority:
Issues

Of all the great issues of politics, among the biggest is the role of the institutions of state power in addressing social and cultural issues. Japan, following in traditions common to other East Asian nations, generally allows greater scope to state guidance than one finds in the West. The scope of authority is determined by the various traditions explored in Chapter 2 under sources of authority. One would not begin any discussion of policy formation in Japan by citing Lockean liberalism or laissez-faire; rather, one would begin by noting the rule of the sages deriving from Confucian tradition and as modified by Shinto, Buddhist, and Western influences. The latter, as noted earlier, includes Lockean liberalism, human rights concerns, certainly a concept of constitutionalism, and laissez-faire considerations. But it is the synthesis of the various traditions that guides assumptions in public policy making. Sages and citizens, represented in administrative and party organs, respectively, and in continuous interaction through structures discussed in Chapter 3, and as shaped by "floating" structures, discussed in Chapter 4, make policy in Japan. One cannot point easily to any one institution or to any one ideological tendency in Japan for answers as to who or what determines policy. This leads to scholarly, as well as civic, frustration. Karel van Wolferen, in his famous, and controversial, study of *The Enigma of Japanese Power* writes of the "elusive state" where "the reality of the Japanese political world has a way of slipping through one's fingers" (1989, 25).

As for the focus of attention, it is always shifting, although some issues are perennial. At the beginning of 1995, one would certainly note the overwhelming importance of issues regarding basic security in Japan. In January, the nation was shocked by the *Kobe* earthquake, which took over 5,000 lives and devastated large sections of one of Japan's biggest and most productive areas. No amount of public planning prepared the national government for the scope of the disaster in Kobe. Similarly, in March, poison sarin gas was released in the Tokyo subway killing 12 people and injuring thousands. Members of the *Aum Shinrikyo*, a religious cult, have been accused and convicted of the unprecedented terrorist attack, and the sect's leader, *Asahara Shoko*, is being tried on 17 charges in Tokyo. The Asahara trial is being called Japan's "trial of the century" in the mass media. Also, in 1995, trade friction between the United States and Japan continued to increase, as did friction within the security alliance. In trade, the United States threatened major tariff sanctions against imported luxury automobiles unless Japan showed more determination to open markets to a wide array of American goods and services, but especially autos, trucks, and vehicle parts. Regarding the security alliance, relations reached new lows due to the arrest, trial, and conviction of three American soldiers on charges of abducting and raping a 12-year-old girl on Okinawa in September. Though crises were averted in both instances, problems continue to exist in trade and defense-related areas with the United States, topics that will be explored in more detail in Chapter 7. Throughout most of 1995 the economy continued to stagnate, although last-quarter figures for 1995 and first-quarter figures for 1996 began to show substantial improvement.

Perennial issues in Japan, as in most modern nation-states, include the following: economic development, social welfare, education, defense, criminal justice, civil rights, and environmental protection. Other issues of increasing concern among policy analysts and legislators include political reform; science and technology funding, particularly in research and development and in a growing space program; energy policy, with particular concern regarding the continued development of nuclear energy; telecommunications; emergency preparedness; and transportation. Three issues of growing concern and, in some respects, unique to Japan are whether, when, and where to move the nation's capital; how to address increasing concerns among Japanese women regarding economic and professional opportunities outside the home; and how properly to remember World War II, events leading up to it, and its aftermath. The latter includes the issue of compensation for so-called "comfort" women.

COMPLIANCE, PERFORMANCE, CONFIDENCE: EDUCATING THE JAPANESE CHILD

Any consideration of education in Japan must begin with observations regarding child development in general. Famous studies of child-rearing practices in Japan, such as by Chie Nakane, and Doi Takeo, emphasize the importance of dependency and indulgence, especially in the relationship of mother and child. Doi's study of *amae* (dependence) is almost always cited as a point of departure. Unlike in most Western societies, Japanese children are indulged somewhat at an early age, creating a close union with the mother. That Japanese children are "spoiled" is a complaint often heard, especially by Westerners visiting Japan. This is part of a larger whole, however, within which habits of the heart are nurtured early, often, and continuously so that the passage from home to school is more the continuation of a process than a sudden break. Raising the good child involves developing habits of mind and feeling expressed in

Japanese terms that are difficult to translate (White and Levine 1986). Concepts such as *sunao* and *yutaka*, for example, point to desired goals usually translated as obedience and fullness, respectively. Yet, *sunao*, as in *sunao na kodomo*, means more than obedient child. It suggests willingly cooperative child and is encouraged as a virtue beyond obedience with the latter's somewhat mechanical connotation of responding to command and prohibition. Similarly, *yutaka*, as in *yutaka na kokoro*, suggests a sensitive, but confident heart. Perhaps in no other area of public policy do cultural distinctions become as subtle and complex as in education. Becoming Japanese, what is usually called political socialization in social science literature, is a process that begins with infancy, continues in the development of parent–child–sibling relations structured by *amaeru* (to depend on the good will of others), *amayakasu* (to indulge), and similar concepts not unique to Japanese culture but uniquely emphasized, and is refined by long established assumptions and procedures in the public schools.

In the public schools, the teaching of language skills, *kokugo*, is central to the educational process through the compulsory years and takes up more class time than any other subject. Elementary school readers that teach language skills play a major role in shaping national identity as well. A recent study of *kokugo* readers shows that the dominant messages in most ministry-approved readers are that Japan is a safe, predictable, and harmonious place, that nature is the "ground of being," and that empathy and feeling are generally more important than analytical skills. In addition, readers traditionally present a mythical Japanese past that idealizes an agrarian and communal society far removed from the realities of late-twentieth-century urban Japan. Stories and lessons tend toward a nature-centered view of reality where nature is almost intimately associated with insects, frogs, fish, monkeys, and other ground-level, nonhuman associations. There is little emphasis on flight, adventure, and challenge as one finds in many American texts. There is much emphasis on those things that suggest the traditional Japanese sensitivity to *aware*, the fragile, almost pitiful, transient and fleeting aspects of life as suggested in poetic references to moon, snow, birds in flight, and the like. Though this is changing in the climate of *kokusaika*, the internationalization of Japanese thought and feeling, it is changing very slowly (Gerbert 1993).

What might be called character education is therefore a central element in Japanese education and is a central concern in government policymaking. Discipline is a primary focus. A student handbook for a middle school in Hitotsubashi, for example, directs students, with detailed pictures, exactly where badges on boys' shirts and buttons on girls' blouses should be placed. Similarly, directions are given on how properly to carry bookbags and on how to get to and from the school properly from each direction. Boys' hair "should not touch the eyebrows, the ears, or the top of the collar"; no student should "have a permanent wave, or dye his or her hair"; young ladies "should not wear ribbons or accessories in their hair"; and for all students, "hair dryers should not be used" and badges should be worn "at all times" and should be "positioned exactly" (White 1993, 223–226). Such rules do not go unchallenged, of course. A recent trend among young Japanese is to color their hair brown or "tea" color, a trend that has caused older students, especially those graduating from college, junior college, or trade school who are seeking job interviews, to spend considerable time coloring and rinsing their hair, depending on the group to which they need to show respect and with whose unwritten rules they must comply.

Strict rules in the public schools illustrate a general tendency in Japanese education that reflects a widely shared cultural priority to give moral weight to all aspects of child development. Performance qualities tend to be secondary to "deeper qualities" that make a child *ningen-rashii* (humanlike). Of paramount importance is the development of a good child (*ii ko*). That children be mild, obedient, cooperative, spirited, and prompt are of primary consideration. Secondarily, children are encouraged to persist, endure, reflect on their weaknesses, and understand logically. According to Merry White and Robert A. Levine (1986), these goals represent "markedly different conceptions than Western ones regarding the proper training of children." In another study, by a Japanese scholar, the concept of *shido* is stressed. Generally translated as "guidance," the concept of *shido* is applied, alternatively, to guidance in academic learning (*gakushushido*), guidance in moral education (*seitoshido*), and guidance in going on to high school and beyond (*shinroshido*). The role of the Japanese teacher in these different forms of guidance includes a much wider field of influence than teachers outside of Japan have (Shimizu 1992). A survey conducted by the *Yomiuri Shinbun* (newspaper) in December 1994 polled Japanese parents regarding what "type of people" they wanted their children to become. The largest response, 43 percent of respondents, identified "not bothersome to others." A similar poll in the United States in the same year asked American parents what they would pick as "the most important" thing for a child to learn as preparation for life. The largest response, 54 percent, picked "to think for himself or herself" (Ladd 1995, 25). Without overgeneralizing, one can still observe in these findings the deeply rooted cultural tendency in Japan to stress harmony and cooperation and the equally entrenched emphasis in the United States to encourage creative individuality.

At the heart of the Japanese school system is the teacher, **sensei**. A recent comparative study of teachers and teaching in the United States and Japan conducted jointly by Tokyo University and Stanford University stresses the importance of "context." The study compared elementary, junior high, and high school teachers in each setting. Major findings included the following: Japanese teachers work longer hours, up to 20 hours more per week. Also, Japanese teachers assume wider duties that carry them beyond the classroom and often into the personal lives of their students. Teachers visit the homes of students at least once a year. These examples reflect cultural differences and society's expectations. In Japan, goals for educational institutions include "social, aesthetic, and interpersonal skills." Great effort is made to encourage cooperative interaction, harmony within groups, and collective responsibility. A striking example is the practice in Japan of promoting students to higher grades despite poor academic achievement. Identity within the group is more important than individual, academic achievement. More attention is generally paid to nonacademic activities, special events, ceremonies, and extracurricular activities. The school year is 240 days, compared to a U.S. average of about 180 days. As more is generally expected of teachers, so also are teachers and teaching held in high regard. They also are generally paid better and for 12 months of work. Teachers in Japan are not permitted to hold second jobs. By comparison, fully a third of American teachers hold second or "moonlighting" jobs, usually with no connection to education. Japanese teachers also feel they have more say in school policy than their American counterparts do (Sato and McLaughlin 1992). This has not always been the case. Immediately after World War II, teachers were often aligned against the government on education policy.

In the years following the war, the American occupation authorities completely reformed public schools. According to R. P. Dore, the changes were indeed "radical." Texts were published with less control from the Ministry of Education in Tokyo, local school boards were made elective with wide authority over personnel and textbook decisions, and ethics education was abolished, along with courses in history and geography. New history courses taught "not of the glorious reigns of former emperors but of class divisions, of economic exploitation, and of struggles for freedom and equality in the face of oppression and despotism" (Dore 1973, 530). In 1952, however, with the return of Japanese sovereignty and the end of the occupation, education issues were among the most important in Japanese politics. Battles over curriculum, textbook content and selection, how local school boards should be chosen, how Japanese history, especially recent history, should be taught, and perhaps most importantly, over how centralized or decentralized public education should be were at the center of political discussion. Many conservatives attempted to "correct the excesses" of occupation reforms by working for appointed rather than elected boards, for laws prohibiting teachers from joining political parties or circulating political literature, and for a restoration of courses in moral instruction. During this period, teachers generally resisted such efforts through their activity in the Japan Teachers' Union, an organization associated with the parties on the political left. In 1956, legislation passed in the Diet making local school boards appointive rather than elective. The conflict over the legislation was so intense that the government placed 500 police officers within and near the Diet chamber during the proceedings (Jansen 1973, 532).

The issue of textbook content and selection has always been of central importance. Prior to World War II, text selection was exclusively the prerogative of the Ministry of Education. A national textbook system was begun in 1903. Texts had to mirror the principles found in the *Imperial Rescript on Education* of 1890. Teachers were expected to stick literally to text materials and to honor the Emperor and his portrait, a symbol of the Japanese state. During the 1960s, the textbook issue received heightened national attention when Ienaga Saburo, a professor of education at Tokyo University, sued the government for censorship of one of his books. A text he had written on Japanese history was rejected in 1963, and after rewrites, resubmissions, and various public hearings given wide exposure in the press, Professor Ienaga was vindicated by a Tokyo district court that ruled certain actions of the Ministry of Education unconstitutional (Dore 1973, 538–545). The textbook issue continues to be a matter of controversy in Japanese politics today. In 1996, the LDP pledged itself to work for an end to the practice of screening high school textbooks by the Ministry of Education. As part of education reform this was seen as a laudable goal in keeping with the larger goals of developing more individualized education and creative thought. It was also in keeping with the diplomatic goals of building closer ties with Asian neighbors, many of which had been pressuring the Diet, ministry officials, and educators for years to write more accurate accounts of Japan's "aggression" during World War II. On the eve of the October election in 1996, however, the LDP withdrew its pledge under pressure from conservative members.

Today, educational reform is much discussed in Japan both inside and outside of government. In 1994, the Ministry of Education authorized the introduction of what are called "comprehensive" high schools. By mid-1996, there were 45 of these in Japan. The basic idea is to give high school students more choice in the courses they take, a wider range of subjects from which to choose, and more choice in setting their own schedules. Underlying the reforms is the desire to encourage more individualism and creative thought in the younger generation. Despite great successes in developing a widely literate citizenry and top achievements on international tests, the Japanese school system has also been roundly criticized for teaching conformity and a lack of creative thought. Reforms are also related to the changing nature of the Japanese economy. As more manufacturing jobs are exported overseas, Japanese companies are actively seeking more creative job applicants. In June 1996, the Ministry of Education's Central Education Council issued a report containing recommendations for reforms appropriate for the next century. A major topic in the report concerns *ijime* (bullying) and the recommendations include the ideas of phasing out all Saturday classes and reducing time in the classroom. If implemented, these reforms would represent dramatic departures in the Japanese school system (Katsukata 1996).

There are 24,676 elementary schools in Japan of which only 171 are private. Of 11,292 junior high schools, only 636 are private. But of 5,501 senior high schools, 1,320 are private schools. This pattern continues into higher education where 390 of a total of 534 universities are private (JISEA 1995, 92). As one gets farther from the world of home and family, one sees more diversity, and parents and students have more options. The exception to this pattern is the high number of private kindergartens in Japan, an exception that might be explained by the desire shared by so many Japanese parents to start their children in school as early as possible. Private kindergartens generally accept children at a younger age than public ones. As for cost, Japan spends about 4.7 percent of its GNP on education. Internationally, this compares with the United States, which spends about 5.3 percent of GNP, Canada 7.6 percent, Italy 5.4 percent, Sweden 8.8 percent, and Australia 5.5 percent, just to name a few (Japan

Information Network). Overseeing all of this is the Japanese Ministry of Education, or *Mombusho*.

Japanese schools generally enjoy a very high reputation in the international community. Discipline, standards, performance, and high graduation rates are often mentioned both in casual conversation and in serious studies. Among criticisms, *ijime* (bullying) and "examination hell" are almost universally pointed to as areas of concern. Bullying is an outgrowth of the emphasis on group bonding and social harmony. As the nail that sticks out is hammered down, so also some students. Often, targets of bullying are students who have spent time overseas and no longer fit into their primary group. Recent high-profile incidents involving the death of young students at school has led to strident government efforts to address the problem at all levels. On December 2, 1994, police in Aichi Prefecture reported the suicide of 13-year-old Okochi Kiyoteru due to bullying. In a four-page note left by the young boy, he wrote details of a three-year routine of bullying by four of his classmates at Tobu Junior High School in Nishio City. He was forced to pay them money for the last year of his life, a situation that became unbearable. The *Asahi* newspaper reported that this was the fifth suicide of the year related to bullying. On December 14, police in Ishikawa in Fukushima Prefecture reported that 15-year-old Sudo Hirotaku hanged himself due to bullying (Ebitsubo and Nakamura 1995, 237, 239). These are but two cases among many in recent years that dramatize the problem of bullying in Japanese schools.

Competitive examinations for entrance into colleges and universities in Japan have also come under stricter scrutiny (see box). Many argue that the effect of such an examination system is to prioritize rote learning in the elementary and secondary schools so that students prepare themselves for test questions rather than life's challenges. Such a system, critics argue, stifles creativity.

SHIKEN JIGOKU: EXAMINATION HELL!

Competitive examinations are a way of life for Japanese youth, a feature of their young lives often referred to as examination hell. Students must take these examinations for entrance into both high school and university. Because of the hierarchical nature of Japanese society and culture and the importance placed on education, achievements later in life are virtually predetermined by where one goes to school and what kind of associates one meets at university. National universities, with Tokyo and Kyoto at the top, and prestigious private schools such as Keio, Waseda, and Doshisha, select entrants on the basis of results from these competitive exams. Related developments in modern Japanese society are the proliferation of after-school schools, or *juku,* which prepare students for the exams, and the pressures on parents, mostly mothers, to look after the study habits of their children. The *kyoiku* mama, "education mother," is a product of this examination subculture in today's Japan. Increasingly, employment is also based on competitive exams.

Sending children to after-school schools, called *juku*, is primarily to prepare students for examinations, especially examinations for entrance to university. These *juku*, and the emphasis on competitive examinations, are part of what some call "shadow education" in Japan. In other words, in addition to the regular schools and the prescribed curricula, there is also an informal "outside" system of preparation that is designed to enhance the "official" schools and provide a sort of pathway to the elite institutions of higher education and success in Japanese society (Stevenson and Baker 1992). A study by James Fallows (1991) identifies the strengths of Japanese schools as emphasizing effort, stressing the importance of education, encouraging collective responsibility, and imparting an overall fairness. Weaknesses include excessive pressure, sexual discrimination, overemphasis on conformity, and a tendency to nurture isolation and separation of individuals.

Higher education in Japan does not enjoy the international reputation of the lower grades. At the top of the university hierarchy is *Tokyo University*, Todai for short. Formerly the Tokyo Imperial University, Todai is today a magnet for Japan's best and brightest. Graduates are practically guaranteed employment by the nation's most prestigious corporations and by national government agencies. After Todai in the hierarchy is Kyoto University and other national universities that can trace their origins back to late nineteenth- or early twentieth-century institutions. Among private universities, *Keio* and *Waseda*, both in Tokyo, are first in rank. Far more students in Japan attend private rather than public universities. The latter, as well as the most prestigious of the private schools, tend to act as midwives for recruiting students into corporate and government positions, rather than as institutions of higher learning. According to one study, higher education in Japan "functions primarily as a filter to certify students for entry into corporations or government." The actual educational process is "secondary." Students, according to this study, are "hired by corporations principally on the basis of which university they attended" (Kempner and Makino 1993, 197).

Japanese colleges and universities are also not known for a high number of foreign exchange students. In 1983, to address this problem, the Ministry of Education set the goal of recruiting 100,000 foreign students per year in institutions of higher education in Japan by the year 2000. Institutions here include junior colleges, technical schools, colleges, and universities. At first, the numbers began to climb rapidly, reaching over 50,000 by 1993. Through 1996, however, the number leveled off in the mid-fifties. Government efforts to improve recruitment include increased appropriations for government scholarships for foreign students, plans to expand campus housing for foreign students, and grants to encourage more short-term stays for students wishing only to study for a year or less while still part of a program in a university in their home country (Iikubo 1996).

A related government concern is the relatively low number of foreign researchers and teachers who come to Japanese universities. In 1994, there were 5,288 foreign researchers in Japan. According to Hayashida Hideki, director-general of the Science and International Affairs Bureau of the Ministry of Education, more researchers will come to Japan when they realize the kinds of cutting edge research that is increasingly being done at places like the National Laboratory for High Energy Physics at Tsukuba and the Institute of Space and Astronautical Science in Kanagawa Prefecture. As for teachers, in 1996 there were only 461 foreign professors in official positions at Japanese public universities, and another 386 lecturers in nonofficial positions. Many of these positions are in foreign-language programs (Iikubo 1996).

CRIME, PUNISHMENT, AND POLICE IN THE JAPANESE STATE

Four things stand out immediately in any observation of the criminal justice system in Japan: The organization of the police and policing is national; crime statistics for the country are remarkably low by Western standards; arrest rates in Japan are high; and the Japanese *koban,* though unique to Japan, is catching on rapidly outside of Japan. Upon closer examination, one might also add that police misbehavior in Japan is miniscule with problems of police corruption rarely, if ever, of national concern. A study of police behavior in Japan and the United States by David Bayley (1976) begins with a chapter on policing in Japan entitled "Heaven for a Cop."

Perhaps few agencies of government reflect cultural traits more dramatically than police agencies. One does not have to be a Hobbesian to recognize security as among the most basic issues within the scope of state authority. Generally speaking, perceptions in the West tend to see all East Asian nations as more authoritarian with respect to security, an image reinforced in recent years by the high-profile caning of an American student in Singapore. Yet, in Japan, the ratio of police officers to citizens is lower than in the United States. Figures for Japan in 1988 show one officer for every 557 Japanese; U.S. figures for 1989 show one officer for every 357 Americans (JETRO 1991, 32). The fact is that crime rates are substantially lower in Japan than in all other developed nations. In 1988, for example, there were 1,400 homicides in Japan compared with 20,700 in the United States. Similarly, in the same year, there were 1,700 rapes in Japan and 92,500 in the United States. Other crime categories show similar differences. Arrest rates show a 97 percent rate for Japan in 1988 compared with 70 percent in the United States for homicides. In rape cases, Japan reported an 86.4 percent arrest rate while United States figures in 1988 show a 52 percent arrest rate in rape cases (JETRO 1991, 30). Most studies that attempt to explain these dramatic differences in crime and arrest rates focus on patrolling activities. Generally, Japanese police are "highly motivated and effectively disciplined and are more intimately involved with their neighborhoods and are more visible than Western police" (Miyazawa 1992, xi). But there are also problems. *New York Times* articles, in the late 1980s, for example, pointed to a tendency in certain high-profile criminal investigations, such as those related to the Recruit Cosmos scandal, for long pretrial detentions. One study, *Policing in Japan,* by the

---

OMAWARISAN

The walking, uniformed police officer who patrols neighborhoods in large cities and mans the police box (*koban*) represents about 40 percent of all Japanese police officers. They visit homes in their jurisdiction one or two times a year to discuss crime prevention and report any problems in the area. This community-based policing is currently gaining in popularity outside of Japan. *Omawarisan* literally means "Mr. walking around." Generally speaking, patrol officers in Japan enjoy wide popularity, and children are taught from an early age to trust and obey *omawarisan*. There is a popular children's song that portrays *omawarisan* as a friendly neighborhood dog in uniform.

Japanese scholar Miyazawa Setsuo, focuses on this problem by examining methods used by detectives. Among his conclusions are that "many detectives may continue to be forced to manipulate the suspect and to otherwise engage in questionable actions" (1992, 242).

Where studies such as Miyazawa's shine a more critical light on policing in Japan, studies of the *koban* continue to draw admiration and emulation. The *koban*, or police box, dates from the early Meiji Period (1868–1912). The structure today is essentially the same. Ten officers are assigned to each *koban*, which are staffed in rotations 24 hours a day. In the rural areas of Japan, the *chuzaisho* (police substations) play the same role as the *koban* in urban areas. In Japan today, there are 6500 *koban* and 8500 *chuzaisho* staffed by 80,000 officers (see accompanying box). These substations are famous for assisting as well as protecting their jurisdictions. It is as likely that officers are busy with lost-and-found problems or citizens temporarily out of money as that they are investigating criminal activity. This community-based approach to patrolling and assisting is currently being adapted in the United States in Philadelphia, Detroit, and Portland, Oregon.

Though one must beware of stereotypes, the *koban* system in Japan tends to illustrate the tendency within the larger culture to emphasize the search for harmony rather than the management of conflict. A recent study of *Everyday Justice* in Japan and in the United States dramatizes the importance of this search as fundamental within Japanese culture. The concept of *wa* or harmony originates in the two kanji, or Chinese characters, for rice and mouth. In other words, the eating of rice produces a harmony that makes all other things possible. According to the authors: "The primacy of wa as a cultural value is usually traced to Prince Shotoku's Seventeen-Article Constitution, circa 604 C.E. As the first article states, when wa is present, 'what is there which cannot be accomplished?'" (Hamilton and Sanders 1992, 213). In a survey conducted by the Prime Minister's Office in 1993, the question was asked what makes people in Japan "proud" of Japan and of being Japanese. The number one response, at 52.1 percent of respondents, was the country's "safety" (Ebitsubo and Nakamura 1995, 358).

ECONOMIC DEVELOPMENT: MEIJI, MITI, AND THE MIRACLE

Among the bigger crises in recent Japanese politics is <u>the issue of government</u> <u>assistance in the rescue of the *jusen*, or housing loan corporations</u>. These companies primarily loan money for home mortgages. The *jusen* were originally created in the 1970s to assist prospective homeowners. But during the *"bubble economy"* of the 1980s, several *jusen* engaged in property speculation and borrowed billions of yen from banks and agricultural cooperatives to finance the projects. A number of the projects were linked to companies with ties to Japanese criminal organizations, notably the *yakuza*. Seven of the *jusen* became all but bankrupt by 1995 and pressures mounted for the Diet to assist the *jusen* by appropriating public funds. The New Frontier Party challenged the proposed bailout and even blockaded committee rooms in the Diet building to frustrate the hearings and focus media and popular attention on the issue.

The proposed government assistance was challenged as improper on a number of points. Critical items included the connections between public money going ultimately to agricultural cooperatives on the vote of a Diet majority controlled essentially by the LDP. Farmers and rural voters generally are traditionally among the most consistent supporters of LDP candidates. Also, many executives of the failed *jusen* were formerly Finance Ministry officials, largely with LDP connections, who upon retirement from the national bureaucracy were hired by the *jusen* in the classic *amakudari* tradition. Public outrage came generally to be split between those critical of the bailout and those critical of New Frontier Party tactics in the Diet. Many were also critical of the opposition party of Ozawa for not offering alternative solutions to the proposed bailout. Eventually, the bailout proposal passed the Diet; it will cost taxpayers 685 billion yen (about $6.85 billion).

This issue not only focused public attention on the continuing problems of money politics, cozy relationships, and the need for political reform; it also sharpened the attacks of critics who had been urging administrative reform. The Finance Ministry had clearly failed to watch developments in the failed *jusens* over the years leading to the crisis. The critical nature of this failure is illustrated by the closing of the main entrance to the Ministry of Finance building at the beginning of 1996 for fear of possible assaults from "ultra-rightists." This failure in the regulatory function of a key government agency was dramatic evidence for many that political reforms of recent years had not gone far enough and that the next big challenge in Japanese politics was reforming the administrative state. In the fall of 1996, this issue became a primary motive force in the creation of the new *Minshuto*, or Democratic Party. It also led Prime Minister Hashimoto to call for cutting the number of government ministries in half. Among the leaders of the *Minshuto* is Kan Naoto, Hashimoto's health and welfare minister. Riding a crest of popular support for his role in leading investigations into another public crisis, that of tainted blood supplies, Kan figured to lend considerable legitimacy to the administrative reform focus of the new party going into the first national election under the new electoral system.

The *jusen* crisis points to the close relationship that traditionally exists between the Japanese government and business organizations. During the early Meiji era, industrial development through state-directed action was the dominant concern of virtually all the *genro*. Through a practice of direct subsidies in key industries such as shipbuilding, foundries, mines, and arsenals the Meiji state built upon its own state-owned enterprises. A law on the "transfer of factories" in 1880 then provided for turning over these state operations to private companies. Early transfers involved cotton-spinning mills, silk mills, glass and cement factories, and sea transportation. All of these enterprises had been targeted by Restoration leaders as critical to building up home manufactures to compete with the onslaught of machine-made overseas products. The latter, such as a stronger, more uniform cotton yarn from Western countries and sugar from China, were virtually destroying Japan's handicraft and small farms domestic economy. Products generally stronger, more efficient, more attractive, and cheaper were threatening the Japanese market with dependency on foreign commerce, an economic dependency that would surely lead to complete subordination. This flood of overseas products was hastened by the so-called *"unequal treaties"* that Japan was compelled to accept and that capped tariffs at 5 percent. To counter all of this, the Meiji oligarchs pressed forward with their modernization and industrialization policies. Among the greatest beneficiaries of these state policies were large family-run "houses" such as those run by Mitsubishi, Sumitomo, Mitsui, and Yasuda, the "big four" of the early *zaibatsu*.

A large element in this "aristocratic revolution" (Smith 1973) was the role of the *samurai*. Educated, literate, spirited, and threatened with extinction by modernization, this elite warrior class of feudal Japan was now split between those who saw opportunity in *"civilization and enlightenment,"* such as the *genro*, and those who felt besieged by it. Among the latter were those *samurai* from **Satsuma** loyal to **Saigo Takamori**. In the last great uprising of the traditional warrior class of Japan, Saigo and his followers were defeated in the *Satsuma Rebellion* of 1877. Other former *samurai* were among those most effective in leading the new Meiji state and large private combinations.

At the beginning of the *Showa* Period, in 1926, Japanese economic development represented a "middle-income industrializing nation with pretensions of being a great power." By the end of Showa, however, Japan had emerged as "a great economic power with doubts about the role it should play in the world" (Lincoln 1992, 191). This was accomplished despite the horrors associated with World War II. Japan's economic growth rate after the war exceeded somewhat the growth of European nations also devastated by war.

Many analyses of Japan's success in developing so rapidly as an industrial power have been presented, each stressing different aspects of Japanese culture, social dynamics, politics, and the rest. David Friedman, in a detailed critique of conventional wisdom regarding the Japanese "miracle," classifies most accounts as falling into two broad categories that he calls the "bureaucratic regulation thesis" and the "market regulation thesis." Those in the former school stress the role of the national bureaucracy in Japan's postwar economic development, especially the role of the Ministry of International Trade and Industry (MITI). Chalmers Johnson's study, *MITI and the Japanese Miracle* (1982), is especially representative of this school. The latter approach, represented by Hugh Patrick (1979), argues that Japanese success has been more the product of key industrialists "disciplined by the market" and driven by competition, especially in domestic markets. Friedman's own view emphasizes the role of mid-size and small businesses in new product development as a larger explanation for Japanese successes in postwar economic development. He also explores in detail the political forces that shape economic decisions with politics understood in a more comprehensive way than most standard definitions. Politics in his view includes basic perceptions about justice and fairness, including and especially in the workplace and within markets (Friedman 1988, 3–20).

Though differing as to degree, most studies, however, agree on the important role of state planning, especially in key bureaucratic organs of the Japanese state. These organs include the Ministry of Finance, the Ministry of International Trade and Industry, and the Ministry of Agriculture, Forestry, and Fisheries. Scholars such as Chalmers Johnson who stress the role of government agencies in Japanese economic development contributed much to the political debate in the United States on "industrial policy" during the late 1970s and into the 1980s. This was presented as a new way of discussing the potential role of national governments in shaping key sectors of economic policy. In Japan, however, certainly since Meiji and the origins of the modern Japanese state, "industrial policy" and the role of the national government in developing a strong economy generally were almost never steeped in controversy. What some call state-centered capitalism has always been but one aspect of a widely held acceptance of state-centered politics in general. When **Ito Hirobumi** and his entourage went to Europe in the early 1880s to study Western political science and law, it was to the state-centered theories of German scholars such as **Rudolf von Gneist, Lorenz von Stein**, and **Hermann Roesler** that they looked for inspiration and guidance. In the specific area of economic development, however, Meiji leaders had much in their own national traditions to draw on as well.

Economic policies during the long **Edo** Period of isolation and feudalism were largely centralized in an administrative state run by the **Tokugawa shoguns**. The **daimyo**, or feudal landlords, had to maintain both sizable properties in their own domains and considerable estates in Edo, the shogunal capital. The required residence of the *daimyo* in Edo in alternating years, the *sankin kotai*, contributed to both a centralized administration and the regular flow of goods, as well as people, between Edo and the various domains. The creation of a national market was among the results, a market with a center at Edo. *Daimyo* were encouraged to produce and market, both at the capital and within their domain's region, surplus items, especially surplus rice. Osaka also emerged during this period as a central economic power in western Japan where surplus goods were also shipped and marketed. Not all economic development was state centered, however. Early in the Edo Period, family-owned businesses such as those controlled by the Mitsui family in Edo also made their first appearance.

The development of a centralized, administrative state and the opening of large family-owned businesses during Edo should not, however, obscure the traditional character traits of the Japanese people that have also contributed greatly to the long history of Japanese economic success. A propensity for hard work, attention to detail, craftsmanship, adaptability, creativity, especially in the arts, and a high regard for education and learning—all of these traits developed by the Japanese during preindustrial times contributed greatly to Japan's transition to an industrial economic power. *Edwin Reischauer's* analysis of Japan's premodern background to economic development stresses in addition two other characteristics of the Japanese people that set them apart from their Asian neighbors: a keen sensitivity to the outside world and the problems and prospects associated with outside pressure and a "historic consciousness" of learning from the outside in previous times (Reischauer and Jansen 1995, 299).

Oe Kenzaburo echoed this theme in a speech on Japanese culture "before a Scandinavian audience" in 1992 where he observed that the "Yamato spirit" which so many critics have identified with militarism in Japan during the years leading up to World War II was actually first spoken of by Murasaki Shikibu in *Tale of Genji* and refers to a "shared sensibility" similar in meaning to the *sensus communis* of Aristotle. Most importantly for Oe, it is something that should be developed only after "book learning," which in traditional Japan meant learning in Chinese culture. After Meiji, it meant learning from the West. The traditional slogan of *wakon-kansai* was replaced by *wakon-yosai*. That is, "Yamato spirit with Chinese learning" developed into the Meiji "Yamato spirit with Western learning" (Oe 1992, 16–20). So much that shaped Japanese culture in the past originated in China. Religion, language, architecture, fine arts, among other elements of Japanese culture, are rooted in Chinese culture. So much that has shaped Japanese culture in the modern era originates in Western culture. The two characteristics, noted by Reischauer, were especially important in Japan's commitment to modernization during the Meiji Period.

A national government's approach to economic policy making naturally reflects the nation's particular history and cultural traditions, the large assumptions that operate somewhat like involuntary muscles. And in Japan, state-directed policy during Meiji became second nature. In the Meiji years, this second nature was substantially enhanced by the so-called unequal treaties imposed by the United States and other Western powers. With the Meiji Restoration, "rich nation, strong military" became the focus of virtually every state action. Numerous laws changing agricultural policies, taxing procedures, the status of *samurai*, the currency system, and banking were implemented in the early years of Meiji to foster economic development. The first national bank was established in 1873, but by 1879 there were 153 national banks in operation. The Bank of Japan was created in 1882. The national government also created a national railway, a modern postal service, and an equally modern telegraph service. The national government directed subsidies to large private companies such as those engaged in shipbuilding, as already noted. The national government began operating coal mines and building factories to produce tools, glass, bricks, cement, reeled silk, spun cotton, and woolen goods (Yamaguchi 1983, 151–154). These actions, among many others, complemented efforts in the private sector. Large financial and industrial combinations, the *zaibatsu,* began to develop during this period. The early political parties **Seiyukai** and **Minseito** were widely regarded as puppets of the Mitsui and Mitsubishi *zaibatsu.* "Money politics" was a concern from the beginning.

The Japanese model for economic development during Meiji, as in almost all other areas, was based on cooperation, specifically cooperation between the public and private sectors. The distinction between public and private, in fact, is not traditionally as important in Japanese cultural traditions. As noted earlier, there is no classical tradition anchored in Rome to which "romantic" longings periodically look for inspiration and the rebirth of *res publica.* There are no admonitions from Voltaire to tend one's own garden as juxtaposition and counter to civic humanist appeals to commit to public duties in the manner of Cincinnatus. The conflict in traditional Japanese culture between obligation and human feelings as explored by Ruth Benedict is not the same as the conflict of interest in the West between public duty and private pursuits. The conflict between public and private leads to walls of institutional separation such as that between church and state and business and government. By contrast, Japanese traditions and culture, emphasizing cooperation and harmony, have nurtured a more cooperative, less adversarial, relationship between private economic organizations and organs of the Japanese state. These cultural traditions are reinforced by paradigms in the social sciences and humanities that deeply influence political socialization processes.

In the United States, the natural law teachings of Charles Darwin, as modified by Herbert Spencer, William Graham Sumner, and other social Darwinists, reinforced laissez-faire economic theories by dramatizing the competitive struggle for survival as a law of nature. This paradigm in the United States extended far beyond the schools with its influence on generations of lawyers and judges during the Lochner Era of jurisprudence. In Japan, the concept of nature that permeates curricula, law, and public perceptions generally is far less Darwinian or Spencerian. As noted in the discussion of education policy, *kokugo* (national language) readers traditionally present images of nature far less hostile to human needs than that presented by Sumner's warning that it is "root, hog, or die." These paradigms also influence perceptions of proper economic development and who decides the paths of that development. There is no general tendency in Japan today for private business interests to compete with agencies of the national government in a competition for survival in a hostile cosmos. This creates an atmosphere within which private corporations, especially large ones like Mitsui or Mitsubishi, can work with government agencies, such as the Ministry of International Trade and Industry, and set an overall industrial policy. Critics liken such cooperation to the earlier relationships between parties, government agencies, and *zaibatsu* in prewar Japan. Critics also contend that such cooperation creates a climate within which consumers, ordinary citizens, workers, the less organized generally, have little input.

Throughout the Showa Period, for example, and especially through the 1970s, government economic policy tended to favor corporations and not address the needs of laborers and their households. Sidewalks and sewers were low priorities. Harbors and railroads topped the agenda. Similarly, environmental protection was lost in the shadows of corporate protectionism. This helped set the scene for the Minamata and *itai itai* tragedies of the 1950s and 1960s. Perhaps most tellingly, the cooperative harmony between large corporate and large government organizations "succeeded" in keeping consumer prices high. This last item is a big element in recent reform proposals involving trade relations, administrative reorganization, deregulation, and traditional "money politics." Today, the Ministry of International Trade and Industry, among other agencies, limits market access for imported products, such as rice; the Ministry of Finance is blamed for much of the *jusen* scandal; critics inside and outside of Japan argue that recent laws adding hundreds of items to the deregulated list are trivial and do not get at major, structural problems such as in the banking and securities sector of the economy; and all accounts are that money politics continues in more creative ways under the election reform law.

Much of economic development depends on monetary and fiscal policy. With respect to the yen, it reached record strength vis-à-vis other currencies in the mid 1990s. The stronger yen resulted in driving up the costs of Japanese goods overseas and making imported goods in Japan more attractive to consumers. Though this has helped reduce trade surpluses with trading partners, thus reducing international friction, and has also stimulated Japanese consumer demand for foreign goods, it has also slowed production within Japanese industries and accelerated pressures to encourage early retirements, discourage hiring, and rethink lifetime employment practices. National government spending for fiscal year 1996 showed interest on the public debt as the leading category, representing 23 percent of total outlays. Second in outlays was spending on social welfare programs at 19 percent. Grants to local governments was third at 18 percent, with public works spending at 13 percent (see Table 5–1). These four categories together accounted for over 70 percent of total outlays. Only education (which includes research and development funding), at 8.2 percent, and defense, at 6.4 percent, represented other categories over 5 percent of the total. Among ministries, Finance, Health and Welfare, Home Affairs, and Construction led spending. Revenues came principally from direct and indirect taxes. Traditionally, the largest single source of tax revenue is the income tax, followed by the corporate tax and the consumption tax (JISEA 1995, 76).

BEYOND MINAMATA: PROTECTING THE ENVIRONMENT

Because of rapid modernization and industrialization, environmental issues usually are not among the Japanese government's highest priorities. Yet, during the 1960s, Japan "had one of the worst pollution problems in the world, if not the worst" (Reed 1986, 63). Four cases of environmental pollution stand out in

TABLE 5–1
General Accounts Budget Expenditures, Fiscal Year 1996

Category	Percent of Total
Government debt expenses	23
Social security expenses	19
Tax allocation to local governments	18
Public works expenses	13
Expenses for education, culture, and the promotion of science and technology	8
National defense	6
Expenses for pensions	2
Expenses for economic cooperation	1
Other	10

SOURCE: Japan Information Network Online, citing the Ministry of Finance.

postwar Japanese politics as especially tragic. The names **Minamata** and Minamata disease are known worldwide among environmentalists and many others as dramatic examples of industrial development regardless of risk to the environment and even to human beings. Minamata is a city on the island of **Kyushu** in southern Japan where a large chemical company, Chisso, dumped mercury sludge into Minamata Bay over many years. Beginning in the mid-1950s, reports of physical ailments in the region, and even death, led to investigations of possible environmental pollution as a cause. Fish contaminated by mercury was discovered as the source of what came to be called Minamata disease. Hundreds died, and thousands were injured by eating contaminated fish, leading to one of the worst environmental disasters on record. Numerous court cases were brought and settled in various ways over the next 30 years. It was not until the spring of 1996, however, that the final resolution of all claims was reached ("Slow Justice" 1996). In a second incident of Minamata disease in Niigata Prefecture in the 1960s, more cases were brought seeking compensation. In December 1995, one of the companies involved in the Niigata case, Showa Denko Chemical Company, "sincerely apologized" to victims and accepted a settlement plan to cover those victims not already compensated by the government. According to the settlement, 231 plaintiffs will receive 2.6 million yen each (Ebitsubo and Nakamura 1996, 233).

Two other famous, and infamous, cases of environmental pollution often recalled in discussions of the issue in Japan are the *itai-itai* disease in Toyama in 1955 and the respiratory disorders that were widespread in Mie Prefecture. It is the pollution issue more than any other that activated citizens' movements in the environmental protests examined in Margaret McKean's study of *Environmental Protest and Citizen Politics in Japan*. According to McKean, the protest movements in Japan not only dramatize the importance of the pollution issue in modern and advanced industrialized democratic states, they also dramatize the existence of "a new avenue of citizen participation" and a "new political force in Japan" (1981, 5).

The earliest major pollution crises were those in the late nineteenth century caused by the Ashio and Besshi copper mines and involved contamination of rivers and noxious fumes. The Ashio copper mine in Tochigi Prefecture dumped acidic chemicals into nearby rivers. When heavy rains would cause these rivers to overflow, huge flooding of contaminated water would pollute vast acreage in sections of the northern Kanto Plain. Protests were heard in the Diet, and government action to limit chemical pollutants from the mine were taken. Not strictly enforced, problems continued right up into the 1970s and the eventual closure of the mine in 1973. A year later, in 1974, area farmers were awarded monetary damages. The Besshi copper mine in Ehime Prefecture (Shikoku) represents an early, 1893, incident of air pollution. Because of the emphasis on industrial development after World War II, the 1960s and 1970s were the peak years of environmental pollution. Numerous chemical complexes, especially, threatened the small towns where they were often located. The turning point in Japan's attitudes toward pollution and protection of the environment, according to Teranishi Shun'ichi, was the battle to stop the construction of petrochemical plants in Mishima, Numazu, and Shimizu in Shizuoka Prefecture in 1963–1964. Residents successfully fought the plans by electing reform candidates to local offices who blocked plant constructions. From this point, hundreds of similar challenges were "repeated over and over again, creating a wave of political reform that swept the metropolitan areas of the Pacific belt" (Teranishi 1992, 326). Also, many court cases ended with victories for environmentalists.

Today, the center of controversy regarding environmental issues in Japan is the Monju fast breeder nuclear reactor in Fukui Prefecture. In December 1995, the Monju reactor was shut down when a coolant compound was discovered leaking. Though no serious damage was done, the Power Reactor and Nuclear Fuel Development Corporation was criticized for the awkward way in which it handled the incident, a response that caused widespread distrust. Japan is almost alone in its continued development of the Monju type of reactor. The prototype reactor uses plutonium as a fuel, a highly toxic and weapons-usable fuel that critics contend is far too risky to develop as an energy source. Being energy resource poor, and heavily dependent on foreign imports for its energy needs, however, the Japanese government continues to support the development of the fast breeder reactor. It is 50 times more efficient than nuclear power plants fueled by uranium (Kumao 1996, 3).

Japan began nuclear power generation with the opening of its first commercial plant in 1966. Since that time, 47 more reactors have begun operation in Japan. In 1992, nuclear power plants were generating approximately 25 percent of the nation's total electric power (see Table 5–2). According to the government's Long Term Program for Research, involving the Development and Utilization of Nuclear Energy, 1994 revision, Japan plans to expand gradually the

TABLE 5–2
Electricity Generated by Nuclear Power, 1992

Country	Nuclear Power Generation (Percent of Total)
Japan	25.10
Canada	15.50
France	73.90
Germany	29.80
United Kingdom	24.10
United States	20.10

SOURCE: Japan Institute for Social and Economic Affairs, *Japan, 1995: An International Comparison* (Tokyo, 1995), 60.

number of reactors that use a mixed-oxide (MOX) fuel, so that by the year 2010 the total will be at least 10 reactors. Mixed-oxide fuels use plutonium that has been recovered from spent fuels. This recovering process has to the present been done in Britain and in France. A Japanese reprocessing plant, however, is under construction in Rokkasho, in Aomori Prefecture. Transportation safety has, of course, been a serious concern here, especially among environmentalists. In 1992, in a highly publicized shipment of recovered plutonium from France to Japan aboard the *Akatsuki-maru,* groups led by Greenpeace dramatized their concerns over potential terrorist highjackings or accidents at sea. Similar concerns were expressed in February 1995 with the sailing of the *Pacific Pintail* from Cherbourg, France, to Japan. That shipment carried 28 canisters of high-level radioactive waste. With Japan's commitment to the development of fast breeder reactors and the use of plutonium in mixed-oxide fuels, these concerns will probably intensify in the years to come (Hayashi 1995, 68–75). In June 1992, Japan was among 180 countries to send delegates to the UN conference on the environment and development, the Earth Summit, in Rio de Janeiro (Teranishi 1992, 321–327).

In March 1997, fears among critics of Japan's nuclear power agenda were intensified when fires and an explosion occurred at a nuclear fuel reprocessing facility in Tokai, in Ibaraki Prefecture. Thirty-five workers were exposed to small amounts of radioactivity. Both Prime Minister Hashimoto and the president of the Power Reactor and Nuclear Fuel Development Corporation offered apologies, but many viewed the accident and slow responses by government authorities as further testimony that Japan's nuclear power plans for the future need serious reconsideration.

An issue related to concerns over environmental pollution is waste management. In a nation as crowded and as productive as Japan, the basic question of what to do with garbage is extremely critical. In most urban areas in Japan, home and institutional trash disposal is carefully regulated and usually closely monitored. A basic procedure is to separate burnable from unburnable trash and to place each type in a different kind of container. Occasionally city officials go to extremes, or what many consider extremes, such as Tokyo officials in September 1993, who began airing television announcements to prepare citizens for a proposed change in the rules. New, transparent, rather than black, bags would be used and people would be asked to attach their names to each bag. This set off "an uproar." The officials decided to delay implementation and to drop the necessity of names on bags. This incident highlights the problematic nature of something as basic as trash disposal in a city the size and density of Tokyo. Every day, in Tokyo, 5,000 truckloads of landfill trash, in 1993, about 9,000 tons, were hauled to landfills. Paper represents about half of the trash and half of the problem. According to Sano Shin'ichi, Japan is, in the mid-1990s, a "garbage superpower, and it's running out of dumping sites" (Sano 1994).

SOCIAL WELFARE IN JAPAN: AN AGING SOCIETY

Japan provides a comprehensive national health care program for its citizens, a program that the Japanese people seem to be generally pleased with. A poll conducted in 1995 by the Ministry of Health and Welfare showed that the overall satisfaction with the system was high. For example, 39.4 percent gave strong approval when asked if they approved of the levels of accessibility of services. Another 47.3 percent indicated moderate approval, while only 3.2 percent gave negative responses. Regarding containment of costs, a particularly large concern in Japan as in other developed nations with large and aging populations, 26 percent gave strong approval to government efforts to keep costs down and 50.4 percent gave moderate approval. Somewhat critical responses came from 5.6 percent of respondents and less than 1 percent expressed strong disapproval. Regarding the overall condition of the health care system in Japan, the same poll indicated that 48.5 percent were generally satisfied, 19.1 percent were slightly dissatisfied, and 3 percent were extremely dissatisfied (Japan Information and Culture Center 1996c, 7).

Social welfare as an issue area in Japan encompasses a complex system of providing minimum standards for all citizens in four basic areas: public assistance, social insurance, basic welfare, and public health. Current policy, as in so many other areas, is related to constitutional provisions. The 1947 Constitution provides, in Article 25, that all "shall have the right to maintain the minimum standards of wholesome and cultured living." It also states, in Section 2, that "the State shall use its endeavors for the promotion and extension of social welfare and security, and of public health." The public assistance programs are designed for those who cannot otherwise maintain themselves at a minimum level. Three-fourths of benefits under this program are provided by the national government with the remainder coming from local governments. Under the Livelihood Protection Law of 1950, recipients of public assistance must take self-help actions and those related who are required to give support under the

Civil Code must do so under a provision called supplementary care. Levels of care are determined by the consideration of many factors and is decided by the Health and Welfare Ministry in cooperation with local welfare commissioners who are appointed to three-year terms. These commissioners, who are volunteers, observe conditions and make recommendations to Health and Welfare officials regarding need. In 1991, public assistance expenditures represented only 2.4 percent of total welfare-related expenditures (JISEA 1995, 89).

Social insurance programs include public pensions, unemployment insurance, workers compensation, and the national health insurance program. All citizens are covered by the national health insurance program, as are many foreign residents. This insurance program is funded by payments from both employers and employees and also from national subsidies. Originating in 1922 in the *Taisho* climate of democratization, the health insurance law has been expanded and amended numerous times since. Today, all citizens are covered under one of six specific plans. Two examples are the employees health insurance and national health insurance programs. The latter term is often used generically to refer to the whole package of specific plans. Members in these plans pay between 10 and 30 percent of medical expenses, according to the treatment, and insurance carriers pay the remainder. Fees are determined by the Ministry of Health and Welfare. The administration of the program is very complex and involves the national government's Health and Welfare Ministry, prefectural governments, and health insurance societies formed by employers and employees at companies with over 300 employees. In 1991, health expenditures in Japan were financed 12 percent by patients, 5.1 percent by local governments, 28.5 percent by the national government, and 54.4 percent by insurance fees (JISEA 1995, 88). Many point with pride to Japan's comprehensive national health insurance program and applaud especially its freedom of choice, where members choose their health care providers and where "deductibles," or out of pocket expenses, are relatively low. Some also point to the early detection of diseases in Japan brought on by easy access to the health care system for all (Ichikawa 1994, 30, 31). Others are critical of staff shortages and the subsequent long waits and compromises on quality care. The number of physicians in Japan in 1991, per 10,000 residents, was 17.0. In the United States, the number is 21.4; in France, 31.9 (JISEA 1995, 87).

A huge problem in the entire social welfare area, but especially in health care, is the rapid "graying" of Japanese society. Japan's projected population of persons 65 years old and over for the year 2025 is 25.8 percent of the total. This compares with a projected 20.5 percent in Germany, 18.5 percent in the United States, and 12.6 percent in China (JISEA 1995, 9). One recent study projects this figure in Japan to be 27 percent and also projects that 57 percent of those aged 65 or older in the year 2025 will be aged 75 or older (Ogawa 1996, 17). This has prompted considerable discussion and planning in health-related agencies for new programs that will address care for the elderly. It has also generated substantial discussions regarding tax policies in Japan. The consumption tax, which was increased in April 1997, was a major election issue in the October 1996 general election. From its beginnings, the consumption tax has been aimed largely at financing increased health care costs.

Public pensions is another major element in the social insurance program and is also a concern given an aging society. There are two major parts to the pension plan: the Employees Pension is paid upon retirement at age 60; the National Pension is paid from age 65. Funding for both programs is from fees paid by participants per month while working. Employees Pension fees are paid half by the employee and half by the employer. About 69 million people today are covered under these plans and 96 percent of households with those aged 65 or over included in the household are currently receiving benefits. In 1993, the average household with senior(s) was receiving just over half of its total annual income from public pensions (Nakamura 1996, 48). The public pension system in Japan also provides disability and survivors' benefits. Public employees are enrolled in a separate Mutual Aid Association Pension.

Workers are protected from unemployment and compensated for injury or death on the job by legislation passed by the Diet in 1947 and by amendments to laws passed early in this century. The Employment Security Law of 1947 provides for employment safeguards, counseling for the unemployed, and assistance in job placement. Companion legislation in the same year provides for unemployment insurance paid for by both employers and employees. Workers compensation laws provide for family protection with survivors' benefits in case of death or injury designed to maintain standards equivalent to those prior to the accident. The often discussed *karoshi,* or death from overwork, is covered under the law.

Other social welfare programs provide for basic welfare funding such as aid for the handicapped, services for the elderly, and aid for fatherless families. In 1973, the Diet passed legislation providing for free medical care for all persons over the age of 70. This was modified in 1983 so that some services require payment. Legislation passed in 1963 provides low-cost or sometimes free nursing home care, free annual physicals, and local welfare centers. Welfare-related government expenditures for health care for the elderly was 11.5 percent of total expenditures for welfare in 1991 (JISEA 1995, 89). The Child Welfare Law of 1947 began a series of laws to protect children from need in all areas—financial, medical, nutritional, and emotional.

Public health is the fourth major element in Japan's social welfare policy and covers sanitation, disease prevention and treatment, and pollution control. Because of the broad nature of public health concerns, a number of agencies outside of the Health and Welfare Ministry administers programs. The Ministries of Labor and Education, for example, deal with sanitation issues, inoculations, and environmental concerns. The Environment Agency of the Prime Minister's Office is primarily responsible for pollution control. The tragedies involving unheated blood products and the spread of the O-157 *E. coli* bacillus through school lunches in 1996 drew national and international attention to public health issues in Japan.

NEW RELIGIONS

One is tempted to tie the rise of new religions in Japan to the vacuum created by the death of the *kokutai* teachings of Meiji, Taisho, and Showa in 1945. The "language" of the *kokutai* state was that of a comprehensive ideology that bound all Japanese subjects together like a large family. The "middle of the message" was that "the village," the "beautiful customs," and the "family" of Japan and the Japanese were morally superior to the institutions, ways, and customs of other nations and cultures (Gluck 1985, 250, 251). A modern state whose foundations were secured in such a mystical philosophy centering in the Imperial Family finds itself populated in the postwar period by generations increasingly alienated and lost. There are at least two major problems with such an analysis, however. First, new religions in Japan are not all that new and may be traced from the early nineteenth-century—long before Meiji, the encounter with the West, and the development of Meiji ideology; second, new religions and cults are increasingly a problem in all modern states, not least of all in the United States. In the spring of 1997, 39 members of Heaven's Gate, including the leader, committed mass suicide in San Diego. Apparent motives centered in a desire to rendezvous with a UFO following in the trail of the Hale-Bopp comet, a rendezvous that would take "travelers" to the "next level."

Within two years of each other, headlines around the world proclaimed mass murder in Japan and mass suicide in the United States, both actions undertaken by "new religions" developed within the world's two most productive economies. In both cases, believers shared visions far beyond the credible by almost any standard. Both events have left scholars in numerous fields searching for answers. One scholar, Yamaori Tetsuo of Tohoku University in Japan, sees the terrorist actions of the *Aum Shinrikyo* in Tokyo as representing the "beginning of the end of Japanese religion." By his view, such terrorist actions will only hasten a widespread suspicion of all religion within Japanese society:

> No matter how hard religious groups try to distinguish between "good" religion and "bad" religion, and no matter how vigorous a case they make for "good" religion, they will not succeed in quelling popular and media criticism. Like a dam breaking, the Aum case has suddenly released people's pent-up dissatisfaction with and suspicion of Buddhism and the other religions of Japan. The torrent of criticism and doubt is bound to swell still further. That is why I suggest that 1995 will probably be looked back upon as year one of the death of religion in Japan. (Yamaori 1995, 48, 49)

Others see the *Aum* sect as somewhat unique, though it shares many features with other new religions. Daniel Metraux, writing in *Asian Survey*, observes that *Aum Shinrikyo* is similar to other new religions that appeared in the 1970s in its appeal to the young, the better educated, and the wealthier in Japanese society (see accompanying box). This contrasts with the new religions of the 1950s and 1960s, which tended to appeal to the impoverished following

---

AUM SHINRIKYO

Aum Shinrikyo dates from 1984, when it began as a small group in Tokyo's Shibuya Ward under the leadership of Asahara Shoko (Matsumoto Chizuo). Licensed by the government as a religious corporation in 1990, it backed 25 candidates for the House of Representatives in the February national election of that year. None were even marginally successful. Membership in Japan grew over the next few years to about 10,000 in 30 branches, including ones in New York, Moscow, Bonn, and Sri Lanka. The Russian branch is estimated to have reached 30,000 members at its peak. The cult's beliefs were borrowed from a mix of Buddhism, Hinduism, Christianity, and Nostradamus. With a growing emphasis on the coming Armegeddon, members began developing communal properties in Yamanishi and Kumamoto prefectures. They also began developing weapons of potential mass destruction such as sarin gas. On March 20, 1995, members were accused by the Japanese government of carrying out a sarin gas attack in the Tokyo subway that killed 12 and injured thousands. Media in Japan referred to the trial of Matsumoto (Asahara) as Japan's "trial of the century."

---

the war. Like other movements of the 1970s, *Aum* drew those looking for meaning in life who sought escape from society. What sets *Aum* apart, however, is its violence and criminal nature. Despite these characteristics, the Tokyo Metropolitan Government, in 1989, recognized *Aum Shinrikyo* as a religious corporation.

Among the appealing features of the sect to the young, educated, and alienated were opportunities to be creative, especially in the sciences (Metraux 1995). This aspect of the whole affair has led to much soul searching in Japan regarding the nature of education, especially higher education, in Japan today. Still other observers see connections between the lure of a sect like *Aum* and the appeal of certain types of computer games. Among the features of the *Aum* sect was the belief in a coming war between the West and Buddhist Asian nations, a belief rooted in traditional Buddhist teachings regarding the last days and as reinforced by elements in Christian millenialism. Simplistic battle scenarios between the forces of good and the forces of evil in high-tech combat are also commonplace features in computer games popular in Japan and the United States. By pushing buttons, one can literally "play God": "The computer game *Simulation Earth,* which is especially popular among youth, offers the player the chance to be God. In the game, the player (programmer) is the Creator, who solves with the push of a button such global problems as the population explosion and environmental pollution" (Kitabatake 1995, 378). In March 1995, members of the *Aum* sect were accused of just such simplistic reasoning in their actions in the Tokyo subway.

But scholars such as Helen Hardacre would caution against too quickly associating the *Aum* sect or its actions with the larger phenomenon of new religions in Japan. She observes that new religions in Japan today "represent an important and distinctive sector of Japanese society" whose members "share a unity of aspiration and world view significantly different from those of secular society and from the so-called established religions." These groups are among the "most vital" sectors in modern Japanese society and include "perhaps 30 percent of the nation's population" (Hardacre 1986, 3). Byron Earhart would issue a similar caution based on his examination of *gedatsu-kai*. Many of the new religions and much of the belief structure within them are motivated less by adapting to or escaping from a high-tech, mass culture, than by a desire to return to a lost "center" in traditional teachings (Earhart 1989).

SCIENCE AND TECHNOLOGY FUNDING

The Japanese government has recently embarked on an ambitious plan to increase science and technology funding by 50 percent, at a time when many governments worldwide are cutting similar funding. In July 1996, the cabinet approved a Science and Technology Basic Plan that includes a five-year strategy for improving basic research and development at Japan's universities and research institutes. Total projected spending is $157 billion. A major focal point in the proposed program is on environmental research. Other major areas targeted for large funding increases are health promotion, disease prevention, nuclear safety, and issues related to population growth. Specific projects include a tenfold increase in funding for brain research, construction of a nuclear magnetic resonance center for analyzing protein molecular structure, research and development funds for studies regarding the next generation of supersonic aircraft, continued funding for the International Space Station project, fellowships for 2,000 foreign researchers to study in Japan, and more funding for computers in the classroom with the target of one for every two students in public school classrooms by the year 2000. Among controversial aspects of the plan, and which reflect changes in Japanese approaches to the "workplace," is the introduction of term contracts for government researchers to replace lifetime employment (Japan Information and Culture Center 1996b, 4, 5).

The government agency that oversees research and development in the sciences is the Science and Technology Agency. The director-general of the cabinet-level agency in the Hashimoto cabinet is Nakagawa Hidenao, a Liberal Democratic Party member of the House of Representatives. Nakagawa was formerly a vice minister of International Trade and Industry. In his remarks to the National Academy of Science in Washington, D.C., in the summer of 1996, Nakagawa seized a political opportunity. The Science and Technology Basic Plan would provide a "new direction" wherein the Japanese government could break through the "walls of ministries and agencies" and also of "existing industrial, academic and governmental organizations," and all under "political leadership." The basic plan represents a dramatic new beginning: "This may well became an important precedent for Japan in working out the new relationship between politicians and the administration" (Japan Information and Culture Center 1996b, 4, 5). Clearly designed as a harbinger of the new Japanese state where elected representatives seize the initiative in policy formation, the basic plan was unveiled after the regular session of the Diet had adjourned on June 19, and in anticipation of a fall election. The election was later called for October. Another feature of the plan is the expansion of joint efforts with the United States and other foreign governments.

In high technology development, two projects gaining support within government planning agencies are floating, offshore airports, and maglev, or superbullet, trains. The floating airports would float on megafloats, massive buoyant platforms, located offshore. The Airport Council supported construction of such airports in its 1996 midyear report projecting plans to the year 2000. First recommendation was to study the feasibility of such an airport as a third airport to supplement Narita, outside of Tokyo, and Haneda, in Tokyo. Among reasons offered in defense of such designs were resistance to earthquakes, fast construction, a minimal environmental impact, and cost-effectiveness. Traditional large airport construction also continues. (See box on Kansai International Airport.) The Ministry of Transport has already approved a research consortium of 17 steel and shipbuilding companies whose plans include feasibility studies of constructing the floating air facilities. An experimental platform consisting of four steel structures 100 meters long and 20 meters wide was scheduled for construction and flotation in the summer of 1996.

The maglev (magnetic levitation) train prototype is scheduled for test runs on a special track in Yamanishi Prefecture in the spring of 1997. Anticipated speed is a maximum 342 miles per hour. The train is designed to "float" above a concrete guideway and move using superconducting electromagnets. The test line, under construction in 1996, is 42.8 kilometers long and, upon completion of testing and approval for service, will become part of a permanent line connecting Tokyo with Osaka. The trains will be automatic with no drivers. The trains will rest on the concrete surfaces on rubber tires, like airplanes, and begin

---

KANSAI INTERNATIONAL AIRPORT

Under construction since 1987, Kansai International Airport, on a 1,300-acre artificial island in Osaka Bay, opened in September 1994. Designed by the Italian architect Renzo Piano, the airport took $14 billion to construct and today charges among the highest landing, concession, and exit fees in the world. Among the design features of the new airport are concourses, gates, and terminals all under one roof and a four-story main building that handles domestic flights on the two middle floors and international flights on the top (departures) and bottom (arrivals) floors. There are 27 restaurants and 48 shops in the airport terminal. Express trains run from the island airport's terminal to Osaka, and a hydrofoil connects the terminal to Kobe. The airport is Japan's first 24-hour airport. Three million passengers a year are expected to pass through the airport at full capacity. Among the expectations of the airport is that it will contribute toward decentralizing transportation and commercial traffic out of the Tokyo area and link the Osaka area, an area of 20 million people, with other major Japanese and East Asian hubs.

their runs on the tires. At approximately 100 kilometers per hour, however, they will rise from the guideways to about 10 centimeters and accelerate to maximum speeds (Japan Information and Culture Center 1996a, 6).

In recent years Japan has also increased development of its space program in ways that do not often grab international headlines but are nonetheless substantial. In 1969, the National Space Development Agency was created. Over the years since, the space agency has worked with the U.S. National Aeronautics and Space Administration on numerous projects. Three Japanese astronauts have flown on Shuttle missions: Mohri Mamoru, Mukai Chiaki, and Wakata Koichi. Dr. Mohri was the first Japanese astronaut in space, Dr. Mukai was the first Japanese woman astronaut in space, and Wakata Koichi was the first mission specialist from Japan in space. Japan is also one of 18 countries participating in the construction of the International Space Station, along with the United States, Canada, Russia, and 14 European nation-states. Japan will contribute 10 percent of the astronauts who serve on the space station when operational. Japan's first satellite was made in and launched by the United States in the mid-1970s. As of February 1996, Japan "ha[d] conducted more than 40 successful launches and orbited more than 40 satellites" (Miyake 1996).

A NEW CAPITAL?

For years there have been numerous plans and advocacy groups promoting the moving of the national capital outside of an increasingly congested Tokyo. In 1992, a poll showed that support for such a move was 58.2 percent with 15.2 percent opposed. Another poll taken two years later showed an increase of support to 73.5 percent and also an increase in opposition to 20.1 percent. A survey of 664 mayors by the Nikkei Institute for Industry and Consumption showed 87 percent in favor of a move. The Prime Minister's Office has released figures based on public correspondence to local government offices showing widespread support for a move ranging from 100 percent support in Hokkaido to 65 percent support in Kyushu and Okinawa. Tokyo has only been the capital since the Meiji Restoration in 1868. Reasons cited for the move are concentration of population, 33 million in the greater Tokyo area and 11 million within the city limits; vulnerability to earthquakes—all remember the great Kanto earthquake of 1923; and political reform. The Commission on Moving the Capital said with respect to the last point that moving the capital would essentially break up the traditionally cozy relationships among government, industry, and politics in Japan.

In 1992, the Diet passed a law creating the Commission on Moving the Capital to draw up designs, processes, and criteria for selecting a site. The commission reported to the prime minister in early summer 1996. Among its recommendations were that the new capital should be dedicated to politics, exclusive of other concerns, especially economic ones; it should have a population of approximately 600,000 persons; it should be accessible by bullet train from

Tokyo within two hours, meaning no more than 300 kilometers away; it must be within 40 minutes' access time to an international airport; be located on land that is earthquake and drought resistant; and be immune to existing urban sprawl. Suggested timetable by the commission is a decision by the Diet on a site within two years—from recommendations of a neutral body of specialists in urban planning; construction to begin in the year 2000; and first Diet session in the new capital for the year 2010. When Prime Minister Hashimoto took office he announced support for moving the capital, along with administrative reform, deregulation, and decentralization of authority. Given the guidelines developed by the commission, strong candidates for the new capital, if it is ultimately approved, are locations in Aichi, Gifu, Fukushima, Tochigi, or Shizuoka prefectures (Hashiyama 1996, 14, 15).

Summary

Among the most important of the traditional and continuing issues in Japan is education. Because the educational process concerns itself with the most basic aspects of culture and socialization, it presents some of the most difficult challenges facing the modern Japanese state. Among basic features in this process are a concentration on the development of language skills in the early grades and a concentration on passing competitive exams for placement both in high schools and colleges and universities in the later grades. The second focus has driven the expansion of *juku*, or after-school schools, in recent years. The competitive exams issue is the focus of most attention outside of Japan and is increasingly the focus within Japan. Teachers in Japan, *sensei*, are generally held in higher regard than in other industrialized nation-states. They also work longer hours and are more involved in the lives of their students outside the classroom. Japanese schools are noted internationally for their standards, the performance and discipline of their students, and high graduation rates. They are also noted for their promotion of rote learning, an "examination hell" system, and problems with bullying (*ijime*). Among recent reform efforts is the creation of "comprehensive" high schools that encourage more choice and independent thought among students. In higher education, there is a strict ranking among institutions based on prestige, with Tokyo University at the top and national public universities generally rated higher than private ones. Recent government efforts have focused on increasing the number of foreign exchange students in Japanese colleges and universities, a goal that has been only partially met.

The criminal justice issue in Japan, like the education issue, draws much attention internationally. Japan is famous for low crime rates and efficient enforcement. Recent high-profile crimes such as those for which leaders in *Aum Shinrikyo* are being prosecuted stand out as highly unusual. Policing in Japan is national. An institution drawing much attention is the *koban* or police box. *Kobans* are famous for offering assistance as well as protection and are increasingly being copied overseas. Japanese policing methods have also come under critical review in recent years, however, for practices such as long pretrial detentions.

The scope of state activities with respect to the economy is a major topic of discussion among scholars outside of Japan. Many revisionist studies of Japan in recent years have focused on the large role of the state, specifically the Ministry of International Trade and Industry and the Ministry of Finance, in industrial development. Much discussion within Japan today centers on deregulation across the wide economic spectrum and includes numerous administrative agencies and thousands of regulations. The *jusen* crisis in particular has accelerated concerns regarding the entire role of the national government in economic planning and development. Monetary policy in recent years has addressed the problems caused by a rising yen. Fiscal policy has largely centered on slowing the national debt, funding the rising costs associated with the health and welfare needs of an aging society, and public works spending.

One of the most controversial issues in Japan today is the future of nuclear power as an energy source. Critics, mindful of earlier tragedies such as that at Minamata in the 1950s and 1960s, warn against what they consider high risk projects, such as the Monju fast breeder reactor in Fukui Prefecture. Among the most complex issues is the further funding of Japan's extensive social welfare system. A similarly complex issue is the recent rise of new religions and the appropriate regulatory role of the state, an issue dramatized by the actions of *Aum Shinrikyo* and the inactions of the national, regional, and metropolitan governments. Higher levels of funding for science and technology have had widespread support in recent Diet sessions, and there is much discussion of moving the national capital out of Tokyo.

Suggested Readings

Calder, Kent E. 1988. *Crisis and Compensation: Public Policy and Political Stability in Japan, 1949–1986.* Princeton, NJ: Princeton University Press.

Doi Takeo. 1973. *The Anatomy of Dependence.* Trans. John Bester. Tokyo: Kodansha International.

Earhart, H. Byron. 1989. *Gedatsu-kai and Religion in Contemporary Japan: Returning to the Center.* Bloomington: Indiana University Press.

Friedman, David. 1988. *The Misunderstood Miracle: Industrial Development and Political Change in Japan.* Ithaca, NY: Cornell University Press.

Hardacre, Helen. 1986. *Kurozumikyo and the New Religions of Japan.* Princeton, NJ: Princeton University Press.

Lewis, Catherine C. 1995. *Educating Hearts and Minds: Reflections on Japanese Preschool and Elementary Education.* Cambridge: Cambridge University Press.

Marshall, Byron K. 1995. *Learning to Be Modern: Japanese Political Discourse on Education.* Boulder, CO: Westview Press.

Miyazawa Setsuo. 1992. *Policing in Japan: A Study on Making Crime.* Trans. Frank G. Bennett, Jr. with John O. Haley. Albany: State University of New York Press.

Nakane Chie. 1970. *Japanese Society.* Berkeley: University of California Press.

Pempel, T. J. 1982. *Policy and Politics in Japan: Creative Conservatism.* Philadelphia: Temple University Press.

Samuels, Richard J. 1987. *The Business of the Japanese State: Energy Markets in Comparative and Historical Perspective.* Ithaca, NY: Cornell University Press.

Tilton, Mark. 1996. *Restrained Trade: Cartels in Japan's Basic Materials Industries.* Ithaca, NY: Cornell University Press.

White, Merry I. 1987. *The Japanese Educational Challenge: A Commitment to Children.* New York: Free Press.

Works Cited

Bayley, David H. 1976. *Forces of Order: Police Behavior in Japan and the United States.* Berkeley: University of California Press.

Dore, R. P. 1973. Textbook Censorship in Japan: The Ienaga Case. In *Postwar Japan: 1945 to the Present,* ed. Jon Livingston, Joe Moore, and Felicia Oldfather, 538–545. New York: Pantheon.

Earhart, H. Byron. 1989. *Gedatsu-kai and Religion in Contemporary Japan: Returning to the Center.* Bloomington: Indiana University Press.

Ebitsubo Isamu, and Tokuji Nakamura. 1995a. Chronology. *Japan Quarterly* 42 (April–June): 237–239.

———. 1995b. Chronology. *Japan Quarterly* 42 (July–September): 358–369.

———. 1996. Chronology. *Japan Quarterly* 43 (April–June): 232–240.

Fallows, James. 1991. Strengths, Weaknesses, and Lessons of Japanese Education. *Education Digest* 57 (October): 55–59.

Friedman, David. 1988. *The Misunderstood Miracle: Industrial Development and Political Change in Japan.* Ithaca, NY: Cornell University Press.

Gerbert, Elaine. 1993. Lessons from the Kokugo (National Language) Readers. *Comparative Education Review* 37 (May): 152–180.

Gluck, Carol. 1985. *Japan's Modern Myths: Ideology in the Late Meiji Period.* Princeton, NJ: Princeton University Press.

Hamada Koichi. 1995. Proposals for the Ailing Japanese Economy. *Japan Echo* 22 (Winter): 36–42.

Hamilton, V. Lee, and Joseph Sanders. 1992. *Everyday Justice: Responsibility and the Individual in Japan and the United States.* New Haven, CT: Yale University Press.

Hardacre, Helen. 1986. *Kurozumikyo and the New Religions of Japan.* Princeton, NJ: Princeton University Press.

Hashiyama Reijiro. 1996. Whither the New Capital? *Look Japan* 42 (June): 14, 15.

Hayashi Akira. 1995. The Safety of Sea Transport for Radioactive Materials. *Japan Echo* 22 (Winter): 68–75.

Ichikawa Heizaburo. 1994. Choosing Priorities in the Health-Care System. *Economic Eye,* 15 (Summer): 30–32.

Iikubo Ryuko. 1996. Rates of Exchange. *Look Japan* 42 (September): 9–11.

Jansen, Marius B. 1973. Education, Values, and Politics in Japan. In *Postwar Japan: 1945 to the Present*, ed. Jon Livingston, Joe Moore, and Felicia Oldfather, 532–537. New York: Pantheon.

Japan External Trade Organization (JETRO). 1991. *U.S. and Japan in Figures.* Tokyo.

Japan Information and Culture Center. 1996a. Science Watch. *Japan Now* 4 (April): 6.

———. 1996b. An Ambitious Science and Technology Plan. *Japan Now* 9 (September): 4, 5.

———. 1996c. Most Japanese Are Happy with Their Health Care. *Japan Now* 2 (February): 7.

Japan Institute for Social and Economic Affairs (JISEA). 1995. *Japan, 1995: An International Comparison.* Tokyo.

Johnson, Chalmers. 1982. *MITI and the Japanese Miracle.* Stanford, CA: Stanford University Press.

Katsukata Shin'ichi. 1996. The Class of 96: Education Today. *Look Japan* 42 (September): 4–8.

Kempner, Ken, and Misao Makino. 1993. Cultural Influences on the Construction of Knowledge in Japanese Higher Education. *Comparative Education* 29 (no. 2): 185–199.

Kitabatake Kiyoyasu. 1995. Aum Shinrikyo: Society Begets an Aberration. *Japan Quarterly* 42 (October): 376–383.

Kogure Fumiaki. 1995. What Nobody Dares to Say About the Banking Crisis. *Japan Echo* 22 (Winter): 43–47.

Kumao Kaneko. 1996. A Call for Cooler Heads. *Look Japan* 42 (July): 3.

Ladd, Everett C. 1995. Japan and America: Two Different Nations Draw Closer. *The Public Perspective: A Roper Center Review of Public Opinion and Polling* 6 (no. 5): 18–36.

Lincoln, Edward J. 1992. The Showa Economic Experience. In *Showa, The Japan of Hirohito*, ed. Carol Gluck and Stephen R. Graubard, 191–208. New York: Norton.

McKean, Margaret A. 1981. *Environmental Protest and Citizen Politics in Japan.* Berkeley: University of California Press.

Metraux, Daniel A. 1995. Religious Terrorism in Japan: The Fatal Appeal of Aum Shinrikyo. *Asian Survey* 35 (December): 1140–1154.

Miyake Masazumi. 1996. Viewpoint. *Japan Now* 2 (February): 5.

Miyazawa Setsuo. 1992. *Policing in Japan: A Study on Making Crime.* Trans. Frank G. Bennett, Jr., with John O. Haley. Albany: State University of New York Press.

Nakamura Shuichi. 1996. Public Pensions for an Aging Population. *Japan Echo* 23 (Special Issue): 48–53.

Oe Kenzaburo. 1992. Speaking on Japanese Culture Before a Scandinavian Audience. In *Japan, the Ambiguous, and Myself: The Nobel Prize Speech and Other Lectures*, 7–38. Tokyo: Kodansha International.

Ogawa Naohiro. 1996. When the Baby Boomers Grow Old. *Japan Echo* 23 (Special Issue): 17–21.

Patrick, Hugh. 1977. The Future of the Japanese Economy: Output and Labor Productivity. *Journal of Japanese Studies* 3 (Summer): 219–249.

Pempel, T. J. 1982. *Policy and Politics in Japan: Creative Conservatism.* Philadelphia: Temple University Press.

Reed, Steven R. 1986. *Japanese Prefectures and Policymaking.* Pittsburgh: University of Pittsburgh Press.

Reischauer, Edwin O., and Marius B. Jansen. 1995. *The Japanese Today: Change and Continuity.* Cambridge, MA: Belknap Press of Harvard University Press.

Sano Shin'ichi. 1994. Japan: The Garbage Superpower. *Japan Echo* 21 (Spring): 86–92.

Sato, Nancy, and Milbrey W. McLaughlin. 1992. Context Matters: Teaching in Japan and the United States. *Phi Delta Kappan* 73 (January): 359–366.

Shimizu Kokichi. 1992. Shido: Education and Selection in a Japanese Middle School. *Comparative Education* 28 (no. 2): 109–129.

Slow Justice. 1996. *Economist,* 25 May, 43.

Smith, T. C. 1973. Japan's Aristocratic Revolution. In *Imperial Japan: 1800–1945,* ed. Jon Livingston, Joe Moore, and Felicia Oldfather, 91–101. New York: Pantheon.

Stevenson, David Lee, and David P. Baker. 1992. Shadow Education and Allocation in Formal Schooling: Transition to University in Japan. *American Journal of Sociology* 97 (May): 1639–1657.

Teranishi Shun'ichi. 1992. The Lessons of Japan's Battle with Pollution. *Japan Quarterly* 39 (July): 321–327.

van Wolferen, Karel. 1989. *The Enigma of Japanese Power: People and Politics in a Stateless Nation.* New York: Knopf.

White, Merry. 1993. *The Material Child: Coming of Age in Japan and America.* New York: Free Press.

White, Merry, and Robert A. Levine. 1986. What Is an *Ii Ko* (Good Child)? In *Child Development and Education in Japan,* ed. Harold Stevenson, Hiroshi Azuma, and Kenji Hakuta, 55–62. New York: W. H. Freeman.

Yamaguchi Kazuo. 1983. Early Modern Economy (1868–1945). In *Kodansha Encyclopedia of Japan,* vol. 2, 151–154.

Yamaori Tetsuo. 1995. Aum Shinrikyo Sounds the Death Knell of Japanese Religion. *Japan Echo* 22 (Autumn): 48–53.

6

Subjects, Citizens, Outsiders

The preface to the Japanese Constitution of 1947 clearly states that "sovereign power resides with the people." Chapter 3 details the "Rights and Duties of the People." Article 14 of Chapter 3 states that all of the people "are equal under the law and there shall be no discrimination in political, economic or social relations because of race, creed, sex, social status or family origin." These are but representative sections in the fundamental law of Japan to illustrate the basic sovereignty of the people and of equal standing before the law. The spirit and letter of the Japanese constitution are firmly embedded in the mainstream of modern democratic theory. Japan's first constitution, the *Meiji Constitution* of 1889, was the product of a very different tradition, however, as discussed in Chapter 2. Scholarly critics, beginning with the promulgation of the 1947 Constitution, have regularly questioned whether and to what extent the postwar constitution really changes the fundamental assumptions that shape day-to-day decisions and attitudes in the modern Japanese state. Some argue that Japanese traditions are so unlike those that have nurtured Western institutions that one may question whether Japan is really governed by *"rule of law"* and "popular sovereignty" in the same sense that modern Western democratic states are governed. One scholar, Tamamoto Masaru, has written of Japan's "ideology of nothingness" (1994, 89–99).

Relations of individual members within states is a fundamental, perennial issue of politics. How are members related to each other and how are the many related to the relative few who actually govern? How are the governors selected? How are they limited by law and how long do they serve? What are the rules governing suffrage; who is eligible for "higher" office; and how are state offices conceptualized—that is, how do they relate to other offices and to the larger, constitutional design? These questions are all linked to the larger issues of defining membership and relationship within the state. Fundamentally, these questions are philosophical and their resolutions are based on the philosophical assumptions of those responsible for laying the foundations and designing the basic institutions of the state. In Japan, the Meiji Constitution of 1889 was designed and implemented by *samurai* leaders from *Satsuma* and *Choshu*—the *Satcho* clique—drawing on a mixture of philosophical and mythic traditions indigenous to Japan, borrowed from China, and as modified by Western European sources, especially German sources. The 1947 Constitution, on the other hand, was written by Americans on General Douglas MacArthur's staff in the early months of the U.S. occupation after the war. The center of gravity in the Meiji Constitution was the Emperor and his relationship with his subjects. The center of the present constitution is the people of Japan in their capacity as citizens. The high drama of Japanese politics in the last hundred years is the evolution of the Japanese subject to today's Japanese citizen.

And yet, in practice, the evolution of the modern Japanese state is nowhere near as neat as the above suggests. In Japanese tradition, the Emperor always reigned, but never ruled. The Shogunate represented military rule in practice. The *Meiji* "restoration" was little more than moving the Emperor to a new, eastern capital (Tokyo) as a legitimizing symbol for the actions of the lower *samurai* of the *Satcho* clique, someone in whose name they could act to bring Japan into the modern world with a strong economy and a stronger army. The Meiji Constitution, then, became a similar symbol for modern parliamentary, democratic governance, or movement in that direction.

JAPANESE SUBJECTS UNDER THE MEIJI CONSTITUTION

The Imperial Rescript accompanying the Meiji Constitution states that the new fundamental law of Japan is a product of "Imperial Ancestors" and for the sake of their "subjects" and "descendants"

> Whereas We make it the joy and glory of Our heart to behold the prosperity of Our country, and the welfare of Our subjects, We do hereby, in virtue of the supreme power We inherit from Our Imperial Ancestors, promulgate the present immutable fundamental law, for the sake of Our present subjects and their descendants.

The second chapter of this "fundamental law" lists the "rights and duties" of "subjects." By contrast, the third chapter of the 1947 Constitution provides for the "rights and duties" of "the people." This shift in conceptualization in Japan's two national constitutions focuses the dramatic change from Imperial to popular sovereignty that occurred between the late nineteenth and mid-twentieth centuries. And though democratic processes and tendencies were nurtured during the *Meiji*, *Taisho*, and *Showa* eras, the Japanese people remained subjects within the Japanese state until the post–World War II era. The Meiji Constitution listed a number of rights, such as that of being appointed to office (Article 19), of the "liberty of abode" (Article 22), of the "right of property" (Article 27), of the "freedom of religious belief" (Article 28), of the "liberty of speech, writing, publication" (Article 29), among many others. But each of these articles, and others pertaining to the rights of Japanese subjects, included qualifying phrases such as "within the limits of the law," or as "determined by law," or "unless according to law." And the sovereign power of determining the law rested constitutionally with the Imperial throne and, practically, in the *genro* acting in the name of the Emperor.

Japanese subjects under the Meiji Constitution organized in parties, agitated for change, and voted in national and local elections. But the limits of the law were wide such that, for example, women neither voted nor held office, men without substantial property holdings neither voted nor held office, and legislation limiting speech and press in the interest of "peace preservation" was not uncommon. For example, just prior to the promulgation of the constitution, a "peace preservation" law was enacted by Imperial decree in 1887. Under this ordinance anyone named by the city of Tokyo police as disturbing public order could be expelled from the city. Within days of the ordinance's announcement, over 500 activists in the *Freedom and People's Rights Movement* were expelled from the capital city. The law was repealed in 1898 only to be replaced by the Public Order and Police Law two years later. This law restricted speech, assembly, and association and was aimed at labor organizers in particular. It also prohibited women from taking part in any political meetings or joining any organizations.

The most famous of these "limiting" laws was the *Peace Preservation Law* of 1925. As in most other parts of the world in the 1920s, political differences in Japan often took the form of ideological differences. Comprehensive, world historic visions such as those represented by various Marxist organizations moved to center political stage. Japan's Peace Preservation Law of 1925 was designed primarily to control the activities of communists and anarchists. In practice, it was used to control virtually all dissent. What sets this law apart in particular is its specific reference to the *kokutai* philosophy of the Imperial state as what is in need of "preserving." Anyone who attempted even to "alter" this state ideology would be punished under this law. Among the first to be prosecuted under the law were student leftists in support of Marxist-Leninist ideas. Soon after the law went into effect, the Justice Ministry created a "thought section" to investigate "thought criminals." These were but the initial actions in a process that would soon lead to mass arrests. In 1928, for example, about 1,600 suspected communists were arrested. Soon after, several other organizations were banned outright, such as the Labor-Farmer Party. In addition, the Peace Preservation Law was amended to include the death penalty for the most serious violations.

All of these strong-hand tactics coincided, ironically, with the first national election under the universal manhood suffrage law that was established in the same year as the Peace Preservation Law. The high water mark in the development of Taisho democracy, universal manhood suffrage, coincided with the appearance of legislation that would be used to club democracy itself into submission. Following the mass arrests of communists, a special section to watch for radical students was created in the Ministry of Education. Rooting out "thought crime" became a major emphasis in the Justice Ministry. Because of the ever growing number of "criminals" and suspects, a policy of conversion or "changing minds" came to replace the policy of punishing offenders. This *tenko* policy was begun after the high-profile "conversion" of two formerly high officials of the Japan Communist Party, Sano Manabu and Nabeyama Sadachika, announced their conversion to the *kokutai* philosophy from prison. This set in motion many other conversions and the new government policy. This happened in 1933, two years after the Japanese army first entered Manchuria, one year after the establishment of *Manchukuo,* and one year after the assassination of Prime Minister *Inukai Tsuyoshi* in the May 15th incident of 1932. The latter was prompted by Inukai's attempts to control the military. The May 15th incident was an attempted coup by naval officers in reaction to the limitations placed on the navy by terms of the *London Naval Treaty* of 1930. All of these events foreshadowed the rise to power of the military, a rise made easier by previous state actions like the Peace Preservation Law that severely limited dissent and organized political action.

All was not state suppression and subsequent military rule, however. Many gains were made by Japanese subjects in the direction of establishing popular participation, if not popular sovereignty. In the first Diet election, noted in Chapter 3, only male adults 25 years of age who paid 15 yen or more annually in taxes were eligible to vote. This meant that only about 1 percent of the population could participate in the suffrage. Beginning in 1897 and moving through stages over the next 25 years, organizations such as the Universal Suffrage League fought for enactment of a universal male suffrage bill. These efforts were often frustrated by incidents that provoked strong government responses to any popular movements. For example, in 1910, a plot to assassinate the Meiji Emperor was exposed and the following year 12 convicted conspirators were executed. Another 12, originally sentenced to death, had their sentences commuted to life in prison. In 1918, rice riots throughout the countryside with an estimated 2 million people rioting in 38 cities over sudden rises in rice prices caused the fall of the Terauchi cabinet. The result was the *Hara Takashi* cabinet, the first party cabinet in Japanese history. But events such as these, which dramatized the potential instability of too much Western-style democratization, had a cooling effect on efforts to widen the suffrage. Still, and in the face of concurrent passage of the Peace Preservation Law, universal manhood suffrage became law in 1925.

Despite these gains in the direction of popular sovereignty, however, the ascendancy of the military in the 1930s culminated in the creation of the *Imperial Rule Assistance Association (IRAA)* in 1940 and the virtual elimination of political parties by 1942. The IRAA was established in October 1940 to provide for a new political order in which all assisted in the *kokutai* idea of true Imperial rule. In concert with the Home Ministry, the IRAA proved an effective organization through which to coordinate the war effort. The visions of those within the Freedom and People's Rights Movement of the early Meiji Period, of the Universal Suffrage League at the turn of the century, and of the party activists during Taisho democracy had all but disappeared in the military's vision of a *kokutai* state centered on the Emperor in which Japanese subjects merely "assisted."

ELECTORAL REFORM: THE GIFT OF THE POLITICIANS

Among the most dramatic changes regarding citizenship in Japan in the postwar era may well be the election reform legislation that passed the Diet in 1994. Because of various scandals during the 1980s and into the 1990s, mostly involving money politics (*kinken seiji*), electoral reform increasingly became a top political issue in Japan. With the scandals surrounding **Kanemaru Shin**, calls for reform intensified in 1992. With the formation of the **Hosokawa** cabinet in 1993, reform became a top priority. Beginning in January 1994, the House of Representatives began passing several major reform bills, completely overhauling the electoral process in Japan. Though doubts have been expressed in many circles of late as to just how permanent these changes will prove to be they continue to enjoy wide popular support.

The reforms begin by redrawing all of the districts for the House of Representatives. From the original 511 representatives elected from 129 multimember districts, Japan is newly divided into 300 single-member districts and 11 regional districts from which 200 party representatives are chosen according to proportional representation. The idea behind single-member districts is to encourage the development of a two-party system somewhat along the lines established in traditional American politics. Under the old system, from two to six members of the House of Representatives were elected from each of the 129 districts, the particular number of representatives depending on the population of the district. One result that developed in practice was the traditional competition of two or three LDP candidates against each other with the opposition parties usually content to win one seat from a reliable constituency within the district. With the only real competition that between LDP candidates, a lot of money was raised and spent and a lot of promises for public moneys to the district were made. Issue differences between candidates of the same party were always kept to a minimum. Two results of this system were money politics and issueless campaigns. The reforms are intended to diminish the need for exorbitant campaign expenditures and to encourage issue debates between and among the candidates and the parties. Smaller campaign budgets are expected to result from the smaller size of the single-member districts and the reduction of campaign time from 14 to 12 days. Head-to-head competition for single seats between and among candidates from rival parties is also expected to encourage policy debates.

Early indications in the fall of 1996, interestingly, suggested rather the development of three parties on the eve of the first national election under the new law. The LDP and the New Frontier parties represent somewhat conservative parties led by Hashimoto and Ozawa. The new *Minshuto*, or Democratic Party, represents former Social Democrats, *Sakigake*, and others on the left desirous of offering alternatives to the parties on the right. In the regional districts, the principle of proportional representation will continue as will the principle of multimember districts. Regional representation will vary from 7 representatives in the **Shikoku** district to 33 from the Kinki region (the Osaka, Kyoto, Kobe, and

Nara areas). In elections, voters will cast two ballots. One vote is for a single individual and the other is a party vote. The individual vote is for representation from the single-member district. The party vote is to determine representation from the regional district. Regional representatives from the 11 regions will be determined according to the percentage of the vote each party gets. For example, in the Kinki region, 33 percent of the vote for a particular party would translate into 11 representatives from that party's list of candidates. Candidate lists, ranked from top to bottom, are developed by each party based on very detailed rules. For example, to win any seats in the regional districts, a party must win at least 3 percent of the national vote.

Among the complicating features of the new election law is the provision that candidates may run concurrently for a single seat and a regional one. That is, a candidate may seek the votes of citizens for a single-member district seat and at the same time be listed on his or her party's proportional representation list for the region encompassing the single-member district. If that candidate wins the single-member seat, his or her name is removed from the regional party list. The effect of this would be to move someone else on the regional list up a spot in the "hierarchy." On the other hand, if a candidate running for a single-member district seat is defeated, he or she might still be elected from the party list for the region. In the October 20, 1996 national House election, the first under the new system, 84 candidates who lost in the single-member district races were nonetheless elected to the House due to being also on party lists in the regional vote. Of the 1,503 candidates running for the 500 House seats in that election, 566 ran both as single-member candidates and as regional candidates. Another controversial aspect of the new law is the provision that names for single-member district representation are not printed on the ballot. Rather, they must be written in. Party names for proportional representation in the regions must also be written in. This continues the traditional practice in Japanese elections to the House of Representatives. In the original version of the reform law, this was changed to require names of candidates to be printed on ballots. But in December 1995, House members allied with the LDP, the Social Democrats, and the New Party Harbinger—the ruling coalition, in short—voted to return to the older method. This was done to place parties that traditionally recruit voters with lesser educational backgrounds, voters traditionally aligned with the *Komei* and Communist parties, for example, at a disadvantage (Christensen 1996, 55).

Still another feature of the election reform legislation is campaign finance reform. The new rules call for national subsidies for the parties, restrictions on individual candidates' fund raising, the phasing out of corporate contributions to individuals after five years, limits on contributions either from individuals or corporations, and threshold levels for parties as a condition for receiving funds.

According to one study of the reform legislation, the following are all among the possible effects: the elimination of smaller parties, the mitigation of problems associated with traditional money politics, more women elected to the House of Representatives from the new regions, more issue-oriented campaigns for House seats, a shrinking role for bureaucrats in the making of public policy, and, ultimately, a more democratic Japan (Christensen 1996, 49–70). Indications following the first election under the new law confirm much of this, though not all. For example, smaller parties did in fact fare poorly in the single-member district races. The Japan Communist Party only won 2 single-member seats, the Social Democrats only 4, the Sakigake 2, and the new *Minshuto* only 17 of its total of 52. Each party did substantially better in the proportional vote, as expected. The Communist Party won an unexpected 24 regional seats in the proportional voting to bring its total to 26. Similarly, the SDPJ won 11 regional seats, and the *Minshuto* won 35 of its 52 seats in the proportional voting. Unexpected outcomes included the poor showing of women candidates, only 23 of the 500 seats being won by women candidates, and less issue debate than had been hoped for.

As the Meiji Constitution was a gift of the Emperor, and the 1947 Constitution was a gift, realistically, of the Supreme Command of the Allied Powers (*SCAP*), one might look on the political reforms initiated by the Hosokawa cabinet in 1994 as a gift of the politicians. As a comprehensive reorganization of the electoral map and electoral process, it represents a potentially dramatic new beginning in the development of true popular sovereignty in Japan. Much will depend on how effective the new laws regulating campaign financing work, how effectively the single-member district design generates issue politics, and how an increasingly cynical Japanese electorate embraces the reforms—that is, will they turn out in large numbers to vote? Gauging by the election in October 1996, the answer to the last question is no. The turnout was a disappointing 59 percent, a record low under the present constitution for a House election. One study of the election pointed out that in 35 of the 300 single-member districts, the victorious candidate won by less than 1 percent of the vote. In another 70 races, the winning margin was less than 2 percent. In 23 of the Liberal Democratic Party victories, the difference with the New Frontier Party candidate was less than 2 percent (Yoshida 1996, 25–31). Gauging by postelection polls, the Japanese electorate is generally unhappy with the whole reform system. A postelection poll by the *Asahi* newspaper, as reported in the *Asahi e News* (23 October, 1996), found that 60 percent of eligible voters were unhappy with the new electoral system. More specifically, 70 percent were against the new dual candidacy system where a candidate can run both in the single-member balloting and concurrently in the regional proportional balloting. Only 19 percent in the poll said that the new electoral system should remain as designed.

CITIZENS TODAY: ATTITUDES, LIFESTYLES, WORK PATTERNS

Polls in Japan suggest that Japanese citizens are generally content with their overall conditions, if not with the election system. Every year since 1969, the Prime Minister's Office has conducted a poll on social attitudes in Japan. In May 1995, 73 percent of Japanese residents, a "record high," said they were "happy with their current living conditions." Similarly, those experiencing dissatisfaction with their lifestyles were a record low of 24.6 percent. Other responses in the survey indicated that residents wanted more government involvement in medical, welfare, and pension programs, with 54.8 percent identifying these concerns first when asked where government should do more. Large numbers also supported more government involvement in developing measures to counter the recession (46.2 percent), in developing programs for the elderly (44.3 percent), and in doing more to prevent crime (26.4 percent). Those saying that the government should do more to prepare for disasters jumped from 7.2 percent in 1994 to 20.4 percent in May 1995 (Ministry of Foreign Affairs, 1995). In another poll, taken in December 1995, responses showed that the *Kobe* earthquake and the sarin gas attack in the Tokyo subway earlier in the year had caused Japanese citizens to have less confidence in Japan as a peaceful and safe society. Only 33 percent said they were satisfied with levels of peace and safety, a drop from 42.6 percent in an earlier survey. Regarding the economy, Japanese citizens expressed cautious optimism in the mid 1990s. The Economic Planning Agency, in a survey conducted in February 1996, reported the following results. Over a third of respondents, 37.4 percent, expected a rise in their income in the next six months, whereas only 13.5 percent did not. Over half expected employment conditions to remain about the same, whereas 24.2 percent expected employment conditions to worsen (Economic Planning Agency, 1996).

Another survey, conducted by the Leisure Development Center and published in a White Paper in 1996, shows a growing generational distinction among Japanese citizens. This survey shows that more Japanese now place leisure ahead of work as a priority and that this is especially true among young men and women. According to the White Paper, the group that most highly values leisure activities is males between the ages of 15 and 19 with females aged 20 to 29 second. Over half of the teen males, 58.1 percent, put leisure first and just over half of the 20-something females, 51.9 percent, put leisure ahead of work. Males in their 50s, by a 59 percent response, put work first. For those actually taking part in leisure activities, the most popular activity reported in the survey was eating out, followed by domestic travel. A noteworthy change from the previous year's survey was the climb from eighth to fourth of "communicating through computer networks" among those who wish they had more time to pursue leisure activities. This reflects the recent surge of personal computer sales and Web sites in Japan (Japan Information and Culture Center, 1996).

Not all agree with the picture presented by such polls, however. Sugahara Mariko, cabinet councillor and chief of the women's affairs office in the Prime Minister's Office, wrote an article expressing deep concern over what she identifies as the "five fatal symptoms" of "Japanese disease." Her major point is that Japan is not immune to the problems that other advanced, industrial democracies have faced and that even as Japanese citizens enjoy the living conditions that go with more affluence and economic success so also must they recognize the symptoms of a growing disease with uniquely Japanese characteristics. The first symptom she identifies is the ever increasing number of Japanese people who "hate work." She contends that the overseas image of Japan as a land of hardworking, industrious people is more image than reality. For Sugahara, other surveys from the Prime Minister's Office indicate that Japanese citizens are taking things too easy of late. New values being expressed are reflected in words like *yasumu* (rest) and *nonbiri suru* (take it easy). She also points to trends in the work force toward shorter working hours and five-day work-weeks. The second symptom she identifies is that of "excessive homogeneity and conformity," symptoms she relates to the highly uniform nature of Japanese education. This emphasis on uniformity also contributes to a third symptom according to which Japanese people lack creativity and vitality. A loss of civic morals and public spirit is a fourth symptom, and society's failure to "tap the potential of women and senior citizens" is the last (Sugahara, 1994).

Recent events tend both to challenge and reinforce Sugahara's observations. Certainly the turnout in both national elections since the summer of 1994, when her article appeared, would confirm her observations regarding public spirit. Both the July 1995 national election for the House of Councillors and the October 1996 election for the House of Representatives set new lows in voter turnout under the 1947 Constitution. Polls similarly confirm rising voter cynicism, as noted above. Other polls, however, suggest that Japanese citizens are far from lax in their attitudes to work. A poll in the early 1990s on aspects of a job that are important showed that 71 percent of those who responded listed "meets my abilities" as important. In the same poll, Sugahara would undoubtedly point to the 52 percent who said "generous holidays" were important. For comparison, 58 percent of Americans said "meets my abilities" and 31 percent said "generous holidays" in a similar poll (Ladd 1995, 29). As for not tapping the potential of women, a 1994 poll by the *Asahi* newspaper showed that 77 percent of respondents approved the "type of woman" who "gives priority to her family life" (Ladd 1995, 26).

Work in Japan is changing to reflect the changes in Japanese social and economic life. Traditionally, Japan is famous for having developed in its economic infrastructure three somewhat unique characteristics: lifetime employment, promotion by seniority, and twice yearly bonuses. Increasingly, another characteristic is becoming more prominent, competitive examinations for job entry at virtually all levels. The three traditional characteristics define the working environment in large corporations, enterprises, and public service. The idea of lifetime employment is tied to the traditional concept of strong family and strong group cohesion as desired social elements. The emphasis is on mutual cooperation and long-term stability. A related fact, however, is that job placement in large corporations or government agencies is usually followed by extensive and continuing training. With so much invested, there is economic incentive to stay with recruits. It also keeps those recruited together over time as a cohesive work group. This tends to build group bonds and loyalty to the company or agency. Lifetime employment is also, however, tied to economic trends. Promotion in Japan is most often by seniority. This, too, keeps internal friction to a minimum. The bonus system provides workers with a summer and winter bonus equal to approximately one fourth of their salary.

All of these traditional features of the work environment in Japan are changing today, though slowly. In the past, Japanese companies cut back in new hires rather than change the pattern of lifetime employment. And this continues. Figures for the spring of 1996 graduates of universities and junior colleges were expected to be down about 4 percent for male liberal arts graduates seeking jobs, and down about 5.5 percent for female liberal arts graduates. Among science graduates, the expectation was for a 5 percent drop among males and an 8 percent drop among females. With the economic downturn of the early 1990s, however, many companies began to introduce early retirement systems as well as cut new placements. About 60 percent, or 140 companies of companies listed on the Tokyo Stock Exchange, had implemented some form of an early retirement policy in 1995. This was up from about 20 percent 15 years earlier. Whether these trends continue depends on the long-term stability of the Japanese economy. According to Wakabayashi Yukinori, a former Ministry of Labor vice minister, successful management of four processes will help keep employment patterns in Japan relatively stable. These four processes are the changes occurring in the industrial structure due to the strong yen, the aging of the Japanese work force reflective of the larger society, the subsequent decline in the number of younger workers, and the increase in the utilization of temporary and part-time workers (Nishimura and Chiba 1995, 4–8).

Lifetime employment and the other features we have discussed are more characteristic of white-collar than blue-collar employment. It was only following World War II that Japanese labor unions began to play a substantial role in the economic sector, and even then it was short-lived due to radical tendencies. The Japan Communist Party was active in boosting union membership after the war and in defining the agenda of the unions. In addition to calls for higher wages and safety on the job, for example, unions were demanding the resignation of the Yoshida Shigeru government in 1947. New labor laws guaranteeing workers the right to collective bargaining, workers compensation, and the right to strike gave a large umbrella of protection to Communist-led demonstrations. A general strike was called for February 1947, only to be prohibited by SCAP. This setback led to other laws strengthening the power of employers to curtail union activities.

Labor unions predated the war and have their beginnings in the late nineteenth century. Early unions were modeled after those in the United States and came to represent metalworkers, railway workers, and printers. These early efforts were very poorly organized, however, and did not last long. The first significant organization was the Japanese Federation of Labor in 1919. During the years following the Peace Preservation Law and the rise of the military to power, union activities virtually ceased altogether until after the war and the release of much and long frustrated energy. Out of the early postwar years developed two major unions, one more radical and one more moderate. The

Sohyo union, or General Council of Trade Unions, tended to confrontation. The *Domei,* or Japan Confederation of Labor, tended to compromise. The Miike coal mine strike in the early 1960s symbolizes even today the potential conflict between management and labor in industries such as coal mining. Gradually, through the 1980s and the years of the bubble economy, *Domei* and *Sohyo* lost their effectiveness, and union workers were reorganized into *Rengou* in 1989.

Today *Rengou* works with the Ministry of Labor to achieve four goals: new rights and benefits for their members; the defense of existing rights and benefits; a macro-economic policy beneficial to workers; and an increase in benefits for the unorganized workers in Japan. In pursuit of these goals, among others, *Rengou* ran its own candidates for the House of Councillors election in 1989 and won 12 seats. Representatives of *Rengou* assisted in efforts to bring political reform to Japan, efforts that culminated in the 1994 electoral reforms first implemented in the 1996 House election in October. The coalition governments beginning in 1993, the merging of the Democratic Socialist Party with the New Frontier Party in 1994, and the virtual disappearance of the Social Democrats following the 1996 House elections have put *Rengou* in an awkward position vis-à-vis party politics in the Diet. Still, with their close ties to the Ministry of Labor and their working relationship with *Nikkeiren* and other employers' associations, *Rengou* continues to affect public policy making in the areas of wages, employment, and working environments in today's Japan (Harari, 1996).

OUTSIDERS IN THE JAPANESE STATE

On rare occasions, outsiders become fully accepted within Japanese society (see box on Lafcadio Hearn). Traditionally, however, outsiders face tremendous obstacles. Two major groups within the Japanese population have not felt completely accepted as members of the modern Japanese state, even though they are born, live, work, and contribute to that state. One group is called the **burakumin**. This term literally means people of the hamlets. The reference, however, is to people whose ancestors in Japan worked in the leather or other trades associated with the slaughter of animals. Because of traditional religious beliefs deriving both from Shinto and Buddhism, people engaged in these activities were looked down upon as engaged in dirty, demeaning, and somewhat impure, even inhuman, work. Over time, due to ostracism and social distancing, these people came to be residentially segregated. During the **Edo Period**, legal discrimination was established. In the strict hierarchy of **Tokugawa** society, the *samurai,* the farmer, the artisan, the merchant, then the people in the animal butchering trades assumed positions in a descending order. During Edo, the *burakumin* became increasingly outcaste within their own society. They were allowed to live only in designated areas or hamlets (*buraku*), hence the term *burakumin.* In 1871, as part of the **civilization and enlightenment** movement characteristic of the Meiji Period, discrimination against the *burakumin* was officially

---

LAFCADIO HEARN (1850–1904)

Koizumi Yakumo, Lafcadio Hearn's adopted Japanese name, was a disillusioned American writer of Greek birth who arrived in Japan in 1890 to begin a new life. He married a *samurai*'s daughter, became a Japanese citizen, taught English in Matsue in Shimane Prefecture, wrote for a Kobe newspaper, taught English literature at Tokyo University, and wrote numerous works on Japan for publication overseas. Among his works are *Glimpses of an Unfamiliar Japan* (1894), *Japan, an Attempt at Interpretation, In Ghostly Japan* (1899), and *Kwaidan* (1904). Though an outsider, Hearn became an insider—a rare accomplishment in Japanese society. His portrayal of a traditional Japan, previously unfamiliar to most Westerners, helped introduce the Japanese people and culture to a more global audience.

---

discouraged through legislation. Social discrimination continued, however, and it was not until the formation of the All Japan Committee for Buraku Liberation after World War II, an organization that changed its name to the Buraku Liberation League in 1955, that major changes began to take place. In 1969, the national government began a process of reviewing problems and legislating in the area of *burakumin* discrimination. Today, according to a recent article published in the *New York Times*, two-thirds of Japanese *buraku* people say that they have not encountered discrimination and 73 percent claim marriage to non-*buraku*. In the same article, however, it is noted that whereas about 40 percent of non-*buraku* Japanese go to college, only 24 percent among *buraku* do (Kristof 1995, 18). *Buraku* issues are not widely discussed in the media in Japan, however. When *Edwin Reischauer*'s classic study *The Japanese* was translated into Japanese in 1979, the section on the *burakumin* was edited out (Guest 1992, 28).

The Korean minority in Japan was 682, 276 as of December 31, 1993. The second largest minority group for the same period was Chinese at 210,138. Next were Brazilians (156,650), Filipinos (73,057), Americans (42,639), Peruvians (33,169), British (12,244), Thai (11,765), Vietnamese (7,609), and Iranian (6,754). Smaller groups included Malaysians, Canadians, Australians, and Indians. The total foreign population registered in Japan in 1993 was 1,320,748 (Hunter 1995).What complicates the situation of the large Korean minority is that the largest number of them are descended from Koreans who came to Japan as workers or as forced laborers during the prewar and war years when Korea was annexed by Japan. Born in Japan, physically similar to Japanese, and fluent in the Japanese language, they nonetheless are not citizens and are sometimes the victim of social prejudices similar to those identified with the *burakumin.* Another complicating factor is that about half of the Korean residents of Japan identify with the South Korean government and about half with North Korea. The ideological gulf separating the two remains despite the easing of ideological tensions in other parts of the world. Koreans born in Japan must carry the alien registration cards (see accompanying box) required of all foreign residents. However, in April 1992, revisions in Japanese law removed the fingerprinting requirement for permanent resident aliens.

A growing problem in Japan today is the increasing number of stateless persons. These are mostly children born to workers in Japan illegally. Estimates are difficult here because there is no formal count of these persons. Some estimates put the number of illegal workers in the country at 300,000. One organization, called HELP, which gives aid to Asian women in Japan, puts the number of illegal women workers alone at 300,000. Under Japanese law, a child must have either a Japanese father or mother at the time of birth. This creates major problems for parents, especially mothers, of children born in Japan of uncertain birth or born outside of Japan to non-Japanese parents and in the country illegally. The Children's Human Rights Charter of the United Nations recommends that every child have a nationality at birth (Sakamaki 1994, 38). In January 1995, the Japanese Supreme Court ruled that when both parents of a child are not known, the child may still become a Japanese citizen.

It may seem somewhat strange to include mention of the *Ainu* people in a discussion of "outsiders" in the Japanese state. They are, historically, the ultimate insiders. The *Ainu* are a small body of people numbering around 20,000 and living on Hokkaido. They once populated large sections of what is now Japan and into the late Edo Period lived in northern Honshu in the Tohoku region. They have their own language, music, arts, and history. In 1984, a museum was opened in Shiraoi on Hokkaido dedicated to the preservation of the *Ainu* culture. On display are the distinctive clothes and other items reflective of *Ainu* traditional lifestyles. Today, one member of the Diet, in the House of Councillors, is of *Ainu* ancestry. They have traditionally been treated as outsiders by many Japanese.

ALIEN REGISTRATION CARD
(*GAIKOKUJIN TOROKU SHOMEISHO*)

Long-term visitors to Japan, beyond tourist stays, must carry with them at all times an alien registration card (*gaijin torokusho*, for short). This card carries information on one's residence while in Japan, one's employer, and one's fingerprints. The card must be carried at all times. Failure to report a change of address or a change of job within two weeks can result in a fine or jail confinement. In 1992, permanent alien residents, such as the large Korean minority in Japan and many of Chinese descent, a total of about 650,000 residents, were exempted by legislation from the fingerprinting requirement. This continues, however, for nonpermanent residents.

WOMEN IN JAPAN TODAY

Stereotypical images of Japanese women are among the most predominant of all images of traditional Japan. The *geisha*, Madame Butterfly, wood-block prints of the ladies of the pleasure quarter in old Edo, and, increasingly, the *kyoiku mama*, or education mother are all familiar portrayals worldwide. Such traditional images present women as aesthetes, entertainers, long-suffering, even tragic victims, and dedicated servants. Counter to these images, however, is Merry White's observation that women in Japan today represent one of the greatest forces for change (see box on Doi Takako). Portraying Japanese women today is a large and complex task, one compounded by the sheer volume of recent studies by and about Japanese women. Some studies take the reader inside the life of one woman, a *Shikoku* farm woman, for example, as in *Haruko's World*, by Gail Lee Bernstein, or an émigré from Hiroshima in the 1920s who begins a new, harsher life in America, as presented by Akemi Kikumara in her portrait of her mother (Bernstein 1983; Kikumara 1981). More recently, Elizabeth Bumiller (1996) explores the *Secrets of Mariko*, a modern, urban Japanese woman whose life transcends all traditional stereotypes, as does her family. Other studies map a larger, more statistical terrain, such as *Technology Change and Female Labour in Japan*, edited by Nakamura Masanori (1994b). Still others explore how basic features of the Japanese language reinforce longstanding stereotypes and gender typing through a separate "woman's speech" within the Japanese language (Abe 1995). Most studies seem to agree, however, in the general observation that the "good wife and wise mother" of prewar psychology—and state policy—is giving way to a more expansive ideal, though slowly. As Iwao Sumiko puts it, Japanese women today are living a "quiet revolution" (Iwao 1993, 2). As she also observes, the gender issue in Japan is complicated by a larger culture that traditionally emphasizes obedience. For example, many studies of Japanese women note the traditional Confucian teaching that women should obey their father in youth, their husband in maturity, and their sons in old age. Yet, she observes, in Japan's modern corporate culture, men must obey

---

WOMAN OF AUTHORITY: DOI TAKAKO

In 1996, Doi Takako was speaker of the House of Representatives of the Japanese Diet. On the eve of the October 1996 national election, she was being courted by members of the rapidly disintegrating Social Democratic Party of Japan to reassume her former role as chairperson of the party. She served as chair from 1986 to 1991 and is the first woman to become head of any political party in Japan's history. She first won a seat in the House in 1969 from Hyogo Prefecture. Doi Takako symbolizes for many the more public roles that women are assuming in today's Japan. She is widely credited with leading the Socialists and their opposition allies to an upset victory over the LDP in the House of Councillors election in 1989.

---

their mother in youth, their companies in maturity, and their wives in retirement (Iwao 1993, 7).

Among the many reforms of the Meiji government in its quest for civilization and enlightenment was the establishment of universal primary education in 1873. This action covered both sexes and represented the Japanese government's first commitment to education for women. In 1899, another law provided that in every prefecture there should be at least one school beyond the primary school for females. Twenty years earlier, the government banned coed schools beyond the primary level. Much of the education of young women during the Meiji Period was provided by private, often Christian missionary schools. Despite increasing opportunities, however, the content of female education reflected the traditional emphasis on a woman's role as that of "good wife, wise mother." Women during Meiji were also expected to be good laborers in the service of building the strong, industrial economic base needed for Japan to compete with the Western powers. Women, in fact, "produced 40 percent of the gross national product and 60 percent of the foreign exchange during the late nineteenth century" (Nolte and Hastings 1991, 153). This was due to the large role women were playing in light industry, especially textiles. But even as women were becoming more literate through education, and contributing to the economic development of the Meiji state, they were being banned from any political involvement. By an act of 1890, issued by the cabinet prior to the first Diet session, women could not attend political gatherings or join organizations with a political purpose. This prohibition was not lifted until 1922, and then only partially to cover the first part of the legislation. Prohibitions against membership in political organizations continued until 1945. The Civil Code established in 1898 required a woman to secure her husband's consent in most legal matters involving domestic relations, family law, and inheritance. When married under the provisions of the Civil Code, a woman lost the independent right to buy or sell property and manage personal property, and was bound to chastity. The husband was not similarly bound.

The Taisho Era, the so called era of Taisho democracy, brought the creation of several women's organizations. Notable examples include the *Bluestocking Society* and the *New Woman's Association*. The first was founded by *Hiratsuka Raicho* and operated between 1911 and 1916. It is often called Japan's first feminist organization. With the ban on political organizations for women in force, the Bluestocking Society focused its activities on literary discussions at first and only slowly branched out into more social issues. Through a literary magazine, this organization promoted the image, concerns, and lifestyles of "new women." Hiratsuka, a graduate of Japan Women's University, was also among the founders of the New Woman's Association in 1920. Unlike the earlier group, the emphasis here was on political rights for women. It was through the efforts largely of this organization that the ban on women from attendance at political gatherings was lifted in 1922.

Three women, in addition to Hiratsuka, who stand out during the Taisho Period for their efforts in defining women's roles in Japan are *Yosano Akiko*,

Yamakawa Kikue, and *Yamada Waka.* Yosano wrote poetry for the literary magazine of the Bluestocking Society, essays on a wide variety of issues, traveled widely in Europe, and was the mother of 11 children, one of whom died a day after birth. She also cofounded a school in which she taught for over 20 years (Rodd 1991, 175–198). Yamakawa was a Socialist active during dangerous times, as noted. She was a graduate of what is today Tsuda College, and wrote numerous essays in journals like the one published by the Bluestocking Society. She also wrote books, among which is her autobiography. After World War II, she became the first director of the Women's and Minors' Bureau of the Ministry of Labor. Yamada Waka, from Kanagawa Prefecture, lived in the United States, on the west coast, and was forced into prostitution as a young woman. She returned to Tokyo in 1906. Before she left the United States she was baptized into the Christian religion and began to write essays that were published in the Bluestocking literary magazine. Later, during early Showa, she wrote responses to letters from women in trouble for what is today the *Asahi Shimbun.* She also established a refuge for mothers and children in Tokyo.

These four women, among many others, worked on behalf of women's concerns in virtually every area of life in a modernizing Japan. Other efforts on behalf of women during the Taisho and early Showa periods focused on acquiring suffrage. The Women's Suffrage League, for instance, was organized in 1924. With the changing political climate brought on by the Peace Preservation Law and the rise of the military to power in the 1930s, these efforts were gradually pushed behind the scenes.

The 1947 Constitution, reflecting the **Potsdam Declaration**'s requirement for a democratic Japan as a precondition for renewed sovereignty, contains a number of passages specifically directed at Japanese women. Article 14 states that there will be "no discrimination in political, economic or social relations because of race, creed, sex, social status or family origin." Article 15 provides for "universal adult suffrage." Article 22 states that "every person" shall be free to choose or change residence and occupation. Article 24 guarantees that marriage will be based "only on the mutual consent of both sexes" and that it will be maintained based on "mutual cooperation." The same article stipulates that with regard to such things as property rights, inheritance, marriage, family, and other basic personal considerations, laws must respect "the essential equality of the sexes." These and other provisions reflect the work of the staff in SCAP headquarters in early 1946 who set to work to write a new, democratic constitution for Japan.

When it comes to certain features of life in Japan today, however, women remain at a substantial disadvantage. One such area is in job placement, especially for recent women college graduates and especially during economic hard times. The number of women university graduates seeking jobs in March 1996 was up 37 percent over the preceding five-year period. Yet the number of jobs available for these women graduates had decreased by 60 percent (Radin 1996). According to one report, there were only 45 openings for every 100 women applicants for jobs, while at the same time there were 133 openings for every

100 men (Iritani 1996). These statistics illustrate a continuing tendency in corporate Japan to see female employees as temporaries. When economic times become difficult, they are the last hired, regardless of qualifications. A related problem is what Kishi Nobuhito calls Japan's "invisible unemployment." Japan and the United States calculate unemployment levels using different methodologies. Using 1994 statistics, the Management and Coordination Agency of the Japanese government, the agency responsible for evaluating unemployment levels in Japan, used a different methodology, one developed by the Bureau of Labor Statistics in the United States. Using this methodology, a category designated as "conventional unemployment" put unemployment in Japan for 1994 at 2.7 percent and in the United States at 6.5 percent. But if one were to include the category of "discouraged workers," those who for various reasons have given up looking for jobs, the jobless rate in Japan for 1994 rises to 8.9 percent and in the United States to 8.8 percent. Of particular note in the category of "discouraged workers" is the very high proportion of women. According to Kishi (1995), women make up 70 percent of the persons in this category in Japan.

Despite these difficulties, Japanese women continue to express levels of satisfaction with conditions in Japan in higher proportions than Japanese men do. Women in their 20s expressed the highest levels of satisfaction in the Prime Minister's Office survey of May 1995. Among women in their 20s, 80.9 percent expressed satisfaction with their present lives. A close second place was women over the age of 70, among whom 79.8 percent expressed satisfaction. Among men over 70, 79 percent also expressed satisfaction. In the survey, women "in every age group (categorized in ten-year increments, beginning with people in their 20s) are more satisfied than men" (Iikubo 1996, 38).

FOREIGN WORKERS

During the late 1980s there was much debate in Japan regarding the increase in illegal immigration and its relationship to the growing demand for cheap labor during the high-growth, bubble economy years. In 1989, the Diet passed the Immigration Control and Refugee Recognition Law to go into effect on January 1, 1990. Among the changes in the law were the expansion of jobs for which foreign workers would be granted visas and legal residence for up to three years. Visa application procedures were also simplified, criminal penalties were stiffened for those who hired illegal aliens, and "long-term" residence status was granted to Japanese descendants up to the third generation who wish to work in Japan. Many who qualify in the latter group tend to come from Brazil and Peru. Among controversies brought by these changes is the opportunity it presents to some to take advantage of overseas Japanese descendants for cheap, dirty, demeaning, even dangerous jobs. It also allows entertainers to enter as professionals, many of whom are actually coming to serve in the "water trade" as bar hostesses. Criticisms have also been directed at the provisions liberalizing work opportunities for company trainees and students. Lured to Japan for career advancement, they end up as cheap laborers. Many of the foreign workers who come to Japan are from China, the Philippines, Thailand, and Malaysia (Morita and Sassen 1994).

The relative status of foreign workers, as well as the *burakumin* and Korean minorities in Japan, is related to those complex aspects of traditional Japanese culture that stress inside and outside relations as primary. The closer one is by blood, such as family, the more "inside" one's status. Foreign workers are *gaijin*, "outside person," by definition. The only exceptions to the maximum three-year contracts on foreign work visas is for up to third-generation Japanese who come to Japan to work. For them, it is not unusual to secure a permanent resident alien status. The *burakumin* and Korean populations, on the other hand, are "outsiders" in a different sense. The *burakumin*'s traditional social distance is ultimately related to Buddhist religious teachings against the slaughtering of animals. The Korean community's troubles are traceable to historical conflicts that remain part of the unique sense of history shared by most Japanese.

The most complex "outside" group in the modern Japanese state is Japanese women. There are those who would say that far from being outside the center, Japanese women define the center. As inside is superior to outside, as *uchi* considerations outweigh all *soto* concerns, so also do women's governing roles in the *uchi* world of the household determine most priorities in the world outside. But this angle of vision comes more from the fixed world of traditional Japanese culture where the state itself is something of a household writ large. In the modern world of democratic and increasingly egalitarian Japan, women are insisting on and increasingly succeeding in finding more places in the traditionally male-governed institutions. All indications are, however, that the pace of change in this area is slower in Japan than in most other advanced, industrialized nations. The October 1996 national election for the House of Representatives makes the point clearly. Of 1,503 candidates running, only 153, about 10 percent, were women. Of that number, only 23 were elected. Recent polls illustrate the continuing power of traditional beliefs in Japan on the roles that women should assume. A 1994 poll, for example, revealed that in Japan the "ideal" of family life is one where the "wife is responsible for the house and children, although the husband also shows concern for his family." Forty percent of respondents chose this ideal. Among less favorable models, chosen by only 19 percent of respondents, was "husband and wife each are deeply involved in their own jobs and activities" (Ladd 1995, 26).

Summary

Under the Meiji Constitution of 1889, the Japanese people were subjects, not citizens. The constitution was a gift from the Emperor. Among provisions in Japan's first constitution was for the "rights and duties" of "subjects." Early legislation by the Diet during this period was to limit citizen involvement. Women neither voted nor held office. The Peace Preservation Law of 1925 was especially restrictive and was designed to protect the *kokutai* philosophy of the state. Mass arrests of leftists and other dissidents were common during early Showa. Some gains were made toward democratization during the Taisho Period, such as the expansion of male suffrage. The 1947 Constitution, by contrast, refers to the rights and duties of citizens, rather than subjects. It protects free expression and association and guarantees the right of women to vote. Recent legislation providing for electoral reform has been seen by some as among the most dramatic of changes in the postwar Japanese state. Districts for the House of Representatives have been completely redrawn, providing for 300 single-member districts and 11 regional districts from which an additional 200 representatives are elected by proportional representation. Expectations are that the new electoral scheme will encourage a two-party system, issue campaigns for the Diet, and a lessening of the role of money and factions in Japanese politics. Under the new system, candidates may run concurrently in a single-member district and on a list in one of the regions.

Japanese citizens today are generally content, according to polls, though some differences exist according to the age of respondents. Younger Japanese generally place leisure ahead of work. Some point to disturbing trends, however, that suggest an increasing number of Japanese citizens who hate work, are overly conforming, lack creativity, show little civic virtue, and fail to appreciate the potential contributions of women and senior citizens to Japanese society. Traditional employment patterns according to which workers enjoy lifetime employment, promotion by seniority, and generous bonuses are changing in the wake of harder economic times. Recent reorganization of labor unions and the decline of the Social Democratic Party of Japan have made labor's voice in the policy process a little weaker than in times past. *Burakumin* and Korean minorities in Japan have traditionally enjoyed the benefits of Japanese citizenship less than others. The traditional *Ainu* have also had to fight for more recognition in recent years. Among the biggest changes in Japanese society today are the roles being assumed by women. Though early organizations such as the Bluestocking Society and early leaders such as Hiratsuka Raicho made significant strides on behalf of women in Japanese society, it is only today that women are assuming positions of leadership across a wide spectrum of Japanese society, and this often slowly. With economic reverses, women are still among the first to be placed at a disadvantage. This has been especially true for recent women graduates of colleges and universities. Foreign workers continue to face problems in Japan due to their status as outsiders, though visa requirements have been eased by recent legislation.

Suggested Readings

Bernstein, Gail Lee. 1983. *Haruko's World: A Japanese Farm Woman and Her Community.* Stanford, CA: Stanford University Press.

———, ed., with an Introduction. 1991. *Recreating Japanese Women, 1600–1945.* Berkeley: University of California Press.

Bumiller, Elizabeth. 1996. *The Secrets of Mariko: A Year in the Life of a Japanese Woman and Her Family*. New York: Times Books.

Fujimura-Fanselow Kumiko, and Atsuko Kameda, eds. 1995. *Japanese Women: New Feminist Perspectives on the Past, Present, and Future*. New York: Feminist Press at the City University of New York.

Iwao, Sumiko. 1993. *The Japanese Woman: Traditional Image and Changing Reality*. New York: Free Press.

Kikumara Akemi. 1981. *Through Harsh Winters: The Life of a Japanese Immigrant Woman*. Novato, CA: Chandler and Sharp.

Naff, Clayton. 1996. *About Face: How I Stumbled onto Japan's Social Revolution*. Tokyo: Kodansha International.

Pharr, Susan J. 1990. *Losing Face: Status Politics in Japan*. Berkeley: University of California Press.

Turner, Christena L. 1995. *Japanese Workers in Protest: An Ethnography of Consciousness and Experience*. Berkeley: University of California Press.

White, Merry. 1993. *The Material Child: Coming of Age in Japan and America*. New York: Free Press.

Works Cited

Abe Hideko Nornes. 1995. From Stereotype to Context: The Study of Japanese Women's Speech. *Feminist Studies* 21 (Fall): 647–671.

Bernstein, Gail Lee. 1983. *Haruko's World: A Japanese Farm Woman and Her Community*. Stanford, CA: Stanford University Press.

Bumiller, Elizabeth. 1996. *The Secrets of Mariko: A Year in the Life of a Japanese Woman and Her Family*. New York: Times Books.

Christensen, Raymond V. 1996. The New Japanese Election System. *Pacific Affairs* 69 (January): 49–70.

Economic Planning Agency of Japan. 1996. Main Results of EPA Information Network Survey on Household Views of the Economy. April 4.

Guest, Robert. 1992. From the Cutting Room. *Far Eastern Economic Review* 155 (9 July): 28, 29.

Harari, Ehud. 1996. Japanese Labor Organization and Public Policy. *Social Science Japan*, no. 6. University of Tokyo: Institute of Social Sciences.

Hunter, Brian, ed. 1995. *The Statesman's Yearbook, 1995–1996*. New York: St. Martin's Press.

Iikubo Ryuko. 1996. Satisfied? *Look Japan* 41 (February): 38.

Iritani, Evelyn. 1996. Japanese Fleeing a Thick Glass Ceiling. *Los Angeles Times*, 5 April, A-1.

Iwao Sumiko. 1993. *The Japanese Woman: Traditional Image and Changing Reality*. New York: Free Press.

Japan Information and Culture Center. 1996. Lifestyle Trends Show Generational Divide. *Japan Now*, July 8.

Kikumura Akemi. 1981. *Through Harsh Winters: The Life of a Japanese Immigrant Woman*. Novato, CA: Chandler and Sharp.

Kishi Nobuhito. 1995. Japan's Invisible Unemployment Problem. *Japan Echo* 22 (Autumn): 38–43.

Kristof, Nicholas D. 1995. Japan's Invisible Minority: Better Off Than in the Past, but Still Outcasts. *New York Times,* 30 November, 18.

Ladd, Everett C. 1995. Japan and America: Two Different Nations Draw Closer. *The Public Perspective: A Roper Center Review of Public Opinion and Polling* 6 (no. 5): 18–36.

Ministry of Foreign Affairs. 1995. Three of Four Happy with Current Living Standards. Information Bulletin, no. 39, September 14.

Molony, Barbara. 1995. Japan's 1986 Equal Employment Opportunity Law and the Changing Discourse on Gender. *Signs* 20 (Winter): 268–302.

Morita Kiriro, and Saskia Sassen. 1994. The New Illegal Immigration in Japan, 1980–1992. *International Migration Review* 28 (Spring): 153–163.

Nakamura, Masanori. 1994a. *Japanese Women and Technology in the Work Place.* Tokyo: United Nations University Press.

———, ed. 1994b. *Technology Change and Female Labour in Japan.* Tokyo: United Nations University Press.

Nishimura Kunio, and Hitoshi Chiba. 1995. Headed for Trouble? Restructuring and Unemployment in Japan. *Look Japan* 41 (December): 4–8.

Nolte, Sharon N., and Sally Ann Hastings. 1991. The Meiji State's Policy Toward Women, 1890–1910. In *Recreating Japanese Women, 1600–1945,* ed. with an Introduction by Gail Lee Bernstein, 151–174. Berkeley: University of California Press.

Radin, Charles A. 1996. Women Fight a Stubborn Bias in Japan. *Boston Globe,* 8 May, 1.

Rodd, Laurel Rasplica. 1991. Yosano Akiko and the Taisho Debate over the "New Woman." In *Recreating Japanese Women, 1600–1945,* ed. with an Introduction by Gail Lee Bernstein, 175–198. Berkeley: University of California Press.

Sakamaki Sachiko. 1994. Stateless Children: Offspring of Illegal Aliens in Japan Force Legal Limbo. *Far Eastern Economic Review,* 157 (20 January): 38.

Sugahara Mariko. 1994. Five Fatal Symptoms of the Japanese Disease. *Japan Echo* 21 (Summer): 68–74.

Tamamoto Masaru. 1994. The Ideology of Nothingness: A Meditation on Japanese National Identity. *World Policy Journal* 11 (Spring): 89–99.

Yoshida Shinichi. 1996. Behind the Vote: Whither the Will of the Voters, Politicians Ask. *Asahi e News,* 23 October, 25–31.

7

Kokusai-ka
(Internationalization)

Historical differences are especially important when considering issues of the relations between states. Japan, as a major force in twentieth-century global politics, has a unique past and may, thereby, have a unique future. *Article 9* of the 1947 Constitution renounces war, a feature unique in the history of constitutional democratic governance. Few constitutional provisions, however, in any nation, have generated as much internal debate and controversy as this famous provision in the Japanese constitution. Following World War II, Marxists in the communist and socialist traditions of Japanese politics, and as later organized in the postwar Japan Communist Party (JCP) and the Japan Socialist Party (JSP), supported this pacifist aspect of the modern Japanese state. The Liberal Democratic Party, on the other hand, which would rule Japan from 1955 through 1993, considered the entire constitution the product of outside forces and called for constitutional revision. Both traditions have since modified their views. But Article 9 remains as a unique, if often debated, provision of the Japanese constitution. It is a symbol of reaction to the militaristic state that brought Japan into the Pacific War and brought unprecedented ruin on Japan in the closing years of the war.

The Pacific War continues to haunt Japan. In the summer of 1995, debates in the Diet on how to memorialize the fiftieth anniversary of the end of the war divided the Diet and, according to the *Mainichi Shimbun,* produced a resolution that "does not reflect a strong will on the part of the Diet, the highest organ of state power, to send a clear message to the world, including Asia." With less than half of the lower House supporting the resolution—many members being absent for the vote, and with no vote at all in the upper house—the resolution conveyed no "heartfelt message" (*Japan Times Weekly* 1995, 20).

ISOLATION, MODERNIZATION, POLARIZATION

Modern Japanese history may be divided into three large segments, each defined by a center of gravity that defines virtually all else, especially relations with other nation-states. During the *Edo Period,* Japan consciously isolated itself from the rest of the world. Except for the trade allowed with the Dutch and the Chinese at Nagasaki, all communications in Japan were focused inward. One result was the strengthening of cultural traits unique to Japan. Another result was a deep reluctance to embrace a wider, more universal, global point of view. Many observe that this is precisely what is changing so rapidly today. *Ozawa Ichiro*'s "blueprint," for example, stresses the epochal nature of the times and the need for Japan to embrace international challenges. *Oe Kenzaburo*'s literary art, celebrated at Stockholm with the Nobel Prize for literature in 1994, points dramatically in the same direction. These challenges from the mainstream in Japanese politics and aesthetics illustrate only more poignantly what seems to be on everyone's mind in Japan at the opening of the twenty-first century. As the political challenge in the immediate postwar environment was to rebuild a devastated nation, the consequence of which was a national focus inward, so also did the literary world focus on national character, tradition, and Japanese-ness. *Kawabata Yasunari*'s work explores the exotic world of old Japan in almost inverse proportion as Oe's work examines the postwar, post-modern, global environment of Japan today. That Kawabata and Oe have become the symbols of Japanese literary art may well be more the result of Western perceptions of Japan than internal perceptions; still, they symbolize the poles of experience in the largest cultural sense noted by Oe in his Nobel acceptance speech. There is a deep scar in the Japanese psyche with very different worlds on either side. The nature of the healing process will determine the direction of Japanese foreign policy priorities, among other developments.

Isolation nurtures uniqueness. And the Japanese of the Edo Period developed and nurtured a language, aesthetics, religious sensibilities, and social dynamics that continue to puzzle outsiders. The language is famous for its complexity, even to the Japanese themselves. Japanese writing combines indigenous *syllabaries*—*hiragana* and *katakana*—with Chinese characters (*kanji*) to form a complex of symbols that to many outside of Japan represent nothing less than an insurmountable wall designed to baffle and frustrate outsiders. Japanese relations with other nations are indeed somewhat complicated by the language barrier. Many in official positions in Japan will note that Japanese education, business, and politics encourage the learning of foreign languages, especially English, while English-speaking nation-states tend to give Japanese passing glances at best in their efforts to teach other languages. It is true that a large number of the members of the Japanese Diet and leaders in the business and education communities speak English, as well as French, German, Chinese, or Russian. Few members of the U.S. Congress or executives in large corporations that do business in Japan, by comparison, are conversant in any foreign language and very few can communicate in Japanese. But the difficulties are enormous for non-Japanese. To read a newspaper in Japanese, one would need to know approximately 1,900 *kanji,* or Chinese characters. In addition, one would have to master the 50 or so *hiragana* and *katakana* characters as well. Confining ourselves only to American and Japanese exchanges, it should be noted here that thousands of Japanese exchange students flock to American universities every year—over 24,000, for example, in 1988—while very few American students study in Japan—less than 1,000 in 1989 (JETRO 1991, 7). Most of the latter are in Japan to study the language.

The Japanese language is a reflection of Japanese uniqueness. One could, of course, note here that any number of nation-states in the world today speak a unique language. But in the case of Japan one is looking at a nation-state that is also a civilization (Huntington 1993); one is looking at the second most productive economy in the world, and by the measure of per capita income, the most productive; one is looking at the first modern democratic state in East Asia; and one is looking at a nation-state whose experience in the twentieth century includes experience with democratization, militarization, global war, nuclear bombing, occupation by a foreign power, and an economic about face perhaps unequaled in world history, a turnabout from total desperation in the wake of devastation from war to the second most productive economy in the world within two generations. To understand Japanese successes and failures, to comprehend its experiences, and to engage in meaningful dialogue in a shrinking global environment, one must attempt to understand the Japanese as they understand themselves, a task that requires an understanding of the language, the history, and the religious, philosophic, and aesthetic traditions and sensibilities of the Japanese people. As for the Japanese people, they have, in the past at least, invested a great deal more in understanding the ways of the West, certainly the defining element in the great *Meiji Restoration*.

If isolation nurtures uniqueness, then certainly the engagement of the West characteristic of the *genro* of the early *Meiji Period* nurtured a dramatic, and for Japan, an unprecedented internationalism. The *Iwakura* mission (see Chapter 2) is but the first dramatic illustration of a tendency that characterized the entire quarter century between the opening of the Meiji era in 1868 and the Sino-Japanese War in 1894–1895. Science, art, technology, fashion, educational theories, architecture, manners, music—virtually all aspects of Western culture—were studied, sifted, reexamined, and adopted or discarded as considered appropriate during the early years of Meiji. At the beginning of Meiji, not everyone was enthusiastic about learning from the West. The expression *sonno joi*, meaning "honor the emperor, expel the barbarian," captured the feelings of many in the early years. Nonetheless, the dominant theme of the Meiji era was the one championed by *Fukuzawa Yukichi* and that went by the name of *civilization and enlightenment*. Japan had moved from isolation as a center of gravity to modernization.

Some in Japan today may be said to embrace the thinking of "honor the Constitution, expel the barbarian." On September 8, 1996, the people of Okinawa voted on a nonbinding referendum regarding whether they wanted to continue to support existing leasing arrangements with the U.S. military or consolidate and reduce American military forces in Okinawa. Almost 60 percent of Okinawans eligible to vote voted in the referendum and over 89 percent voted for changes. Governor Ota Masahide brought the "message" of the Okinawan people to Tokyo and Prime Minister *Hashimoto* two days later. The referendum vote represented but the latest development in a complex foreign policy issue in Japan with a long history. Even as Tokyo was pondering the implications of the vote on Okinawa, the Chinese government in Beijing sent a request to Prime Minister Hashimoto asking that he not visit the *Yasukuni Shrine* in October. The prime minister earlier visited the shrine to Japan's war dead in July, as a "private" citizen, and announced his intention to return in October to honor the memory of a cousin who died during the war. As relations with the United States have been strained in recent years over the Okinawa bases and trade disputes, relations with China have been complicated by war remembrances, post–Cold War regional tensions, a Chinese military buildup, and rival claims to the *Senkaku Islands*.

Relations between Japan and the United States and between Japan and China are among Japan's most important. Yet, in the background of both relationships are the lingering and bitter memories surrounding all of the events leading up to and including the Second World War. Complicating relations further is the famous Article 9, a unique constitutional feature produced by the same complex events of twentieth-century war and diplomacy.

ARTICLE 9: BEFORE AND AFTER

Japan as an actor on the world stage begins in July 1853, when Commodore *Perry* and his "black ships" arrived in Edo Bay with the intention of opening Japan to international trade. The issue of how to respond to this initiative led to the famous call for honoring the Emperor and expelling the barbarian and the internal clash between *Tokugawa* forces and forces loyal to the outer *daimyo*. With the Meiji Restoration and all of the dramatic internal reforms undertaken at the new capital of Tokyo, the focal point of Japanese state policy came to be to build a stronger, richer economy and a more powerful military that could stand up to any external power. Rich country, strong military was the rallying phrase of late nineteenth-century Japanese politics. With victories over China and Russia, the Japanese military established itself internationally as a non-Western power that could indeed rival Western powers. By the end of the Meiji Period in 1912, the isolated world of the Edo Period had given way completely to a Japanese state seeking its "proper place" in global affairs. Many scholars, both Japanese and non-Japanese, have observed that from approximately the beginnings of the *Showa* Period, the Japanese "changed." Donald Keene, in a recent tribute to the Japanese writer Shiba Ryotaro, who died in early 1996, observed that for Shiba the Japanese became "insane" from about 1926, the beginning of Showa. Oe Kenzaburo, as noted earlier, referred to a "split" in the Japanese psyche related to Showa. The popular film *The Mystery of Rampo* (explored in Chapter 1) begins in 1926. Others refer to the "dark valley" leading up to the Pacific War. The rise of the military to power is, of course, the primary drama of the period. And the purging of any possible repeat of such a tragedy was among the primary motives in the design of the postwar 1947 Constitution. Article 9 says that the Japanese people "forever renounce war" and, in Section 2, that "land, sea, and air forces, as well as other war potential, will never be maintained."

But in the climate of postwar global tensions brought on by the ideological confrontations between the Soviet Union and the United States and their respective allies, Japan found itself in a dilemma. Many Japanese citizens admired, openly or clandestinely, the courage of young Marxists prior to the war. Hardly anyone else, certainly not the writers, artists, and scholars of the prewar generation, attempted to resist the military assumption of power. Many, too, supported the pacifist aims expressed in Article 9. Others, however, especially those within the government section of the American military in *SCAP*, recognized the need for "self-defense."

JAPAN AND INTERNATIONAL TRADE

In the fall of 1994, President Bill Clinton and Japanese Prime Minister *Murayama Tomiichi* met with other leaders of the Asia Pacific Economic Cooperation (APEC) summit in Bogor, Indonesia. This was only the second such summit where leaders of the 18-member organization gathered to discuss a common agenda regarding future economic ties. APEC was founded in 1989, and by 1995 included the following countries: Australia, Brunei, Canada, Chile, China, Chinese Taipei (Taiwan), Hong Kong, Indonesia, Japan, Malaysia, Mexico, New Guinea, New Zealand, the Philippines, Singapore, South Korea, Thailand, and the United States. Per capita income in member nations ranges from about $400 to $30,000 a year. Japan's stake in APEC is considerable, as the following observations show. Japanese trade with the Asia Pacific region represented almost 80 percent of all exports and almost 70 percent of all imports in 1993. Both percentages were up over two-thirds from the figures for the previous year. At the Bogor Conference, a declaration was issued that pledged member states to the goal of free trade between and among all members by the year 2020. It called for Japan and the United States to achieve that goal by the year 2010. Though the agreement is nonbinding, it points to the growing importance of the Asia Pacific region in global trade. If the timetable is kept, APEC would represent in 2020 the largest free trade area in the world, covering 2.2 billion people and involving four continents. The free trade area would cover half of the world's industrial output and over 40 percent of global trade (Japan Information and Culture Center 1994). One year later, APEC met in Osaka, Japan, to draw up more specific plans.

Following World War II, Japanese trade was seriously imbalanced toward imports. So much of the productive capacity of Japanese industry had been destroyed or damaged by the war that it would take nearly 20 years for Japanese trade to show a surplus. In the mid-1960s, trade figures began to show balances favoring exports, especially in products related to heavy industry. To help the Japanese economy get reestablished after the war, government restrictions such as high tariffs were allowed by the U.S. occupation forces (SCAP). Upon regaining sovereignty in 1952, Japan attempted to join the General Agreement on Tariffs and Trade (GATT), created in 1947 to build cooperation and rules to coordinate world trade. It took three years, however, because several member nations of GATT objected to Japanese tariff policies. With membership in 1955, the Japanese government began a long process of liberalizing its trade regulations. This process included a number of tariff reductions and the removal of tariffs on hundreds of products as the result of the so-called Kennedy and Tokyo Rounds of GATT-sponsored negotiations during the 1960s and 1970s. During the 1980s, however, due to ever increasing trade surpluses, especially with the United States, many observers both inside and outside Japan began to challenge the Japanese government's commitment to free trade and fair competition. Trade friction between the United States and Japan reached critical levels in the late 1980s and mid 1990s.

Japanese trade in the 1990s revealed two basic aspects of Japan that figure in all discussions of Japanese politics: Japan's geographic character as a somewhat crowded, somewhat isolated, island nation and Japan's socioeconomic character as a highly productive nation of hardworking people. With respect to the first, or geographic, point, Japan imports heavily in particular areas. For example, in agriculture, with so much of Japan's available farmland dedicated to rice production, most of the cereals, such as wheat and corn, are imported. In 1992, Japan produced only 12.1 percent of its needs in wheat consumption. The rest had to be made up in imports, principally from the United States. Only 3.9 percent of annual needed corn is produced in Japan. Bean production is 6.1 percent of domestic needs. By contrast, Japan exports no wheat, corn, or beans. Beef consumption has gone up considerably in recent years in Japan, as have beef imports. Japan imports 34.8 percent of its annual consumption needs in beef products. Over half of America's exports of beef and veal go to Japan. With respect to agriculture, Japan is the number one destination of American agricultural exports, with Canada second and Mexico third. With respect to foodstuffs as a whole, 16.1 percent of all imports in Japan, in 1992, were food products. This is the highest percentage of foodstuffs to total imports among all advanced, industrialized, G-7 nations. By comparison, only 5.5 percent of American imports are food products. For the United Kingdom the figure is 10.7 percent, and for Germany, 9.7 percent. What these figures show is a nation heavily dependent on imports for basic aspects of the national diet (JISEA 1995, 16–19). The great exception to this picture is rice. In 1992, Japan produced 100 percent of its consumption needs in rice. This is, of course, an international trade issue and is discussed below.

Another area where Japan is heavily dependent on imports is energy. Japan's import dependency here is 82.6 percent. In other words, Japan imports over 80 percent of its total energy resources. This compares with dependency percentages in other countries as follows: United States, 22.8 percent; Germany, 50.3 percent; France, 52.3 percent; and the United Kingdom, 39.1 percent. Focusing only on oil dependency, Japan must import 99.6 percent, according to 1991 figures originating with the Organization for Economic Cooperation and Development (OECD). This compares with an import dependency in the United States of 46.6 percent and in the United Kingdom of 54.9 percent. By place of origination, over three-fourths of Japanese oil imports, in 1993, came from the Middle East. Regarding other natural resources, Japan imports 100 percent of its iron ore, tin, bauxite, and nickel (JISEA 1995, 64).

Internationally, Japan is more famous for its exports and its consequent trade surpluses than for its import dependencies. Who cannot name the automotive and electronics giants in Japan whose products are known the world over for high performance, durability, reliability, and styling? Toyota, Mitsubishi, Honda, Matsushita, Canon, Hitachi, Nissan, Toshiba, Sony, NEC—all of these names represent companies in the top 100 of the Fortune 500 rankings of companies as of July 1994. All of them have international reputations as producing among the best cars, trucks, stereos, televisions, copiers, cameras, VCRs, and, more and more, computers and computer-related products. Japanese consumers only began in the mid-1990s to court the home computer as a necessity, and Japanese companies have been among the slower in advanced nations to develop Internet programming and Web pages. As is historically true, however, Japan is fast catching up in these developments as any regular user of the worldwide Web knows.

Japan's leading trading partner, both for exports and imports, is the United States (see Table 7-1). In 1993, 29.2 percent of Japanese exports went to the United States, with the European Union second at 15.6 percent. The second position goes to Hong Kong (then independent) at 6.3 percent if one disregards "bloc" destinations such as the European Union. Taiwan, South Korea, and Germany are next, with each getting from 6 to 5 percent of Japan's total exports. China is next at 4.8 percent and the fastest growing export destination (JISEA 1995, 38). Japan's overall balance of trade surplus has been shrinking in recent years. From 1992 to 1993, the balance of trade surplus fell by just under 1 percent.

TABLE 7–1
Japan's Leading Trading Partners, 1993

Country	Exports to (percent)	Country	Imports from (percent)
United States	29.20	United States	23.00
European Union	15.60	European Union	12.50
Hong Kong	6.30	China	8.50
Taiwan	6.10	Indonesia	5.20
Korea, Republic of	5.30	Australia	5.10
Germany	4.80	Korea, Republic of	4.90
China	4.80	Germany	4.10
Singapore	4.60	Taiwan	4.00
Thailand	3.40	Saudi Arabia	3.70
United Kingdom	3.30	United Arab Emirates	3.70

SOURCE: Japan Institute for Social and Economic Affairs, *Japan, 1995: An International Comparison* (Tokyo, 1995), p. 38.

The following year showed a fall of 7.3 percent. From 1994 to 1995, according to Finance Ministry figures, the surplus, meaning the difference between overall exports and overall imports, fell a substantial 19.3 percent.

Changes in individual categories are also worth noting. Motor vehicle exports, Japan's traditional big source of export revenues, was down for 1995 by 14.7 percent. These vehicles continued, however, to represent the largest share of Japan's exports at 12 percent. The export of integrated circuits, by contrast, the second largest share of export items by category, was up in 1995 by 27.8 percent. Other categories showing decreases in exports for 1995 were office machines, auto parts, ships, and visual apparatuses. Other categories showing increases in exports were optical instruments, iron and steel products, power generating machinery, and organic chemicals. Among imports, the year 1995 showed increases in clothing, office machines, integrated circuits, nonferrous metals, meat products, liquefied natural gas, and road motor vehicles. The last, a major concern of U.S. trade negotiators in recent years, was up a healthy 29.9 percent. Yet these vehicles still only represent 3 percent of total imports. The single largest category of imports, not surprisingly, is petroleum products. Second among imports is clothing, followed by fish, office machines, and integrated circuits (Kubota 1996, 34–35).

These figures regarding changes in the overall surplus for 1995 are calculated in yen. The overall drop in the surplus, calculated in dollars, is 11.4 percent from 1994. Similarly, automobile imports were up 40.6 percent by dollar calculations. Other highlights of Japan's international trade picture, using dollars for 1995, are a 73.8 percent increase in imports of office equipment, which includes personal computers, and an overall increase in imports of 22.3 percent. This compares with an overall increase in exports of 12 percent (Japan Information and Culture Center 1996b, 3).

JAPAN AND THE UNITED STATES

Policymakers in both Tokyo and Washington often say that there is no more important bilateral relationship in the world today than that between the United States and Japan. Such a statement points beyond the obvious economic ties that bind the world's two most productive economies. Today, despite changes in global politics brought on by the end of the Cold War, security issues involving Japan and the United States and the Pacific region are among the most important issues for both nations. The relationship has a clear beginning in Commodore Perry's visit to Edo Bay. It also has dramatic aspects with attendant images, many dark and haunting. War images of Pearl Harbor, the Bataan death march, jungle fighting, fierce sea battles, kamikaze attacks, and the mushroom clouds at the end are indelibly etched in the minds of both Japanese and American citizens. Prewar images lack the same clarity but suggest stresses and strains more than harmonious interactions. The *unequal treaties*, the gentlemen's agreements, foreign expansion, talk of "yellow perils," and immigration restrictions in the United States—all contributed to difficult relations. Still, not everything was negative. From Meiji, through early Showa, there were many exchanges between the countries involving diplomatic missions, scholars, students, sports figures, and, of course, trade and tourism. After the catastrophic Kanto earthquake of 1923, Americans sent millions of dollars in relief. Following the rise of the military to power in Japan, Japanese-American relations entered a period of growing mutual distrust and fear that ended in devastation and death for millions.

The U.S. occupation of Japan from September 2, 1945 to April 1952 represents a transitional period, one major highlight of which was the rewriting of the Japanese constitution. Prior to regaining sovereignty, Japan signed the San Francisco Peace Treaty and the United States–Japan Security Treaty in September 1951. Under the first, Japan signed with 48 other countries to secure an international peace that would last. Under it, Japan lost all claims to territories gained since 1895, territories that included Taiwan, parts of Sakhalin, Korea, and islands such as those in the Kurile chain. The last item has since been contested, with Japan claiming what it considers the Northern Territories. The Soviet Union did not sign the treaty, a circumstance that continues to complicate Japan–Russian relations to this day. Japan, under the San Francisco Peace Treaty, also accepted American occupation of the Ryukyu Islands, which includes Okinawa, and agreed to pay war reparations. Both of these events also continue as issues. The Ryukyus were returned to Japan by treaty in 1972, but U.S. military forces continue to be a large presence in Okinawa. In September 1996, the Okinawan people voted overwhelmingly in a referendum on the continuation of American bases for a substantial revision of the agreements.

The Okinawan issue, in fact, has become in the mid and late 1990s one of the biggest issues in Japanese domestic politics. In the October 1996 national House election, LDP candidates running in the three single-member districts on Okinawa were all unsuccessful. Also, the jump in Japan Communist Party representation from 15 to 26, one of the surprises in the election, may be explained partially by the party's position on the Okinawan bases. It campaigned on a platform that included removal of all American bases from the island. In this sense, even outside of Okinawa, the party became a lightning rod for sentiments focused by the rape committed by American soldiers on Okinawa in September. Approximately 75 percent of American military base facilities in Japan are located on Okinawa and about half of the approximately 48,000 American troops in Japan are stationed there. The United States has agreed to return lands presently used for the Futenma Air Station within five to seven years, as well as reduce overall land use in Okinawa by 20 percent. In the spring of 1997, the LDP, with the support of the New Frontier Party, sponsored an amendment to the 1952 law regarding land leases to ease the government's extension of leases on Okinawa over the protests of some 3,000 property owners and the Social Democratic Party. The latter, in speeches opposing the revision of the law, stressed the unfortunate coincidence of such actions taking place in the year of the fiftieth anniversary of the Peace Constitution and the twenty-fifth

anniversary of the return of Okinawa to Japanese sovereignty. Political alignments over the Okinawa land lease issue were reminiscent of the traditional
alignments under the *55 system* from 1955 to 1993.

On the subject of war reparations, the Japanese government today claims
that they are all settled. This view has been rejected by many surviving "comfort women" and their supporters, who argue that direct government payments—reparations, not funds from private sources, be paid. Under the United
States–Japan Security Treaty, signed at the same time as the San Francisco Peace
Treaty, Japan agreed to the presence of U.S. military forces within Japan to assist
in case of attacks against Japan, among other provisions. This security treaty
went into effect in 1952. Eight years later, a Treaty of Mutual Cooperation and
Security was signed, but only after much dispute and turmoil within Japan. In
the most critical confrontation in Japanese domestic politics since the war, supporters and opponents of the new treaty clashed in often violent confrontations.
The 1960 treaty contains many specifics the primary intent of which is to clarify
the mutual security positions of each government and to give more recognition
to the sovereign status of the Japanese government. During the 1960s and the
Vietnam War, protests against the treaty were periodically voiced in street
demonstrations. In 1970, the security treaty was extended.

In April 1996, President Clinton went to Tokyo to sign a joint declaration
with Prime Minister Hashimoto that pledged both governments to "common
security objectives." The declaration agreed to the continuing need of approximately 100,000 American troops in the Pacific and the maintenance of "about
the current level" in Japan. Both sides agreed also to review guidelines regarding military cooperation (Mitchell 1996, l). Some Japanese scholars and policy
analysts have expressed concerns that the joint declaration actually changes
Japan's commitments under the *Mutual Security Treaty* or, at least, opens the
door to major changes. The Japanese government's current interpretation is that
under the Japanese constitution Japan only has the right to defend itself, a position called "individual self-defense." This forbids any "collective self-defense."
There is, however, a large gray area involving possible rear guard and logistical
cooperation during emergencies. According to one American policy analyst,
much in the bilateral security arrangements between Japan and the United
States remains vague. One critical question, among many, is "What role can and
should the Japanese *Self Defense Forces* play to deter aggression in the region
beyond attacks on Japan proper?" (Mochizuki 1996, 4–16). Spring 1996 military
operations by the People's Republic of China off the coast of Taiwan and the
subsequent rise of anxiety worldwide about potential military conflict over the
status of Taiwan dramatize the importance of such questions regarding Japan's
security commitments. Though the joint declaration is vague on particulars, it
nonetheless points in the direction of Japan's assuming an increased role in
international affairs.

As for Japan's defense forces, they were being downsized in the mid-
1990s. In 1995, the Self Defense Forces, which includes ground, air, and maritime forces, were reduced from 180,000 to 145,000 troops. For fiscal year 1996, a

cap was placed on increases for defense at 2.9 percent. That year's military budget was approximately $50 billion, making Japan the second or third ranking nation in the world in terms of amount spent on the military, after the United States and maybe Russia. In November 1995, the Self Defense Forces also modified formal descriptions of their role so as to clarify responsibilities in the areas of crisis management and counter terrorist activities (Blaker 1996, 41–52). The first modification is based on the slow response to the *Kobe* earthquake in January 1995, which took over 5,000 lives (see box on The Great Hanshin Earthquake, 1995). Though most observers have been critical of the government's response, some have urged caution on giving too much emergency powers to the state. Shimokobe Atsushi, the chair of the Committee for the Reconstruction of the Hanshin-Awaji Region, reminds readers in an article on "Rebuilding Kobe" that the elaborate procedures required for calling out the Self Defense Forces were written into law in 1961 in the climate of opinion surrounding the security treaty revisions of 1960. Most analysts feared at the time giving too much emergency power to the national government for fear of overreaction or abuse in highly charged political situations like the one in Tokyo in 1960 where hundreds of thousands of protestors filled the streets (Shimokobe 1996, 51, 52). Once the Self Defense Forces were mobilized, public opinion gives them high marks. In a survey on the future role of the SDF, the Prime Minister's Office asked respondents if the SDF had "produced results" in their work in disaster relief in Kobe. Among respondents, 90.2 percent said that the SDF had produced results and only 7.7 percent disagreed. When asked the same question with respect to response to the Tokyo gas attack, the responses were 76.6 percent favorable and 16.1 percent critical. These very high favorable ratings help explain why in another poll 66 percent of Japanese citizens expressed the

---

THE GREAT HANSHIN EARTHQUAKE, 1995

On January 17, 1995, at 5:46 A.M., Kobe, a city of 1.5 million people and Japan's second largest port after Yokohama, was hit by one of the worst earthquakes in Japan's history, leaving over 5,500 dead, scores of thousands injured, and 340,000 homeless. The great Hanshin earthquake, as it is often called, was recorded at a magnitude of 7.2 on the Richter scale. Property damage was estimated to be in the area of $100 billion. Among the aftershocks of the tragedy were realizations that Japan's "state of the art" quake-resistant engineering technology was far from expected reliability. Approximately 55,000 homes collapsed and another 30,000 were badly damaged. Fires broke out in 140 different locations following the quake. The Kobe quake was the most devastating since the Tokyo quake in 1923, which left over 120,000 dead. In addition to exposing engineering problems, the Kobe quake also dramatized problems in the Japanese government's crisis management capabilities, both in Tokyo and in the Hyogo prefectural government. The Self Defense Forces were not mobilized until four hours after the quake, a situation that brought severe criticism to the Murayama cabinet and those in ministry positions responsible for emergency preparedness.

view that the "purpose" of the SDF is "disaster relief." This compared with 57.2 percent who said the primary purpose was "national security" (Nishimura and Chiba 1996, 7).

This illustrates a powerful dilemma with respect to state power in general in Japan. Because of Japan's geography and its vulnerability to natural disasters, particularly powerful earthquakes in urban areas, emergency preparedness requires rapid, efficient, centralized response. Because of Japan's political history, however, cautions abound in the manner expressed by Shimokobe. Regarding counterterrorist strategies, the same dilemma presents itself. Still, under current global political conditions, effective counterterrorist strategies are essential as elements in any modern, industrialized, democratic nation-state's self-defense. The subway gas attack in March 1995 in Tokyo attributed to the *Aum Shinrikyo* religious cult dramatized the point for Japanese policy-makers. A related issue in Japanese defense policy deliberations is the threat of nuclear missile attack and what realistic cost-effective measures might be implemented as part of a long-term defense strategy. With China continuing underground nuclear tests and North Korea periodically hinting at its potential in strategic weapons development, with images of Chinese M-9 missiles splashing into the sea 30 miles off the coast of Taiwan in March 1996, during the presidential election there, and, perhaps most dramatically, with Japan's own historic images consequent to its unique experience as victim of nuclear attack, public officials are debating whether and to what extent Japan should develop a missile defense system (Crowell 1996, 14, 15). Japanese citizens appear relatively unconcerned with defense issues, however. A poll conducted by the *Yomiuri* newspaper in the spring of 1995 found that more than 40 percent of Japanese citizens, and about 52 percent of those in their 20s, were "unconcerned" regarding defense issues (Blaker 1996, 41–52).

THE TRADE ISSUE

Little was discussed on President Clinton's April 1996 visit regarding trade issues. Yet relations between Japan and the United States in recent years have more often involved trade than security issues. And the relationship has been bumpy at best. The United States is the number one export destination of Japanese goods. The United States is also the number one source of Japanese imports. In 1993, 29.2 percent of all Japanese exports went to the United States. Similarly, 23 percent of all imports originated in the United States (JISEA 1995, 38). The biggest source of friction has been the large trade surplus that Japan showed, especially in the 1980s and continuing into the 1990s. Though trade balances showed fluctuations, the big picture was that the United States had chronic trade deficits with Japan. Much of this was caused by Japanese exports of automobiles that became increasingly popular in the United States after the oil embargoes of the 1970s and the various OPEC policies drove up the cost of gasoline at the pump. Japanese cars proved both reliable and efficient, especially regarding gasoline consumption, and sales picked up dramatically in the late 1970s and into the 1980s. Despite voluntary export limits on the number of Japanese-manufactured cars sent to the United States, the volume remained high. The volume of exported American manufactured vehicles going to Japan, on the other hand, remained low. In 1992, Japan imported 181,417 passenger cars. In the same year, it exported 4,655,000 cars. Of the cars Japan imported, about 20 percent, just over 37,000 units, came from the United States. But 58 percent of cars entering Japan as imports in 1992 came from Germany (JISEA 1995, 21, 22).

These figures, and others related to auto parts, are part of the background to the near crisis over Japanese luxury autos and America's threatened tariffs in the summer of 1995 (see accompanying box). These problems led to the auto agreement later in the year according to which Japan agreed to take active steps to open showrooms and garages to more American-made automotive products. In 1996, the United States once again became the world's leading automobile producer, a status it had lost to the Japanese for several years. Also, in late 1995, sales of American automobiles in Japan were up as much as 50 percent. According to the *New York Times,* American-made auto sales in Japan for the last quarter of 1995 were averaging 15,000 units per month. This was an increase from about 10,000 per month before the auto accords in August. In addition, 730 independent garages in Japan were selling American-made auto parts for the first time (Sanger 1996).

Other areas where trade friction between the United States and Japan has been troublesome are in textiles, steel, agricultural products, insurance, airline services, and semiconductors. Textiles were a problem in the 1950s, before Japan began large-scale exports in automotive and electronic products. Because of the importation of large amounts of Japanese-produced textile products, the

---

LUXURY AUTO TARIFFS

Problems between Japan and the United States over trade issues were dramatically illustrated by the clash over Japanese luxury auto sales in the U.S. market and American threats to levy heavy—100 percent—tariffs on them. Punitive tariffs on 13 models, including Lexus, Acura, and Infiniti, were threatened by the United States unless Japan made specific provisions for opening its markets to more American-built cars and trucks and American-made auto parts. The last-minute agreement in late June 1995 provided for the phased opening of Japanese car dealerships to more American vehicles and repair garages to more American parts, but without specific numerical targets. Both sides claimed victory. The American negotiator was Mickey Kantor, who presented the Japanese negotiator with a *Kendo* sword at the beginning of the talks. After Ron Brown died in a plane crash, President Clinton named Kantor the new secretary of commerce. The negotiator for Japan in the talks was the minister of international trade and industry, Hashimoto Ryotaro. Hashimoto holds the equivalent of a black belt in *Kendo.* In January 1996, Hashimoto became Japanese prime minister.

United States successfully pressured Japan to voluntarily reduce its exports. In the 1960s and 1970s, steel exports presented a similar threat to the U.S. steel industry, and similar voluntary agreements were established, though not without some difficulty. Agricultural products such as beef, oranges, and rice were major problems into the 1980s. Japanese import restrictions on these items, and the complete exclusion of foreign rice from Japanese markets, were the central issues. Import restrictions on beef and oranges were later lifted, though tariffs were temporarily raised. Hailed as something of a breakthrough by American negotiators was the 1986 semiconductor agreement which required Japan to guarantee a 20 percent share of the market in Japan to chips manufactured by American companies. Years later, American negotiators often attempted to strike similar deals for other markets, a tactic the Japanese labeled "managed trade." Many of the negotiations that affect Japan–United States trade relations have been done through GATT authorities and will increasingly be done through World Trade Organization authorities in the future. Other negotiations, however, are strictly bilateral.

Among the more important bilateral talks were the Structural Impediments Initiative (SII) talks that began in 1989. These were designed to look at the various structural factors in each economy that contributed to economic and trade problems and to develop strategies for dealing with them. Important topics with respect to Japanese structures were the *keiretsu,* the complex distribution system, and restrictions on foreign businesses in Japan. Important U.S. topics included management procedures, the education of workers, and research and development practices. *Keiretsu* are groupings of mutually dependent enterprises with sometimes vague and sometimes clear past associations with the prewar ***zaibatsu***. According to one study, there are today six "big" and "horizontal *keiretsu*" with close connections to earlier *zaibatsu* (Maruyama 1992). *Keiretsu* companies borrow from the same banks and do business with other members of the *keiretsu*. There are many types and variations of *keiretsu*, but essentially they form close associations with each other and with parent companies. One result is the virtual impossibility of foreign subcontractors to break into the market in question. Defenders emphasize the traditional importance of trust and familiarity over time in Japanese business practices. Critics use terms like cartel, trust, and *zaibatsu* to point to the closed nature of *keiretsu* associations.

The distribution system in Japan involves sometimes myriad "middle people." Most retailers in Japan, traditionally, are small businesses. These businesses often depend on wholesalers for a broad range of services, such as inventory and frequent deliveries. The patterns that have been established are related also to the traditional patterns of life in urban Japan and to things as basic as eating habits. For example, the traditional diet of vegetables and seafood requires freshness. Trips to the grocery store, therefore, are daily. These trips are most often made on foot or by bicycle as well because the small food retailers, "mom and pops," are scattered all over large cities and always nearby. What is true of grocery outlets is also true of dry cleaners, small appliance stores, noodle shops, hair cutters, bakeries, and the rest. With such an emphasis on small retail stores, there is a consequent need for much distribution, and often. Economies of scale are not the primary object. In 1973, the Diet passed the Large Scale Retail Stores Law in an effort to protect these small businesses. Under the law, long and complex procedures are required before large retail stores can open. Defenders point to the mom and pops and the need to preserve the patterns that go with them. Critics, often though not always foreign critics, charge that the law makes it almost impossible for large, overseas retailers to crack Japanese markets. Yet, Toys 'Я' Us opened its first large retail toy store in Osaka in December 1991, and first-year sales figures were more than double the target set by the company of $51 million. Early success prompted the American company to open five more Japanese stores in 1992, with another eight planned for 1993 ("Toys 'R' Us" 1993).

Other American companies, such as Kodak, have had great difficulties with the subtleties and frustrations of doing business in Japan. Kodak sales of film in Japan, in the mid-1990s, represented about 10 percent of the market, a much smaller share than the large Japanese manufacturer Fuji. In Tokyo, however, Kodak did better at 14 percent of the market. Frustrated by years of poor sales in small retail stores, Kodak began to publicize claims that subtle forms of collusion were keeping the company from being competitive. For example, for customers in Japan who just ask for film, without designating a brand, large numbers of retailers tend to hand them Fuji. Also, the four largest wholesale film distributors in Japan do not handle Kodak. The problem is compounded by the fact that what barriers exist are subtle and do not involve tariffs or import quotas or bureaucratic red tape involving permits necessary to build a large retail outlet. The prospect of bringing the dispute to the World Trade Organization, consequently, does not appeal to Kodak. This case illustrates several of the characteristics of internal Japanese market conditions such as relationships based on trust over time and small retailers dependent on large wholesalers (Sugawara 1996, 1).

GLOBALIZATION AND NATIONAL SECURITY

The Japanese government is involved in several land disputes with China and South Korea, mostly island claims and potentially rich oil and mineral resources. The *Senkaku Islands*, southwest of Okinawa, are among the disputed islands. But in different areas beneath the East China Sea are potentially large oil pools that both China and Japan would like to tap. Presently, the Foreign Ministry of Japan is discouraging Japanese oil companies from exploration of the region so as not to provoke the Chinese. The Chinese, on the other hand, began limited exploration in the fall of 1995. Japanese officials claim that Japanese sovereignty over the Senkaku Islands was never challenged by China until reports of oil and natural gas reserves began circulating. For the national House election in October 1996, the Liberal Democratic Party put the Japanese claim to

HIROSHIMA'S ASIAN GAMES

In October 1994, Hiroshima was host in Japan to the Twelfth Asian Games. Over 7,000 athletes from 42 countries competed in the first games to be held outside of a national capital. The Hiroshima games were also the second hosted by Japan, the first being in 1958 in Tokyo. As the games in Tokyo prepared the Japanese government for hosting the Tokyo Olympics in 1964, so also did the Hiroshima games serve as a warmup for the Nagano Winter Olympics in 1998. The Asian Games symbolize Japan's increasing diplomatic focus on building more Asian ties. Among events at the games were a number of native Asian games such as the Korean *taekwando.* The games also were an economic boost for the city of Hiroshima and the surrounding region. A new railway system, airport, hotels, and athletic complex were all built for the games.

the Senkaku Islands in its platform. The official *China Daily* in Beijing warned that Japan was "embarking on the road to confrontation" ("Troubled Waters" 1996). Similarly, South Korea and Japan both claim jurisdiction over waters between them, waters that also could contain large underwater oil pools. Disputes with both China and South Korea increased in recent years due to pressure on all three countries to delineate economic zones under the 1994 UN Convention on the Law of the Sea. With Japanese energy dependence as high as it is, and China's developing industrial economic base needing ever larger energy sources, the stakes are high and the pressures building for diplomatic resolutions in order to avoid potential military confrontation later. Increasingly, foreign initiatives in Japan focus on improving relations with other nations as well (see box on Hiroshima's Asian Games).

Another land dispute, longer and more contentious, is the one with Russia over what the Japanese call the **Northern Territories**. In 1951, Japan renounced claims of sovereignty over the Kurile Islands as part of the San Francisco Peace Treaty. In the years that followed, Japan revised its position several times before agreeing on a "four-island" position in 1955. Under this position, developed by the Ministry of Foreign Affairs, Japan claimed historic ties to and sovereignty over the islands of Etorofu, Kunashiri, Shikotan, and Habomais in the "northern territories." The Soviet Union had earlier agreed to return Shikotan and Habomais, islands outside the Kurile chain, but were unwilling to agree to the new four-island position. Talks between the Soviet Union and Japan in London broke down over this issue. When the LDP was formed in 1955, return of all four islands was in the party platform. Though revisions to the Japanese position were periodically presented during the 1950s, the Japanese government's position today is that all four islands are part of Japan. In September 1992, Boris Yeltsin was scheduled to visit Tokyo but canceled the visit at the last minute. The cancellation was widely believed to be over the four-island issue and Yeltsin's fragile base at home. The islands issue has been dormant since 1992. A complicating issue in the claims is the shadow of the final days of World War II. The

Soviet Union joined the war against Japan only on August 9, 1945. In the closing days of the war Soviet forces occupied the Kurile Islands among other territories which included Manchuria, Korea, and parts of Sakhalin. About 640,000 Japanese, by one account, were taken to the Soviet Union as prisoners of war (Hasegawa 1995, 23). The Kurile Islands, north of Hokkaido, represent a stark contrast to Okinawa, south of Kyushu. While the former remains in the hands of an enemy from the war, the latter has been returned to Japan by another former enemy. This juxtaposition represents a powerful image in the minds of many Japanese who see in the return of the Northern Territories a final closure to the events of the war. As one Japanese scholar has put it: "For the Japanese, this issue acts as an irritating reminder that the legacy of the war has not yet been laid to rest" (Hasegawa 1995, 23).

Beyond relations with the United States, Japanese foreign policy in the closing years of the twentieth century was focused on creating a vision and a framework consistent with a post–Cold War international climate and with hosting the Winter Olympics (see box on Nagano 1998). Regional conflicts based on religious, ethnic, and historical tensions were among the greatest concerns for their potential to escalate into wider conflicts. Other concerns include the economic difficulties of former socialist states, of developing nations (see box on Peruvian Rebels), of the potential spread of nuclear weapons, and of the increasing threat to global stability due to threats to the environment and the spread of infectious diseases. More specifically, Japanese foreign policy is sensitive to regional developments in North Korea, Taiwan, East Asian waters, Russia, and, of course, the People's Republic of China.

With respect to China, in particular, many observers inside and outside of Japan have expressed concerns over the possible repercussions of a veiled "containment policy." By this view, a U.S.–Japan alliance will attempt to contain China in the post–Cold War climate in much the same way that American

---

NAGANO 1998

The Winter Olympic Games took place February 7–22, 1998 in Nagano City, Japan. Located in what is called the "Japanese Alps," Nagano City is the second Japanese city to host the Winter Olympics. In 1972, the Games were held in Sapporo on the island of Hokkaido. The five main facilities in Nagano City were given nicknames in a competition among junior and senior high school students in Japan. The two ice hockey stadiums are called "Big Hat," and "Aqua Wing." The speed skating arena is called "M Wave." The arena housing the figure skating rink is called "White Ring," and the bobsled/luge track is named "Spiral." For the games, a new line for the *shinkansen* (bullet train) was built to connect Nagano with Tokyo. The trip takes about 90 minutes. For the official poster of the XVIII Winter Games, a thrush that migrates every year to Japan from Siberia is the central image and symbol. The intention is to symbolize the special care that has been taken to preserve the natural habitat in the mountains surrounding the location for the Games.

PERUVIAN REBELS TAKE HOSTAGES

On December 18, 1996, approximately 20 armed rebels attacked the Japanese ambassador's residence in Lima, Peru, and took hundreds of guests as hostages. Identifying themselves as the Tupac Amaru movement, they demanded that their imprisoned colleagues be released. Hundreds were at the residence during the attack, which took place during a party in celebration of Japanese Emperor Akihito's sixty-third birthday. Over the next several days, scores of hostages were released leaving a core of 72 hostages, which included the Japanese ambassador. Talks between the rebels and the Peruvian government were broken off in early March due to rebel allegations that the government was digging a tunnel under the residence. On April 22, Peruvian troops stormed the residence and rescued all but one of the hostages. All of the Tupac Amaru rebels and two of the soldiers were killed in the raid.

foreign policy during the Cold War aimed at "containing" the Soviet Union. Chalmers Johnson, for example, has suggested that among the "implications of containment" is the "possibility of war" (1996, 12). For Johnson, many Chinese feel victimized historically by both the West and Japan. This is particularly true with respect to Japan. According to Johnson, "no politically sentient Chinese will ever fully forgive the Japanese" (1996, 12). It was the Japanese military in China during the 1930s, after all, which set the stage for the communist drive to power in China. Scholars such as Johnson see a report for the U.S. Department of Defense by Joseph Nye, published in 1995, as the real impetus to the Japanese and American agreements of April 1996, which pledge both nations to an expanded military alliance to prevent "instability" in East Asia. To these observers preventing "instability" looks remarkably like "containment." One Chinese official has been quoted as saying that "whether or not the Japanese government admits, the two countries are trying to turn the Japan–U.S. Security Treaty against China" (Johnson 1996, 13). President Clinton, largely to allay concerns over America's China policy, stressed the need to improve relations with China in his first State of the Union Address following his reelection to a second term. In March 1997, Vice President Al Gore visited China to discuss these and other issues, such as the transfer of Hong Kong to Chinese sovereignty and new trade relations. He stopped in Tokyo for discussions with Prime Minister Hashimoto on the way to Beijing.

Throughout all of these considerations are two more global concerns: the major and especially vexing problem of Japan's future role within the United Nations' peacekeeping operations and within the Security Council and the role of the new World Trade Organization in monitoring global trade patterns.

Clouding virtually all of Japan's efforts, most notably with neighbors in East Asia, are memories that linger and continue to haunt from World War II. Periodic comments by Japanese ministers and subministerial administrators that show insensitivity to war legacies make international news. The "comfort women" issue remains unresolved to the satisfaction of many. Visits by the prime minister and members of the cabinet to Yasukuni Shrine in 1996 were considered especially insensitive to Asian neighbors that were victimized by the Imperial Army during the war. Special attention was focused on the war's legacies by the occasion of the fiftieth anniversary of the end of World War II in 1995. A resolution passed by the House of Representatives was thought anemic by most and was not even taken up by the House of Councillors. This weak signal takes on more dramatic meaning when measured by Japan's stated desire to build stronger ties with regional Asian governments and peoples. The Diplomatic Bluebook of the Ministry of Foreign Affairs for 1995 states clearly that Japan's foreign policy will develop beyond the Cold War framework where Japan was a "member of the West" and toward nations with "common values." The tone and context of the remarks are such as to emphasize the importance of regional cooperation and development. Noted by many in 1995 was the gap between the resolution of the House regarding the war and remarks in the Bluebook regarding "mutual trust" and the importance for Japan to "look squarely at the history of its relations with neighboring Asian countries" (Ministry of Foreign Affairs 1995).

Under the revisions to guidelines for dispatching Self Defense Forces in the International Peace Cooperation Law passed by the Diet in 1992, Japan has sent troops to Rwanda, the Golan Heights, Angola, Cambodia, Mozambique, and El Salvador through 1996. Despite early opposition by many, public opinion, as expressed in polls, seems to accept these operations without much controversy. One poll, for example, showed 75 percent "in favor" of "future SDF participation in UN peacekeeping operations," with only 14.2 percent saying they were against future missions. An earlier poll, in 1991, had shown only 45.5 percent support and 37.9 percent opposition to UN peacekeeping operations (Nishimura and Chiba 1996, 7). The Self Defense Forces operate under strict limits regarding the use of weapons or, in some instances, of the weapons they are permitted to carry. Other limits in the 1992 legislation require that there must be an agreement to a cease-fire by the parties in conflict; the rival parties must give consent to peacekeeping forces and to Japanese forces in particular; and the peacekeeping forces must pledge themselves to strict neutrality in the conflict. Also, if any of the restrictions are compromised, Japan reserves the right to withdraw its forces, and the use of weapons is restricted to the minimal level necessary to protect the lives of Self Defense Forces (Takai 1996). The emphasis in the missions has been on humanitarian aid, assistance in road building and other civil engineering projects, and monitoring elections. The debate regarding the constitutionality of these operations continues and is the background for various calls to revise Article 9 of the Japanese constitution so as to clarify the legal status of the SDF.

The turnabout on this issue by the Social Democratic Party under Prime Minister Murayama as part of the coalition with the LDP and *Sakigake* is among the main reasons for the demise of Japan's leading opposition party under the 55 system. As for the LDP, two leaders stand out: Kono Yohei, as deputy prime minister and minister of foreign affairs, spoke to the UN General Assembly in September 1994 regarding Japan's continued commitment to its "peace" constitution. In September 1995, the LDP chose its new president from a contest between Kono and Hashimoto Ryutaro. The latter won, and in January 1996 became prime minister. In the following summer, Hashimoto made the controversial appearance at Yasukuni Shrine. There is much internal debate and discussion within the LDP as there is within Japan as a whole on the complex issue of Japan's potential military role in peacekeeping operations. This issue also clouds Japan's stated goal of seeking a permanent seat on the United Nations Security Council. In Japan's favor in its quest for a permanent seat is its disbursements of foreign aid in recent years through its Official Development Assistance (ODA) program. Japan's foreign aid disbursements, as tracked by the OECD, has been the highest among all nations for five straight years through 1996. In 1995, disbursements were $14.5 billion. Largest recipients of the aid were countries in Asia (57 percent), Africa (12 percent), Central and South American states (9 percent), and the Middle East (8 percent) (Japan Information and Culture Center 1996a, 3).

Among regional developments posing the largest potential threat to Japan are North Korea's possible development of nuclear weapons and, of course, the continuing emergence of China as an economic and military power. With respect to North Korea, the United States and North Korea signed an Agreed Framework in 1994 to resolve problems regarding inspections in North Korea and to provide for international agency monitoring of future actions in North Korea. The United States agreed to supply North Korea with light-water nuclear reactors to substitute for other types, fuel for which being potentially useful in the development of strategic weapons. The Japanese government fully supports these developments. Japan's relations with both Korean governments is complicated by a long history of regional conflict between Japan and Korea, Japan's annexation of Korea between 1910 and 1945, and the presence in Japan of a large Korean minority that does not enjoy the privileges of Japanese citizenship and maintain close ties with family and friends in both Koreas. Large amounts of money are sent by Koreans living in Japan to family members living in both parts of Korea, but especially North Korea. With North Korea under a communist government, under international suspicion for its moves toward developing a nuclear capability, and with its people living mostly in impoverished conditions, the unofficial movement of large sums of money from private residents in Japan to North Korea represents a type of unofficial foreign aid with few precedents. As for China, Japan's relationship is long, complex, and today, fragile. Friction stems from territorial disputes, war and prewar "colonial" memories, China's recent development as an economic and military power, and the continuing conflict involving the status of Taiwan.

Summary

Especially prominent in modern Japanese history are the long isolation of the Edo Period, the modernization of the Meiji Period, and the Pacific War and its aftermath. The isolation contributed to the development of Japanese uniqueness. The rush to modernization contributed to internal dissent, the civilization and enlightenment movement, a constitution based on a blend of Western and indigenous Japanese ideas, and imperialism. The Pacific War and its aftermath created a polarization within Japanese society with many complex features. Japan's modern involvement in global affairs begins with Commodore Perry's visit to Edo in 1853. Following the Meiji Restoration and victories over China and Russia on the battlefield, Japan established itself as a rival to Western powers at the opening of the twentieth century. With defeat in World War II, Japan entered a period of foreign occupation and national rebuilding. Among the most dramatic products of this period is the 1947 Constitution with its renunciation of war. With respect to global affairs, the postwar years were characterized mostly by Japan's alliance with the United States during the Cold War and the concurrent drive to rebuild a devastated economy. Increasingly, with the gradual economic recovery of the 1950s and 1960s, Japan became more involved with world trade. In the early postwar years, Japanese trade was imbalanced toward imports. In the mid-1960s, trade balances began to move in Japan's favor. In the 1990s, Japanese trade is dominated by dependency in critical areas, notably agriculture and oil, and success in other areas. Especially successful for Japan have been the exports of automotive and electronic products, as consumers the world over are aware.

Relations with the United States have been especially problematic for Japan in recent years. The Okinawan base is an especially difficult problem, and a resolution satisfactory to all sides will be hard to come by. In the spring of 1996, President Clinton went to Tokyo to sign a joint declaration with Prime Minister Hashimoto pledging both sides to continued cooperation regarding defense issues in the Pacific region. Concerns that the new agreement pledges Japan to "collective self-defense" have been raised by many, especially inside Japan. Japan's Self Defense Forces currently number around 145,000 personnel, a reduction from recent numbers closer to 180,000. Many Japanese citizens see the primary purpose of the SDF as disaster relief more than defense. Polls also show that a large number of Japanese citizens, especially younger ones, are unconcerned with defense issues. Problems also exist in trade relations with the United States. The United States is the number one destination of Japanese exports and also the largest source of Japanese imports. Frictions surrounding trade imbalances with huge surpluses going to Japan and allegations from the United States that Japanese markets remain closed or heavily regulated have increased in recent years. Auto parts, luxury autos, semiconductors, and photographic film have been especially high-profile problem areas. Bilateral talks combine with multilateral discussions associated with GATT and APEC to address these and other trade problems between Japan and the United States.

With respect to other nations, Japan has growing problems connected to land disputes. Japanese claims to the Senkaku Islands are challenged by China; other claims to islands in the area are challenged by South Korea. The largest dispute is with Russia over the status of what the Japanese call the Northern Territories, islands off the north coast of Hokkaido presently occupied by Russia. Relations with China have become particularly sensitive in recent years due to the changing dynamics of a post–Cold War global climate. Some in China see Japan allying with the United States to "contain" China today much in the same way that a containment policy was formulated against the Soviet Union during the Cold War. Clouding all of Japan's actions in foreign policy are memories of the war years. With the International Peace Cooperation Law of 1992, Japan is again sending troops overseas. Though the missions are highly restricted and for the purpose of peacekeeping operations, some see precedents being set whereby Japanese troops will once again be dispersed overseas on different and more dangerous missions. North Korea remains a major concern for the Japanese government due to proximity, traditional hostilities, and North Korea's alleged nuclear potential. Among Japan's biggest goals today is a permanent seat on the United Nations Security Council.

Suggested Readings

Calder, Kent E. 1996. *Pacific Defense: Arms, Energy, and America's Future in Asia.* New York: William Morrow.

Cohen, Stephen D. 1985. *Uneasy Partnership: Competition and Conflict in United States–Japan Trade Relations.* Cambridge, MA: Ballinger.

Green, Michael J. 1995. *Armed Japan: Defense Production, Alliance Politics, and the Postwar Search for Autonomy.* New York: Columbia University Press.

Holland, Harrison M. 1992. *Japan Challenges America: Managing an Alliance in Crisis.* Boulder, CO: Westview Press.

Lincoln, Edward J. 1993. *Japan's New Global Role.* Washington, DC: Brookings Institution.

Samuels, Richard J. *Rich Nation, Strong Army: National Security and the Technological Transformation of Japan.* Ithaca, NY: Cornell University Press.

Steven, Rob. 1996. *Japan and the New World Order: Global Investments, Trade and Finance.* New York: St. Martin's Press.

Williams, David. 1994. *Japan: Beyond the End of History.* London: Routledge.

Yasutomo, Dennis T. 1995. *The New Multilateralism in Japan's Foreign Policy.* New York: St. Martin's Press.

Works Cited

Blaker, Michael. 1996. Japan in 1995: A Year of Natural and Other Disasters. *Asian Survey* 36 (January): 41–52.

Crowell, Todd. 1996. Target: Star Wars. *Asiaweek* 22 (12 July): 14, 15.

Dower, John. 1973. The U.S.–Japan Military Relationship. In *Postwar Japan: 1945 to the Present*, ed. Jon Livingston, Joe Moore, and Felicia Oldfather, 232–244. New York: Pantheon.

Hasegawa, Tsuyoshi. 1995. Rethinking the Russo-Japanese Territorial Dispute. *Japan Echo* 22 (Winter): 23–31.

Huntington, Samuel P. 1993. The Clash of Civilizations? *Foreign Affairs* 72 (Summer): 22–49.

Japan External Trade Organization (JETRO). 1991. *U.S. and Japan in Figures*. Tokyo.

Japan Information and Culture Center. 1994. Sweeping APEC Free-Trade Plan Is Born; Murayama, Clinton Meet. *Japan Now* 12 (December): 1.

———. 1996a. How U.S. Firms Can Join in Japan's ODA. *Japan Now* 7 (July): 3.

———. 1996b. Trade Surplus Drops 11.4% from 1994. *Japan Now* 3 (March): 3.

Japan Institute for Social and Economic Affairs (JISEA). 1995. *Japan, 1995: An International Comparison*. Tokyo.

Japan Times Weekly International Edition. 1995. 3–9 July, 20.

Johnson, Chalmers. 1995. *Japan: Who Governs?* New York: Norton.

———. Containing China: U.S. and Japan Drift Toward Disaster. *Japan Quarterly* 43 (October–December): 10–18.

Kubota Isao. 1996. Structural Change and the Trade Surplus. *Look Japan* 42 (June): 34, 35.

Maruyama Yoshinari. 1992. The Big Six Horizontal Keiretsu. *Japan Quarterly* 39 (April–June): 186–199.

Ministry of Foreign Affairs of Japan. *Japan's Foreign Policy on CD-ROM: January 1992–March 1995.* Toppan Printing Co.

Mitchell, Alison. 1996. U.S. Military Role in East Asia Gets Support in Tokyo. *New York Times*, 17 April, 1 (A).

Mochizuki, Mike M. 1996. Toward a New Japan–U.S. Alliance. *Japan Quarterly* 43 (July–September): 4–16.

Nishimura Kunio, and Hitoshi Chiba. 1996. Today's SDF. *Look Japan* 42 (June): 6–10.

Sanger, David E. 1996. International Business; Sales of U.S. Autos up 50% in Japan Since Trade Accord. *New York Times*, 12 April, 1 (A).

Sansom, G. B. 1973. *The Western World and Japan: A Study in the Interaction of European and Asiatic Cultures.* New York: Vintage Books.

Shimokobe Atsushi. 1996. Rebuilding Kobe: The "Impossible Dream." *Japan Echo* 23 (Spring): 48–52.

Sugawara, Sandra. 1996. In Japan, a Trade Fight over Film Gets Fuzzy with Overt Barriers Gone. *Washington Post*, 7 April, 1 (H).

Takai Susumu. 1996. Japan's Contribution to U.N. Peacekeeping. *Social Sciences Japan*, no. 6. University of Tokyo: Institute of Social Sciences.

Toys 'R' Us Reports Strong Sales for 1992 in Japan. 1993. *New York Times*, 4 March, 4 (D).

Troubled Waters. 1996. *Economist*, 12 October, 37, 38.

8

Conclusion: Between Yamato and Ukiyo

It might appear strange to conclude an exploration of contemporary Japanese politics with a quotation from Ralph Waldo Emerson. Yet the following insight from Emerson's essay on "Self Reliance" seems especially appropriate:

> Traveling is a fool's paradise. Our first journeys discover to us the indifference of places. At home I dream that at Naples, at Rome, I can be intoxicated with beauty, and lose my sadness. I pack my trunk, embrace my friends, embark on the sea and at last wake up in Naples, and there beside me is the stern fact, the sad self, unrelenting, identical, that I fled from. I seek the Vatican, and the palaces. I affect to be intoxicated with sights and suggestions, but I am not intoxicated. My giant goes with me wherever I go. (Emerson 1967, 1146)

Nations, too, take journeys. And their "giants" go with them. Few nations have taken a bolder journey than Japan in the last 150 years or so. Beginning with the *Meiji Restoration*, and continuing to the present, Japan has undertaken a journey deep into modernity and what many increasingly refer to as postmodernity, with all of the uniquely Western connotations associated with both terms. In just 130 years, six and a half generations, Japan has developed from a regional East Asian power self-consciously cut off from the rest of the world to the second most productive economic power in the world deeply involved in global socioeconomic and political issues. Inasmuch as the most dramatic economic gains have been made in the wake of World War II and its catastrophes, it has become commonplace to refer to recent Japanese history as that of the "Japanese miracle." A large, much debated factor in these developments is the Japanese government. A very large factor in the government has been the *55 system* with the Liberal Democratic Party and its connections in both the corporate and bureaucratic worlds.

Among other things, a journey into modernity means democratization. By the *Taisho* Period (1912–1926), Japan was well on its way in developing toward this largely Western ideal. On March 5, 1919, the American philosopher and educator John Dewey wrote to his children from Japan: "There is no doubt a great change is going on; how permanent it will be depends a good deal upon how the rest of the world behaves. If it doesn't live up to its peaceful and democratic professions, the conservative bureaucrats and militarists, who of course are still very strong, will say we told you so and there will be a backset. But if other countries, and especially our own, behave decently, the democratizing here will go on as steadily and as rapidly as is desirable" (Dewey 1920, 52). Five years later the U.S. government would shut the door to Japanese immigration, an action that led to a day of national mourning in Japan. Within one generation of Dewey's letter, the "bureaucrats and militarists" were leading Japan on a very different journey under an enhanced *kokutai* philosophy. Parties were disbanded, public discussion was limited, military preparedness was heightened, and on December 7, 1941, Hawaii time, the Japanese military government took the irrevocable steps at Pearl Harbor that would lead to destruction and despair. Out of the devastation of the war, however, Japan has built a modern democratic state that most observers see as both a continuation of prewar developments toward a more democratic state and dramatic departures that place Japan among the most democratic of states. Women are granted suffrage and "essential equality" by the 1947 Constitution, the Emperor is clearly to be a "symbol of the state," and, most dramatically, "war as a sovereign right" is renounced.

There is a scene in *Dazai*'s *Setting Sun* where Kazuko, the young woman protagonist, is face to face with a young officer during the war. The young man has loaned her a book and given her an easy duty assignment. He has just returned to release Kazuko from her duties and retrieve his book. Their eyes meet and both Kazuko and the young officer become teary eyed, though no words are spoken. They part and never meet again. Periodically Kazuko thinks about a "special someone" though she knows that they will never meet again in the world of sorrows of postwar Japan. Later, Kazuko is with Uehara, a corrupted, somewhat decadent artist in failing health with whom she will have a child. Uehara, attempting to secure a room for them, tells the innkeeper that the "princess" and the "prince" are in need of a room. In one sense, Uehara is mocking Kazuko's aristocratic family under the *Meiji Constitution*. He hates aristocrats, as he often says. But in another sense, Kazuko represents a no longer "shining" princess and Uehara her might-have-been prince. Uehara is also not the young officer of Kazuko's earlier longings. But Uehara, the artist, represents in decadent form one half of the artist/warrior of *bushido* tradition who is equally talented in the ways both of the sword and the brush. In the postwar milieu of Dazai's literary world of characters, the way of the warrior is a discredited path, a circumstance reflected in the real, political world in *Article 9* of the new constitution.

Today, in the film about the world of the literary artist Rampo (explored in Chapter 1), the princess and the artist are united in the end after a painful search for answers to the many-layered mysteries of *Showa* Japan. These artistic sequences point to a progression in which aspects of a traditional Japanese archetype are slowly, painfully cast aside. Among the biggest challenges for Japan today is to reconcile its growing desire to play a larger role in global affairs without bringing back the ghosts of its militarist past. Japan continues to rely heavily on the presence of U.S. forces for its defense, even as protests grow louder in Okinawa and in Tokyo. Many point out that no world power has ever achieved such status without a strong military.

As is so often the case in studying Japan, scenes such as the above in artistic presentations point to dramatic themes in Japanese history known so well to Japanese audiences. *The Tale of the Heike,* which dates from the early thirteenth century, tells the story of the great twelfth-century struggle between two families: the Taira (also called Heike) and the Minamoto (also called Genji). The victory of the latter ushered in the world and ways of the **Shogun** beginning in 1185. The ensuing **Kamakura** Period (1185–1333) is the beginning of the development of the **samurai**'s status and the **bushido** (way of the warrior) culture. Though there is much in *The Tale of the Heike* about the glorification of military prowess and loyalty unto death, there is also much about tragic lovers and doomed intimacies more characteristic of earlier literature such as *The Tale of Genji.* Both famous tales draw from Buddhist concepts regarding the illusory and ephemeral nature of life. *The Tale of Heike,* however, is saturated with sadness and a sense of the "last days" as taught by Buddhism. The Kamakura Shogunate and the culture of the warrior emerge from this sense of a culture in decay to point the way to a new beginning. Over time the way of the warrior came to be somewhat codified in the *Hagakure,* something of a guidebook for *samurai* published in the early eighteenth century. This warrior ideal came to blend with the aesthetic ideal of the **Heian** Court as dramatized in *The Tale of Genji* and which is usually called **mono no aware.**

Today, as noted in *Oe*'s Stockholm speech, there is much ambiguity within the Japanese people's feelings and within the state. Japan's journey has been toward democratization; but there is Emerson's "giant" that continues to accompany Japan's modern and postmodern journey, a giant that symbolizes all of the complex, enduring elements in the fixed world of traditional Japanese culture.

THE DEMOCRATIC IDEAL IN POSTMODERN CONTEXT

However prescient George Orwell might have been regarding the more distant horizon of political development, the contemporary global frontier is defined by democracy and democracy movements as far as one can see. The democratic ideal is the very cornerstone of post–Cold War political development from images of Tianenman Square to elections in Bosnia Herzegovina in 1996. Democracy as ideal and democracy "movements" as reality define political dynamics in every corner of the globe. Some, such as Francis Fukuyama, have even proclaimed an "end of history." Presumably there will be no more "movements" other than that of democratization. Only "technical problems" remain, by this view. We find ourselves at last at the "end point of mankind's ideological evolution and the universalization of Western liberal democracy as the final form of human government" (Fukuyama 1989, 4). If liberal democracy is the logic of history, then the ruling party during the better part of Japan's postwar rediscovery of democracy has chosen its English name well. The Liberal Democratic Party continues to be the dominant party in Japanese politics going into the twenty-first century. The party's very name assures its harmony with the larger *weltgeist.* The future of democracy in Japan, midwifed by such a party and such a spirit, seems to be assured.

But what of Emerson's insight? He would, perhaps, have us consider the giant that accompanies this modern and democratic journey. And as this giant within Emerson's individual is all of the ghosts and habits, the "can't help but thinks," the unconscious or subconscious of modern psychotherapies, so also is it in the life of nations the cultural centers of gravity—seriousness—that make a people actors in history. Emerson's insight beckons the scholar in search of meaning within Japanese political tradition and practice to consider also the insights of the cultural anthropologist. In this spirit, our concluding observations will focus on four issues: the meaning of democracy in its contemporary idiom; the effect of selected features of Japanese culture on the development of democracy in Japan; the role of the Liberal Democratic Party in mediating essential distinctions between the two under the 55 system; and the direction of change as Japan enters the twenty-first century and the challenges of what many scholars increasingly refer to as a "postmodern" global political environment.

"Democratization" is the great political ideal of the modern era. Yet, according to Giovanni Sartori, we live in an age of "confused democracy" (1987, 3–6). And although conceptual clarity is critical, the prospect of effective communication appears to be jeopardized by an integral feature of modern democracy itself—the growth, development, and international diffusion of mass communications. To tune in or overhear representative media accounts of events in Bosnia Herzegovina, Iraq, Poland, Hungary, the People's Republic of China, the Czech Republic, Russia, Nicaragua, Mexico, or any other nation, including the United States and Japan, one would think that democracy is both simple and self-evident as to its meaning. Erich Kahler's analysis of what he called the "overpopulation of the surfaces," noted in Chapter 6, suggests the nature of the problem (1989, 93–97). By definition, mass communications sacrifice depth and dialogue to surface images and apparent self-evident conclusions. When Thomas Jefferson, within the context of the evolution of modern democracy, appealed to self-evident truths in the Declaration of Independence of the American states, the climate of opinion in the American states was far removed from that of the so-called global village of contemporary telecommunications technology. The appeal was more to the Socratic "know thyself" of ancient and classical Western civilization than to the industrial or postindustrial world's "know thy work and do it."

The distinction is from Thomas Carlyle's *Sartor Resartus,* and it was one heavy on the mind of Henry Adams in his writing *The Education of Henry Adams.* Adams, whose great grandfather, John, was the second president of the United States, whose grandfather was President John Quincy Adams, and whose father was English Ambassador Charles Francis Adams, was a historian interested in the extraordinary distance between his world and the world of his famous ancestors. The *Education of Henry Adams* explores, among a rich variety of topics, the demands of a new world of forces, a world symbolized by the image of the dynamo, and the inadequacy of traditional education to prepare public servants, or citizens, for such a world. The "know thyself" challenge of traditional education became, by the late nineteenth century, somewhat outdated. Modern politics had become, in Adams's view, "a struggle not of men but of forces." He observed men becoming "more and more creatures of force, massed about central power-houses." For Adams, the "height of knowledge" was still to know "not only the forces but also the men" (1973, 421–424).

The relevance of Adams's insights to an understanding of the development of modern democracy in the West is difficult to state concisely. But at the center of his vision was a seam, perhaps a split, that divided politics in the West according to a pre- and postindustrial style. And, for Adams, appeals to "self-evident truths" in the latter "style" would become increasingly difficult. As Emerson warned of the "giants" we carry with us, Adams warned of the giants that stalk citizens in the modern world. And one very important aspect of the giant stalking modern democracy was the message that people ought to know their "work" and "do it," in Carlyle's phrase. It was about the time of this transition, one that might be concisely captured as a transition from citizenship to production and consumption as the central focus of the democratic ideal in the West, that Japanese "voyagers" embarked on their Western journeys in search of Western concepts, practices, designs, and details regarding democratic governance. The "surfaces" of democracy in America during this time, and to some degree in other Western nation-states, were somewhat commercial surfaces. And these commercial surfaces had a tendency to obscure somewhat the deeper traditions of thought and experience that continued to nurture Western concepts of good governance and healthy political practice in the late nineteenth century.

One could make the case that the commercialization of Western concepts of good government and the democratic ideal in particular led in large measure to the imperialist tone, texture, and essential substance in some cases of the foreign policies emanating from Western capitals. This is among the themes in Hannah Arendt's study of the *Origins of Totalitarianism* published after World War II (1951). Any consideration of the democratic ideal today must give passing glances, at least, to the early modern dimensions in the development of democratization in the West, if for no other reason than that so much of the tone of postmodern discussion regarding the concept of democracy has premodern overtones. One reasonable place to focus a brief examination of early modern Western democratic theory is on Thomas Jefferson's faith in self-evident truths. Such a focus should give the broadest outline of the meaning of democracy in its early modern meaning. Also, Jefferson is often cited today, internationally, as a symbol for all that is implied in references to the concept of democracy. As a grass-roots example, one can visit even the remotest parts of Japan, and despite a limited knowledge of things Western or American in particular, the name of Thomas Jefferson somehow captures an essential spirit, a common sense, of modern and American politics.

For Jefferson, four essential truths are self-evident: that all men are created equal; that all men are endowed with natural and inalienable rights; that legitimate governments exist only by consent of the governed; and that governments that become destructive of their proper ends may be altered or abolished. In political science, much traditional and continuing research probes the meaning and applications, the theory and practices, of these Jeffersonian "truths." As for the first of these truths, some concept of equality has always been associated with democracy. Sartori calls it a "protest ideal." In the evolution of the concept from Jefferson's day and its role in the revolutionary psychology of the French Declaration of Rights, it has come to mean primarily equal universal suffrage, social equality of status and consideration, and equality of opportunity. Recent legislation and adjudication in the United States involving the extension of suffrage opportunities, such as the "motor voter" provisions for registration, involving the social equality of women in their applications to military academies, and in the debates surrounding affirmative action are all related to the continuing development of this democratic concept of equality.

But these are the primary meanings of equality within the context of a liberal democratic tradition. With respect to a social democratic tradition, one must add economic equality. And this makes an important point in any discussion of the democratic ideal in the modern, or postmodern, world. The existence of a distinction between liberal and social democratic traditions must be acknowledged at the outset and care given to the use of appropriate, or at least reasonable, adjectives. In Japan, for example, the Liberal Democratic Party represents, however inconsistently at times, and always as filtered through Japanese experiences and traditions, a liberal democratic tradition that echoes American themes and English parliamentary practice. The Social Democratic Party of Japan, the former Democratic Socialist Party, which folded itself within the New Frontier Party in 1994, and the Japan Communist Party all, in varying degrees, and also as measured by Japanese historical experiences, identify with social democratic ideas that center more on economic equality than individual rights as an ideal. It is illustrative of the strong measuring role that Japanese history plays on political ideology to note here that throughout its history the Liberal Democratic Party has been somewhat critical of the 1947 Constitution and has called for major revisions, and, similarly, the Japan Socialist Party (today's SDPJ) has supported the document despite its "bourgeois" origins. The essential point with respect to any global consideration of the idea of democracy, or certainly in the Japanese experience with democracy, is that the distinction between liberal and social democratic traditions be kept near the center of discussion. It is a distinction that the mass media, as a matter of course, tend to avoid.

Another point with respect to the meaning of democracy in general and the principle of equality in particular has to do with the institutional context within which ideals and principles become measures of reality in society. In the United States, for example, and perhaps reflecting the development of the democratic ideal there out of an earlier republicanism, it is a constitutional/legal tradition centered in higher law thinking that shapes the particular meaning of ideals like equality. The constitutional guarantee of equal protection of the law in the Fourteenth Amendment to the U.S. Constitution is a practical, legal expression of the Jeffersonian appeal to the principle of equality. In the brighter light of courtroom dialogue, measured by the continuing dialogue of previous courts considering similar issues, equality in America today has come to mean, among other things, that no majority in the U.S. Congress, nor any majority in any of the state legislatures, may pass laws containing "suspect classifications." Race is a suspect classification, age is not; sex is "quasi-suspect" (Burns, Peltason, and Cronin 1989, 108–110). The importance of all this for an evaluation of democracy in the modern world and for Japan in particular lies in the fact that it is not always, or perhaps even often, that political, legislative, electoral, or party competitive factors determine the meaning and operation of basic democratic ideals.

With respect to Jefferson's appeal to inalienable rights to life, liberty, and the pursuit of happiness, the modern development would be the centrality of human rights to the idea of democracy. For democracy in America, these ideals are embodied in the Bill of Rights of the U.S. Constitution, the various bills of rights in the constitutions of the 50 states, and in court interpretations of specific provisions in each. The center of gravity in contemporary debates is the right of privacy and its boundaries. Issues of sexual preference, censorship, search and seizure, electronic surveillance, drug testing, and news gathering have all forced public debates on the meaning and limits of privacy. Research on precedents and historical developments with respect to this critical issue have given a sort of renaissance to the importance of public and private as an essential distinction in the development of modern democratic thought. The centrality of this distinction, expressed or implied, in the development of Western ideals of democracy and its relative absence in traditional Japanese culture represent an important East/West distinction related to a wide range of issues and will be returned to in the following section on democratic development in Japan.

Privacy has not always been the implied center of rights thinking. In the late nineteenth-century, the so-called Lochner era of American jurisprudence, rights suggested "property" rights. That part of the Constitution's Fourteenth Amendment that might be called the "life, liberty, and property" clause came to be called the "due process clause." Instead of drawing attention to the Lockean and Jeffersonian legacies of a broad-based concept of natural rights, the U.S. Supreme Court, under the pressures of a dominant social Darwinist psychology, honed its interpretation of the meaning of "liberty" as liberty of trade and contract. Due process came to mean substantive due process, and the court assumed the role of midwife to the industrial revolution and its needs. These observations are important in the context of evaluations of democracy in Japan. Many critics, notably those among so-called "revisionist" writers, lament the absence of democratic public policy making in Japanese government circles pointing invariably to the role of the bureaucracy—MITI and the Ministry of Finance in particular—as evidence to support their views. Curiously, some public and party officials in Japan today, in their zeal to reform *kasumigaseki*, sound remarkably like these revisionist scholars. The suggestion in both cases is that, unlike true democracies, Japan is run by bureaucratic and corporate elites to the detriment of Japanese citizens and consumers and also to the ruin of equitable foreign trade relations. Yet, a similar objection can be made to developments in the United States during the height of its advance toward an industrialized economic base. The difference, perhaps reflecting different cultural and historical roots, is that in the American case the elite institution allied with corporate interests was the legal profession and its social Darwinist voice on the bench at the highest levels. Both nation-states carry their giants with them.

That legitimacy is conferred by consent, Jefferson's third self-evident truth, is the very cornerstone of democratic theory. Most contemporary accounts of democracy stress the importance of party competition as the essential prerequisite for structuring political choice for voters in regular elections. This is the context, too, of much of the reform debate and the ensuing reform legislation that created a new electoral system in Japan, first implemented in the October 1996 House election. Most analysts before and after the new legislation argued that it would encourage party competition, issue politics, and voter participation. Early reviews of the first election under the reforms include numerous critics, however. Consent of the governed is also the spirit of popular sovereignty, the guiding principle of the 1947 Constitution. An increasingly common conceptualization of democratic politics, one that also integrates the other dimensions of Jefferson's vision, is called *polyarchy*. Scholars such as Robert Dahl, Charles Lindblom, and Harmon Zeigler have used this term to identify a kind of minimal definition of democracy. According to Dahl, for example, polyarchy requires the freedom to create and join organizations, to express oneself, to vote, to seek office, to seek support for public policies, to access alternative sources of information, to take part in free and fair elections, and to be governed by institutions that depend on fair votes and the choosing of preferences. Harmon Zeigler sums up the meaning this way: "All systems that assign positions of formal authority in response to a routinized indication of citizen's wishes—that is, an election—and do so in a manner that ensures that each vote counts equally are polyarchies, and since that term is unfamiliar, we call them democracies" (1990, 79). This definition underscores the centrality of the concept of consent in contemporary democratic, or polyarchal, theory. Whether one uses the term *polyarchy* or *democracy*, reform efforts in Japan are rooted in this point of view as are continuing efforts that focus on reforming the bureaucracy.

Though not presented explicitly as a "self-evident truth" by Jefferson, the modern concept of democracy also includes the idea of an essential distinction between public and private activities. When John Locke began his *Second Treatise of Government*, he was especially concerned with distinguishing between the claim of Sir Robert Filmer that "Adams' Private Dominion and Paternal Jurisdiction" was the "Fountain of all power" and the claim that political power was, in truth, "a Right of making Laws with Penalties of Death, and consequently all less Penalties, for the Regulating and Preserving of Property, and of employing the force of the Community, in the Execution of such Laws, and in the defence of the Common-wealth from Foreign Injury, and all this only for the Publick Good" (Locke 1963, 307, 308). The power of a magistrate over a subject or, perhaps, a citizen is to be distinguished from the power of a "Father over his children" or a "Master over his Servant." From this distinction between private and public forms of power, Locke begins his famous discussion "Of the State of Nature," a discussion that has as its principal concern the identification of perfect freedom and equality as the state "all Men are naturally in" (Locke 1963, 308, 309). This is, of course, the *axis mundi* of liberalism and of liberal democratic theory. The essential point is that political relationships should not be confused with private ones. In Hannah Arendt's terms, the "distinction between a private and a public sphere of life corresponds to the household and the political realms, which have existed as distinct, separate entities at least since the rise of the ancient city-state" (1958, 28).

Modern democratic theory and practice is heir to Locke on this point. And Locke is heir to a distinction basic to ancient political theory in the West. Modern expressions of this essential distinction are open meetings laws, ethics legislation, public disclosure statutes, public financing reform proposals, and, perhaps most importantly, public dialogue regarding real or potential conflicts of interest. What is especially important is the realization that in modern discussions of democracy and democracy movements, it is as much corruption and potential corruption that warrants and receives attention as the fear of centralized power. The real or imagined corruption of the public trust through a conflict of interest remains a constant concern in modern democratic forms of government, whether heirs to a liberal or social democratic tradition. One might argue that democracy, with all of its complexity and diversity of form in practice, whether presidential or parliamentary, has as its spiritual substance an essential distinction between private and public things that cannot be compromised. The former, writ large, is undemocratic. The latter is the very spirit of the laws in modern democracies regardless of institutional particulars. That corruption of the public trust is a major concern of Japanese citizens is, in today's world, a "self-evident truth."

DEMOCRACY JAPANESE STYLE

To listen to some revisionist scholars, one is tempted to think that there can be little future for democracy in Japan, for the simple reason that there has never been any. A primary reason often given for the incompatibility of democratic visions and Japanese experience is that the latter begins with and continues to be steeped in social ranking, a vertical assumption regarding proper human relationships. Social ranking is also, of course, an integral feature of Western societies historically. The appeal of Marxism, East or West, has always been rooted at least in part in its challenges to established class rankings. One can see the faded legacy of these rankings in contemporary British government resting as it still does on a psychology of the one (monarch), the few (lords), and the many (commons). Although political power is firmly established in the Commons, the residue of an ancient culture persists in the very constitution of the state. And not a little attention is paid to the royal family. Similarly, in the United States constitutional scheme, which is almost universally presented as a system of separating, checking, and balancing power, one can see the faded traces of the same cultural psychology. The president is a symbol of the one, the chief of state, and has virtually unrestrained power in war and diplomacy, the Senate is still regarded as the "upper" house with all of the class connotations that go with it, and the House is the voice—in theory at least—of the many. More tellingly, the Supreme Court has come to play the role of the few "wise" whose deeper understanding of higher law, precedent, and founding intention gives them the power of judicial review. These and other examples in Western national experience—the three estates of French tradition, for example—all point to the weight of tradition and its hierarchical structures in modern democratic states. In Japanese society, *amae* (dependency), *on* (obligation), and *iegara* (lineage), complex terms referring to personal relationships and their larger effects, certainly continue to play important roles. But the large forces of historical change are in the direction of egalitarian, or horizontal, relations. As Edwin Reischauer put it: "The traditional sense of hierarchy of the Japanese has been fitted very smoothly into what is now a basically egalitarian society, and thus it remains a major and efficiently functioning feature of contemporary Japanese society" (1981, 237).

Attributes often singled out in Japanese studies are hierarchy, social relativism, and the importance of the group and group identification. Nakane Chie's 1970 study of Japanese society, for example, stresses the importance of social hierarchy in Japan. Takie Sugiyama Lebra, in her study of *Japanese Patterns of Behavior* (1976), emphasizes social relativism as the "ethos" of Japanese society. And Ishida Takeshi's 1983 study of the political culture in Japan gives special recognition to "group cohesiveness." Frequently mentioned, Doi Takeo's study (1973) of *amae* often frames discussions of Japanese uniqueness and a particular kind of hierarchical orientation. Less often explored is the relationship between the public and private aspects of life in Japan. At the beginning of the modern state in early *Meiji*, an unusual concept of "public" and "public man" began to make its appearance in Japan. This is one of the arguments in a contemporary work by Andrew Barshay on the public man in crisis in imperial Japan. The following is an excerpt:

The creation and the development of the modern state in Japan simultaneously redefined both politics and society. In this process, a vast area of social thought and practice concerned with the national life, one that fed and transcended official and purely private activity, also emerged. This was the "public" sphere, whose emergence also produced the type of intellectuals I call "public men." Owing to the heavily bureaucratic character of Japan's political and institutional evolution, however, "publicness" soon ramified into positions distinctly "inside" and "outside." Public life pursued in large, especially official, organizations was accorded greater value and prestige; independent (and dissident) activity, while public, did not enjoy such approbation. Indeed, *public* tended to be identified with the state itself. (1988, xiii)

According to Barshay, even though the 1868 Charter Oath specified that "all measures (shall be decided by) public discussion," this meant in practice that only "inside" members of official organizations would engage in such "discussions." The oldest meaning that attaches to the Japanese concept for "public" (*oyake*) "seems to be that of 'sovereign' (imperial), 'palace,' 'court,' and 'government.'" In other words, "public" and "public men" referred more to "inside" ministry officials and, by the 1890s, inside meant within the higher positions of the "family state" (*kazoku kokka*). This conceptualization of "public" in early Meiji seems closer to the vertical relationships in Robert Filmer's *Patriarcha* than the horizontal ones of Locke's *Second Treatise*, as discussed above.

In a related study, *Palace and Politics in Prewar Japan*, David Titus contrasts the privatized decision-making process in prewar Japan with democratic policy processes. Drawing on the work of E. E. Schattschneider, he presents Japanese politics of the prewar period as the inverse of Schattschneider's definition of democracy as the "socialization of conflict." During this period, "policy initiative, policy advocating, and conflict resolution were basically privatized processes, despite the growth of modern institutions, such as the Diet and the mass media, for socializing conflict" (Titus 1974, 332, 333). What all of this suggests is that early experiences with democracy, from Meiji through Taisho and into Showa, were frustrated by powerful and complex forces among which was a tradition of privatizing rather than socializing conflict. In such a climate, a concept of "public" that is higher than "private" or more than the sum of private interests could not develop. Another way of framing this is to observe that there is no tradition of republicanism prior to Japan's experience with Westernization, modernization, and democratization. The desire of *genro* to catch up with the West and undo **unequal treaties** squeezed out any interest in probing the deeper mysteries of Western political theory. The supporters of **civilization and enlightenment** saw but glimpses of the older civilization and the more traditional forms of enlightenment. In the development of popular sovereignty in Japan, an essential element in modern democratic theory and practice, the distinction between public and private spheres developed only slowly. Even today, public debate and public policy making through discussion, dissent, and deliberation is a new experience.

THE LIBERAL DEMOCRATIC PARTY REVISITED

One reason often given for the slow and incomplete development of democratic practices in Japan during the postwar 55 system is the relationship that developed among Diet committees, national administrative agencies (the bureaucracy), and interest groups. Centering on what are often called *zoku-giin* (hooked in lawmakers), these critics contend that the real public policy decisions were made by long-tenured LDP specialists who worked closely with appropriate civil servants in the bureaucracy to serve well-organized and LDP supporting special interests. On balance, according to most accounts, it is the bureaucracy from which most legislation actually comes. A particularly expressive example of this view is given by Asai Motofumi, professor of international relations at Tokyo University and former career civil servant in the Ministry of Foreign Affairs: "There is no system in Japan, even the Diet, that can assure an effective popular check against the bureaucracy" (1990, 7). Gerald Curtis compares the operation of *zoku-giin* to the "iron triangles" in the U.S. policy process of politicians, bureaucrats, and interest groups. Still, he concedes that the bureaucracy in Japan is autonomous and insulated in degrees "unimaginable in a country like the United States" (Curtis 1988, 110).

With respect to Jefferson's self-evident truth that legitimate government rests on the consent of the governed, then, the nominal regular elections in postwar Japan obscure what some observers regard as poorly developed party competition, a personalistic or compensatory politics, and public policy making by specialists isolated from parliamentary or electoral debate. As recently as October 1996, on the eve of the national election for the House of Representatives, a reporter covering the election from a small town in Japan for the *New York Times* offered this assessment: "Electoral politics in places like Omiya rests on much deeper concepts of Japanese behavior that long predate ballots or democracy: notions of group identity, of hereditary entitlement, and especially of 'giri', the sense of owing someone a debt or obligation" (Kristof 1996, 1). Perhaps all of these characteristics of electoral politics and public policy making in contemporary Japan are residues of the incompletely developed distinction between public and private activities. It is tempting to see in the LDP politics of compensation and *zoku-giin* the contemporary political manifestation of Barshay's "public men" and Titus's privatization of conflict—a temptation that is encouraged further still by late 55 system developments in the internal politics of the Liberal Democratic Party.

The title of the lead article in the Summer 1989 issue of the *Japan Quarterly* summarizes the political center of the late 55 system: "The Liberal Democratic Party in Crisis" (Takabatake 1989). The LDP, due to a combination of scandal and poor judgment, was at its lowest popularity since 1955. In 1989, it was defeated in four straight elections: a by-election in Fukuoka Prefecture in February; another by-election in Niigata Prefecture in June; the Tokyo Metropolitan Assembly elections early in July; and, most surprisingly and seriously, in the national House of Councillors election on July 23, 1989. In the latter election, the

LDP lost a majority for the first time since 1955, falling from 142 seats to 109 (18 less than a majority). The reasons given for this sudden decline included unpopular agricultural policies that put domestic farmers in a pinch; the consumption tax of 3 percent; the liaison of Prime Minister Sosuke Uno with a *geisha* and the subsequent éxposé of the details; and the Recruit Cosmos scandal.

Although all four crises cut deeply into traditional LDP support among farmers, women, and young urban adults, the most serious long-term damage was that created by the Recruit Cosmos scandal. Unlisted stocks were sold to private secretaries, assistants, and family members of government officials and to those officials themselves, all of whom reaped huge profits when the stocks were later listed on the stock exchange. In all, and following a nine-month Public Prosecutor's Office investigation, numerous politicians, civil servants, businessmen, and journalists resigned. The events surrounding the Recruit Cosmos scandal pointed to a larger issue—the role of money in Japanese politics. This is, of course, an issue in all modern democracies, not least in the United States. The traditional conceptualization of the problem is that of conflict of interest, an angle of vision that stresses the centrality of distinguishing private from public activities. Reflecting on the "crisis" in the LDP at the time, Asai Motofumi observed that Japan "is not a mature democracy." With respect to the bureaucracy, he saw little change from the prewar period of David Titus's analysis: "The basic assumption, traditional to officialdom since long before the Occupation's democratic reforms, that the people need not be informed about public policy but should simply obey, is still alive and well in the bureaucracy." Finally, on the LDP, he observed that they were as "indifferent to true democracy as ever" (Asai 1990, 4–7). The Recruit Cosmos scandal turned out to be but the preface to later scandals involving money politics, conflicts of interest, and the rest that reached a peak with the **Kanemaru Shin** revelations. It all set the stage for the end of the 55 system in the summer of 1993 and the introduction of electoral reform legislation the following year that completely redesigned the Japanese political landscape. Few have missed the irony that the turnout in the October 1996 national election for the House of Representatives was the lowest under the present constitution, and, more remarkably, those who did vote all but delivered the new system into the hands of the Liberal Democratic Party.

EXPERIENCE AND SYMBOLIZATION: *YAMATO* AND *UKIYO*

This study began with an image of Japanese politics—reflecting a long and complex cultural experience—as embodying a dynamic relationship between more "fixed" and more "floating" worlds. The former world encompasses all of the older, deeper, more complex traditions within the Japanese experience and as reflected, minimally, in language, religion, aesthetics, literature, and a particular sense of history. In Oe Kenzaburo's terms, the more fixed world represents one side of the "split between two opposite poles of ambiguity" (Oe 1995, 117). The floating world, referring to the traditional Buddhist image of life as ephemeral, encompasses the more democratic experience associated with modern, mostly Western challenges to the fixed world of traditional Japanese experience. Neither of these "poles" represents Japanese politics by itself. Japanese politics is the interplay between these worlds, the "in-between." By this reading, reforming electoral politics in Japan will not lead to a more democratic Japan or, in Ozawa's terms, a "normal" democracy. Not by itself. By this reading, severe critiques of Japanese politics today, such as van Wolferen's often cited *Enigma of Japanese Power,* or Tamamoto Masaru's brilliant essays on politics in Japan, overstate the continuing power of the fixed world on current dynamics. Analyses that begin with assumptions that Japan is a typical modern democracy, or that ignore cultural traits not characteristic of other systems, similarly overstate one of the "poles" that defines Japanese politics. By this reading, the ability to balance the demands of the fixed and floating aspects of Japanese politics since the Meiji Restoration is among the great strengths of the modern Japanese state. This is not to wink and dismiss the seriousness of recent scandals involving both money politics and arrogant administration. It is to suggest that reforms of institutions in the electoral arena will be balanced by reforms in the administrative institutions, and that over time these reforms will be stabilizing, the one by drawing electoral politics into more "fixed" patterns, and the other by reorganizing and opening administrative structures that have become too fixed and rigid. Out of this interplay the modern Japanese state will probably continue to develop into a more mature democracy with a citizenry less conscious of being split in the ways that Oe's remarks in Stockholm, and indeed Oe's works, suggest.

In traditional Japanese culture, there are two particularly expressive linguistic symbols that capture the spirit of the fixed and floating world concepts. The first is **Yamato**. This refers to a place, a time, and a spirit. The place is a plain east of Osaka where **Nara**, the ancient capital, is located. The time is the early beginnings of the Japanese state at Nara in the seventh and eighth centuries, though the term is more suggestive of distant beginnings than any precise time period. The spirit is the spirit of Japan itself and suggests a similar ambiguity. In prewar Japan references to the "*Yamato* spirit" had overtones of the *kokutai* philosophy, and today references sound antiquated and suspicious. Yet the concept may be more properly traced to the *Tale of Genji* where its meaning is "not unlike what Aristotle calls *sensus communis,* that is, a shared sensibility." During Meiji, the concept of *Yamato* spirit, though surely used by the *genro* to rally people in support of Meiji goals, was more importantly combined with the encouragement of Western learning as in the appeal for "*Yamato* spirit with Western learning" (Oe 1995, 16–20). This is not far removed from the suggestion here that it is only in the combination of both the fixed and floating aspects of Japanese politics that we see the subject matter. The term *Yamato,* then, is highly suggestive of all the complex particulars that make up traditional Japan, complex particulars that do not exclude foreign sources. Of all the organs of the modern Japanese state, it is the administrative world that represents more all that is suggested by the *Yamato* symbol. *Ukiyo* refers to the floating, sometimes called the "fleeting," world, as discussed in some detail in Chapter 1. As *Yamato* does not suggest complete resistance to change, so also does *ukiyo* have substantive features. Participants in the particular worlds of electoral politics, mass-mediated analyses and images, even citizens' action groups concentrate energies on things more ephemeral and localized. Japanese politics is a dynamic in-between with *yamato* and *ukiyo* symbolizing the poles of experience that define the political boundaries.

TWENTY-FIRST CENTURY JAPAN

Japan in the twenty-first century will likely be a place of maglev bullet trains, floating airports, floating video arcades, ever faster and more sophisticated developments in communications and transportation technology, and ubiquitous *manga* characters populating urban spaces, rural spaces, and cyberspaces. It will also be a place of traditional Shinto shrines, Buddhist temples, and Confucian assumptions about the place of education and administration in the larger scheme of things. It will continue to be a place where the challenges of the new, much of it proving to be ephemeral, will be balanced with the challenges of the old, much of it proving to be discardable. It will undoubtedly continue to be a place much admired but also much questioned. Politically, it will likely continue rebuilding parties in the manner of rebuilding the shrine at Ise, and protecting administrative agencies and all of the competitive institutional infrastructure, much of it educational, that attends them. Reforms will be incremental and as midwifed by angst and agitation in the floating structures profiled in Chapter 4.

Returning to the perennial issues identified by Leslie Lipson as the essence of politics and that have structured this introductory study of Japanese politics, the modern Japanese state in the twenty-first century, as all modern states, will be placed under considerable strain by forces and features unique to the times. Population growth continues to be among the greatest challenges. For Japan, with limited resources and already among the most concentrated populations in the world, there are good and bad projections. The good news is a leveling off of the population as a whole followed by a decrease somewhere around 2030. The bad news is the graying of Japanese society and the reshaping of what used to be called the population pyramid. A plot of Japan's population by age in 1920 shows a pyramid structure with a large base of youthful citizens and a small pinnacle at the top. With improvements in medicine, nutrition, quality of life, leisure activities, and the like, Japanese people live longer today than anyone in the world. The pyramid projected for the year 2025 is actually more in the shape of a tall fire hydrant. Age brackets have similar numbers until the very tip where the oldest die (JISEA 1995, 8). This, of course, will put great pressure on the governments, national and local, to provide services or, working with the private sector, assist in the development of creative programs and financing. This is already among the bigger issues in Japanese politics. Bureaucrats in ministries such as Health and Welfare, working with local administrators and engaging in research, develop policy strategies somewhat in isolation. Elected officials, theoretically at least closer to the people through constituency contacts in their communities, develop strategies based on interaction with citizens, interest groups in the health field, and ministry officials in the bureaucracy. Out of this interaction, strategies are developed, plans are funded, and incremental changes take place. There is little likelihood of a Japanese-style assault on health care reform similar to the thousand-page-plus proposal that emerged from the early Clinton White House in the United States. There is somewhat the likelihood, however, that the problems associated with *amakudari* will continue. What is likely true with respect to health care and taking care of an aging population is also likely in other areas where twenty-first-century challenges will be keenest: education, criminal justice, protecting the environment, developing energy independence, promoting more professional and business opportunities for women, economic development, and public financing. All of these issues will come under the scope of national government authority, but increasingly as qualified by inputs at the prefectural and municipal levels. Devolution of authority is an international trend to which Japan is far from immune.

As for the other perennial issues, change will occur but incrementally. Japan's traditional sources of authority will be little contested in all likelihood, though Western sources may be challenged in key areas. There is talk even today of writing a new constitution, even as there is talk of moving the capital out of Tokyo, that symbol of a "westering" Japan. There is frustration in the wake of single-member district House elections, modeled after American precedents. There is much talk of the Japan that can say "no" to outside pressure, *gaiatsu*, which traditionally means Western pressure. Whether the talk swells into a chorus that urges Japan into leading a "Pacific Century" in the manner of what some call the "American Century," now passing, remains to be seen. More likely, Japan will continue to nurture its East Asian, indigenous, and Western sources of authority in somewhat the same balance one finds today, though this balance will likely be accompanied by increased trade with Asian neighbors, a trend already under way. The structures of authority in Japan are already under review, a process that will likely continue. The focus has already begun to shift toward the administration and away from the electoral institutions. But reform talk will likely be louder than reform actions. One is tempted to see in the floating structures an ever accelerating focus on ever more ephemeral aspects of the environment, a sort of *manga* future where "info-" and "edutainment" replace traditional media and schools. Yet, a more sober expectation is for electoral politics, business, and entertainment as usual, only more of it. It will, however, be interesting to see if citizen action groups are able to mobilize in the future against corruption in their political communities with the same vigor that they brought to fighting corruption, pollution, in the environment. Among the biggest challenges for Japan heading into the twenty-first century are in foreign policy as noted in Chapter 7. And as with all the other challenges awaiting Japan in the next century, global challenges will likely be met by drawing equally on the resources of the moment and the lessons of a very long past. Donald Richie once wrote that in Japan there is a "pattern" for everything, and that among the more striking patterns was one wherein nothing is ever old. He observed that in Japan there are no antique stores, only secondhand stores. "Precious, old objects existed," he wrote, "but always in the context of the present" (1987, 22). And so it is also, perhaps, with Japanese politics. Old, fixed worlds of thought and habit exist, but only in the context of a floating present.

Works Cited

Adams, Henry. 1973. *The Education of Henry Adams,* ed. and with an Introduction by Ernest Samuels. New York: Houghton Mifflin.

Arendt, Hannah. 1951. *The Origins of Totalitarianism.* New York: Harcourt, Brace.

———. 1958. *The Human Condition.* Chicago: University of Chicago Press.

Asai Motofumi. 1990. Democracy, an Unintended Victim. *Japan Quarterly* 37 (January–March): 4–13.

Barshay, Andrew E. 1988. *State and Intellectual in Japan: The Public Man in Crisis.* Berkeley: University of California Press.

Burns, James MacGregor, J. W. Peltason, and Thomas Cronin. 1989. *Government by the People* (13th ed.). Englewood Cliffs, NJ: Prentice Hall.

Curtis, Gerald. 1988. *The Japanese Way of Politics.* New York: Columbia University Press.

Dewey, John, and Alice Chipman Dewey. 1920. *Letters from China and Japan,* ed. Evelyn Dewey. New York: Dutton.

Doi Takeo. 1973. *The Anatomy of Dependence,* trans. John Bester. Tokyo: Kodansha International.

Emerson, Ralph Waldo. 1967. Self-Reliance. In *The American Tradition of Literature,* ed. Sculley Bradley, Richmond Croom Beatty, and E. Hudson Long, vol. 1, 1129–1149. New York: Norton.

Fukuyama, Francis. 1989. The End of History? *The National Interest* (Summer): 3–18.

Ishida Takeshi. 1983. *Japanese Political Culture: Change and Continuity.* New Brunswick, NJ: Transaction Books.

Japan Institute for Social and Economic Affairs (JISEA). 1995. *Japan, 1995: An International Comparison.* Tokyo.

Kahler, Erich. 1989. *The Tower and the Abyss: An Inquiry into the Transformation of the Individual.* New Brunswick, NJ: Transaction Books.

Kristof, Nicholas D. 1996. Main Street, Japan: Heading to the Polls; Family and Friendship Guide Japanese Voting. *New York Times,* 13 October, 1.

Lebra Takie Sugiyama. 1976. *Japanese Patterns of Behavior.* Honolulu: University of Hawaii Press.

Locke, John. 1963. *Two Treatises of Government.* Introduction and Notes by Peter Laslett. New York: New American Library.

Nakane Chie. 1970. *Japanese Society.* Berkeley: University of California Press.

Oe Kenzaburo. 1995. *Japan, the Ambiguous, and Myself: The Nobel Prize Speech and Other Essays.* Tokyo: Kodansha International.

Reischauer, Edwin. 1981. *The Japanese.* Cambridge, MA: Harvard University Press.

Richie, Donald. 1987. *A Lateral View: Essays on Contemporary Japan.* Tokyo: Japan Times, Ltd.

Sartori, Giovanni. 1987. *The Theory of Democracy Revisited.* Chatham, NJ: Chatham House.

Takabatake Michitoshi. 1989. The Liberal Democratic Party in Crisis. *Japan Quarterly* 36 (July–September): 244–251.

Titus, David Anson. 1974. *Palace and Politics in Prewar Japan.* New York: Columbia University Press.

Zeigler, Harmon. 1990. *The Political Community: A Comparative Introduction to Political Systems and Society.* New York: Longman.

Glossary

Akihito Heisei Emperor, ascending the throne on November 12, 1990; son of the Showa Emperor Hirohito.

Akishino Second son of the Heisei Emperor.

Amae A Japanese term meaning dependence, often discussed in characterizations of Japanese personality. A famous study of Japanese psychology that stresses the importance of this concept is by Doi Takeo, *The Anatomy of Dependence.*

Amakudari Literally, descent from heaven, this term refers to retired members of the senior civil service of the national government who take high positions in private corporations to serve as advisers. They are critical links in the relationship between the national government and business activity in Japan.

Amaterasu Omikami Female deity who, according to Shinto mythology, and as recorded in the *Kojiki* (712), is the goddess from whom Japan's Imperial line descends. She is worshipped, traditionally, at the Ise Shrine.

Article 9 Provision of the 1947 Constitution that states: "Aspiring sincerely to an international peace based on justice and order, the Japanese people forever renounce war as a sovereign right of the nation and the threat or use of force as a means of settling international disputes." Section 2 states: "In order to accomplish the aim of the preceding paragraph, land, sea, and air forces, as well as other war potential, will never be maintained. The right of belligerency of the state will not be recognized."

Asahara Shoko Head of *Aum Shinrikyo;* was tried in 1996–1997 on 17 criminal counts related to the Tokyo gas attacks in the spring of 1995.

Bakufu Tent government. This term is often used to refer to the shogunate as the center of Japanese government through the end of the Edo Period. It is sometimes still used today to refer simply to the Japanese government.

Benedict, Ruth (1887–1948) Professor of anthropology for many years at Columbia University and famous for her study of Japanese national character, published as *The Chrysanthemum and the Sword.*

Bluestocking Society Primarily a literary association that published a magazine called *Bluestocking* (1911). The Bluestocking Society was the forerunner of the New Woman's Association, a more politically active women's rights organization.

Bubble Economy Reference to the Japanese economy during the 1980s when land values, widely used for collateral on loans, skyrocketed.

Bunraku Traditional Japanese puppet theater developed by urban commoners during the Edo Period. *Bunraku* performances combine puppets, puppet operators, shamisen music, and chanters and deal with both comic and tragic themes.

Burakumin Japanese minority group historically discriminated against because of their association with the leather trades and the slaughtering of animals; about 2 percent of the population today. *Burakumin* discrimination is illegal but continues in many quarters.

Charter Oath An Imperial oath in five articles given by the Emperor Meiji in 1868. Among the items in the oath is Imperial support for a representative assembly.

Choshu The western and southern region of Honshu with Hagi at its center. This region, along with Satsuma and Tosa, produced many of the leaders of the Meiji Restoration. Ito, Kido, and Yoshida were all from Choshu.

Chu Hsi (Zhu Xi; 1130–1200) Chinese, neo-Confucianist scholar who stressed metaphysical concepts and founded *shushigaku,* a neo-Confucianist school especially influential in Japan during the Edo Period.

Chushingura The story of the 47 *ronin.* Has been dramatized many times, from *bunraku* theater during the Edo Period to movie remakes in recent years.

Civilization and Enlightenment Reference to the Westernization tendency during the Meiji Period.

Confucius Chinese philosopher (551–479 B.C.), author of *The Analects* and is widely regarded as the most influential teacher of East Asia and whose influence continues to this day.

Consumption Tax A sales tax supported by the Liberal Democratic Party in the late 1980s to generate revenues for social programs, mostly in health care, for a rapidly aging population. In the beginning the tax was set at 3 percent.

Daimyo Feudal lords of Japan who dominated the Edo Period as local and regional rulers. *Daimyo* were classified as *shimpan* (related to the Shogun), *fudai* (hereditary landholders), and *tozama* (outside allies). *Daimyo* lands were replaced by modern prefectures in 1871.

Dazai Osamu (1909–1948) Japanese writer of short stories and novels whose real name was Tsushima Shuji. His father was a member of the House of Peers. Dazai's best known works are *The Setting Sun* (1947) and *No Longer Human* (1948).

Democratic Socialist Party Founded in 1960 after breaking away from the Japan Socialist Party.

Dogen (1200–1253) Founder of the *Soto* sect of Zen Buddhism in 1227. Born in Kyoto, educated in China, Dogen wrote several works now considered classics of Zen Buddhist literature.

Dutch Learning During the Edo Period, knowledge of the West was largely knowledge of Dutch Learning because of Dutch access to Japan during the period of Edo isolation. From their settlement on Dejima Island at Nagasaki, Dutch influence spread throughout Japan as "Western" learning. Medical science was an especially important element in Dutch Learning.

Edo The old name for Tokyo and the name given to the long period of Japanese isolation under the Tokugawa Shoguns.

Edo Period A long period (1600–1868) of isolation under the Tokugawa Shogunate; a time of relative internal peace in Japanese history.

Eisai (1141–1215) Founder of the *Rinzai* sect of Zen Buddhism. He wrote *Essentials of the Monastic Life.*

55 System Reference to the rule of the Liberal Democratic Party from 1955 to 1993.

Freedom and People's Rights Movement A political movement in early Meiji made up of former *samurai* and commoners who sought Western-style democracy in Japan. Came to be called the Popular Rights Movement and was led by Itagaki Taisuke.

Fujiwara Family that effectively ruled Japan during the Regency period of the tenth and eleventh centuries. The last 300 years of the Heian Period are often called the Fujiwara Period after the influence of the Fujiwara family in the Heian Court.

Fukuda Hideko (1865–1927) One of Japan's first feminists, from Okayama Prefecture. She was active in the Freedom and People's Rights Movement, as well as in the Japanese socialist movement in its early stages. She wrote *Half of My Life* (1904).

Fukuzawa Yukichi (1835–1901) Best known promoter of Western culture and enlightenment during the Meiji Period; author of numerous works, most notably *Conditions in the West.* He also founded what is now Keio University in Tokyo.

Genro The name given to the oligarchs who led the Meiji Restoration and continued to be a dominant force in Japanese government through the Taisho and into the Showa period.

Genshin (942–1017) *Tendai* Buddhist monk influential in the spread of Pure Land Buddhism in Japan.

Gneist, Rudolf von (1816–1895) German law professor and political theorist especially influential in shaping Ito Hirobumi and his entourage in their views on Western constitutional theory. He was a professor at the University of Berlin and a representative in the Prussian National Assembly. He also served on the German Supreme Court.

Haiku A 17-syllable form of poetry indigenous to Japan and very popular worldwide today. Matsuo Basho (1644–1694) is considered the great master.

Hara Takashi (1856–1921) Prime minister from 1918–1921 and one of the proponents of the party government principle in Japan. He is also known as the "commoner" prime minister. He was assassinated at Tokyo Station in 1921 by an ultra-right radical.

Hashimoto Ryutaro Prime minister of Japan from January 1996. He is head of the Liberal Democratic Party and former minister of finance and international trade and industry. His rise to head of the LDP and prime minister is certainly related to his strong positions representing Japan in trade talks with the United States in 1995.

Hata Tsutomu Prime minister very briefly in 1994, in the transition between the Hosokawa and Murayama cabinets.

Hayashi Razan (1583–1657) Leader of the neo-Confucianist school during the early years of Edo and principal adviser to the Tokugawa Shogunate.

Heian (794–1185) Period of Heian or Kyoto Court when aristocratic court life defined many of the traditional aspects of Japanese culture; time of *Tale of Genji* and other renowned literary works.

Heisei (1989–present) The name of the reign of Akihito, the present Emperor.

Hiratsuka Raicho (1886–1971) Born in Tokyo, a founder of the Bluestocking Society (*Seitosha*) in 1911 and a cofounder of the New Woman's Association in 1920.

Hirohito (1901–1989) The Showa Emperor and father of the present Emperor Akihito. Hirohito reigned longer than any other Japanese Emperor in history.

Hizen A domain during the Edo Period, parts of today's Nagasaki and Saga prefectures on Kyushu. Hizen was the home of several leaders of the Meiji Restoration, including Okuma Shigenobu.

Hokusai (1760–1849) Among the most prominent *ukiyo e* artists. He is best known for his *Thirty-six Views of Mt. Fuji* and his *One Hundred Views of Mt. Fuji.* Early in his career he worked under other names.

Honen (1133–1212) Founder of the *Jodo* sect of Japanese Buddhism.

Horyuji Temple A Buddhist Temple built in the early seventh century in today's Nara Prefecture by order of Prince Shotoku.

Hosokawa Morihiro Prime Minister in 1993–1994; founder of the Japan New Party and a leader today in the New Frontier Party (*Shinshinto*).

Ibuse Masuji (1898–1993) Japanese writer of short stories and novels, best known for his novel *Black Rain* (1966).

Iegara Japanese concept meaning one's family lineage or ancestry.

Ijime Bullying; refers specifically to bullying in the schoolyard and is a huge problem in Japan today as well as traditionally. With the traditional emphasis on conformity and fitting in, children who go overseas or who otherwise stand out are sometimes subjected to bullying. Extraordinary instances where children commit suicide make national headlines.

Imperial Rescript on Education Imperial order of October 1890, outlining major goals of the school system in Japan with a heavy emphasis on Confucianist and *kokutai* teachings. These guidelines remained in effect until the end of World War II.

Imperial Rule Assistance Association Founded in 1940 to promote state goals and consolidate the power of the ruling elite. The IRAA came to include all Japanese subjects and led to the abolition of all political parties. It was disbanded in 1945.

Inukai Tsuyoshi (1855–1932) Longtime member of the House of Representatives, first elected in the 1890 election (first Diet election). He was prime minister in 1931–1932. During the May 15 incident of 1932, he was assassinated.

Ippen (1239–1289) Founded the *Ji* sect of Japanese Buddhism.

Itagaki Taisuke (1837–1919) One of the pioneers of democratic politics in Japan. He founded Japan's first political party, the *Jiyuto* (Liberal Party), and was active in the Freedom and People's Rights Movement.

Ito Hirobumi Japan's first prime minister and often regarded as the architect of the Meiji Constitution. He served as prime minister on several occasions and was assassinated in China by a Korean dissident, an event that helped lead Japan to annex Korea in 1910.

Iwakura Tomomi (1825–1883) A leader of the Meiji Restoration; instrumental in the issuing of the Charter Oath by the Meiji Emperor; influential in the transition from *daimyo* to prefectures; leader of the Iwakura Mission overseas.

Jimmu Tenno First Emperor of Japan, according to legend, and ruler from 660 to 585 B.C. According to legend he is descended from the sun goddess Amaterasu Omikami.

Juku After-school cram schools to help students prepare for entrance examinations to colleges and universities.

Kaifu Toshiki (1931–) Prime minister from 1989 to 1991 as LDP reform candidate in the wake of several scandals. In the mid-1990s, a leader of the New Frontier Party.

Kamakura (1185–1333) The first shogunal period, dominated largely by the Hojo family. A period of military rule.

Kanemaru Shin (1914–1996) Former vice president of the LDP and deputy prime minister; indicted and tried for accepting bribes. He symbolizes for many the "money politics" and corruption characteristic of much postwar Japanese political activity.

Kansai Literally, west of the pass. This is the region around the city of Osaka. The new international airport on the water in Osaka is called the Kansai International Airport.

Katayama Tetsu (1887–1978) First Socialist prime minister of Japan, 1947–1948. A founder of the Japan Socialist Party and later the Democratic Socialist Party in 1960.

Kawabata Yasunari (1899–1972) Japanese writer of short stories and novels and winner of the Nobel Prize for Literature in 1968, Japan's first Nobel winner in literature. He is best known for his novels *Snow Country, Thousand Cranes,* and *Sound of the Mountain.*

Kawashima Kiko Princess, wife of Akishino; a popular member of the royal family.

Keene, Donald (1922–) Prolific author of works on Japan and noted translator of Japanese literary works. Among his books are *World Within Walls* (1976) and *Dawn to the West* (1984).

Keio University Private university in Tokyo founded in 1858 by Fukuzawa Yukichi and widely regarded as among Japan's most prestigious private schools.

Kido Takayoshi (1833–1877) One of the leaders of the Meiji Restoration from Choshu. He led the efforts to unite Satsuma and Choshu against the Tokugawa government in Edo. He also led the effort to replace feudal *daimyo* estates with modern prefectural governments.

Kishida Toshiko (1863–1901) Political activist and writer, she is the author of *Shoen's Diary* (1903). She was active in the Freedom and People's Rights Movement and in the first Liberal Party.

Kobe Large city, population about 1.5 million, in Hyogo Prefecture in western Honshu and Japan's second largest port, after Yokohama. The Kobe earthquake in 1995 exposed problems in the Japanese government's crisis management procedures.

Kojiki *Record of Ancient Matters,* from the year 712. Contains myths regarding the Japanese founding and the earliest rulers of Japan.

Kokugaku (national learning) A seventeenth-century focus by Japanese scholars on the classical writings of Japan dating from the Nara Period. Motoori Norinaga (1730–1801) is the most famous of the Kokugaku scholars.

Kokutai (national polity) This term captured the essence of a mystic state under the Emperor and unique to Japan. It is usually associated with Japan during the period 1890–1945.

Kukai (A.D. 774–835) Buddhist priest who founded the *Shingon* sect of Japanese Buddhism. He is also known for introducing the Japanese *kana* syllabary and for designing the Buddhist pilgrimage to 88 temples on Shikoku, popular to this day.

Kuya (A.D. 903–972) Popularized Pure Land Buddhism and the idea of universal salvation.

Kyushu The southernmost of the four main islands of Japan. Kyushu is home to Fukuoka, Nagasaki, and Kitakyushu (a consolidation of the old cities of Kokura, Yahata, Tobata, Wakamatsu, and Moji).

Lockheed Scandal A scandal from the mid-1970s involving the purchase of aircraft from the American Lockheed Corporation by a Japanese airline. Seventeen people were prosecuted for illegal activities.

Manchukuo State created by the Japanese army in 1932 that covered all of Manchuria and part of Inner Mongolia.

Marquis One of five ranks established by the Peerage Act of 1884. The ranks, in order, were prince, marquis, count, viscount, and baron, and were conferred by the Emperor. Abolished by the 1947 Constitution.

Meiji Name of the emperor in whose name the great reforms of the late nineteenth century took place; also the name for the period from 1868 to 1912.

Meiji Constitution The first constitution for Japan in 1889. It was a gift from the Emperor to the Japanese people.

Meiji Restoration Reference to the return of the national government to the Emperor from the Tokugawa Shogunate and the beginning of the Meiji era (1868–1912).

Mencius (371–289 B.C.) Ancient Chinese philosopher whose emphasis on the obligations of rulers dramatized the political content of the teachings of Confucius.

Michiko Wife of Emperor Akihito and Empress of Japan. She is the first commoner to become Empress.

Minamata A city in Kyushu, Kumamoto Prefecture, which is today an international symbol for the need for environmental protection against chemical and other hazards. Site of one of the world's worst environmental disasters in the 1950s.

Minseito Full name, *Rikken Minseito,* the Constitutional Democratic Party; one of the two main parties during the early Showa Period.

Miyazawa Kiichi (1919–) Prime minister from 1991 to 1993. The last of the LDP prime ministers under the 55 system. A graduate of Tokyo University, he is from Hiroshima Prefecture; he also served as finance and foreign minister and as director of the Economic Planning Agency.

Mizuko Jizo A Buddhist spiritual being who assists those in distress. The Mizuko Jizo is particularly compassionate toward children and is regarded as the protector of children.

Mombusho A colloquial term for the Ministry of Education.

Momotaro ("Peach Boy") A popular children's story known to all Japanese children today and by many the world over.

Mono no aware An aesthetic ideal roughly meaning the deep feeling one has regarding the conjunction of beauty and sadness. It is a central concept in *kokugaku* and in the works of Motoori Norinaga.

Motoori Norinaga (1730–1801) Central scholar in the *kokugaku* movement during the Edo Period. He is especially known for his study of Japanese Shinto and the *Kojiki.*

Murasaki Shikibu, Lady Author of *Tales of Genji,* one of the world's great literary classics written around A.D. 1000.

Murayama Tomiichi Prime minister of Japan from summer of 1994 to early January 1996. He headed the Social Democratic Party of Japan (SDPJ).

Mutual Security Treaty A shorthand reference to the U.S.–Japan Security Treaty implemented in 1952 and revised in 1960. The 1960 revision set the context for the bitterest confrontations in postwar Japanese politics.

Nara A city in central Honshu and the oldest capital of Japan during the Nara Period (710–794).

Naruhito, Crown Prince The oldest son of the Emperor Akihito and Empress Michiko. The Crown Prince married Owada Masako in June 1993.

New Woman's Association The first woman's rights association in Japan to focus on political issues, founded in 1920. It led the fight to give women the right to join political associations.

Noh Japanese drama, largely aristocratic, dating from the fourteenth-century and heavily influenced by Buddhist sources.

Northern Territories Four islands north of Hokkaido that the Japanese claim and Russia occupies and also claims. In the early 1990s, this was an especially topical issue. With the return of the LDP to a more influential position in the Diet, it may well become an issue again in the near future.

Oda Nobunaga (1534–1582) One of the three great unifiers of sixteenth-century Japan. He took control of Kyoto and the surrounding areas and is especially known for confiscating weapons and for providing for a comprehensive land survey.

Oe Kenzaburo (1935–) One of Japan's two Nobel writers, receiving the Nobel Prize for Literature in 1994. A graduate of Tokyo University, Oe has written such works as *A Personal Matter, The Silent Cry,* and *A Quiet Life.*

Ogyu Sorai (1666–1728) Confucian scholar of the Edo Period who criticized the neo-Confucianist teachings of his time. Sorai called for a return to the Chinese classics.

Okubo Toshimichi (1830–1878) A leader in the Meiji Restoration with Saigo and Kido, Okubo led the land tax reforms, and later led the government's resistance to Saigo's Satsuma Rebellion. He was assassinated by Satsuma *samurai.*

Okuma Shigenobu (1838–1922) Leader in early Meiji politics and later founder of Waseda University. He was from Hizen and served as prime minister and also led the first Party cabinet under the Meiji Constitution. He was a leading critic of the Satcho clique.

On A Japanese term meaning obligation. It refers to a feeling of debt as in the term *onjin,* that is, a person to whom one feels indebted for a large favor.

Onna daigaku Higher learning for women popularly taught during the Edo Period; based on the teachings of Confucius and published in manual form in 1716. This view was attacked by Fukuzawa during the civilization and enlightenment movement.

Owada Masako Married Crown Prince Naruhito in June 1993. Future Empress of Japan.

Ozawa Ichiro Former LDP leader who broke away and formed the Japan Renewal Party (*Shinseito*) in the early 1990s. In 1994, he created the New Frontier Party (*Shinshinto*) and became the leader of the conservative alternative to the LDP. He is the author of *Blueprint for a New Japan.*

Paris Commune An insurrection against the French government in Paris between March and May 1871. About 20,000 in the insurrection were killed and over 700 government soldiers. Thousands were arrested after the insurrection and many were deported.

Peace Preservation Law A law passed in 1925 aimed at communist and other left wing groups. It was used by the government to stifle dissent during World War II.

Perry, Matthew C. (1794–1858) Commanded naval forces in the Mexican War prior to his leading the expeditions to Japan in 1853 and 1854. With four ships he entered Japanese waters at Edo on July 8, 1853, to force diplomatic and trade talks. He returned in February 1854 with nine ships, and in March the first treaty between Japan and the United States was signed.

Potsdam Declaration This agreement defined the terms of Japan's surrender in late July 1945. It was the product of an Allied conference outside Berlin involving the United States, Great Britain, and the Soviet Union.

Privy Council Created by Imperial Ordinance in 1888 primarily to direct preparation of the Meiji Constitution. Under the latter, this council was given substantial powers to "deliberate upon important matters of state."

Rai Sanyo (1781–1832) Author of *An Unofficial History of Japan,* which placed the Emperor in the center of Japanese history and greatly influenced the young *samurai* of the *sonno joi* movement.

Reischauer, Edwin (1910–1990) Japanese historian and U.S. ambassador to Japan under the Kennedy and Johnson administrations (1961–1966). He published many studies of Japan and Japanese–U.S. relations. He was born in Tokyo and spent most of his professional career at Harvard University.

Revisionist Studies A general reference to the trend in the 1980s to revise scholarly assessments of Japan's commitment to democracy and free market economics by several leading, mostly American, scholars.

Roesler, Karl Friedrich Hermann (1834–1894) German adviser to the Japanese leadership during the writing of the Meiji Constitution of 1889. He also helped draft the commercial codes.

Ronin Masterless *samurai* in traditional Japan; today, also refers to students who fail to gain acceptance to the college of their choice upon first try. *Ronin* literally means "floating" man.

Rule of Law A concept at the center of Western democracies according to which no person or persons rule, only settled law as expressed in a constitution. Rule of law is sometimes also expressed as "constitutionalism."

Ryonin (1073–1132) Studied at Mt. Hiei and later founded a Buddhist sect in Kyoto.

Saicho (767–822) Founded *Tendai* Buddhism, one of the major early sects of Japanese Buddhism.

Saigo Takamori (1827–1877) A member of the Satcho clique (from Satsuma) which overthrew the Tokugawa and established the Meiji Restoration. Later he led the Satsuma rebellion and died in the last great battle of the samurai.

Saionji Kimmochi (1849–1940) Prime minister on two occasions during the late Meiji Period and one of the original *genro;* a founder of Meiji University; served in numerous government posts including as minister of education and as a member of the Privy Council.

Salarymen Middle-class businessmen.

Samurai A premodern Japanese warrior, also called *bushi.* Dating from the tenth-century and officially dissolved in early Meiji, *samurai* were at the top of the social hierarchy in traditional Japan.

Sankin Kotai Alternating attendance of *daimyo* in Edo to wait on the Shogun every other year. This practice was used to control the *daimyo* all over Japan.

Satsuma Region surrounding what is now Kagoshima Prefecture at the southern end of Kyushu. With Choshu, Satsuma *samurai,* most famously Saigo Takemori, led the Meiji Restoration.

Satsuma Rebellion Rebellion led by Saigo in 1877, representing the last great action of Japanese *samurai,* against the new Meiji state. The rebellion was put down by national government troops.

Sayako Daughter and youngest child of Emperor Akihito and Empress Michiko, born in 1969.

SCAP Supreme Commander of the Allied Powers, a term used both for General Douglas MacArthur and General Headquarters during the U.S. occupation of Japan from 1945 to 1952.

Seami (also Zeami) (1363–1443) One of the great *Noh* playwrights; also a Zen monk and author of treatises on aesthetic principles.

Seiyukai Early political party founded by Ito Hirobumi in 1900; also the party of Hara Takashi. It was dissolved with all other parties in 1940, but today's LDP traces part of its beginnings to this party.

Self Defense Forces SDF, or Jieitai, refers to the armed forces of Japan. Though officially created by the Self Defense Forces Law in 1954, the SDF evolved from a National Police Reserve created by General MacArthur during the U.S. occupation (1945–1952).

Senkaku Islands Uninhabited islands northeast of Taiwan and south of Okinawa claimed by the Japanese government as Japanese territory; also by China. The contested islands were hardly mentioned by either side until recent explorations suggested large oil, gas, and mineral deposits in the vicinity.

Sensei Teacher; also, one to whom one owes respect. Physicians, Diet members, leaders in the community, and others are also called *sensei.*

Seppuku Often called also *harakiri* (usually outside of Japan). Ritual suicide associated with the *samurai* and made famous in the dramatization of the 47 ronin in Chushingura.

Shikoku The smallest of the four main islands of Japan and home to the 88 temples in the traditional pilgrimage of Buddhist faithful and tourists today.

Shingon One of the major Buddhist sects in Japan, founded by Kukai.

Shogun Military rulers of Japan from the twelfth to the nineteenth centuries. Kamakura (1192–1333), Muromachi (1338–1573), and Edo (1603–1867) were the centers of Shogunate rule.

Shotoku Taishi (574–622) Prince of sagely virtue who promulgated the 17-article constitution in the seventh century.

Showa The period in Japanese history from 1926 to 1989 under the Emperor Hirohito.

Siddhartha (Gautama) (c. 563–c. 483 B.C.) Buddha, the enlightened one; founder of Buddhism. Born in the area of contemporary Nepal, became a wandering monk at 29. He dedicated his life to finding enlightenment, and inspired countless followers. Came to be revered worldwide as the founder of Buddhism.

Sohei Armed monks who protected Buddhist temples and other lands and sometimes rivaled even Shogunate forces. They were the target of Oda Nobunaga's campaign against Buddhism in the late sixteenth century.

Soka Gakkai A "new religion" founded in 1930 as a Buddhist sect whose founder, Makiguchi, died in prison during World War II. Today this religion has several million members and is a force in Japanese party politics.

Stein, Lorenz von (1815–1890) Law professor in Vienna influential on the Japanese *genro* who went to Europe in 1882 seeking knowledge of Western constitutionalism.

Structural Impediments Initiative Also called SII, these are negotiations between Japan and the United States that began in 1989, focusing on internal, structural barriers to more balanced trade between the two countries.

Syllabary Kana characters, both *hiragana* and *katakana*, do not represent "letters" as in English; rather, they represent syllables. For example, *ka, ga, shi, sa, ku, te,* and the like.

Taisho The period in Japanese history from 1912–1926. The term *Taisho democracy* is often used to refer to reforms during this period.

Takeshita Noboru Prime minister from 1987 to 1989; an LDP Diet member representing Shimane Prefecture. He was prime minister during the introduction of the consumption tax in 1988 and resigned during the Recruit Cosmos scandal in 1989.

Taketori Monogatari "Tale of the Bamboo Cutter," which tells the story of the shining princess, Kaguyahime. It dates from the ninth century and is one of Japan's oldest and most favorite folktales.

Tanaka Kakuei Prime minister from 1972–1974, a symbol for many of corruption in Japanese politics and in the Liberal Democratic Party in particular. He was implicated in the Lockheed Scandal. The Tanaka faction of the LDP continued to have tremendous influence long after Tanaka left the scene. His daughter was recently reelected from a district in the Niigata area to the House of Representatives in the October 1996 election.

Tanizaki Junichiro (1886–1965) Japanese writer, famous in the West for *Some Prefer Nettles* and *The Makioka Sisters*.

Tanka Short poems of 31 syllables in five lines and a style characteristic of classical Japanese poetry and still popular today.

Tendai The Buddhist sect founded by Saicho in the ninth century and popular at court during the Heian Period (794–1185). A rival sect to Kukai's *Shingon* sect.

Tokugawa The ruling Shogun family from 1600 to 1868. The period is alternatively called Edo and Tokugawa. Tokugawa Ieyasu is considered the great unifier of modern Japan for his victory at Sekigahara in 1600 and his subsequent inauguration of 250 years of relative peace.

Tokugawa Ieyasu (1543–1616) Founder of the Tokugawa Shogunate and hero of Sekigahara in 1600. He is sometimes called the Napoleon of Japan.

Tokyo University Oldest and most prestigious of the public institutions of higher education in Japan. Todai graduates traditionally assume roles in upper government administration and in corporate management. It was formerly known as Tokyo Imperial University.

Tosa Domain in present Kochi Prefecture on Shikoku that played a prominent role, with Satsuma and Choshu, in the Meiji Restoration.

Toyotomi Hideyoshi (1537–1598) Military leader of nonaristocratic birth and a general under Oda Nobunaga, Toyotomi succeeded in unifying late sixteenth-century Japan. He instituted many reforms and never took the title of Shogun.

Transcendental Cabinets Term used early in the development of the Meiji Constitution of 1889 to refer to cabinets above party politics in the making of policy and run by the *genro* of the Satcho clique.

Tsuda Umeko (1864–1929) Founder of the English School for Women in 1900, now Tsuda College for women. She went on the Iwakura mission in 1871 and later served as a tutor in Ito Hirobumi's household.

Uchi Japanese word meaning "inside"; also "home." This term is often juxtaposed with *soto*, or "outside."

Ukiyo e Floating world pictures made from woodblocks during the Edo Period and made famous by artists like Utamaro, Hokusai, and Hiroshige.

Unequal Treaties Various commercial treaties between Japan and the U.S., Dutch, Russian, French, and British governments that limited Japan's power to raise tariffs and provided for the trial of foreigners by their own courts within Japan. A major focus of the Meiji government's policy was to revise and abolish these treaties.

U.S.–Japan Security Treaty The treaty of 1951, implemented in 1952, which sets the framework for the operation of U.S. troops in Japan and the protection of Japan from armed attack. It includes today the Treaty of Mutual Cooperation and Security, signed in 1960.

Utamaro Kitagawa (1753–1806) Famous *ukiyo e* artist who specialized in portraying the women of the Edo Period, notably women of the pleasure quarters.

Waseda University A large private university in Tokyo and one of Japan's most prestigious institutions of higher education. It was founded in 1882 by Okuma Shigenobu.

Watsuji Tetsuro (1889–1960) Professor of philosophy at Kyoto and Tokyo universities who emphasized the uniqueness of Japanese ethical philosophy, in contrast to the West.

Yakuza Japanese organized crime and the subject of much discussion within and outside of Japan. There are estimated to be about 3,300 different gangs each of which consider themselves *yakuza*. These organizations trace their history back 250 years and more.

Yamada Waka (1879–1957) Writer who published in *Seito* (*Bluestocking*) literary magazine during early Taisho and later advised women in trouble from a newspaper position during Showa. She founded a refuge for mothers and children in Tokyo and was the first president of the Motherhood Protection League.

Yamakawa Kikue (1890–1980) Born in Tokyo, became a socialist and activist and wrote for *Seito* (*Bluestocking*) literary journal. The first director of the Women's and Minors' Bureau of the Ministry of Labor.

Yamato Old name for Japan and, specifically, for the area around Nara. It is also the name often used for the period prior to Nara (710–794). Japan's largest battleship, completed in 1941, was also called *Yamato*.

Yasukuni Shrine Famous Shinto shrine in Tokyo where Japan's military war dead are buried.

Yosano Akiko (1878–1942) Poet, essayist, teacher, mother of 11 children; published widely during the Taisho and early Showa periods on women's concerns in modern Japan.

Yoshioka Yayoi (1871–1959) Founder of Japan's first medical school for women in 1900. Today, this institution is called Tokyo Women's Medical College.

Zaibatsu Large business and financial combinations during Japan's industrialization during Meiji, Taisho, and early Showa. They were dissolved after World War II.

Zen Buddhist school that emphasizes meditation; originated in China but is most often identified with Japanese Buddhism. This Buddhist school was especially popular with *samurai* during the feudal times and during the Edo Period in particular. There are over 21,000 Zen Buddhist temples in Japan.

Index